The Institute of Chartered Accountants in England and Wales

# ACCOUNTING

For exams from 1 August 2016 to 31 December 2017

Study Manual

www.icaew.com

Accounting

The Institute of Chartered Accountants in England and Wales

ISBN: 978-1-78363-388-3

Previous ISBN: 978-1-78363-197-1

First edition 2007

Tenth edition 2016

The content of this publication is intended to prepare students for the ICAEW examinations, and should not be used as professional advice.

British Library Cataloguing-in-Publication Data
A catalogue record for this book is available from the British Library

Originally printed in the United Kingdom by Polestar Wheatons on paper obtained from traceable, sustainable sources.

Polestar Wheatons
Hennock Road
Marsh Barton
Exeter
EX2 8RP

The publishers are grateful to the IASB for permission to reproduce extracts from the International Financial Reporting Standards including all International Accounting Standards, SIC and IFRIC Interpretations (the Standards). The Standards together with their accompanying documents are issued by:

The International Accounting Standards Board (IASB)
30 Cannon Street, London, EC4M 6XH, United Kingdom.
Email: info@ifrs.org Web: www.ifrs.org

**Disclaimer:** The IASB, the International Financial Reporting Standards (IFRS) Foundation, the authors and the publishers do not accept responsibility for any loss caused by acting or refraining from acting in reliance on the material in this publication, whether such loss is caused by negligence or otherwise to the maximum extent permitted by law.

**Copyright © IFRS Foundation**

All rights reserved. Reproduction and use rights are strictly limited. No part of this publication may be translated, reprinted or reproduced or utilised in any form either in whole or in part or by any electronic, mechanical or other means, now known or hereafter invented, including photocopying and recording, or in any information storage and retrieval system, without prior permission in writing from the IFRS Foundation. Contact the IFRS Foundation for further details.

The IFRS Foundation logo, the IASB logo, the IFRS for SMEs logo, the 'Hexagon Device', 'IFRS Foundation', 'eIFRS', 'IAS', 'IASB', 'IFRS for SMEs', 'IASs', 'IFRS', 'IFRSs', 'International Accounting Standards' and 'International Financial Reporting Standards', 'IFRIC' 'SIC' and 'IFRS Taxonomy' are **Trade Marks** of the IFRS Foundation.

Further details of the Trade Marks including details of countries where the Trade Marks are registered or applied for are available from the Licensor on request.

# Welcome to ICAEW

I am delighted that you have chosen ICAEW to progress your journey towards joining the chartered accountancy profession. It is one of the best decisions I also made.

The role of the accountancy profession in the world's economies has never been more important. People making financial decisions need knowledge and guidance based on the highest technical and ethical standards. ICAEW Chartered Accountants provide this better than anyone. They challenge people and organisations to think and act differently, to provide clarity and rigour, and so help create and sustain prosperity all over the world.

As a world leader of the accountancy and finance profession, we are proud to promote, develop and support over 145,000 Chartered Accountants worldwide. Our members have the knowledge, skills and commitment to maintain the highest professional standards and integrity. They are part of something special, and now, so are you. It's with our support and dedication that our members and hopefully yourself, will realise career ambitions, maintain a professional edge and contribute to the profession.

You are now on your journey towards joining the accountancy profession, and a highly rewarding career with endless opportunities. So, if you are studying for our Certificate in Finance, Accounting and Business (ICAEW CFAB) or our world-leading chartered accountancy qualification, the ACA, you too have made the first of many great decisions in your career.

You are in good company, with a network of over 28,000 students around the world made up of like-minded people. You are all supported by ICAEW as you progress through your studies and career; we will be with you every step of the way. Visit page viii to review the key resources available as you study.

I wish you the best of luck with your studies and look forward to welcoming you to the profession in the future.

Michael Izza
Chief Executive
ICAEW

# Contents

Questions within the study manual should be treated as preparation questions, providing you with a firm foundation before you attempt the exam standard questions. The exam standard questions are found in the question bank.

# 1 Introduction

## ACA qualification

The ICAEW chartered accountancy qualification, the ACA, is a world-leading professional qualification in accountancy, finance and business.

The ACA has integrated components that will give you an in-depth understanding across accountancy, finance and business. Combined, they help build the technical knowledge, professional skills and practical experience needed to become an ICAEW Chartered Accountant.

Each component is designed to complement each other, which means that you can put theory into practice and you can understand and apply what you learn to your day-to-day work. Progression through all the elements of the ACA simultaneously will enable you to be more successful in the workplace and exams.

The components are:

- Professional development
- Ethics and professional scepticism
- Three to five years practical work experience
- 15 accountancy, finance and business modules

To find out more on the components of the ACA and what is involved in training, visit your dashboard at icaew.com/dashboard

## ICAEW Certificate in Finance, Accounting and Business

The ICAEW Certificate in Finance, Accounting and Business (ICAEW CFAB) teaches essential skills and knowledge in the three key areas of finance, accounting and business.

ICAEW CFAB consists of the same six modules as the first level of our world-leading qualification, the ACA. This means, it can serve as a stand-alone qualification or as a stepping stone on your journey towards chartered accountancy.

You can find out more about the ICAEW CFAB exams and syllabus at icaew.com/cfabstudents

To learn more about the ACA qualification and chartered accountancy, visit icaew.com/careers

# 2 Accounting

The full syllabus and technical knowledge grids can be found within the module study guide. Visit icaew.com/exams if you're studying the ACA or icaew.com/cfabstudents if you're studying ICAEW CFAB.

## 2.1 Module aim

To ensure that students have a sound understanding of the techniques of double entry accounting and can apply its principles in recording transactions, adjusting financial records and preparing non-complex financial statements.

On completion of this module, candidates will be:

- Proficient in the use of double entry accounting techniques and the maintenance of accounting records

- Able to identify and correct omissions and errors in accounting records and financial statements

- Able to specify the components of financial statements, and prepare and present non-complex accounts for sole traders, partnerships and limited companies

## 2.2 Specification grid

This grid shows the relative weightings of subjects within this module and should guide the relative study time spent on each. Over time the marks available in the assessment will equate to the weightings below, while slight variations may occur in individual assessments to enable suitably rigorous questions to be set.

|  | Weighting (%) |
| --- | --- |
| Maintaining financial records | 30 |
| Adjustments to accounting records and financial statements | 35 |
| Preparing financial statements | 35 |
|  | 100 |

# 3 Key Resources

We provide a wide range of fantastic resources and services to help you in your studies. Here is a taster of what we have to offer.

## Student support team

Our student support team are here to help you, providing full support throughout your studies.

**T** +44 (0)1908 248 250
**E** studentsupport@icaew.com

## Student website

The student area of our website provides the latest information, guidance and exclusive resources to help you as you progress through the ACA. These include exam webinars, interactive sample assessments, errata sheets and guidance for your computer-based assessments. Find everything you need at icaew.com/dashboard.

If you are studying for the ICAEW CFAB qualification, you can access exam resources and support at icaew.com/cfabstudents.

## Online student community

The online student community provides support and practical advice – wherever you are, whenever you need it. With regular blogs covering a range of work, life and study topics as well as a forum where you can post your questions and share your own tips. ACA and ICAEW CFAB students can join the conversation at icaew.com/studentcommunity.

## Faculties and Special Interest Groups

These groups are designed to support you in specific areas of work and industry sectors of interest.

Our seven faculties provide knowledge, events and essential technical resources. As an ACA or ICAEW CFAB student, you can register to receive a complimentary e-newsletter from a faculty of your choice.

Our 14 special interest groups provide practical support, information and representation within a range of industry sectors. As an ACA student, you can register for provisional membership to one special interest group of your choice.

Find out more about faculties and special interest groups at icaew.com/facultiesandsigs.

## Library & Information Service

The Library & Information Service is ICAEW's world-leading accountancy and business library. The library provides access to thousands of resources online and a document delivery service, you'll be sure to find a useful eBook, relevant article or topic-based guide to help you. Find out more at icaew.com/library.

## Tuition

The ICAEW Partner in Learning scheme recognises tuition providers who comply with our core principles of quality course delivery. If you are receiving structured tuition with an ICAEW Partner in Learning, make sure you know how and when you can contact your tutors for extra help. If you are not receiving structured tuition and are interested in classroom, online or distance learning tuition, take a look at our recognised Partner in Learning tuition providers in your area, on our website icaew.com/dashboard.

# CHAPTER 1

# Introduction to accounting

Introduction

Examination context

**Topic List**

Summary and Self-test

Technical reference

Answers to Interactive questions

Answers to Self-test

## Learning objectives

- Specify why an entity maintains financial records and prepares financial statements ☐

- Specify the ethical considerations for preparers of financial statements ☐

- Record and account for transactions in accordance with the laws, regulations and accounting standards applicable to the financial statements ☐

- Specify the key aspects of the accrual basis of accounting, cash accounting and break-up basis of accounting ☐

Specific syllabus learning outcomes are: 1a, b, d, 3b

## Syllabus links

The material in this chapter will be developed further in this paper, and later in the Professional level module of Financial Accounting and Reporting.

## Examination context

Questions on topics in this chapter will be knowledge-type multiple choice questions. In the exam you may be required to:

- Identify capital as opposed to revenue expenditure
- Specify the distinctions between the different qualitative characteristics
- Identify the principles that relate to each qualitative characteristic
- Identify the different interests of stakeholders
- Identify the differences between IFRS and UK GAAP

# 1 The purpose of accounting information

## Section overview

- Accounting is a way of recording, analysing and summarising the transactions of an entity.
- The three main types of business entity are sole traders, partnerships and companies.
- Users who need financial information include: managers, owners, customers, suppliers, lenders, employees, trade unions, HM Revenue and Customs, financial analysts and advisers, government agencies and the public.
- Managers and (present and potential) owners are the prime users of published financial statements.
- People need financial information on a company to make economic decisions, to assess managers' stewardship of the company's resources, and to assess the level, timing and certainty of its future cash flows.

## 1.1 What is accounting?

**Accounting** is a way of recording, analysing and summarising transactions of an entity (a term we shall use to describe any business organisation).

- The transactions are **recorded** in 'books of original entry' (see Chapter 3).
- The transactions are then **analysed** and posted to the ledgers (see Chapter 4).
- Finally the transactions are **summarised** in the financial statements (see Chapter 5).

One of the roles of an accountant is to measure the revenue and expenditure of an entity and, if it is a business, its profit. This is not as straightforward as it may seem and in later chapters we will look at some theoretical and practical difficulties.

## 1.2 Types of business entity

There are three main types of profit-making business entity.

- Sole traders
- Partnerships
- Limited liability companies

**Sole traders** are people who work for themselves. Examples include a local shopkeeper, plumber or hairdresser. The term sole trader refers to the **ownership** of the business; sole traders can have employees.

**Partnerships** occur when two or more people decide to share the risks and rewards of a business together. Examples include an accountancy, medical or legal practice. A partnership can take one of two forms: a **general partnership** (like two or more sole traders) and a Limited Liability Partnership LLP (more like a company).

**Limited liability companies** are incorporated to take advantage of 'limited liability' for their owners (shareholders). This means that, while sole traders (always) and partners (usually) are **personally responsible** for the amounts owed by their businesses, the owners (shareholders) of a limited liability company are only responsible for the **amount to be paid for their shares**.

## 1.3 The objective of financial statements

Why do businesses need to produce accounting information in the form of financial statements? If a business is being run efficiently, why should it have to go through all the bother of accounting procedures in order to produce financial information?

A business should produce information about its activities because there are user groups who want or need to know that information in order to make **economic decisions**.

When making economic decisions, users need to assess:

- The ability of the business to generate cash
- The timing and certainty of cash flows

Whether the business can generate cash of the right amount determines whether it can:

- Pay its employees and suppliers
- Meet interest payments
- Repay loans
- Pay something to its owners

Large businesses are of interest to a greater variety of people and so we will consider the case of a large public company, whose shares can be purchased and sold on a stock exchange.

## 1.4 Who needs financial information?

The following people are likely to be interested in financial information about a large company with listed shares.

- **Managers/directors** appointed by the company's owners to supervise the day to day activities of the company. They need information about the company's present and future financial situation. This enables them to manage the business efficiently (exercising the stewardship function) and to make effective decisions about matters such as pricing, output, employment and financing.

- **Owners of the company** (shareholders) want to assess management performance. They want to know how profitable the company's operations are and how much profit is available for distribution to the shareholders through a dividend. In addition, the value of their investment in the company is affected by the company's profitability.

- **Trade contacts** include suppliers who provide goods on credit and customers who purchase goods or services. **Suppliers** want to know about the company's ability to pay its debts; **customers** need to know that the company is a secure source of supply, so that repeat purchases and after-sales care will be available.

- **Finance providers** include banks which allow the company to operate an overdraft, or provide longer term loan finance secured on the company's assets. A bank wants to ensure that the company is able to keep up loan payments.

- **HM Revenue and Customs (HMRC)** want to know about business profits in order to assess the company's tax liabilities.

- **Employees** have an interest in the company's financial situation, because their careers and remuneration depend on it.

- **Financial analysts and advisers** need information for their clients or audience. For example, stockbrokers need information to advise investors; credit agencies want information to advise potential suppliers of goods to the company; and journalists need information for their reading public.

- **Government agencies** are interested in the efficient allocation of resources and therefore in the activities of enterprises. They also require information in order to provide a basis for national statistics.

- **The public**. Business entities affect members of the public in a variety of ways. For example, they may make a substantial contribution to a local economy by providing employment and using local suppliers. Another important factor is the effect of an entity on the natural environment, for example as regards pollution.

- **Bodies** such as the Financial Conduct Authority (FCA) who regulate the financial services industry, require information to ensure compliance with regulations and the law.

Accounting information is summarised in financial statements to satisfy the **information needs** of these different groups. However, some of these individual users of financial information may have conflicting needs, therefore, the information provided should meet the needs of the maximum number of primary users.

**Managers** of a business need the most information, to help them make planning and control decisions. They have greater access to business information, because they are able to review internally produced statements. Managers can obtain extra information through the **cost and management accounting system**.

### Interactive question 1: Accounting information

It is easy to see how 'internal' people get hold of accounting information. A manager, for example, can just go along to the accounts department and ask the staff there to prepare whatever accounting statements she needs. But external users of accounts cannot do this. How, in practice, can a business contact or a financial analyst access accounting information about a company?

See **Answer** at the end of this chapter.

In addition to management information, additional financial statements are prepared for the benefit of other user groups, who may demand particular information.

- **HMRC** will receive information to make tax assessments.
- A **bank** might demand a cash flow forecast as a pre condition of granting an overdraft.

### 1.4.1 Not-for-profit entities

It is not only businesses that need to prepare financial statements. **Charities and clubs**, for example, prepare financial statements every year. Financial statements also need to be prepared for **government (public sector) organisations**.

## 1.5 Users and their information needs

Below we consider potential users of financial statements, and the aspects of financial statements they are likely to be interested in.

- **Investors** (current and potential owners) are the providers of risk capital for the company, so they are interested in the **risk** to their capital presented by the investment, and the **return** they will get for taking that risk. They need information to help them determine whether they should buy, hold or sell shares. Owners are also interested in information which enables them to assess the ability of the entity to pay dividends.

- **Employees** and their representative groups need information about the stability and profitability of their employers, so they can assess the entity's ability to provide remuneration, retirement benefits and employment opportunities.

- **Lenders** need information that enables them to determine whether their loans, and the interest attached to them, will be paid when due.

- **Suppliers and other creditors** need information that enables them to determine whether amounts owing to them will be paid. Trade creditors are likely to be interested in an entity over a shorter period than lenders, unless they are dependent upon the continuation of the entity as a major customer.

- **Customers** need information about the entity's continuance, especially when they have a long-term involvement with, or are dependent on, the entity.

- **Governments and their agencies** have the needs listed in section 1.4. They also require information in order to regulate the activities of entities, and determine taxation policies.

- **Public**. Members of the public have the needs listed in section 1.4, that is they wish to see how the company will be able to continue employing local people and using local suppliers. Financial statements may assist the public by providing information about the trends and recent developments in the prosperity of the entity and the range of its activities.

The management of a reporting entity will be interested in financial information about the entity but does not need to rely on general purpose financial reports because it is able to obtain the financial information it needs internally.

Therefore instead of being thought of as users of the financial statements, management are primarily responsible for the **preparation and presentation** of the financial statements.

### 1.5.1 Ethical considerations

Ethical considerations should underpin the work of all professional accountants, including those in business who prepare financial statements and those who set the rules and regulations of financial reporting.

In order for the work of accountants to continue to be valuable, the financial information that they provide must be perceived as being trustworthy. If this reliability becomes compromised then users will no longer depend on the information and the value of the profession will be damaged.

By adhering to a code of conduct and ethical behaviour, accountants can maintain public confidence in the profession and thus maintain the value of accounting. Ethical considerations are discussed further in section 7 of this chapter.

## 2 The regulation of accounting

**Section overview**

- In the UK all companies must comply with the provisions of the Companies Act.

- In the UK financial statements must be prepared in accordance with either the UK GAAP or IFRS. They must also give a true and fair view.

A number of factors have shaped the **development of accounting**.

The regulatory framework of accounting, and the technical aspects of the changes made, will be covered later in this Study Manual and in your professional studies. The purpose of this section is to give a **general picture** of some of the factors which have shaped accounting. We will concentrate on the financial statements of limited liability companies, as these are the ones most closely regulated by statute or otherwise.

The following factors can be identified.

- Legislation
- Accounting concepts and individual judgement
- Accounting standards
- Generally accepted accounting practice (GAAP)
- True and fair view/fair presentation

**UK GAAP alert!**

The *Conceptual Framework* that underlies IFRS is very similar to that used to develop GAAP. However the elements identified and their definitions under IFRS are different. The UK GAAP alert! will give some insight into these differences throughout this Study Manual.

### 2.1 Generally Accepted Accounting Practice (GAAP)

GAAP is a term used to cover all the rules, from whatever source, which govern accounting in various jurisdictions. The requirement that financial information is relevant, reliable, comparable and understandable is common to both IFRS and GAAP.

### 2.2 Legislation

A listed company is one whose shares can be traded on a stock exchange, for example the London Stock exchange. Unlisted companies tend to be smaller than listed companies and their shares cannot be traded on a stock exchange. Limited liability companies are required by the Companies Act 2006 to prepare and publish financial statements annually. Their form and content are regulated by legislation but must comply with **accepted accounting and financial reporting standards**. For listed groups this means compliance with IAS and IFRS. Non-listed companies generally follow UK accounting standards which are substantially converged with international ones. The nature of a limited company and the issue of shares are dealt with in more detail in chapter 11.

### 2.2.1 Accounting standards

While ethical principles underpin financial accounting, different people could still interpret situations differently. In order to deal with some of this subjectivity, and to achieve comparability between different organisations, **accounting standards** were developed. These were developed at an international level, by the IASB and at a UK level by the Accounting Standards Board (ASB), an operating body of the Financial Reporting Council (FRC). The FRC changed its structure recently and the responsibility for accounting standards is now with the Accounting Council of the FRC

## 2.3 International Financial Reporting Standards (IFRS)

The IASB (International Accounting Standards Board) is responsible for setting international financial reporting standards (IFRS).

The standards and interpretations that are issued by the IASB comprise:

* International Financial Reporting Standards (IFRS)
* International Accounting Standards (IAS)
* IFRS Interpretations committee
* SIC Interpretations

The *Conceptual Framework* sets out concepts that underlie the preparation and presentation of financial statements for a wide range of users, many of whom have to rely on financial statements as their major source of financial information on an entity.

All standards (IASs and IFRSs) stem from the concepts set out in the *Conceptual Framework*. The *Conceptual Framework* states that:

'The objective of general purpose financial reporting is to provide financial information about the reporting entity that is useful to existing and potential investors, lenders and other creditors in making decisions about providing resources to the entity.'

### UK GAAP alert!

The examinable standards for Certificate Level Accounting are the IFRSs, however, as you continue your studies to FAR level you may choose to study UK GAAP as an alternative. It is important, therefore, to be familiar with UK GAAP.

## 2.4 UK GAAP

Companies in the UK can choose IFRS or UK financial reporting standards (FRS). References to UK GAAP in this Study Manual refer to the use of UK Companies Act 2006 and UK FRS. Whilst IFRS have different standards for different issues, there is one main accounting standard in the UK – FRS 102 – covering all issues. FRS 102 also contains the underpinning concepts and principles, which are similar to those which guide IFRSs.

So, UK GAAP rules derive from:

* The Companies Act 2006
* UK and international accounting and financial reporting standards

UK GAAP uses different terminology in many important respects regarding financial statements. FRS 102 actually uses international terminology, while the Companies Act 2006 uses terminology that is UK specific. In their published financial statements, UK non-listed companies tend to follow Companies Act 2006 and use the UK specific terminology which is as follows:

| International term | UK GAAP term |
| --- | --- |
| Statement of profit or loss | Profit and loss account |
| Statement of financial position | Balance sheet |
| Non-current asset | Fixed asset |
| Carrying amount | Net book value |
| Inventories | Stock |
| Receivables | Debtors |
| Irrecoverable debt | Bad debt |
| Irrecoverable debt expense | Bad and doubtful debts expense |
| Allowance for irrecoverable debts | Allowance for doubtful debts |
| Retained earnings | Retained profits (reserve) |
| Payables | Creditors |
| Non-current liabilities | Creditors: amounts falling due after more than one year |
| Current liabilities | Creditors: amounts falling due in less than one year |
| Revenue | Turnover |
| Finance costs | Interest payable |
| Property, plant and equipment | Tangible fixed assets |

## 2.5 True and fair view/faithful representation

Financial statements are required to give a **true and fair view**. True and fair view or **present fairly in all material respects** the financial results of the entity. These terms are not defined and tend to be decided in courts of law on the facts.

- *The Conceptual Framework*: Conceptual Framework states that if financial information is to be useful, it must be relevant and faithfully represent what it purports to represent.

- The Companies Act: Companies Act 2006 requires that the financial statements should give a **true and fair** view of the financial position of the entity at a particular point in time.

- In terms of IAS 1, financial statements should present fairly the financial position and performance, and the cash flows, of the entity. This requires faithful representation of the effects of transactions.

## 2.6 How to use this Study Manual

The study manual will use IFRS throughout this study manual as these are the examinable standards. However, you should be aware that chapters 2 to 10 contain the building blocks for creating financial statements. The aim of the UK GAAP alert! is to highlight the differences or in most cases, the similarities between IFRs and FRS (UK GAAP). Therefore, whether you go on to study UK GAAP or IFRS the skills you learn in these building block chapters will equip you to prepare both sets of accounts. Remember that the UK GAAP alert! is designed to assist you in your studies beyond this course, and that **the only examinable standards are the IFRSs**.

# 3 The main financial statements

## Section overview

- Financial statements prepared under IASs collectively comprise a statement of financial position, a statement of comprehensive income including a statement of profit or loss (previously referred to as an income statement), a statement of changes in equity, a statement of cash flows, notes and (in certain circumstances) a revised statement of financial position from an earlier period.

- IAS 1 *Presentation of Financial Statements* sets out the form and content of the financial statements.

IAS 1 *Presentation of Financial Statements* identifies a complete set of financial statements for a reporting period (typically a year) as comprising:

- A **statement of financial position** as at the end of the reporting period (as we shall see in Chapter 14, under UK GAAP this is called a **balance sheet)**,

- A statement of comprehensive income for the reporting period, which can be in a two-part format including a separate **statement of profit or loss** (as we shall see in Chapter 14, under UK GAAP this is called a **profit and loss account)**,

- A statement of changes in equity for the reporting period,

- A **statement of cash flows** for the reporting period,

- Notes comprising a **summary of significant accounting policies** and other explanatory information, and

- A statement of financial position as at the beginning of the earliest comparative period when an entity applies an accounting policy retrospectively, makes a restatement of items in its financial statements, or reclassifies items.

In this Study Manual we are only concerned with the **statement of financial position,** the **statement of profit or loss** part of the statement of comprehensive income, the **statement of cash flows** and the **summary of accounting policies note.**

IAS 1 makes it clear that an entity may use titles for the statements other than those used in the Standard. Many entities will no doubt continue to use the term '**balance sheet**' instead of 'statement of financial position', '**statement of profit or loss**' instead of 'statement of comprehensive income' and '**cash flow statement**' instead of 'statement of cash flows'. However in this Study Manual we shall use the IAS 1 terminology until Chapter 14, when we shall use the terminology of financial statements prepared under UK GAAP ('balance sheet' and 'profit and loss account').

## 3.1 Statement of financial position

### Definitions

**Statement of financial position:** A **list** of all the **assets controlled** and all the **liabilities owed** by a business as at a particular date: it is a snapshot of the **financial position** of the business at a particular moment. Monetary amounts are attributed to assets and liabilities. It also quantifies the amount of the owners' interest in the company: **equity.**

**Equity:** The amount invested in a business by the owners (IAS 1 refers to 'owners' rather than 'equity holders' or 'shareholders').

Assets and liabilities are explained in more detail in Chapter 2. However, the sum of the assets will always be equal to the sum of the liabilities plus equity/capital.

There are a number of factors affecting a company's financial position at any one time which include:

(a) The **economic resources** it controls (cash, labour, materials, machinery, skills)
(b) Its **financial structure** (whether it is funded by owners, lenders, suppliers, or by all three)

(c) Its **liquidity** (short-term availability of cash) and **solvency** (long-term access to funds)

(d) Its **adaptability** to changes in its operating environment

The *Conceptual Framework* focuses on how information about the nature and amounts of an entity's **economic resources** and **claims** (liabilities) can help users to identify the reporting entity's financial strengths and weaknesses.

In particular it points out that information about the nature and amounts of an entity's economic resources and claims can help users to assess:

- The entity's liquidity and solvency
- The entity's need for additional financing
- How successful the entity is likely to be in obtaining that financing

Additionally by gaining knowledge of the economic resources a business controls, users will be in a better position to predict the **entity's ability to generate cash in the future**.

Information about an entity's financial structure and liquidity/solvency can also help financial statement users.

| Factor | Information on this helps users |
|---|---|
| **Financial structure** | • To predict future borrowing needs |
| | • To predict how future profits and cash flows will be distributed among owners and lenders |
| | • To predict how successfully it will be able to raise future finance |
| **Liquidity/solvency** | • To predict its ability to meet financial commitments as they fall due |

## 3.2 Statement of profit or loss

### Definition

**Statement of profit or loss:** A statement displaying items of **income** and **expense** in a **reporting period** as components of **profit or loss for the period**. The statement shows whether the business has had more income than expense (a profit for the period) or *vice versa* (a loss for the period).

The **reporting period** chosen will depend on the purpose for which the statement is produced. The statement of profit or loss which forms part of the published annual financial statements of a **limited liability company** will usually be for the period of a **year**, commencing from the date of the previous year's financial statements. On the other hand, **management** might want to keep a closer eye on a company's profitability by making up **quarterly, monthly, weekly or even daily** statements.

The *Conceptual Framework* sets out how information about the business's financial performance, ie its profits or losses, is needed by users.

- To **understand the return** that the entity has produced on its economic resources
- To assess how well **management has discharged its responsibilities** to make efficient and effective use of the reporting entity's resources
- To help predict the business's **future returns** on its economic resources

The link between the statement of financial position and the statement of comprehensive income is provided by the **statement of cash flows** and the **statement of changes in equity**. These are covered in detail later in your professional studies. However, you will find an introduction to the statement of cash flows in Chapter 13. The statement of cash flows shows the actual cash flowing into and paid out of the business.

**UK GAAP alert!**

Companies reporting under UK GAAP will present their financial statements in accordance with:

- Companies Act 2006
- FRS 102

Details of the different terminology used is outlined in the table above. Generally the profit and loss account formats require less detail than IAS 1. The Companies Act balance sheet formats are less flexible than the IAS 1 formats. The Companies Act formats are enshrined in law.

## 3.3 Presentation of financial statements

Both the statement of financial position and the statement of profit or loss are **summaries of accumulated data**. For example, the statement of profit or loss shows a figure for revenue earned from selling goods and services to customers. This is the total revenue earned from all sales made during the period. An accountant devises methods of recording such transactions, so as to produce summarised financial statements from them.

The statement of financial position and the statement of profit or loss form the basis of financial statements for most businesses. For limited liability companies, other information by way of statements (such as the **statement of cash flows** and the **statement of changes in equity**) and notes is required by statute and accounting standards.

# 4 Capital and revenue items

**Section overview**

- Capital and revenue income and expenditure must be distinguished from each other.

## 4.1 Capital and revenue expenditure

**Definition**

**Capital expenditure:** Expenditure which results in the acquisition of long-term assets, or an improvement or enhancement of their earning capacity.

**Long-term assets** are those which will be kept in the entity for more than one year.

- Capital expenditure is not charged as an expense in the statement of profit or loss (although a '**depreciation**' charge will usually be made to write off the capital expenditure gradually over time; depreciation expense is shown in the statement of profit or loss).

- Capital expenditure on long-term assets appears in the statement of financial position.

**Definition**

**Revenue expenditure:** Expenditure which is incurred either:

- For **trade purposes**. This includes purchases of raw materials or items for resale, expenditure on wages and salaries, selling and distribution expenses, administrative expenses and finance costs, or

- To maintain the **existing earning capacity** of long-term assets.

Revenue expenditure is charged to the statement of profit or loss of a period, provided that it relates to the trading activity and sales of that particular period.

### Worked example: Revenue expenditure

If a business buys ten steel bars for £200 (£20 each) and sells eight of them during a reporting period, it will have two steel bars left at the end of the period. The full £200 is revenue expenditure but only £160 is the cost of the goods sold during the period. The remaining £40 (cost of two units) will be included in the statement of financial position as 'inventory' valued at £40.

### Worked example: Capital expenditure

A business purchases a building for £300,000. It then adds an extension to the building at a cost of £100,000. After a few months the building needs to have a few broken windows mended, its floors polished and some missing roof tiles replaced. These cleaning and maintenance jobs cost £900.

In this example, the original purchase (£300,000) and the cost of the extension (£100,000) are **capital expenditure**, because they are incurred to acquire and then improve a long-term asset. The other costs of £900 are **revenue expenditure**, because these merely maintain the building and thus its 'earning capacity'.

**Capital expenditure** can include costs incurred in bringing a long-term asset to its final condition and location, such as legal fees, duties and carriage costs borne by the asset's purchaser, plus installation costs. Repair, maintenance and staff costs in relation to long-term assets are **revenue expenditure**.

## 4.2 Capital income and revenue income

### Definition

Capital income: Proceeds from the sale of non-current assets.

The profits (or losses) from the sale of long-term assets are included in the statement of profit or loss for the reporting period in which the sale takes place. For instance, the business may sell machinery or property which it no longer needs.

### Definition

Revenue income: Income derived from

- The sale of trading assets, such as goods held in inventory
- The provision of services
- Interest and dividends received from business investments

## 4.3 Capital transactions

The categorisation of capital and revenue items given above does not mention raising **additional funds from the owner(s) of the business**, or raising and repaying **loans**.

- These transactions add to the cash assets of the business and create corresponding capital or liabilities (loans).

- When a loan is repaid, it reduces the liabilities (loan) and the assets (cash).

None of these transactions would be reported through the statement of profit or loss.

## 4.4 Why is the distinction between capital and revenue items important?

Calculating profit for any reporting period depends on the correct and consistent **classification** of revenue or capital items. You must get used to the terminology here as these words appear in the accounting and financial reporting standards themselves.

## Interactive question 2: Capital or revenue?

State whether each of the following items should be classified as 'capital' or 'revenue' expenditure or income.

(a) The purchase of a property (eg an office building)

(b) Property depreciation

(c) Solicitors' fees in connection with the purchase of property

(d) The costs of adding extra memory to a computer

(e) Computer repairs and maintenance costs

(f) Profit on the sale of an office building

(g) Revenue from sales paid for by credit card

(h) The cost of new machinery

(i) Customs duty charged on machinery when imported into the country

(j) The 'carriage' costs of transporting the new machinery from the supplier's factory to the premises of the business purchasing it

(k) The cost of installing the new machinery in the premises of the business

(l) The wages of the machine operators

See **Answer** at the end of this chapter.

# 5 Qualitative characteristics of useful accounting information

### Section overview

- Financial information should be **relevant** and **faithfully represent** what it purports to represent. The usefulness of financial information is enhanced if it is comparable, verifiable, timely and understandable.

What type of information then should financial statements contain? What should its main qualities be from the user's point of view?

## 5.1 The fundamental qualitative characteristics

The *Conceptual Framework* identifies the fundamental qualitative characteristics to be **relevance** and **faithful representation**. Information must be **both** relevant and faithfully represented to be useful.

- **Relevance.** Relevant financial information is capable of making a difference in the decisions made by users. Information may be capable of making a difference in a decision even if some users choose not to take advantage of it or are already aware of it from other sources.

  Financial information can make a difference to decisions if it has:

  - **Predictive value.** It can be used to predict future outcomes.

  - **Confirmatory value.** It provides feedback about previous evaluations (it confirms whether past predictions were reasonable).

  Information's relevance is affected by its nature and **materiality**. (We shall come back to materiality; for now you can think of it as 'important'). You should note that information may become less relevant if there is undue delay in its reporting.

- **Faithful representation**. If information is to be useful, it must represent faithfully the transactions and other events it purports to represent. A faithful representation will be:

  - **Complete**. All information necessary for a user to understand the transactions or events being depicted is included.

  - **Neutral** (unbiased)

  - **Free from error**. Free from error in the context of faithful representation **does not mean** the information is perfectly accurate in all respects. Instead it means there are no errors or omissions in the description of it and the process used to produce the reported information has been selected and applied with no errors in the process.

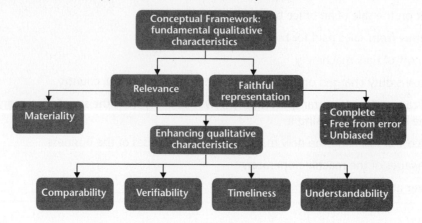

**UK GAAP alert!**

FRS 102 includes qualitative characteristics for companies using UK GAAP which are similar to the characteristics included in the *Conceptual Framework*.

## 5.2 Enhancing qualitative characteristics

According to the *Conceptual Framework* information that is relevant and faithfully represented can be enhanced by the following 'enhancing' qualitative characteristics:

- **Comparability**. Comparability is the qualitative characteristic that enables users to identify and understand similarities in, and differences among, items. Information should be produced so that valid comparisons can be made with information from previous periods and with information produced by other entities (for example, the financial statements of similar companies operating in the same line of business). Comparability should not be confused with **consistency**. Applying consistency (using the same methods for the same items) is a means of achieving comparability (comparability is the goal).

- **Verifiability**. Verifiability helps to assure users that information is a faithful representation of the transactions or events it purports to represent. If information is verifiable it essentially means that it can be proven, for example you may be able to check it is true by examination, inspection or comparison. The *Conceptual Framework* states that 'verifiability means that different knowledgeable and independent observers could reach consensus, although not necessarily complete agreement, that a particular depiction is a faithful representation'.

- **Timeliness**. Timeliness means having information available to decision-makers in time to be capable of influencing their decisions. As a general rule older information is less useful than recent information. However, you should note that some information may still be timely for a long time after the end of a reporting period. This is true of information for users of financial information who need to identify and assess trends.

- **Understandability**. Information is understandable if it is classified, characterised and presented clearly and concisely. When considering whether information is understandable you should bear in mind that financial reports are prepared for users who have a **reasonable knowledge of business and economic** activities.

# 6 Accounting concepts and conventions

**Section overview**

- The fundamental assumptions behind ledger accounting and the preparation of financial statements are contained in IAS 1 and the *Conceptual Framework.*

- IAS 1 is concerned with the presentation of financial statements so that they are comparable across time and with other companies.

- The objective of financial statements is to provide useful information to users making economic decisions. To achieve this information must be presented fairly or faithfully, which generally means it should be presented in accordance with IASs.

- Each entity needs to select and apply accounting policies in order to present its financial statements. The result will be information that is relevant and faithfully represents what it purports to represent.

Many accounting procedures are operated automatically by people who have never questioned whether alternative methods exist which have equal validity. In fact the procedures in common use imply the acceptance of certain concepts which are by no means self evident, nor are they the only possible concepts which could be used to build up an accounting framework.

Our next step is to look at some of the more important concepts which are used in preparing financial statements.

We begin by considering the **fundamental assumptions** which are the subject of IAS 1 *Presentation of Financial Statements* (and which are also covered in the *Conceptual Framework*).

## 6.1 Fair presentation

In this section we look at the general requirements of IAS 1's **assumptions**. The rest of IAS 1, on the format and content of financial statements will be covered in Chapter 11 and 12 when we look in detail at the preparation of company financial statements.

### 6.1.1 Objectives and scope of IAS 1

The main objective of IAS 1 is:

'to prescribe the basis for presentation of general purpose financial statements, to ensure comparability both with the entity's financial statements of previous periods and with the financial statements of other entities.'

IAS 1 applies to all **general purpose financial statements** prepared and presented in accordance with International Financial Reporting Standards (IFRSs – this refers to IASs as well, the collective term that we use in this Study Manual). General purpose financial statements are those intended to meet the needs of users who are not in a position to demand reports tailored to meet their particular information needs.

### 6.1.2 Purpose of financial statements

The **objectives of financial statements** are:

- To provide information about the financial position, performance and cash flows of an entity that is useful to a wide range of users in making **economic decisions**

- To show the result of **management's stewardship** of the resources entrusted to it

- To assist users in **predicting the entity's future cash flows** and, in particular, their timing and certainty

To fulfil these objectives, financial statements must provide information about the entity's:

- Assets
- Liabilities
- Equity
- Income and expenses (including gains and losses)
- Other changes in equity
- Cash flows

As defined in Chapter 2, these are called the **elements of financial statements**

A complete set of financial statements includes:

- Statement of financial position
- Statement of profit or loss (part of the statement of comprehensive income)
- Accounting policies note
- Statement of cash flows

Covered in the *Accounting* syllabus

- Statement of changes in equity
- Explanatory notes

Covered in the *Financial Accounting and Reporting* syllabus

- A further statement of financial position from an earlier period where there has been retrospective application of an accounting policy, a reclassification or a retrospective restatement – issues that we shall come back to in Chapter 11.

Preparation of the financial statements is the responsibility of the **board of directors**. IAS 1 also recognises the value of a **financial review** by management and the production of any other reports and statements which may aid users, but these fall outside the *Accounting* syllabus scope.

### 6.1.3 Fair presentation and compliance with IASs

Most importantly, financial statements should **present fairly** the financial position, financial performance and cash flows of an entity. **Applying IASs** is presumed to result in fair presentation.

### Definition

**Fair presentation:** The faithful representation of the effects of transactions, other events and conditions in accordance with the *Conceptual Framework*.

The following points made by IAS 1 expand on this principle.

- Compliance with IASs should be explicitly stated in a note to the financial statements.
- All relevant IASs must be followed if compliance with IASs is disclosed.
- Use of an inappropriate accounting treatment cannot be rectified either by disclosure of accounting policies or notes/explanatory material.

IAS 1 states what is required for a fair presentation.

- Selection and application of **accounting policies.**
- **Presentation of information** in a manner which provides relevant, reliable, comparable and understandable information.
- **Additional disclosures** where required to enable users to understand the impact of particular transactions, events and conditions on the entity's financial position and performance.

### 6.1.4 Departures from IASs

There may be (very rare) circumstances when management decides that compliance with a requirement of an IAS would be so misleading that financial statements would not meet their objectives. **Departure from the IAS** may therefore be required to achieve a fair presentation. The following should be disclosed in such an event.

- Management confirmation that the financial statements fairly present the entity's financial position, performance and cash flows.

- Statement that all IASs have been complied with *except* in respect of departure from individual IASs, required to achieve a fair presentation.

- Details of the nature of the departure, why the IAS treatment would be misleading, and the treatment adopted.

- Financial effect of the departure.

## 6.2 Going concern (IAS 1)

### Definition

**Going concern:** The entity is viewed as continuing in operation for the foreseeable future. It is assumed that the entity has neither the intention nor the necessity of liquidation or ceasing to trade.

This concept assumes that, when preparing a normal set of financial statements, the business will **continue to operate** in approximately the same manner for the foreseeable future (at least, but not limited to, the next 12 months). In particular the entity will not go into liquidation or cease trading, or have no realistic alternative but to liquidate or cease trading.

When an entity is not a going concern, the financial statements must state that they are prepared on a basis other than going concern, and clarify what this basis entails. When presenting financial statements using a break up basis of accounting, an entity's assets are **valued at their 'break up' value**: the amount they would sell for (their **net realisable value**) if they were sold off individually in a forced sale and the business were broken up. Since this forced sale is necessary because the business has foreseen problems in the next 12 months, financial statements prepared on a break-up basis will contain neither non-current assets nor non-current liabilities. All assets will be deemed to be for sale and all liabilities will be treated as becoming due within 12 months of the date of the statement of financial position.

### Interactive question 3: Going concern

A retailer commences business on 1 January and buys 20 washing machines, each costing £100. During the year he sells 17 machines at £150 each. How should the remaining machines be valued at 31 December in the following circumstances?

(a) He is forced to close down his business at the end of the year and the remaining machines will realise only £60 each in a forced sale.

(b) He intends to continue his business into the next year.

See **Answer** at the end of this chapter.

**If the going concern assumption is not followed**, that fact must be disclosed, together with:

- The **basis** on which the financial statements have been prepared.
- The **reasons** why the entity is not considered to be a going concern.

When there is uncertainty as to whether the entity is a going concern, this should be disclosed along with the nature of the uncertainty.

## 6.3 Accrual basis of accounting (IAS 1)

An entity should prepare its financial statements, except for cash flow information, using the accrual basis of accounting.

## Definition

**Accrual basis of accounting:** Items are recognised as assets, liabilities, equity, income and expenses (the elements of financial statements) when they satisfy the definitions and recognition criteria for those elements in the *Conceptual Framework*.

Entities should prepare their financial statements on the basis that transactions are recorded in them, not as the cash is paid or received (**cash accounting**), but as the income or expenses are **earned or incurred** in the reporting period to which they relate.

According to the accrual basis, when computing profit **income earned must be matched against the expenses incurred in earning it**.

## Worked example: Accrual basis

Emma purchases 20 T-shirts in her first month of trading (May) at a cost of £5 each on credit. She sells all of them on credit for £10 each. Emma has therefore made a profit of £100, by matching the income (£200) earned against the cost (£100) of acquiring them.

If, however, Emma only sells 18 T-shirts, it is incorrect to charge her statement of profit or loss with the cost of 20 T-shirts, as she still has two T-shirts in hand. If she sells them in June, she is likely to make a profit on the sale. Therefore, only the purchase cost of 18 T-shirts (£90) should be matched with her sales income (£180), leaving her with a profit of £90.

Her statement of financial position will look like this at the end of May.

|  | £ |
|---|---|
| *Assets* | |
| Inventory (two T-shirts at cost, ie 2 × £5) | 10 |
| Receivables (18 × £10) | 180 |
| | 190 |
| *Capital and liabilities* | |
| Proprietor's capital (profit for the period) | 90 |
| Payables (20 × £5) | 100 |
| | 190 |

However, if Emma had decided to give up selling T-shirts at the end of May, then the going concern assumption would no longer apply and the two T-shirts in the statement of financial position should be at their break up valuation, not cost. Similarly, if the two unsold T-shirts are unlikely to be sold at more than their cost of £5 each (say, because of damage or a fall in demand) then they should be recorded on the statement of financial position at their **net realisable value** (ie the likely eventual sales price less any expenses incurred to make them saleable) rather than cost.

In this example, the concepts of **going concern and accrual are linked**. Since the business is assumed to be a going concern, it is possible to carry forward the cost of the unsold T-shirts as a charge against profits of the next period.

## Definition

**Cash accounting basis of accounting:** Under this method, a company records customer receipts in the period that they are received, and expenses in the period in which they are paid. It is easier to use and can be useful for a smaller company, especially for tax purposes where cash flow may be an issue. Under the accruals basis, a company may have to pay tax on profits before the cash is actually received by the business.

Applying the cash accounting basis to the above example, no profit or expenses would be recorded until cash changed hands. Therefore, if Emma bought 20 tshirts on credit for £5 each, and sold them on credit for £10 each in May, no profit or loss would be recorded in May. If, in June Emma received payment for the tshirts she had sold on credit, and in July she paid for the tshirts she had purchased on credit, a profit of £200 would be recorded in June, and a loss of £100 would be recorded in July.

## 6.4 Consistency of presentation (IAS 1)

To maintain consistency, the presentation and classification of items in the financial statements should **stay the same from one period to the next**, unless:

- There is a significant change in the **nature of the operations**, or a review of the financial statements indicates a **more appropriate presentation.**

- A change in presentation is **required by an IAS.**

By having consistent presentation the **comparability** of financial statements is enhanced, both over a period of time, and also between different companies.

## 6.5 Materiality and aggregation (IAS 1)

### Definition

**Material:** Omissions or misstatements of items are material if they could, individually or collectively, influence the economic decisions of users taken on the basis of the financial statements. **Materiality** depends on the size and nature of the omission or misstatement judged in the surrounding circumstances. The size or the nature of an item, or a combination of both, could be the determining factor.

Each **material class of similar items** shall be presented **separately** in the financial statements. Items of a dissimilar nature or function shall be presented separately unless they are immaterial.

A specific disclosure requirement in an IAS need **not** be satisfied if the information is immaterial.

The *Conceptual Framework* links materiality particularly to the qualitative characteristic of **relevance**.

Financial statements result from processing large numbers of transactions or other events that are then **aggregated** into classes according to their nature or function, such as 'revenue', 'purchases', 'trade receivables' and 'trade payables'. The final stage in the process of aggregation and classification is the presentation of condensed and classified items on the face of the statement of financial position or statement of profit or loss. If an item is not individually material it is aggregated with other items on the face of financial statements, though it may be separately classified in the notes.

There is no absolute measure of materiality. In relation to **materiality by size** it is common to apply a convenient rule of thumb (for example material items are those with a value greater than 5% of net profits). However some items are regarded as particularly sensitive and therefore as being **material by nature**. Even a very small misstatement of such an item is taken as a material error; an example is the amount of remuneration paid to directors of a company.

## 6.6 Offsetting (IAS 1)

**Assets** and **liabilities**, and **income** and **expenditure** must be presented **separately** in the financial statements. IAS 1 does not allow these items **to be offset** against each other unless such a treatment is required or permitted by another IFRS.

**Income and expenses** can be offset only when:

- An IFRS requires or permits it, **or**

- Gains, losses and related expenses arising from the same/similar transactions are not material (in aggregate).

## 6.7 The business entity concept

This concept has already been discussed in the context of the **separate entity principle**: that accountants regard a business as a separate entity, distinct from its owners or managers. The concept applies whether the business is a limited liability company (and so recognised in law as a separate entity), a sole trader or a partnership (in which case the business is not legally recognised as separate from its owners).

## 6.8 The historical cost convention

A basic principle of accounting is that the monetary amount at which **items are normally measured in financial statements is at historical cost**, ie at the amount which the business paid to acquire them. An important advantage of this concept is that the objectivity of financial statements is maximised: there is usually a **source document** to prove the amount paid to purchase an asset or pay an expense.

### Definition

Historical cost: Transactions are recorded at their cost when they occurred.

It is easier to deal with costs when measuring items, rather than with 'values', as valuations tend to be subjective and to vary according to what the valuation is for.

### Worked example: Cost or valuation

A company acquires a machine to manufacture its products. The company expects to use the machine for four years. At the end of two years the company is preparing a statement of financial position and has to decide what monetary amount to give the machine (the *Framework* refers to this process as 'measurement').

Numerous possibilities can be considered.

- The original cost (historical cost) of the machine

- Half of the historical cost, on the ground that half of its useful life has expired

- The amount the machine might fetch on the secondhand market (**realisable value**)

- The amount needed to replace the machine with an identical machine (**replacement cost**)

- The amount needed to replace the machine with a more modern machine incorporating the technological advances of the previous two years

- The machine's economic value, ie the amount of the profits it is expected to generate for the company during its remaining life (**present value**)

All of these valuations have something to commend them, but the great advantage of the first two is that they are based on a figure (the machine's historical cost) which is **objectively verifiable**.

There are many problems associated with the use of historical cost valuations but these are outside the scope of the *Accounting* syllabus.

### Interactive question 4: Accounting concepts

(a) Your office equipment will be used, on average, for five years, so you charge 20% of its cost as depreciation each year in your statement of profit or loss . This year your business profitability is down and you think you can squeeze an extra year's life out of your equipment. Is it acceptable not to make any charge this year?

(b) You have recently paid £4.95 for a waste paper bin which should be used for about five years. Should you treat it as a non-current asset?

See **Answer** at the end of this chapter.

# 7 Ethical considerations

> **Section overview**
>
> * Application of judgement required in applying fundamental accounting concepts.
>
> * The IESBA Code of Ethics for Professional Accountants describes five fundamental principles of professional ethics that accountants must adhere to: integrity, objectivity, professional competence and due care, confidentiality, and professional behaviour.
>
> * ICAEW Code of Ethics is a principles based system.

## 7.1 Accounting concepts and individual judgement

Many figures in financial statements are derived from the **application of judgement** in applying **fundamental accounting concepts**.

Different people exercising their judgement on the same facts could arrive at very different conclusions.

### Interactive question 5: Value of reputation

An accountancy training firm has an excellent **reputation** amongst students and employers. How would you value this and include this asset in the financial statements?

See **Answer** at the end of this chapter.

Other examples of areas where the judgement of different people may vary are as follows.

* **Valuation of buildings** in times of changing property prices.

* **Research and development** (R&D): is it right to treat this only as an expense? In a sense it is an investment to generate future revenue.

* **Brands** such as 'Snickers' or 'iPod'. Are they assets in the same way that a fork lift truck is an asset?

Working from the same data, different groups of people may produce very different financial statements, but if judgement is completely unregulated, there will be no comparability between the financial statements of different organisations. This will be all the more significant in cases where deliberate manipulation occurs, in order to present financial statements in the most favourable light.

The exercise of judgement in accounting matters should always be underpinned by ethical principles. To this end both the International Ethics Standards Board for Accountants (IESBA) and the ICAEW have produced codes of ethics that state the fundamental ethical principles that all professional accountants should adhere to.

## IESBA Code of Ethics for Professional Accountants – fundamental principles

The International Ethics Standards Board for Accountants (IESBA) develops ethical standards and guidance for use by professional accountants. The IESBA code applies to all professional accountants, whether in public practice, in business, education and the public sector. It serves as the foundation for codes of ethics developed and enforced by member bodies. The IESBA Code of Ethics for Professional Accountants describes five fundamental principles of professional ethics that accountants must adhere to. These are:

* **Integrity.** A professional accountant should be straightforward and honest in all professional and business relationships.

* **Objectivity.** A professional accountant should not allow bias, conflict of interest or undue influence of others to override professional or business judgements.

- **Professional competence and due care**. A professional accountant has a continuing duty to maintain professional knowledge and skill at the level required to ensure that a client or employer receives competent professional service based on current developments in practice, legislation and techniques. A professional accountant should act diligently and in accordance with applicable technical and professional standards when providing professional services.

- **Confidentiality**. A professional accountant should respect the confidentiality of information acquired as a result of professional and business relationships and should not disclose any such information to third parties without proper and specific authority unless there is a legal or professional right or duty to disclose. Confidential information acquired as a result of professional and business relationships should not be used for the personal advantage of the professional accountant or third parties.

- **Professional behaviour**. A professional accountant should comply with relevant laws and regulations and should avoid any action that discredits the profession.

The structures and processes that support the operations of the IESBA are facilitated by the International Federation of Accountants (IFAC). IFAC is the global organisation for the accounting profession. It aims to ensure that the global accountancy profession is valued in the development of strong and sustainable organisations.

### Interactive question 6: Ethics

Susan works as an auditor for a client called Plasma Screen Ltd. During the audit, the CEO of Plasma Screen Ltd offers Susan their newest model of television, which is about to be released on the market, for free as a thank you for carrying out the audit. If Susan accepts the television, which of IESBA's fundamental principles of professional ethics may be threatened?

See **Answer** at the end of this chapter.

## ICAEW Code of Ethics

The ICAEW Code states that 'Chartered Accountants are expected to demonstrate the highest standards of professional conduct and to take into consideration the public interest and to maintain the reputation of the accounting profession'.

It should be noted that the guidance applies to ICAEW members, students, affiliates, employees of member firms and member firms themselves. All of these are 'expected to follow the guidance contained in the fundamental principles in all of their professional and business activities whether carried out with or without reward and in other circumstances where to fail to do so would bring discredit to the profession.'

Therefore, the Code may apply not only to the paid activities of the professional accountant but also to the life of the professional accountant, particularly if he is involved in matters relevant to his profession, such as being a Trustee of a charity or club.

The Code also states that professional accountants are required to follow the spirit as well as the letter of the guidance. In other words, a specific matter being excluded from the guidance does not mean that the accountant does not have to think about it; rather he must determine if the spirit of the guidance would also apply to that situation.

### Professional competence and due care

The principle of professional competence and due care is of particular relevance to preparers of financial statements.

Professional accountants have a duty to achieve a level of professional knowledge and skill and must ensure that they do not operate beyond their current level of competence.

In order to continue offering services in a particular field the professional accountant must maintain their competence. This can be achieved through a continued awareness of the relevant technical, professional and business developments.

As part of the requirement for diligence the professional accountant should do what is required to deliver the agreed service, should ensure that any staff working under their authority are competent and adequately trained and supervised and where appropriate should ensure that the client or employer understands the limitations of the services that are being provided.

## 7.2 Principles based system

Rather than containing a set of rules, the ethics codes discussed above are principles based. There are a number of advantages to a framework over a system of ethical rules. These are outlined in the table below.

| Advantages of a principles based over a rules based system of ethics |
| --- |
| A principles based system places the **onus on the individual** to actively consider independence for every given situation, rather than just agreeing a checklist of forbidden items. Even if something is not expressly stated in the guidance, professional accountants are required to follow the spirit as well as the letter of the guidance. |
| A principles based system **prevents individuals interpreting legalistic requirements narrowly** to get around the ethical requirements. There is an extent to which rules engender deception, whereas principles encourage compliance. |
| A principles based system **allows for** the variations that are found in every **individual situation**. Each situation is likely to be different. |
| A principles based system can accommodate a **rapidly changing environment**, such as the one that professional accountants regularly face. |
| A principles based system **can contain prohibitions** where these are necessary as safeguards are not feasible. |

### Interactive question 7: ICAEW Code of Ethics

Discuss the merits and drawbacks of the ICAEW Code of Ethics being a principles based system.

See **Answer** at the end of this chapter.

## Summary

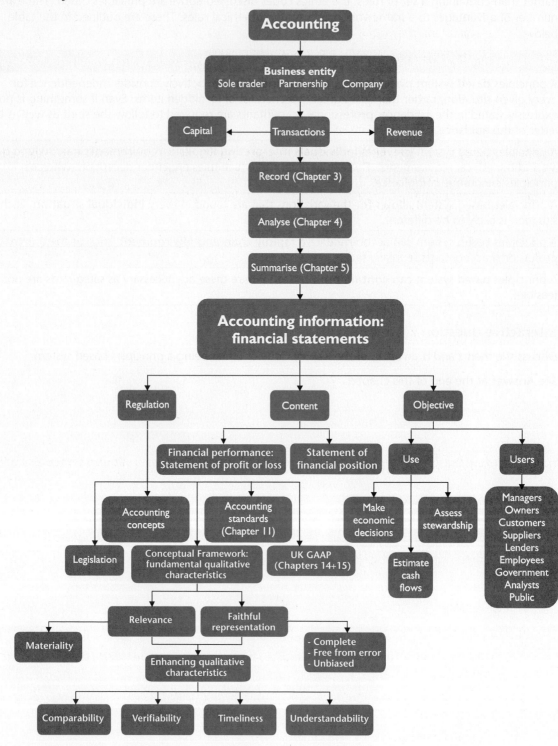

**Accounting**

**Business entity**
Sole trader  Partnership  Company

Capital ← Transactions → Revenue

Record (Chapter 3)

Analyse (Chapter 4)

Summarise (Chapter 5)

**Accounting information:
financial statements**

Regulation    Content    Objective

Financial performance:
Statement of profit or loss

Statement of
financial position

Use

Users

Accounting
concepts

Accounting
standards
(Chapter 11)

Make
economic
decisions

Assess
stewardship

Legislation

Conceptual Framework:
fundamental qualitative
characteristics

UK GAAP
(Chapters 14+15)

Estimate
cash
flows

Managers
Owners
Customers
Suppliers
Lenders
Employees
Government
Analysts
Public

Relevance

Faithful
representation

Materiality

- Complete
- Free from error
- Unbiased

Enhancing qualitative
characteristics

Comparability    Verifiability    Timeliness    Understandability

ICAEW

# Self-test

Answer the following questions.

1 An entity's transactions are recorded first in

 A Books of original entry
 B Ledger accounts
 C The statement of profit or loss
 D The statement of financial position

2 Liability for the debts of the business does **not** fall on

 A A sole trader
 B Partners in a general partnership
 C A limited liability company
 D Owners of a limited liability company

3 According to IAS 1 which of the following does **not** represent an objective of financial statements?

 A To provide information to investors in making economic decisions
 B To provide information to managers in making business decisions
 C To show the results of management's stewardship of the resources entrusted to it
 D To help users predict the entity's future cash flows

4 Which one of the following issues in an entity's financial statements is likely to be of most interest to an entity's lender?

 A Whether the entity has paid a dividend
 B Whether the entity will repay a loan when it falls due
 C Whether the entity will continue to be able to employ people
 D Whether the entity patronises local suppliers

5 A statement of financial position is best described as:

 A A snapshot of the entity's financial position at a particular point in time
 B A record of an entity's financial performance over a period of time
 C A list of all the income and expenses of the entity at a particular point in time
 D A list of all the assets and liabilities of the entity over a period of time

6 In applying fundamental accounting concepts the preparers of financial information are also using

 A Legislation
 B Accounting standards
 C Judgement
 D Financial reporting standards

7 Match the fundamental ethical principle to the characteristic.

 A Integrity

 B Objectivity

 (i) Members should be straightforward and honest in all professional and business relationships.

 (ii) Members should not allow bias, conflict or interest or undue influence of others to override professional or business judgements.

8 Which of the following would NOT be a suitable question to ask yourself when resolving an ethical dilemma?

 A Would my colleagues think my solution is reasonable?
 B Have I thought about all the possible consequences of my solution?
 C Could I defend my solution under public scrutiny?
 D Does my solution benefit my career?

9   The ICAEW Code only applies to the paid activities of the professional accountant.

    True    ☐

    False   ☐

10  Which of the following is **not** a source of the accounting rules embodied in UK GAAP?

    A   The Companies Act 2006
    B   UK accounting standards
    C   Listing requirements of the London Stock Exchange
    D   Accounting requirements of an entity's US parent company

11  Which of the following factors have **not** influenced financial reporting?

    A   National legislation
    B   Economic factors
    C   Accounting standards
    D   GAAP

12  Materiality is an entity-specific aspect of which qualitative characteristic?

    A   Relevance
    B   Understandability
    C   Faithful representation
    D   Comparability

13  Which of the following is an item of capital expenditure?

    A   Cost of goods sold
    B   Purchase of a machine
    C   Repairs to a machine
    D   Wages cost

Now, go back to the Learning Objectives in the Introduction. If you are satisfied that you have achieved these objectives, please tick them off.

# Technical reference

## 1 The purpose of accounting information

- The objective of general purpose financial reporting is to provide financial information about the reporting entity that is useful to existing and potential investors, lenders and other creditors in making decisions about providing resources to the entity.

  *Conceptual Framework Para OB2*

- To provide information about the financial position, performance and cash flows of an entity that is useful to a wide range of users in making economic decisions

  IAS 1 para 9

- To show the results of management's stewardship of the resources entrusted to it

  IAS 1 para 9

- Assists users of the financial statements in predicting the entity's future cash flows and, in particular, their timing and certainty

  IAS 1 para 9

## 3 The regulation of accounting

- A statement of financial position, a statement of comprehensive income, a statement of changes in equity, a statement of cash flows, notes and (in certain circumstances) a revised statement of financial position from an earlier period

  IAS 1 para 10

  IAS 1 para 15;

- Fair presentation/faithful representation

  *Conceptual Framework paras QC12 - QC16*

## 4 The main financial statements

- Information about the nature and amounts of an entity's economic resources and claims can help users to assess the entity's liquidity and solvency, its need for additional financing and how successful the entity is likely to be in obtaining that financing.

  *Conceptual Framework para OB13*

- Information about a reporting entity's financial performance is needed by users to understand the return that the entity has produced on its economic resources. Information about the return the entity has produced provides an indication of how well management has discharged its responsibilities to make efficient and effective use of the reporting entity's resources. Information about the variability and components of that return is also important, especially in assessing the uncertainty of future cash flows.

  *Conceptual Framework para OB16*

## 4 The qualitative characteristics of useful financial information

- Fundamental qualitative characteristics: relevance and faithful representation.
- Enhancing qualitative characteristics: comparability, verifiability, timeliness and understandability.

  *Conceptual Framework paras QC6-QC34*

## 5 Objectives and scope of IAS 1

- To prescribe the basis for presentation of general purpose financial statements, to ensure comparability both with the entity's financial statements of previous periods and with the financial statements of other entities

  IAS 1 para 1

- To be applied to all general purpose financial statements prepared and presented in accordance with International Financial Reporting Standards (IFRSs)

  IAS 1 para 2

- General purpose financial statements are those intended to meet the needs of users who are not in a position to demand reports tailored to meet their particular information needs.

  IAS 1 para 7

## 6 The purpose of financial statements

- To provide information about the financial position, performance and cash flows of an entity that is useful to a wide range of users in making economic decisions

  IAS 1 para 9

  - To show the results of management's stewardship of the resources entrusted to it

  - To assist users in predicting the entity's future cash flows and, in particular, their timing and certainty

  - To provide information about the entity's assets, liabilities, equity, income and expenses (including gains and losses), other changes in equity and cash flows

## 7 Components of financial statements

- A statement of financial position at the end of the reporting period, a statement of profit or loss, an accounting policies note, a statement of changes in equity, a statement of cash flows, explanatory notes and a statement of financial position at an earlier date where there has been retrospective application, retrospective restatement or reclassification

  IAS 1 para 10

## 8 Fair presentation (IAS 1)

- The faithful representation of the effects of transactions, other events and conditions in accordance with the definitions and recognition criteria in the *Framework*. The application of IASs, with additional disclosure when necessary, is presumed to result in financial statements that achieve a fair presentation.

  IAS 1 para 15

- Compliance with IASs must be explicit and complete.

  IAS 1 para 16

- For there to be fair presentation:

  IAS 1 para 17

  - Accounting policies must be selected and applied.

  - Information must be presented in a manner which provides relevant, reliable, comparable and understandable information.

  - To enable users to understand the impact of particular transactions, events and conditions on the entity's financial position and performance additional disclosures may be required.

- Use of an inappropriate accounting treatment cannot be rectified either by disclosure of accounting policies or notes/explanatory material

  IAS 1 para 18

- In some circumstances departure from the IASs may be required to achieve a fair presentation

  IAS 1 para 23

## 9 Underlying assumptions

- Financial statements shall be prepared on a **going concern** basis unless management either intends to liquidate the entity or to cease trading, or has no realistic alternative but to do so. Assessment of whether the going concern assumption is appropriate must take into account all available information for at least 12 months from the end of the reporting period. Any uncertainty must be disclosed.

  IAS 1 para 25 and 26

- An entity should prepare its financial statements using the **accrual basis** of accounting, recognising the elements of financial statements in line with the *Framework.*

  IAS 1 para 27 and 28

- To maintain **consistency**, the presentation and classification of items in the financial statements should stay the same from one period to the next, unless there is significant change in the nature of the operations, or a review of the financial statements indicates a more appropriate presentation, or a change in presentation is required by an IAS.

  IAS 1 para 45

- Omissions or misstatements of items are material if they could, individually or collectively, influence the economic decisions of users taken on the basis of the financial statements. **Materiality** depends on the size and nature of the omission or misstatement judged in the surrounding circumstances. The size or the nature of an item, or a combination of both, could be the determining factor.

IAS 1 para 7

- Each material class of similar items shall be presented separately in the financial statements. Items of a dissimilar nature or function shall be presented separately unless they are immaterial, but a specific disclosure requirement in an IAS need not be satisfied if the information is immaterial.

IAS 1 paras 29 and 31

# Answers to Interactive questions

## Answer to Interactive question 1

Limited liability companies (though not other forms of business such as general partnerships) are required to make certain accounting information public. This is done by filing information centrally, as a Companies Act 2006 requirement.

## Answer to Interactive question 2

(a) Capital expenditure

(b) Depreciation is revenue expenditure

(c) Legal fees associated with purchasing a property may be added to the purchase price and classified as capital expenditure

(d) Capital expenditure (enhancing an existing long-term asset)

(e) Revenue expenditure (restoring an existing long-term asset)

(f) Capital income (net of the costs of sale)

(g) Revenue income

(h) Capital expenditure

(i) If customs duties are borne by the purchaser of the long-term asset, they should be added to the purchase cost of the machinery and classified as capital expenditure

(j) If carriage costs are paid for by the purchaser of the long-term asset, they should be included in the cost of the long-term asset and classified as capital expenditure

(k) Installation fees of a long-term asset are also added to cost and classified as capital expenditure

(l) Revenue expenditure

## Answer to Interactive question 3

(a) If the business is to be closed down, the remaining three machines must be valued at the amount they will realise in a forced sale, ie 3 × £60 = £180.

(b) If the business is regarded as a going concern, the machines unsold at 31 December will be valued as an asset at cost, 3 × £100 = £300.

## Answer to Interactive question 4

(a) No, because of the need for consistency. Once the depreciation policy has been established, it should not be changed without good cause.

(b) No, because of the materiality concept. The cost of the bin is very small. Rather than cluttering up the statement of financial position for five years, treat the £4.95 as an expense in this year's statement of profit or loss.

## Answer to Interactive question 5

The firm may have relatively little in the form of things you can touch, perhaps a building, desks and chairs. If you simply drew up a statement of financial position showing the cost of the things owned, then the business would not seem to be worth much, yet its income earning potential might be high. This is true of many service organisations where the people are among the most valuable assets, but justifying their exact value is extremely problematic.

## Answer to Interactive question 6

Objectivity. Unless the value of the gift/hospitality is clearly insignificant, a firm or a member of an assurance team should not accept it. It clearly threatens objectivity. In addition there may also be an intimidation threat if there is a suggestion that the receipt of the gift will be made public.

## Answer to Interactive question 7

The key merit of the code being principles based is that it is flexible. Professional accountants must consider the spirit of the guidance, even where there is no explicit guidance for a given scenario. This is necessary in the rapidly changing environment in which ICAEW members operate.

Rules based systems tend to give rise to checklists, which are often unsuitable when considering the ethical implications of decisions. Under the principles based system, members cannot simply engage in a box-ticking exercise, and the risk of loopholes arising in ethical guidance is reduced.

Disadvantages

Critics would argue that the principles based system may allow individuals to get away with non-compliance unchallenged, as they apply their own individual interpretation to the guidance.

1  A  Books of original entry form the primary record of transactions. These are analysed and posted to the ledger accounts and summarised in the financial statements, including the statement of profit or loss and the statement of financial position.

2  D  Sole traders and partners bear full liability for the debts of the business entity, as does a limited liability company itself. The liability of the shareholders or owners for the debts of a company is, however, limited.

3  B  IAS 1 identifies A, C and D as an objective  The use of accounting information by managers in making business decisions is not identified as an objective.

4  B  A is of interest to investors; C is of interest to employees, D is of interest to suppliers.

5  A  A statement of financial position is a list of assets and liabilities which represent the entity's financial position at a particular point in time. D is wrong because it refers to 'a period of time'; C refers to income and expenses, not assets and liabilities; B defines the statement of profit or loss.

6  C  Many figures in financial statements are derived from the application of judgement in putting fundamental accounting concepts into practice.

7  A  (i)

   B  (ii)

8  D  The best solution to an ethical dilemma should be taken whether or not it improves your career.

9  False. The Code may apply not only to the paid activities of the professional accountant but also to the life of the professional accountant, particularly if he is involved in matters relevant to his profession, such as being a Trustee of a charity or club.

10  D  UK GAAP relates to **generally** accepted accounting practice; the rules applied as a result of internal requirements can therefore not be part of GAAP.

11  B  Economic factors do not influence the development of financial reporting; all the others do (see section 3).

12  A  Information is material if omitting or misstating it could influence the decisions of the users. If information is deemed material then it is relevant to the users. The *Conceptual Framework* states that materiality is an entity-specific aspect of relevance.

13  B  This results in the acquisition of a long-term asset. All the others are revenue expenditure.

# CHAPTER 2

# The accounting equation

Introduction

Examination context

**Topic List**

Summary and Self-test

Technical reference

Answers to Interactive questions

Answers to Self-test

## Learning objectives

- Record and account for transactions and events resulting in income, expenses, assets, liabilities and capital in accordance with the appropriate basis of accounting and the laws, regulations and accounting standards applicable to the financial statements ☐

- Identify the main components of a set of financial statements and specify their purpose and interrelationship ☐

Specific syllabus learning outcomes are: 1d, 3a

## Syllabus links

The material in this chapter will be developed further in this paper, and then in the Professional Level module of Financial Accounting and Reporting.

## Examination context

Questions on the topics in this chapter will be set as multiple choice questions, some of which may involve calculations so that the correct answer can be selected.

In the exam you may be required to:

- Identify and manipulate the accounting equation

- Specify transactions affecting the elements of financial statements: assets, liabilities, capital, income and expenditure

# 1 Assets, liabilities and the business entity concept

**Section overview**

- An asset is a resource controlled by the entity as a result of past events from which future economic benefits are expected to flow.

- Assets may be held for the long-term (non-current assets) or for the short term as trading assets (current assets).

- A liability is a present obligation arising from past events, the settlement of which is expected to result in an outflow of resources from the business embodying economic benefits.

- Liabilities may be current or non-current.

- A business entity is a separate entity from its owners from an accounting point of view, whatever the legal position may be.

## 1.1 Assets and liabilities

**Definition**

Asset: The *Conceptual Framework* states that an asset is a resource controlled by the entity as a result of past events from which future economic benefits are expected to flow to the entity. **Assets are key elements of financial statements**.

---

Examples of assets:

- **Land and buildings:** factories, office buildings, storage and distribution centres (warehouses)

- **Motor vehicles**

- **Plant and machinery**

- **Fixtures and fittings:** computer equipment, office furniture and shelving

- **Cash:** in a bank account or held as notes and coins

- **Inventory:** goods held in store awaiting sale to customers, and raw materials and components held in store by a manufacturing business for use in production

- **Receivables:** amounts owed by customers and others to the entity

Some assets are held and used in operations for a long time. An office building is occupied by administrative staff for years; similarly, a machine has a productive life of many years before it wears out. These are long-term or **non-current assets**.

Other assets are held for only a short time. A newsagent, for example, has to sell his newspapers on the same day that he gets them. The quicker a business sells goods, the more profit it is likely to make, provided, of course, that the goods are sold at a higher price than what it cost the business to acquire them. Short-term assets are called **current assets**.

**Definition**

Liability: The *Conceptual Framework* states that a liability is a present obligation arising from past events, the settlement of which is expected to result in an outflow from the entity of resources embodying economic benefits. **Liabilities are key elements of financial statements**.

---

Examples of liabilities:

- A **bank loan** or **overdraft**. The liability is the amount eventually repaid to the bank.

- **Payables**: amounts owed to suppliers for goods purchased but not yet paid for (purchases 'on credit'). For example, a boatbuilder buys some timber on credit from a timber merchant, so that the boatbuilder does not pay for the timber until some time after it has been delivered. Until the boatbuilder pays what he owes, the timber merchant is a creditor for the amount owed.

- **Taxation** owed to the government. A business pays tax on its profits but there is a gap in time between when a business declares its profits (and becomes liable to pay tax) and the payment date.

## 1.2 The business as a separate entity

You may have wondered whether an intangible entity, such as a business, can own assets or have liabilities in its own name. There are two aspects to this question: the **strict legal position** and the **convention adopted by accountants**.

Many businesses are carried on in the form of **limited liability companies**. The owners of a limited company are its shareholders, who may be few in number (as with a small, family owned company) or very numerous (as with a large public company whose shares are listed on a stock exchange).

The law recognises a **company as a legal entity**, quite separate from its owners. A company may, in its own name, acquire assets, incur debts, and enter into contracts. If a company's assets became insufficient to meet its liabilities, the company as a separate entity becomes 'insolvent'. However, the owners of the company are not usually required to pay the debts from their own private resources: the debts are not debts of the owners, but of the company.

The case is different when a business is carried on by an individual (a sole trader). There is **no legal separation** between a **sole trader** and the business he/she runs. In most **partnerships**–, there is also no legal distinction.

### Worked example: Sole trader

Rodney Quiff starts business as a hairdresser, trading under the business name 'Quiff's Hair Salon'. The law recognises no distinction between Rodney Quiff, the individual, and the business known as 'Quiff's Hair Salon'. Any debts of the business which cannot be met from business assets must be met from Rodney's personal resources.

However in **accounting, any business is treated as a separate entity from its owner(s)**. This applies whether or not the business is recognised in law as a separate entity, ie it applies whether the business is carried on by a company or by a sole trader. This is known as the **business entity concept** (or separate entity concept, or just entity concept).

### Definition

**Business entity concept:** A business is a separate entity from its owner.

Although this may seem illogical and unrealistic you must try to appreciate it, as it is the basis of a fundamental rule of accounting, which is that the **liabilities** plus the **capital** of the business must always equal its **assets**. We will look at this rule in more detail later in this chapter, but a simple example now will clarify the idea of a business as a separate entity from its owners.

### Worked example: The business as a separate entity

On 1 July 20X6, Liza Doolittle opened a flower stall. She had saved up £2,500 and opened a business bank account with this amount.

When the business commences, an accountant's picture can be drawn of what it **owns** and what it **owes**. The business begins by owning the cash that Liza has put into it, £2,500.

**The business is a separate entity in accounting terms.** It has obtained assets, in this example cash, from Liza Doolittle. It therefore **owes this amount of money to Liza**. If Liza changed her mind and decided not to go into business, the business would be dissolved by the 'repayment' of cash to Liza.

The amount owed by a business to its owners is known as (equity) **capital**.

### Definition

**Capital:** The *Conceptual Framework* states that capital (which it calls **equity** in the context of a company, as we shall see in Chapter 11) is the residual interest in the assets of the entity after deducting all its liabilities. **Equity is a key element of financial statements.**

## 2 The accounting equation

### Section overview

- The basic accounting equation states that assets = capital + liabilities.
- Capital is the amount that the entity owes to its owners.

### 2.1 What is the accounting equation?

### Definition

Accounting equation: ASSETS = CAPITAL + LIABILITIES.

We will use an example to illustrate the **accounting equation**, ie the rule that the assets of a business will at all times equal its liabilities plus capital. This is also known as the **balance sheet equation.**

### 2.2 Assets = capital + liabilities

### Worked example: Assets = capital

The business began by owning the **cash** that Liza has put into it, £2,500. The business is a separate entity in accounting terms and so it owes the money to Liza as **capital**.

In accounting, **capital** is an investment of money (funds) with the intention of earning a return. A business owner invests capital with the intention of earning **profit**. As long as that money is invested, accountants will treat the capital as money owed to the owner by the business.

When Liza Doolittle sets up her business:

|  | £ |
|---|---|
| Cash at bank | 2,500 |
| Capital invested | 2,500 |

We can express Liza's initial accounting equation as follows:

For Liza Doolittle, as at 1 July 20X6:

| Assets | = | Capital | + | Liabilities |
|---|---|---|---|---|
| £2,500 (cash at bank) | = | £2,500 | + | £0 |

## Worked example: Different types of asset = capital

Liza purchases a market stall from Len Turnip for £1,800.

She also purchases some flowers from a trader in the wholesale market, at a cost of £650.

This leaves £50 in cash, after paying for the stall and goods for resale, out of the original £2,500. Liza keeps £30 in the bank and holds £20 in small change for trading. She is now ready for her first day of market trading on 3 July 20X6.

The assets and liabilities of the business have now altered, and at 3 July, before trading begins, the state of her business is as follows.

| Assets | | = | Capital | + | Liabilities |
|---|---|---|---|---|---|
| | £ | | | | |
| Stall | 1,800 | = | £2,500 | + | £0 |
| Flowers | 650 | | | | |
| Cash at bank | 30 | | | | |
| Cash in hand | 20 | | | | |
| | 2,500 | | | | |

The stall and the flowers are physical items, but they must be given a money value. This money value is usually what they cost the business (called **historical cost** in accounting terms).

## Definition

**Historical cost:** Transactions are recorded at their cost when they were incurred.

## 2.3 Where do profits/losses fit into the accounting equation?

## Worked example: Assets = capital + profit

On 3 July Liza sells all her flowers for £900 cash.

Since Liza has sold goods costing £650 to earn income of £900, we can say that she has **earned a profit of £250 on the day's trading**.

**Profits** are added to the owner's capital. In this case, the £250 belongs to Liza Doolittle. However, so long as the business retains the profits and does not pay anything out to its owner, the **retained profits are accounted for as an addition to the owner's capital**.

| Assets | | = | Capital | | + | Liabilities |
|---|---|---|---|---|---|---|
| | £ | | | £ | | |
| Stall | 1,800 | | Original investment | 2,500 | | |
| Flowers | 0 | | | | | |
| Cash in hand and at | | | Retained profit | | | |
| bank (30+20+900) | 950 | | (900–650) | 250 | | |
| | 2,750 | | | 2,750 | + | £0 |

We can re arrange the accounting equation to help us to calculate the capital balance.

Assets – liabilities (net assets) = Capital

At the beginning and end of 3 July 20X6, Liza Doolittle's financial position was as follows.

| | | Net assets | = | Capital |
|---|---|---|---|---|
| (a) | At the beginning of the day: | £(2,500 – 0) = £2,500 | | £2,500 |
| (b) | At the end of the day: | £(2,750 – 0) = £2,750 | | £2,750 |

There has been an increase of £250 in net assets, which is the amount of profit earned during the day.

ICAEW

## Definitions

**Profit**: The excess of income over expenses.

**Loss**: The excess of expenses over income.

**Income**: Increases in economic benefits over a period in the form of inflows or increases of assets, or decreases of liabilities, resulting in increases in equity/capital (*Conceptual Framework*). It can include both revenue and gains. **Income is a key element of financial statements**.

**Expenses**: Decreases in economic benefits over a period in the form of outflows or depletion of assets, or increases in liabilities, resulting in decreases in equity/capital (*Conceptual Framework*). **Expense is a key element of financial statements**.

Thus:    **Profits are added** to owner's capital
         **Losses are deducted** from owner's capital

Note that the *Conceptual Framework* identifies **income** and **expenses**, and **assets**, **liabilities** and **equity**, as the **elements of financial statements**. Each element represents a class of transactions or other events that are grouped together according to their economic characteristics.

## 2.4 Appropriation of profits: sole trader drawings

The owner of a sole tradership does not get paid a wage; they '**draw out**' or **appropriate** some of their capital as drawings.

## Definition

**Drawings**: Money and goods taken out of a business by its owner.

## Worked example: Assets = capital + profit – drawings

Business owners, like everyone else, need income for living expenses. Liza therefore decides to pay herself £180 in 'wages'.

The payment of £180 is regarded by Liza as a fair reward for her day's work and she might think of the sum as 'wages'. However, the £180 she draws is not an expense to be deducted in arriving at the figure of net profit because any amounts paid by a business to its owner are treated by accountants as **withdrawals or appropriations of profit** and **not as expenses** incurred by the business. In the case of Liza's business, the true position is:

|  | £ |
|---|---|
| Net profit earned by the business | 250 |
| Less profit withdrawn by Liza | (180) |
| Net profit **retained** in the business | 70 |

Profits are capital as long as they are retained in the business. Once they are **appropriated,** the business suffers a reduction in capital.

The withdrawals of profit are taken in cash, and so the business loses £180 of its cash assets. After the withdrawal has been made, the accounting equation would be restated.

(a)

| Assets | £ | = | Capital | £ | + | Liabilities |
|---|---|---|---|---|---|---|
| Stall | 1,800 | | Original investment | 2,500 | | |
| Goods | 0 | | Retained profit | | | |
| Cash (950 – 180) | 770 | | (250 – 180) | 70 | | |
| | 2,570 | | | 2,570 | + | £0 |

(b)  Alternatively

| Net assets | = | Capital |
|---|---|---|
| £(2,570 – 0) | = | £2,570 |

The increase in net assets since trading operations began is now only £(2,570 – 2,500) = £70, which is the amount of the retained profits.

---

## Worked example: Assets = capital

On 10 July Liza purchases flowers for cash, at a cost of £740. She decides to employ her cousin Ethel for a wage of £40 for the day.

On 10 July Liza and Ethel sold all their flowers for £1,100 cash. Liza paid Ethel £40 and drew out £200 for herself.

After the purchase of the goods for £740 the accounting equation is:

| Assets | | = | Capital | + | Liabilities |
|---|---|---|---|---|---|
| | £ | | | | |
| Stall | 1,800 | | | | |
| Flowers | 740 | | | | |
| Cash (770 – 740) | 30 | | | | |
| | 2,570 | = | £2,570 | + | £0 |

On 10 July, all the flowers are sold for £1,100 cash, and Ethel is paid £40. The profit for the day is calculated as follows:

| | £ | £ |
|---|---|---|
| Sales | | 1,100 |
| Less   cost of goods sold | 740 | |
| Ethel's wage | 40 | |
| | | (780) |
| Profit | | 320 |

| Assets | | = | Capital | | + | Liabilities |
|---|---|---|---|---|---|---|
| | £ | | | £ | | |
| Stall | 1,800 | | At beginning of 10 July | 2,570 | | |
| Flowers | 0 | | Profits earned on | | | |
| Cash (30 + 1,100 – 40) | 1,090 | | 10 July | 320 | | |
| | 2,890 | = | | 2,890 | + | £0 |

After Liza has withdrawn £200 in cash, retained profits will be only £(320 – 200) = £120.

| Assets | | = | Capital | | + | Liabilities |
|---|---|---|---|---|---|---|
| | £ | | | £ | | |
| Stall | 1,800 | | At beginning of 10 July | 2,570 | | |
| Flowers | 0 | | Retained profits for | | | |
| Cash (1,090 – 200) | 890 | | 10 July | 120 | | |
| | 2,690 | = | | 2,690 | + | £0 |

---

## Interactive question 1: Capital

Fill in the missing words.

Capital = ...................................... less ....................................

See **Answer** at the end of this chapter.

---

ICAEW

# 3 Credit transactions

## Section overview

- A creditor is any person to whom the entity owes money.
- A trade payable is a creditor which has arisen following a purchase on credit by the entity.
- A trade payable is a liability of the entity.
- A debtor is any person who owes money to the entity.
- A trade receivable is a debtor that has arisen following a sale on credit by the entity.
- A trade receivable is an asset of the entity.
- The matching or accruals concept requires that income is matched with the expenses incurred in earning it. This concept is the reason why we account for credit transactions before they are realised in the form of cash.

## 3.1 Trade payables

### Definition

**Creditor:** Person to whom a business owes money.

A **trade creditor** is a person to whom a business owes money for trading debts. In the accounts of a business, debts still outstanding which arise from the purchase from suppliers of materials, components or goods for resale are called **trade payables**.

A business does not always pay immediately for goods or services it buys. It is common business practice to make credit purchases, with a promise to pay within 30/60/90 days, of the date of the bill or 'invoice' for the goods. For example, A buys goods costing £2,000 on credit from B, B sends A an invoice for £2,000, dated 1 March, with credit terms that payment must be made within 30 days. If A then delays payment until 31 March, B will be a creditor of A between 1 and 31 March for £2,000. From A's point of view, the amount owed to B is a **trade payable.**

A trade payable is a **liability** of a business. When the debt is finally paid, the trade payable 'disappears' as a liability and the balance of cash at bank and in-hand decreases.

### Definition

**Trade payables:** The amounts due to credit suppliers.

## 3.2 Trade receivables

### Definition

**Debtor:** Person who owes money to the business.

Suppose that C sells goods on credit to D for £6,000 on terms that the debt must be settled within two months of the invoice date, 1 October. D will be a debtor of C for £6,000 from 1 October until the date payment is made. In the accounts of the business, amounts owed by debtors are called **trade receivables**.

A debtor is an **asset** of a business. When the debt is finally paid, the debtor 'disappears' as an asset, to be replaced by 'cash at bank and in hand'.

## Definition

Trade receivables: The amounts owed by credit customers.

## Worked example: Assets = capital + liabilities

Look at the consequences of the following transactions in the week to 17 July 20X6. (See Worked example: Assets = capital for the situation as at the end of 10 July.)

(a) Liza Doolittle realises that she is going to need more money in the business and so she makes the following arrangements.

  (i) She invests a further £250 of her own capital.

  (ii) She persuades her Uncle Henry to lend her £500. Uncle Henry tells her that she can repay the loan whenever she likes, but in the meantime, she must pay him interest of £5 each week at the end of the market day. They agree that it will probably be quite a long time before the loan is eventually repaid.

(b) She decides to buy a van to pick up flowers from her supplier and bring them to her market stall. She finds a car dealer, Laurie Loader, who agrees to sell her a van on credit for £700. Liza agrees to pay for the van after 30 days' trial use.

(c) During the week, Liza's Uncle George telephones her to ask whether she would sell him some garden furniture. Liza tells him that she will look for a supplier. She buys what Uncle George has asked for, paying £300 in cash. Uncle George accepts delivery of the goods and agrees to pay £350, but he asks if she can wait until the end of the month for payment. Liza agrees.

(d) Liza buys flowers costing £800. Of these purchases £750 are paid in cash, with the remaining £50 on seven days' credit. Liza decides to use Ethel's services again, at an agreed wage of £40 for the day.

(e) On 17 July, Liza sells all her goods, for £1,250 (cash). She decides to withdraw £240 for her week's work. She also pays Ethel £40 in cash. She decides to make the interest payment to her Uncle Henry the next time she sees him.

(f) There are no van expenses for the week.

## Solution

Deal with transactions one at a time in chronological order. (In practice, it is possible to do one set of calculations which combines all transactions.)

(a) **The addition of Liza's extra capital and Uncle Henry's loan**

An investment analyst might call Uncle Henry's loan a capital investment, on the grounds that it will probably be for the long term. Uncle Henry is not the owner of the business, however, even though he has made an investment in it. He would only become an owner if Liza offered him a partnership in the business, and she has not done so. To the business, Uncle Henry is a long term creditor, and it is appropriate to define his investment as a liability and not business capital.

The accounting equation after £(250 + 500) = £750 cash is put into the business will be:

| Assets | | = | Capital | | + | Liabilities | |
|---|---|---|---|---|---|---|---|
| | £ | | | £ | | | £ |
| Stall | 1,800 | | As at end of 10 July | 2,690 | | Loan | 500 |
| Goods | 0 | | Additional capital | 250 | | | |
| Cash (890 + 750) | 1,640 | | | | | | |
| | 3,440 | = | | 2,940 | + | | 500 |

ICAEW

(b) The purchase of the van (cost £700) on credit

| Assets | | = | Capital | | + | Liabilities | |
|---|---|---|---|---|---|---|---|
| | £ | | | £ | | | £ |
| Stall | 1,800 | | As at end of 10 July | 2,690 | | Loan | 500 |
| Van | 700 | | Additional capital | 250 | | Payables | 700 |
| Cash | 1,640 | | | | | | |
| | 4,140 | = | | 2,940 | + | | 1,200 |

(c) The sale of goods to Uncle George on credit (£350) which cost the business £300 (cash paid)

| Assets | | = | Capital | | + | Liabilities | |
|---|---|---|---|---|---|---|---|
| | £ | | | £ | | | £ |
| Stall | 1,800 | | As at end of 10 July | 2,690 | | Loan | 500 |
| Van | 700 | | Additional capital | 250 | | Payables | 700 |
| Receivable | 350 | | Profit on sale to | | | | |
| Cash (1,640 – 300) | 1,340 | | Uncle George | | | | |
| | | | (350 – 300) | 50 | | | |
| | 4,190 | = | | 2,990 | + | | 1,200 |

(d) After the purchase of goods for the weekly market (£750 paid in cash and £50 of purchases on credit)

| Assets | | = | Capital | | + | Liabilities | |
|---|---|---|---|---|---|---|---|
| | £ | | | £ | | | £ |
| Stall | 1,800 | | As at end of 10 July | 2,690 | | Loan | 500 |
| Van | 700 | | Additional capital | 250 | | Payables | |
| Goods (750 + 50) | 800 | | Profit on sale to | | | (van) | 700 |
| Receivable | 350 | | Uncle George | 50 | | Payables | |
| Cash (1,340 – 750) | 590 | | | | | (goods) | 50 |
| | 4,240 | = | | 2,990 | + | | 1,250 |

(e) After market trading on 17 July

Goods costing £800 earned income of £1,250 in cash. Ethel's wages were £40 (paid), Uncle Henry's interest charge is £5 (not paid yet) and drawings were £240 (paid). The profit for 17 July may be calculated as follows, taking the full £5 of interest as a cost on that day.

| | | £ | £ |
|---|---|---|---|
| Sales | | | 1,250 |
| Cost of goods sold | | 800 | |
| Wages | | 40 | |
| Interest | | 5 | |
| | | | (845) |
| Profit earned on market trading on 17 July | | | 405 |
| Profit on sale of goods to Uncle George | | | 50 |
| Profit for the week | | | 455 |
| Drawings | | | (240) |
| Retained profit | | | 215 |

| Assets | | = | Capital | | + | Liabilities | |
|---|---|---|---|---|---|---|---|
| | £ | | | £ | | | £ |
| Stall | 1,800 | | As at end of 10 July | 2,690 | | Loan | 500 |
| Van | 700 | | Additional capital | 250 | | Payables | |
| Goods (800 – 800) | 0 | | Profits retained | 215 | | (van) | 700 |
| Receivable | 350 | | | | | Payables | |
| Cash (590 + | | | | | | (goods) | 50 |
| 1,250 – 40 – 240) | 1,560 | | | | | Payables | |
| | | | | | | (interest | |
| | | | | | | payment) | 5 |
| | 4,410 | = | | 3,155 | + | | 1,255 |

## 3.3 Accruals concept

The **accruals** (or matching) **concept** requires that income earned is matched with the expenses incurred in earning it.

In Liza's case, we have 'matched' the income earned with the expenses incurred in earning it. So in part (e), we included all the costs of the goods sold of £800, even though £50 had not yet been paid in cash. Also the interest of £5 was deducted from income, even though it had not yet been paid.

### Interactive question 2: The accounting equation

How would each of these transactions affect the accounting equation in terms of increase or decrease in asset, capital or liability?

(a)  Purchasing £800 worth of goods on credit
(b)  Paying the telephone bill £25
(c)  Selling £450 worth of goods for £650
(d)  Paying £800 to a supplier

See **Answer** at the end of this chapter.

We shall look now at how the business entity concept and accruals together result in the statement of financial position.

# 4 The statement of financial position

### Section overview

- The statement of financial position shows the entity's financial position at a particular moment in time.

- The statement of financial position represents the accounting equation: assets are in one half and capital and liabilities in the other.

- The more detailed accounting equation, represented in the IAS 1 format for the statement of financial position, states that non-current assets + current assets = capital + profit – losses – drawings + non-current liabilities + current liabilities.

- Net assets = assets – liabilities, therefore net assets = capital.

- A non-current asset is acquired for long term use in the business, with a view to earning profits from its use, either directly or indirectly.

- Non-current assets may be tangible (with a physical reality) or intangible.

- Current assets are either cash or items which are held by the entity to be turned into cash shortly.

- Capital comprises opening capital + capital introduced + profits – losses – drawings of capital/profits taken by the owners.

- Non-current liabilities are payable after one year, such as secured loans.

- Current liabilities are payable within one year, such as trade payables and bank overdrafts.

## 4.1 What is a statement of financial position?

The business's **statement of financial position** shows its financial position at a given moment in time. It contains three key **elements of financial statements: liabilities, capital and assets** at that moment. It is a 'financial snapshot', since it captures on paper a still image of something which is dynamic and continually changing. Typically, a statement of financial position is prepared at the end of the reporting period to which the financial statements relate.

A statement of financial position is very similar to the accounting equation. In fact, the only **differences between a statement of financial position and an accounting equation** are:

- The manner or **format** in which the liabilities and assets are presented.
- The extra **detail** which is usually contained in a statement of financial position.

The details shown in a statement of financial position will not be described in full in this chapter. Instead we will make a start in this chapter and add more detail in later chapters as we go on to look at other ideas and methods in accounting.

A statement of financial position is divided into two halves, and is presented in either of the following ways.

- **Capital and liabilities** in one half and **assets** in the other (the IAS 1 format that we adopt in this Study Manual).

- **Capital** in one half and **net assets** in the other (the UK GAAP format for the balance sheet that is looked at in Chapters 14 and 15).

 **Definition**

Net assets: Assets less liabilities

In this Study Manual we will follow the assets = capital + liabilities format given by IAS 1 *Presentation of Financial Statements*.

NAME OF BUSINESS
STATEMENT OF FINANCIAL POSITION AS AT (DATE)

|  | £ |
|---|---|
| Assets (item by item) | X |
|  |  |
| Capital | X |
| Liabilities | X |
|  | X |

The total value in one half of the statement of financial position equals the total value in the other half. Since each half of the statement of financial position has an equal value, one side **balances** the other.

Capital, liabilities and assets are usually shown in some detail in a statement of financial position. The following paragraphs describe the sort of detail we might expect to find.

## 4.2 Capital (sole trader)

The sole trader's capital is usually analysed into its component parts.

|  | £ | £ |
|---|---|---|
| Capital at the beginning of the reporting period (ie **capital brought forward**) |  | X |
| Add additional **capital introduced** during the period |  | X |
|  |  | X |
| **Add profit** earned during the period (or **less losses** incurred in the period) | X |  |
| Less **drawings** | (X) |  |
| **Retained profit** for the period |  | X |
| Capital as at the end of the reporting period (ie **capital carried forward**) |  | X |

'**Brought forward**' means that the amount is brought forward from the previous period. Similarly, '**carried forward**' means carried forward to the next period. The carried forward amount at the end of one period is therefore the brought forward amount of the next period.

### 4.2.1 Equity (company)

The capital or equity side of a company's **statement of financial position** is more complicated than a sole trader's. We shall look at it in detail in Chapter 11.

## 4.3 Liabilities

A distinction is required by IAS 1 in the statement of financial position between **non-current liabilities** and **current liabilities**.

- **Current liabilities** are debts which are payable within one year
- **Non-current liabilities** are debts which are payable after one year

### 4.3.1 Non-current liabilities

**Definition**

**Non-current liability:** A debt which is not payable within one year. Any liability which is not current must be non-current.

Examples of non-current liabilities:

- **Loans** which are not repayable for more than one year, such as a bank loan or a loan from an individual to a business.

- **Loan stock or debentures.** These are common with limited companies. Loan stocks or debentures are securities issued by a company at a fixed rate of interest. They are repayable on agreed terms by a specified date in the future. Holders of loan stocks are therefore lenders of money to a company. Their interests, including security for the loan, are protected by the terms of a trust deed. If the loan is repayable over several years then the portion repayable within one year is shown as a current liability (see below).

### 4.3.2 Current liabilities

**Definition**

**Current liabilities:** Debts of the business that must be paid within **one year**, or within the entity's normal operating cycle, or that are held to be traded.

Examples of current liabilities:

- **Loans** repayable within **one year**, including the element of a long term loan that is repayable within one year.

- A bank **overdraft**, which is usually **repayable on demand.**

- **Trade payables** represent suppliers to which the business owes money for goods or services bought on credit as part of the business's trading activities.

- **Other payables** are due to anyone else to whom the business owes money, such as HM Revenue and Customs (HMRC) in respect of VAT, pension trustees in respect of pension contributions, and employees in respect of unpaid remuneration, for example sales commissions.

- **Taxation payable** to HMRC with respect to corporation tax on the company's profits.

- **Accruals.** These are expenses already incurred by the business, for which no invoice has yet been received, or for which the date of payment has not yet arrived. An example of accrued charges is the cost of gas or electricity used. If a business ends its accounting year on 31 December, but does not expect its next quarterly gas bill until the end of January, there will be two months of accrued gas charges to record in the statement of financial position as a liability. Accruals will be described more fully in Chapter 9.

## 4.4 Assets

The statement of financial position distinguishes between **non-current assets** and **current assets** (again as required by IAS 1).

- **Non-current assets** are acquired for **long-term** use within the business. They are normally valued at cost less accumulated depreciation.

- **Current assets** are expected to be converted into cash within **one year**.

## 4.4.1 Non-current assets

### Definition

**Non-current assets:** Assets acquired for continuing use within the business, with a view to earning income or making profits from their use, either directly or indirectly, over more than one reporting period.

Non-current assets in the statement of financial position usually comprise:

- **Property, plant and equipment** (ie 'Tangible' assets)
- **Intangible non-current assets** such as goodwill
- **Long-term investments**

A non-current asset is not acquired for sale to a customer.

- In a manufacturing industry, a production machine is a non-current asset, because it makes goods which are then sold.

- In a service industry, equipment used by employees giving service to customers is a non-current asset (eg the equipment used in a garage, or furniture in a hotel).

- Less obviously factory premises, office furniture, computer equipment, company cars, delivery vans or pallets in a warehouse are all non-current assets.

To be classed as a non-current asset in the business's statement of financial position, an item must satisfy two further conditions.

- It must be **used by the business**. For example, the owner's own house would not normally appear on the business statement of financial position.

- The asset must have a 'life' in use of **more than one reporting period** or year.

A **tangible non-current asset** is a physical asset that can be touched. All of the examples of non-current assets mentioned above are 'tangible' assets. They are often referred to as **property, plant and equipment**.

**Intangible non-current assets** are assets which do not have a physical existence; they cannot be 'touched'. An example is a **patent**, which protects an idea, and **goodwill**.

An **investment** can also be a non-current asset. Company A might invest in another company, B, by purchasing some of B's shares. These investments will earn income for A in the form of dividends paid out by B. If the investments are purchased by A with a view to holding on to them for more than one year, they would be classified as non-current assets of A.

In this chapter, we shall restrict our attention to **tangible non-current assets**.

## 4.4.2 Non-current assets and depreciation

Non-current assets are held and used by a business for a number of years, but they wear out or lose their usefulness in the course of time. Every tangible non-current asset has a limited life. The only exception is **freehold land**, although this too can be exhausted if it is used by extractive industries (eg mining).

The financial statements of a business reflect that the cost of a non-current asset is gradually consumed as the asset wears out. This is done by gradually 'writing off' the asset's cost in the statement of profit or loss over several reporting periods. For example, in the case of a machine costing £1,000 and expected to wear out after ten years, it is appropriate to reduce the value in the statement of financial position by £100 each year. This process is known as **depreciation**.

If a statement of financial position were drawn up four years after the asset was purchased, the amount of depreciation accumulated over four years would be 4 × £100 = £400. The machine would then appear in the statement of financial position as follows.

|                              | £     |
|------------------------------|-------|
| Machine at original cost     | 1,000 |
| Less accumulated depreciation | (400) |
| **Carrying amount** *        | 600   |

* ie the value of the asset in the books of account, net of accumulated depreciation. After ten years the asset would be fully depreciated and would appear in the statement of financial position with a carrying amount of zero.

The amount that is written off over time does not have to be the full cost of the asset if it is expected to have a resale – or 'residual' – value at the end of its useful life.

### Interactive question 3: Residual value

Suppose a business buys a car for £10,000. It expects to keep the car for three years and then to sell it for £3,400. How much depreciation should be accounted for in each year of the car's useful life?

See **Answer** at the end of this chapter.

We shall study non-current assets in detail in Chapter 10.

### 4.4.3 Current assets

**Current assets** take one of the following forms.

(a) Items owned by the business with the intention of **turning them into cash in a short time**, usually within one year (see the worked example below).

(b) **Cash**, including money in the bank, owned by the business.

These assets are 'current' in the sense that they are continually flowing through the business; they are always realisable in the near future.

### Definition

**Current asset:** An asset is current when it is expected to be realised in, or intended for sale or consumption in, the entity's normal operating cycle, or it is held for being traded, or it is expected to be realised within 12 months of the date of the statement of financial position, or it is cash or a cash equivalent.

### Worked example: Current assets

David Wickes runs a business selling cars. He purchases a showroom, which he stocks with cars for sale. He obtains the cars from a manufacturer and pays for them in cash on delivery.

- If he sells a car in a **cash sale**, the goods are immediately converted into cash. The cash can then be used to buy more cars for re sale.

- If he sells a car in a **credit sale**, the car will be given to the customer, who then becomes a trade receivable. Eventually, the customer will pay what they owe and David Wickes will receive cash. Once again, the cash can then be used to buy more cars for re-sale.

Current assets are as follows.

- The cars (goods) held in **inventory** for re-sale are current assets, because David Wickes intends to sell them within one year in the normal course of trade.

- Any **trade and other receivables** are current assets, if they will be paid within the usual cash operating cycle of less than one year.

- **Cash** is a current asset.

## Interactive question 4: Asset classification

Identify which of the following assets falls into the non-current category and which should be treated as current. Could any be treated as either?

| Asset | Business | Current or non-current |
|-------|----------|------------------------|
| Van | Delivery firm | |
| Machine | Manufacturing company | |
| Car | Car trader | |
| Investment | Any | |

See **Answer** at the end of this chapter.

Cars are current assets for David Wickes because he is in the business of buying and selling them, ie he is a car trader. If he also has a car which he keeps and uses for business purposes, this car would be a non-current asset. The distinction between a non-current asset and a current asset is not what the asset is physically, but for what **purpose it is obtained and used** by the business.

There are some other categories of current asset.

- **Short term investments**. These are stocks and shares of other businesses, owned with the intention of selling them in the near future. For example, if a business has a lot of spare cash for a short time, its managers might decide to invest short-term in the stock exchange. The shares will later be sold when the business needs the cash. If share prices rise in the meantime, the business will make a profit from its short term investment. Such shares must be readily realisable (ie easy to sell) to be short-term.

- **Prepayments**. These are amounts of money paid by the business in one reporting period for benefits which have not yet been enjoyed, but which will be enjoyed within the next reporting period. For example, a business pays an annual insurance premium of £240, and the premium is payable annually in advance on 1 December. If the business has an accounting year end of 31 December, it will pay £240 on 1 December but only enjoy one month's insurance cover by the year end. The remaining 11 months' cover (£220 cost, at £20 per month) will be enjoyed in the next year. The prepayment of £220 is shown in the statement of financial position, at 31 December, as a current asset. Prepayments will be described more fully in Chapter 9.

### 4.4.4 Trade and other receivables

A receivable can be due from **anyone** who owes the business money. For example, if a business makes an insurance claim, the insurance company is a receivable for the money payable on the claim. If the business makes loans to staff to buy rail season tickets, staff are receivables for the amount outstanding.

A distinction can be made between two types of receivable.

- **Trade receivables** represent customers who owe money for goods or services bought on credit in the course of the trading activities of the business.

- **Other receivables** are due from anyone else owing money to the business, such as an insurance company, HMRC for VAT, or employees for season ticket loans.

# 5 Preparing the statement of financial position

### Section overview

- The statement of financial position lists out and totals non-current plus current assets, then it lists out and totals capital plus non-current liabilities plus current liabilities.

## 5.1 How is a basic statement of financial position prepared?

We shall now look at how the various types of assets and liabilities are shown in a business's statement of financial position (IAS 1 format). You might like to attempt to prepare it yourself from the information provided before reading the solution which follows.

### Worked example: Statement of financial position

Prepare a statement of financial position for Sunken Arches as at 31 December 20X6, given the information below.

|  | £ |
|---|---|
| Capital as at 1 January 20X6 | 51,100 |
| Profit for the year to 31 December 20X6 | 8,000 |
| Premises, carrying amount at 31 December 20X6 | 50,000 |
| Motor vehicles, carrying amount at 31 December 20X6 | 9,000 |
| Fixtures and fittings, carrying amount at 31 December 20X6 | 8,000 |
| Non-current loan | 25,000 |
| Bank overdraft * | 2,000 |
| Inventories | 16,000 |
| Trade receivables | 500 |
| Cash in hand * | 100 |
| Trade payables | 1,200 |
| Drawings | 4,000 |
| Accrued costs of rent | 600 |
| Prepayment of insurance premium | 300 |

\* A shop might have cash in its cash registers, but an overdraft at the bank.

### Solution

SUNKEN ARCHES
STATEMENT OF FINANCIAL POSITION AS AT 31 DECEMBER 20X6

|  | £ | £ |
|---|---|---|
| ASSETS | | |
| *Non-current assets* | | |
| *Property, plant and equipment* | | |
| Premises | | 50,000 |
| Fixtures and fittings | | 8,000 |
| Motor vehicles | | 9,000 |
| | | 67,000 |
| *Current assets* | | |
| Inventories | 16,000 | |
| Trade and other receivables | 500 | |
| Prepayments | 300 | |
| Cash and cash equivalents | 100 | |
| | | 16,900 |
| *Total assets* | | 83,900 |
| CAPITAL AND LIABILITIES | | |
| *Capital* | | |
| As at 1 January 20X6 | 51,100 | |
| Profit for the year | 8,000 | |
| Less drawings | (4,000) | |
| At 31 December 20X6 | | 55,100 |
| *Non-current liabilities* | | |
| Long-term borrowings | | 25,000 |
| *Current liabilities* | | |
| Short-term borrowings (bank overdraft) | 2,000 | |
| Trade and other payables | 1,200 | |
| Accrued costs | 600 | |
| | | 3,800 |
| *Total capital and liabilities* | | 83,900 |

The layout is in the preferred format from IAS 1, adapted for a sole trader, and we will use it throughout this Study Manual, for sole traders as well as companies, until we look at UK GAAP in Chapters 14 and 15.

### Interactive question 5: Preparing a statement of financial position 1

You are given the following information about Liza Doolittle at the end of her first full month of trading, 31 July 20X6:

|  | £ |
| --- | --- |
| Capital at 1 July 20X6 | 2,500 |
| Additional capital introduced | 250 |
| Profit for the month | 3,620 |
| Stall at cost | 1,800 |
| Van at cost | 700 |
| Drawings in month | 960 |
| Loan | 50 |
| Inventories | 1,250 |
| Cash in hand | 20 |
| Trade payables | 675 |
| Cash at bank | 1,475 |
| Trade receivables | 890 |

**Requirement**

Prepare a statement of financial position for Liza Doolittle as at 31 July 20X6.

See **Answer** at the end of this chapter.

# 6 The statement of profit or loss

### Section overview

- The statement of profit or loss sets out the entity's financial performance over a period of time.
- It matches income and expenses to arrive at a figure for profit or loss.
- Trading income less the costs of trading represents gross profit.
- Gross profit less expenses represents net profit.
- Profit for the period per the statement of profit or loss is added to the capital section in the statement of financial position; drawings are deducted as appropriations of profit in order to arrive at the owner's total capital.

## 6.1 What is the statement of profit or loss?

The **statement of profit or loss** is a statement in which two key **elements of financial statements** – **income** and **expenses** – are matched to arrive at profit or loss. Many businesses distinguish between:

- **Gross profit** earned on trading (revenue less cost of sales)
- **Profit for the period (sometimes referred to as net profit)** after other income and expenses

In the first part of the statement of profit or loss **revenue** from selling goods is compared with direct costs of acquiring or producing the goods sold to arrive at a **gross profit** figure. From this, deductions are made in the second half of the statement (which we will call the **expenses** section) in respect of indirect costs (overheads). Additions may also be made to gross profit in respect of **non-trading income**.

| **Gross profit** | = | revenue from sales, less cost of sales |
| --- | --- | --- |
| **Profit for the period** | = | gross profit less expenses plus non-trading income |

Business owners want to know how much profit or loss has been made, but there is only limited information value in the profit figure. In order to exercise financial control effectively, managers must know how much revenue and other income has been earned, what costs have been, and whether the performance of sales or the control of costs appears to be satisfactory.

The statement of profit or loss **matches income earned to the expenses of earning that income**. This is why prepayments and accrued expenses appear in the financial statements. **Prepayments** are excluded from expenses in the statement of profit or loss and are included in receivables in the statement of financial position, because they relate to future periods.

**Accrued expenses** are added to expenses in the statement of profit or loss and shown as payables in the statement of financial position, because they relate to the current period but have not been paid as cash in the period.

### 6.1.1 Gross profit

Gross profit is the difference between:

- The value of sales revenue and
- The purchase or production cost of the goods sold: **cost of sales**

In a retail business, the cost of the goods sold is **their purchase cost** from suppliers. In a manufacturing business, the production cost of goods sold is the **cost of raw materials** in the finished goods, plus **labour costs** required to make the goods, plus an amount of production 'overhead' costs. In many types of business the cost of sales also includes:

- The cost of employing those people directly involved in making or providing a service

- Maintenance and depreciation on non-current assets used directly in making sales, plus losses on their disposal

Gross profit represents the profit made directly from the sale of goods or services. It can be represented as a percentage of revenue, called the **gross profit margin**.

$$\textbf{Gross profit margin} = \frac{\text{Gross profit}}{\text{Revenue}} \times 100$$

The gross profit margin can be used to compare the results of different periods to see how well the costs of sales are being controlled as revenue changes. It can also be used to compare the results of different businesses in the same industry.

We shall see more about margins in Chapter 7.

### 6.1.2 Profit for the period

The second part of the statement of profit or loss shows the **net profit** for the reporting period. The net profit is:

| | |
|---|---|
| Gross profit | X |
| **Plus** any other income from sources other than the sale of goods | X |
| **Minus** other business expenses, not included in the cost of goods sold | (X) |
| | X |

**Income from other sources** will include:

- Profit on disposals of non-current assets

- Dividends or interest received from investments

- Rental income from property owned but not otherwise used by the business

- Amounts due in respect of insurance claims

- **Discounts received** from suppliers for early payment of their debt. (See under administrative costs below for a brief explanation of discounts.)

**Business expenses** not directly related to cost of sales appear in the statement of profit or loss under one of three headings.

- **Distribution costs.** Expenses associated with selling and delivering goods to customers. They include the following.

    - Salaries, wages and sales commission of employees

    - Marketing costs (eg advertising and sales promotion expenses)

    - The costs of running and maintaining delivery vans, including **depreciation** on these and any **losses** on their disposal

- **Administrative costs.** Expenses of providing management and administration for the business. Examples include:

    - Management and office staff salaries

    - Rent and local business or property taxes

    - Insurance

    - Telephone and postage

    - Printing and stationery

    - Heating and lighting

    - Discounts allowed to customers for early payment of their debt. For example, a business sells goods to a customer for £100 and offers a 5% discount for payment in cash. If the customer takes the discount, record revenue at the full £100, with an administrative cost for discounts allowed of £5. Discounts are described more fully in Chapter 3.

    - Irrecoverable debts written off. Sometimes customers fail to pay what they owe and a business has to decide at some stage that there is now no prospect of ever being paid. The debt has to be written off as 'irrecoverable'. The amount of the debt written off is charged as an expense in the statement of profit or loss. Irrecoverable debts are also described more fully in Chapter 8.

    - The cost of running and maintaining other non-current assets such as office buildings, plus depreciation and losses on disposal of these.

- **Finance costs.** These include:

    - Interest on loans
    - Bank overdraft interest

As far as possible, items of expense should be grouped (distribution costs, administrative expenses, and finance costs) but this is not something that you need worry about at this stage.

## Worked example: Preparing a statement of profit or loss

On 1 June 20X5, Jock Heiss commenced trading as an ice cream salesman, using a van.

(a) He borrowed £2,000 from his bank, and the interest cost of the loan was £25 per month.

(b) He rented the van for £1,000 for three months. Running expenses for the van averaged £300 per month.

(c) He hired an assistant for £100 per month.

(d) His main business was to sell ice cream to customers in the street, but he also did special catering for business customers, supplying ice creams for office parties. Sales to these customers were usually on credit.

(e) For the three months to 31 August 20X5, his total sales were as follows.

    (i)   Cash sales       £8,900
    (ii)  Credit sales     £1,100

(f) He purchased his ice cream from a local manufacturer, Floors Co. The purchase cost in the three months to 31 August 20X5 was £6,200, and at 31 August he had sold every item. He still owed £700 to Floors Co for unpaid purchases on credit.

(g) One of his credit sale customers has gone bankrupt (insolvent), owing Jock £250. Jock has decided to write off the debt in full, with no prospect of getting any of the money owed.

(h) He used his own home for his office work. Telephone and postage expenses for the three months to 31 August were £150, which he paid in cash.

(i) During the period he paid himself £300 per month.

A statement of profit or loss can be presented in various formats, but here we will use a vertical format similar to the one used in IAS 1. (It is not exactly the same.)

JOCK HEISS
STATEMENT OF PROFIT OR LOSS
FOR THE THREE MONTHS ENDED 31 AUGUST 20X5

|  | £ | £ |
|---|---|---|
| Revenue (8,900 + 1,100) |  | 10,000 |
| Cost of sales |  | (6,200) |
| *Gross profit* |  | 3,800 |
|  |  |  |
| *Expenses* |  |  |
| Wages (3 × 100) | 300 |  |
| Van rental | 1,000 |  |
| Van expenses (3 × 300) | 900 |  |
| Irrecoverable debt written off | 250 |  |
| Telephone and postage | 150 |  |
| Interest charges (3 × 25) | 75 |  |
|  |  | (2,675) |
| *Profit for the period* |  | 1,125 |

## 6.2 Relationship between the statement of profit or loss and the statement of financial position

- **The profit for the period is the amount by which revenue exceeds expenses during the reporting period**. For a sole trader it is transferred to the statement of financial position as an addition to the owner's capital. A loss for the period, whereby expenses exceed revenue, would be transferred as a deduction from capital in the statement of financial position.

- **Drawings** are **appropriations of profit** and not expenses. They must **not** be included in the statement of profit or loss. The payments that Jock Heiss makes to himself (£900) are shown as **deductions from capital** in the statement of financial position.

- The cost of sales is £6,200, even though £700 of the costs have not yet been paid for. The £700 owed to Floors Co will be shown in the balance sheet as a trade payable. This is an example of the **accruals concept**.

### Interactive question 6: Preparing a statement of financial position 2

Prepare a statement of financial position as at 31 August 20X5 for Jock Heiss, using the information from the Worked example above.

See **Answer** at the end of this chapter.

## Summary

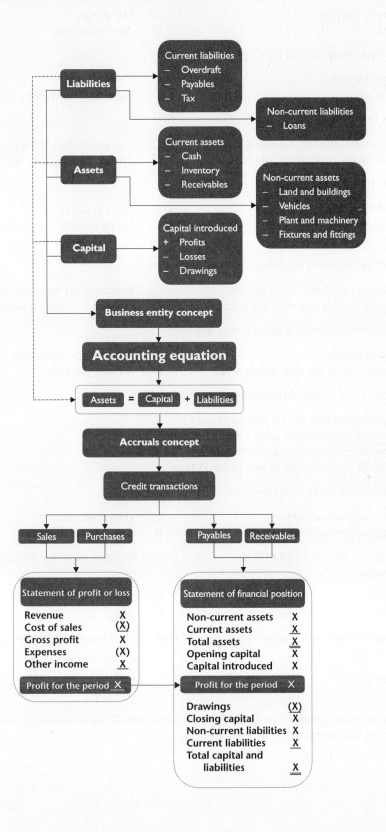

CHAPTER 2

## Self-test

Answer the following questions.

1 Which of the following is an asset?

| | | | |
|---|---|---|---|
| A | A trade payable | C | Drawings |
| B | A loan | D | A prepayment |

2 Which of the following is a liability?

| | | | |
|---|---|---|---|
| A | Depreciation | C | Cash at bank |
| B | An accrual | D | Plant and machinery |

3 Capital is the amount:

| | | | |
|---|---|---|---|
| A | The entity's owners owe to it | C | The entity owes to its creditors |
| B | The entity's customers owe to it | D | The entity 'owes' to its owners |

4 Which of the following are assets of an entity?

| | | | |
|---|---|---|---|
| A | Trade payables | D | Cash in hand |
| B | Trade receivables | E | Funds introduced by the owner |
| C | Bank overdraft | | |

5 Which of the following best describes the accruals concept?

| | | | |
|---|---|---|---|
| A | Assets are matched with liabilities | C | Expenses are matched with assets |
| B | Income is matched with expenses | D | Income is matched with liabilities |

6 Which of the following is a non-current liability?

| | | | |
|---|---|---|---|
| A | A bank overdraft | C | A mortgage repayable in five years' time |
| B | A bank loan repayable within a year | D | A trade payable |

7 The statement of financial position sets out the entity's

A Financial position over a period of time
B Financial performance over a period of time
C Financial position at one point in time
D Financial performance at one point in time

8 Which of the following expenses is included in cost of sales?

| | | | |
|---|---|---|---|
| A | Sales people's salaries | C | Overdraft interest |
| B | Management salaries | D | Cost of raw material |

9 A business has sales of £100,000, cost of sales of £60,000 and expenses of £20,000. The gross profit margin is:

| | | | |
|---|---|---|---|
| A | 60% | C | 20% |
| B | 40% | D | 80% |

10 Which figure from a sole trader's statement of profit or loss would appear in its statement of financial position?

| | | | |
|---|---|---|---|
| A | Gross profit | C | Revenue |
| B | Drawings | D | Net profit |

Now, go back to the Learning Objectives in the Introduction. If you are satisfied you have achieved the objectives, please tick them off.

# Technical reference

- Basic format of the statement of financial position and statement of profit or loss

  IAS 1
  IG

- Elements of financial statements

  *Conceptual*
  *Framework*
  paras 4.2 to 4.3

- Definition of asset, liability, equity

  *Conceptual*
  *Framework*
  para 4.4

- Definition of income, expense

  *Conceptual*
  *Framework*
  para 4.25

- Current/non-current distinction in the statement of financial position

  IAS 1
  paras 60/61

- Definition of current asset

  IAS 1
  para 66

- Definition of current liability

  IAS 1
  para 69

### Answer to Interactive question 1

Assets = capital + liabilities. Therefore capital = assets − liabilities

### Answer to Interactive question 2

| | | |
|---|---|---|
| (a) | Increase in liabilities (payables) | £800 |
| | Increase in assets (inventory) | £800 |
| (b) | Decrease in assets (cash) | £25 |
| | Decrease in capital (an expense reduces profit) | £25 |
| (c) | Decrease in assets (inventory) | £450 |
| | Increase in assets (cash) | £650 |
| | Increase in capital (profit) | £200 |
| (d) | Decrease in liabilities (payables) | £800 |
| | Decrease in assets (cash) | £800 |

### Answer to Interactive question 3

The point in this case is that the car has a residual value of £3,400. It would be inappropriate to account for depreciation in such a way as to write off the asset completely over three years; the aim should be to account only for its loss of value (£10,000 − £3,400 = £6,600), which suggests depreciation of £2,200 per year.

### Answer to Interactive question 4

| Asset | Business | Current or non-current |
|---|---|---|
| Van | Delivery firm | Non-current |
| Machine | Manufacturing company | Non-current |
| Car | Car trader | Current |
| Investment | Any | Either* |

\* The classification of the investment will depend on the purpose for which it is held. If the intention is to make a non-current investment it will be a **non-current asset**, but if it is a short-term way of investing spare cash it will be a **current asset**.

## Answer to Interactive question 5

LIZA DOOLITTLE
STATEMENT OF FINANCIAL POSITION AS AT 31 JULY 20X6

| | £ | £ |
|---|---|---|
| **ASSETS** | | |
| *Non-current assets* | | |
| Stall | | 1,800 |
| Van | | 700 |
| | | 2,500 |
| *Current assets* | | |
| Inventories | 1,250 | |
| Trade receivables | 890 | |
| Cash in hand | 20 | |
| Cash at bank | 1,475 | |
| | | 3,635 |
| *Total assets* | | 6,135 |
| **CAPITAL AND LIABILITIES** | | |
| *Capital* | | |
| Opening capital | 2,500 | |
| Additional capital introduced | 250 | |
| | | 2,750 |
| Profit for month | 3,620 | |
| Less drawings | (960) | |
| | | 2,660 |
| | | 5,410 |
| *Non-current liabilities* | | |
| Loan | | 50 |
| *Current liabilities* | | |
| Trade payables | | 675 |
| *Total capital and liabilities* | | 6,135 |

## Answer to Interactive question 6

JOCK HEISS
STATEMENT OF FINANCIAL POSITION AS AT 31 AUGUST 20X5

| | £ |
|---|---|
| **ASSETS** | |
| *Current assets* | |
| Trade receivables (1,100 – 250) | 850 |
| Cash at bank and in hand | |
| (2,000 + 8,900 – (6,200 – 700) – 300 – 1,000 – 900 – 150 – 75 – 900) | 2,075 |
| *Total assets* | 2,925 |
| **CAPITAL AND LIABILITIES** | |
| *Capital* | |
| Opening capital | 0 |
| Profit for the period | 1,125 |
| Drawings | (900) |
| Closing capital | 225 |
| *Non-current liabilities* | |
| Loan | 2,000 |
| *Current liabilities* | |
| Trade payables | 700 |
| *Total capital and liabilities* | 2,925 |

1  D  A and B are liabilities; C is an appropriation of profit.

2  B  C and D are assets, depreciation is an expense and a reduction in the value of an asset.

3  D  B is an asset while C is a liability; A is the wrong way round. A better way of thinking of capital is that it is the owners' residual interest in the entity's net assets.

4  B and D. A and C are current liabilities; E is capital.

5  B  The accruals concept is best described as the matching of income with expenses.

6  C  The mortgage is repayable in over a year's time and, therefore, is a non-current liability. The bank overdraft is repayable on demand, a trade payable is usually paid within a year and the bank loan is repayable within one year, so these are all current liabilities.

7  C  B describes the statement of profit or loss accurately.

8  D  The others are examples of selling expenses (A), administration expenses (B) and finance cost (C).

9  B  Gross profit margin $= \dfrac{\text{Gross profit}}{\text{Sales}} \times 100\% = \dfrac{(100,000 - 60,000)}{100,000} \times 100\% = 40\%$

10  D  Gross profit (A) and revenue (C) are included in the calculation of net profit; drawings are appropriations of net profit that appear in the statement of financial position only.

# CHAPTER 3

# Recording financial transactions

Introduction

Examination context

**Topic List**

# Introduction

## Learning objectives

- Identify the sources of information for the preparation of accounting records and financial statements ☐

- Record transactions and events resulting in income, expenses, assets, liabilities and equity ☐

Specific syllabus learning outcomes are: 1c, d

## Syllabus links

The material in this chapter will be developed further in this paper, and then in the Professional Level module of Financial Accounting and Reporting.

## Examination context

Questions on the topics in this chapter will be set as multiple choice questions, some of which may involve calculations so that the correct answer can be selected.

In the exam you may be required to:

- Specify source documents for the accounting system
- Identify the purpose of books of original entry
- Identify the books of original entry in which specific transactions are recorded
- Identify an accurate description of the petty cash imprest system
- Calculate net or gross pay, or the amounts owed to HMRC

# 1 Source documents for recording financial transactions

**Section overview**

- Credit sales make use of sales orders, delivery notes to the customer and sales invoices (which is the source document that is then recorded).

- Credit purchases make use of purchase orders, goods received notes and sales invoices from the supplier (which become purchase invoices to be recorded).

- Invoices show, among other things, what has been sold at what price. Trade discounts and VAT are also shown, so that the total reflects the full amount that remains to be paid.

- Credit notes are negative invoices.

## 1.1 What are source documents used for?

Whenever a business transaction takes place involving sales or purchases, receiving or paying money, or owing or being owed money, it is usual for the transaction to be recorded on a **source document**. These documents are the source of all information recorded by a business, but only invoices and credit notes are source documents for the accounting system.

| CREDIT SALE | CREDIT PURCHASE |
|---|---|

**CREDIT SALE**

Receive sales order from customer — Sales order (received from customer)

↓

Prepare goods and delivery note; deliver to customer — Delivery note

↓

Prepare sales invoice and send to customer — SOURCE DOCUMENT FOR ACCOUNTING SYSTEM — Sales invoice

**CREDIT PURCHASE**

Purchase order — Send purchase order to supplier

↓

Goods received note — Receive goods with supplier's delivery note; prepare goods received note (GRN)

↓

Purchase invoice (received from supplier) — Receive purchase invoice from supplier, and match to GRN — SOURCE DOCUMENT FOR ACCOUNTING SYSTEM

CHAPTER 3

In many businesses a customer writes out or signs a **sales order** for goods or services he requires. Similarly, a business will place **purchase orders** with other businesses for goods or services, such as material supplies.

While sales and purchase orders are very important from a practical point of view, they are **not** treated as source documents for recording financial transactions in the business accounts.

## 1.2 Invoices

Invoices are used to record transactions which have been made on credit. This is where goods or services are supplied but payment is not made straight away as there is a 'period of credit' before they are actually due for payment.

- When a business sells goods or services on credit to a customer, it sends out a **sales invoice**. The invoice details should match the sales order details. The invoice is a request for the customer to pay what is owed.

- When a business buys goods or services on credit it receives a **purchase invoice** from the supplier. The details on the invoice should match the details on the purchase order.

An **invoice** may relate to a sales or purchase order. **Invoices are source documents for credit transactions**.

Most **sales invoices** are numbered, so that the business can keep track of all the **sales invoices** it sends out. Information usually shown on an invoice includes the following.

- Invoice number

- Name and address of seller and purchaser

- Sale date

- Product/service description

- Quantity and unit price of what has been sold (eg 20 pairs of shoes at £25 a pair)

- Details of trade or bulk discount, if any (eg 10% reduction in cost if buying over 100 pairs of shoes)

- Total invoice amount including (usually) VAT details

- The date by which payment is due, and other terms of sale

- A tear-off remittance advice, for the customer to send to the business along with payment so that the business can identify what outstanding amounts are being settled.

**Purchase invoices** received will show exactly the same details as a sales invoice – because it is of course the supplier's sales invoices to us! Most businesses will give unique reference numbers to purchase invoices received so that they can be 'tracked' within the business.

## 1.3 Credit notes

Suppose China Supplies sent out a sales invoice to a customer (a shop) for 20 dinner plates, but the person creating the invoice accidentally typed in a total of £162.10, instead of £62.10. The shop has been **overcharged** by £100. What is China Supplies to do?

Another shop received 15 plates from China Supplies but found that they had all been broken in the post. Although the shop has received an invoice for, say, £45.60, it has no intention of paying it because the plates were substandard. Again, what is China Supplies to do?

The answer is that China Supplies sends out a **credit note**. It will be made out in the same way as an invoice, but with a 'credit note number' instead of a 'sales invoice number'.

**Definition**

**Credit note:** A document issued to a customer relating to returned goods, or refunds when a customer has been overcharged for whatever reason. It can be regarded as a **negative invoice**. **It is a source document for credit transactions.**

### 1.3.1 Debit notes

A **debit note** might be issued to a supplier as a means of formally requesting a credit note from that supplier. A debit note is **not a source document.**

## 1.4 Delivery notes

When goods or services are delivered to a customer in respect of a sale, they are usually accompanied by a **delivery note** prepared by the seller. This sets out:

- The goods/service delivered
- The quantities delivered
- The date of the delivery and
- The delivery address

The delivery note is most often prepared with reference to the sales order. Once the delivery is complete the delivery note is used to provide information for creating the **sales invoice**. The delivery note is **not** a source document for credit transactions.

## 1.5 Goods received notes

A **goods received note** (GRN) records a receipt of goods purchased, most commonly in a warehouse. They may be used in addition to suppliers' delivery notes. Often the accounts department will ask to see the GRN before paying a purchase invoice. Even where GRNs are not routinely used, the details of a delivery from a supplier which arrives without a delivery note must always be recorded. A GRN is **not** a source document for credit transactions.

**Interactive question 1: Credit note**

Fill in the blanks.

'China Supplies sends out a ........................................ to a credit customer in order to correct an error where a customer has been overcharged on a ........................................ .'

See **Answer** at the end of this chapter.

## 1.6 VAT

Value added tax (VAT) is a sales tax added to most sales invoices in the UK. Details for calculating and recording VAT are discussed in Chapter 4. As well as the sale or purchase amount, the business also normally needs to record VAT on each invoice or credit note. This amount will ultimately be paid to or received from HMRC.

## 1.7 Other source documents

So far we have only considered source documents for initial recording of sales and purchases on credit, ie sales and purchase invoices and credit notes. Other source documents for transactions involving settlement of credit transactions (by cheque, debit card or transfer), cash, wages and other matters are also used, as we shall see.

# 2 Books of original entry

**Section overview**

- Books of original entry record information about a transaction shown in a source document.

- The key books of original entry are sales and purchases day books, the cash book, the petty cash book, the journal and the payroll.

## 2.1 What are books of original entry used for?

Source documents need to be summarised, as otherwise the business might forget to ask for some money, forget to pay some, or pay something twice. It needs to keep records of transactions as documented in invoices and credit notes. Such records are made in **books of original (or prime) entry**.

**Definition**

**Books of original entry:** The records in which the business first records transactions.

The main books of original entry are:

- Sales day book
- Purchases day book
- Cash book

- Petty cash book
- The payroll
- The journal

To help you visualise what is going on, this chapter describes books of original entry as if they are actual books written by hand. In fact, books of original entry are nearly always computer files. However, the principles remain the same whether they are manual or computerised.

# 3 Sales and purchases day books

**Section overview**

- Sales invoices and credit notes are recorded in the sales day book.
- The sales day book is usually analysed to show the types of sale and VAT.
- Purchase invoices and credit notes are recorded in the purchases day book.
- The purchases day book is usually analysed to show the types of purchase and VAT.

Invoices and credit notes are recorded in **day books**.

## 3.1 Sales day book

**Definition**

**Sales day book:** The book of original entry in respect of credit sales, including both invoices and credit notes.

The sales day book lists all invoices and credit notes sent out to customers. An extract from a sales day book might look like this.

SALES DAY BOOK

| Date | Invoice/credit note number | Customer | Total £ |
|---|---|---|---|
| 20X0 | | | |
| Jan 10 | I 247 | Jones & Co | 107.04 |
| | I 248 | Smith Co | 88.32 |
| | CN 004 | Alex & Co | (32.16) |
| | I 249 | Enor College | 1,291.68 |
| | | | 1,454.88 |

Most businesses 'analyse' their sales. For example, this business sells boots and shoes. The invoice to Smith Co was entirely boots, the credit note to Alex & Co was entirely shoes, and the other two invoices were a mixture of both. All contained an element of VAT. We look at VAT in detail in Section 9 of Chapter 4 and in particular we cover VAT rates in Section 9.3 of Chapter 4. However at this stage you should note that VAT is typically charged at a rate of 20% of the related sales value and is analysed separately on sales invoices. A separate column is used in the sales day book to account for VAT.

The analysed sales day book might look like this.

SALES DAY BOOK                                                       Folio: SDB 48

| Date | Invoice/credit note number | Customer | Total £ | VAT £ | Boots £ | Shoes £ |
|---|---|---|---|---|---|---|
| 20X0 | | | | | | |
| Jan 10 | I 247 | Jones & Co | 107.04 | 17.84 | 50.00 | 39.20 |
| | I 248 | Smith Co | 88.32 | 14.72 | 73.60 | – |
| | CN 004 | Alex & Co | (32.16) | (5.36) | – | (26.80) |
| | I 249 | Enor College | 1,291.68 | 215.28 | 800.30 | 276.10 |
| | | | 1,454.88 | 242.48 | 923.90 | 288.50 |

The analysis gives business managers useful information which helps them to decide how best to run the business. It also fulfils in part their duty to record and account for VAT.

## 3.2 Purchases day book

### Definition

**Purchases day book:** The book of original entry in respect of credit purchases, including both invoices and credit notes.

An extract from a purchases day book might look like this. VAT on purchases is also separately analysed on purchase invoices and a VAT column is included in the purchase day book.

PURCHASE DAY BOOK                                                    Folio: PDB 37

| Date | Invoice/credit note number | Supplier | Total £ | VAT £ | Purchases £ | Expenses £ |
|---|---|---|---|---|---|---|
| 20X8 | | | | | | |
| Mar 15 | I 4192 | Cook | 321.60 | 53.60 | 268.00 | – |
| | CN 048 | Butler | (30.24) | (5.04) | (25.20) | – |
| | I 4193 | Telcom | 119.04 | 19.84 | – | 99.20 |
| | I 4194 | Show | 102.24 | 17.04 | 85.20 | – |
| | | | 512.64 | 85.44 | 328.00 | 99.20 |

In the 'invoice/credit note number' column a number is allocated by the business; the purchases day book records **other people's invoices**, which have all sorts of different numbers which it cannot usually record.

The purchases day book analyses invoices and credit notes which have been received. In this example, two of the invoices and the credit note related to goods which the business intends to re sell (called simply 'purchases') and the third invoice was a phone bill. All included VAT.

# 4 Cash book

## Section overview

- The cash book records all payments from and receipts into the entity's bank account.

- Payments and receipts may be via cash, cheque, card payment, BACS transfer or online transfer.

- Ideally, payments and receipts should be evidenced by a remittance advice as the source document.

- The cash book is analysed to show the types of payment and receipt, and any VAT.

- Discount allowed and received is recorded in memorandum columns in the cash book.

## Definition

Cash book: The book of original entry for receipts and payments in the business's bank account.

## 4.1 What is the cash book used for?

The cash book is used to record money received and paid out by the business through the business **bank account**. This could be money received on the business premises in notes, coins and cheques, and subsequently paid into the bank. The source documents for such items are usually remittance advices, which identify what is being settled. There are also receipts and payments made by card, bank transfer, standing order, direct debit and online transfer, plus bank interest and charges made directly by the bank. The source documents for such items are remittance advices or receipts, though the first the business may know of some transactions is when they appear on the business's bank statement.

Some cash, in notes and coins, is usually kept on the business premises in order to make occasional payments for odd items of expense. This cash is usually accounted for separately in a **petty cash book**.

One part of the cash book records cash receipts, and another part records payments. The best way to see how the cash book works is to follow through an example.

## Worked example: Cash book

At the beginning of 1 September 20X7, Robin Plenty had £900 in the bank.

On 1 September, Robin had the following receipts and payments.

- (a) Cash sale: receipt of £96 (including VAT of £16)
- (b) Payment from credit customer Hay £380
- (c) Payment from credit customer Been £720
- (d) Payment from credit customer Seed £140
- (e) Cheque received as a short term loan from Len Dinger £1,800
- (f) Cash sale: receipt of £144 (including VAT of £24)
- (g) Cash received for sale of machine £200 (no VAT)
- (h) Payment to supplier Kew £120
- (i) Payment to supplier Hare £310
- (j) Payment of telephone bill £384 (including VAT of £64)
- (k) Payment of gas service charge £288 (including VAT of £48)
- (l) £100 in cash withdrawn from bank for petty cash
- (m) Payment of £1,500 to Hess for new plant and machinery (no VAT)

The receipts part of the cash book for 1 September would look like this.

### CASH BOOK (RECEIPTS)

| Date | Narrative | Total receipts £ | VAT £ | Receivables £ | Cash sales £ | Other £ |
|------|-----------|-----------------|-------|---------------|--------------|---------|
| 20X7 | | | | | | |
| 1 Sept | Balance b/d* | 900 | | | | |
| | Cash sale (a) | 96 | | | | |
| | Receivables: Hay (b) | 380 | | | | |
| | Receivables: Been (c) | 720 | | | | |
| | Receivables: Seed (d) | 140 | | | | |
| | Loan: Len Dinger (e) | 1,800 | | | | |
| | Cash sale (f) | 144 | | | | |
| | Sale of non-current assets (g) | 200 | | | | |
| | Total | 4,380 | | | | |

* 'b/d' = brought down (ie brought forward)

There is usually space on the right hand side of the cash book so that the receipts can be analysed – for example, 'VAT', '(cash from) receivables', 'cash sales' and 'other (receipts)'.

The cash received in the day amounted to £3,480. Added to the £900 at the start of the day, this comes to £4,380. This is not the amount to be carried forward to the next day, because first we have to subtract all the payments made on 1 September.

The payments part of the cash book for 1 September would look like this.

### CASH BOOK (PAYMENTS)

| Date | Narrative | Total payment £ | VAT £ | Payables £ | Petty cash £ | Wages £ | Other £ |
|------|-----------|----------------|-------|------------|--------------|---------|---------|
| 20X7 | | | | | | | |
| 1 Sept | Payables: Kew (h) | 120 | | | | | |
| | Payables: Hare (i) | 310 | | | | | |
| | Telephone bill (j) | 384 | | | | | |
| | Service charge bill (k) | 288 | | | | | |
| | Petty cash (l) | 100 | | | | | |
| | Machinery purchases (m) | 1,500 | | | | | |
| | Total payments | 2,702 | | | | | |
| | Balance c/d | | | | | | |
| | (4,380 – 2,702) | 1,678 | | | | | |
| | Total | 4,380 | | | | | |

The analysis on the right would be under headings like 'VAT', '(payments to) payables, '(payments into) petty cash', 'wages' and 'other (payments)'.

Payments during 1 September totalled £2,702. We know that the total of receipts was £4,380. That means that there is a balance of £4,380 – £2,702 = £1,678 to be 'carried down' to the start of the next day. As you can see this 'balance carried down' is noted at the end of the payments column, so that the total receipts and total payment columns show the same figure of £4,380 at the end of 1 September.

With analysis columns completed, the cash book given in the example above would look as follows.

## CASH BOOK (RECEIPTS)

| Date | Narrative | Total receipts £ | VAT £ | Receivables £ | Cash sales £ | Other £ |
|---|---|---|---|---|---|---|
| 20X7 | | | | | | |
| 1 Sept | Balance b/d | 900 | | | | |
| | Cash sale (a) | 96 | 16 | | 80 | |
| | Receivables: Hay (b) | 380 | | 380 | | |
| | Receivables: Been (c) | 720 | | 720 | | |
| | Receivables: Seed (d) | 140 | | 140 | | |
| | Loan: Len Dinger (e) | 1,800 | | | | 1,800 |
| | Cash sale (f) | 144 | 24 | | 120 | |
| | Sale of non-current assets (g) | 200 | | | | 200 |
| | | 4,380 | 40 | 1,240 | 200 | 2,000 |

## CASH BOOK (PAYMENTS)

| Date | Narrative | Total payment £ | VAT £ | Payables £ | Petty cash £ | Wages £ | Other £ |
|---|---|---|---|---|---|---|---|
| 20X7 | | | | | | | |
| 1 Sept | Payables: Kew (h) | 120 | | 120 | | | |
| | Payables: Hare (i) | 310 | | 310 | | | |
| | Telephone bill (j) | 384 | 64 | | | | 320 |
| | Service charge bill (k) | 288 | 48 | | | | 240 |
| | Petty cash (l) | 100 | | | 100 | | |
| | Machinery purchases (m) | 1,500 | | | | | 1,500 |
| | Total payments | 2,702 | 112 | 430 | 100 | – | 2,060 |
| | Balance c/d | | | | | | |
| | (4,380 – 2,702) | 1,678 | | | | | |
| | | 4,380 | | | | | |

## 4.2 VAT in the cash book

In the cash book VAT was included in only the cash sales and the telephone and service charge payments. There are two reasons:

- Some transactions did not fall under the scope of VAT at all (the sale of non-current assets, the loan receipt, the petty cash payment and the purchase of machinery).

- For all other transactions the VAT had already been recorded in the sales or purchases day book. Subsequent receipts from customers or payments to suppliers are simply of the total amount owed.

The cash book only records VAT in respect of receipts or payments which:

- Fall under the scope of VAT, and
- Are not recorded in any other book of original entry, because they are not credit transactions.

## 4.3 Discounts in the cash book

Discounts may be offered in respect of credit transactions.

- A **discount allowed** arises when a business records one amount as being due from a customer, but then allows the customer to pay slightly less in full settlement (in return for the customer paying early).

- A **discount received** arises when a business records one amount as being due to a supplier, but then receives notice from the supplier that slightly less can be paid in full settlement (again, usually in return for paying early).

When a receipt is for less than the total amount owed by the customer, the amount of the discount (the difference between the amount owed and the receipt) is recorded in a special 'memorandum' column of the cash book.

### Worked example: Discount allowed

Suppose that in the example above, Hay's payment of £380 was in full settlement of an invoice that had been recorded at £385 in total in the sales day book. The cash book would be written up as follows, with an additional 'discount allowed' column.

| Date | Narrative | Total receipts £ | VAT £ | Receivables £ | Cash sales £ | Other £ | Discount allowed £ |
|------|-----------|------------------|-------|---------------|--------------|---------|--------------------|
|      | Receivables: Hay | 380 | | 380 | | | 5 |

There is usually a vertical line to separate discounts, as the discount column is not included in the addition to the total receipts column (it is not 'cross-cast').

### Worked example: Discount received

Suppose now that, in the example above, the payment to Kew of £120 was in full settlement of an invoice which had been recorded in the purchases day book at £123 in total. The cash book would be written up as follows, with an additional 'discount received' column.

#### CASH BOOK (PAYMENTS)

| Date | Narrative | Total payments £ | VAT £ | Payables £ | Petty cash £ | Wages £ | Other £ | Discount received £ |
|------|-----------|------------------|-------|------------|--------------|---------|---------|---------------------|
|      | Payables: Kew | 120 | | 120 | | | | 3 |

## 5 Petty cash book

### Section overview

- The petty cash book records all payments out of and receipts into petty cash.

- Petty cash is the cash (notes and coins) that an entity keeps on the premises for incidental expenditure.

- Under an imprest system, petty cash is kept at a fixed 'float' amount, which is made up of notes, coins and vouchers representing payments from and receipts of petty cash.

- The amount of notes and coins used to 'top up' petty cash will be equal to the total of the vouchers issued for petty cash receipts and payments.

- The petty cash book is analysed to record the different types of petty cash expense plus VAT on petty cash purchases.

### 5.1 What is the petty cash book used for?

Most businesses keep a small amount of 'petty cash' on the premises to make occasional small payments in cash, eg staff refreshments, postage stamps, taxi fares, etc. This is often called the **cash float** or **petty cash**. Petty cash can also be the resting place for occasional small receipts, eg cash paid by a visitor to make a phone call, etc.

### Definition

**Petty cash book:** The book of original entry for small payments and receipts of cash.

Petty cash transactions – including VAT on payments where relevant – still need to be recorded, otherwise petty cash could be abused for personal expenses or even stolen.

There are usually more payments than receipts, and petty cash must be 'topped up' from time to time with cash from the business bank account. A typical layout is as follows.

### PETTY CASH BOOK

| Receipts £ | Date | Narrative | Payments £ | VAT £ | Milk £ | Postage £ | Travel £ | Other £ |
|---|---|---|---|---|---|---|---|---|
| | 20X7 | | | | | | | |
| 250 | 1 Sept | Bal b/d | | | | | | |
| | | Milk bill | 25 | | 25 | | | |
| | | Postage stamps | 5 | | | 5 | | |
| | | Taxi fare | 10 | | | | 10 | |
| | | Flowers - sick staff | 15 | | | | | 15 |
| | | Bal c/d | 195 | | | | | |
| 250 | | | 250 | 0 | 25 | 5 | 10 | 15 |

Under what is called the **imprest system**, the amount of money in petty cash is kept at an agreed sum or 'float' (say £250). Expense items are recorded on vouchers as they occur, so that at any time:

| | £ |
|---|---|
| Cash still held in petty cash | 195 |
| Plus vouchers for payments (25 + 5 + 10 + 15) | 55 |
| Must equal the agreed sum or float | 250 |

The total float is made up regularly (to £250, or whatever the agreed sum is) by means of a cash payment from the bank account into petty cash. The amount of the 'top up' into petty cash will be the total of the voucher payments since the previous top up.

### Interactive question 2: Books of original entry

State which books of original entry the following transactions would be entered into.

(a)   Your business pays A Brown (a supplier) a cheque for £450.00.
(b)   You send D Smith (a customer) an invoice for £650.
(c)   Your accounts manager asks you for £12 to buy envelopes.
(d)   You receive an invoice from A Brown for £300.
(e)   You pay D Smith £500 by online transfer.
(f)   F Jones (a customer) returns goods valued £250.
(g)   You return goods to J Green valued £504.
(h)   F Jones pays you a cheque for £500.

See **Answer** at the end of this chapter.

# 6 The payroll

## 6.1 What is the payroll used for?

### Definition

**Payroll:** The book of original entry for recording staff costs.

The payroll records all the individual amounts that appear on employees' payslips, namely:

- Gross pay to employees:
    - PAYE income tax
    - Employee's NI contributions
    - Employee's pension contributions
    - Net pay (cash paid to employees)

- Additional costs for the employer:
    - Employer's NI contributions
    - Pension contributions

Gross pay is **not** the amount paid to the employee. The employer needs to make deductions from gross pay before **paying net pay to the employee**.

### Worked example: Payroll

Sunny Climes Ltd employs three people: Anja earns £36,000 a year, Mark earns £33,000 a year and Dipak earns £30,000 a year. The gross pay in September for each employee is as follows.

|  | £ |
|---|---|
| Anja | 3,000 |
| Mark | 2,750 |
| Dipak | 2,500 |

However, these are not the amounts that each employee will receive. Sunny Climes Ltd first of all has to deduct income tax from gross pay under the PAYE scheme to be paid to HMRC. It deducts National Insurance (employee NI) from gross pay, again to be paid to HMRC. As it runs a pension scheme, it has to deduct each employee's pension contribution, to be paid to pension fund trustees.

| | Deductions | | | | |
|---|---|---|---|---|---|
| | PAYE | NI | Pension | Net pay | Gross pay |
| | £ | £ | £ | £ | £ |
| Anja | 550 | 250 | 150 | 2,050 | 3,000 |
| Mark | 500 | 230 | 135 | 1,885 | 2,750 |
| Dipak | 460 | 210 | 125 | 1,705 | 2,500 |
| | 1,510 | 690 | 410 | 5,640 | 8,250 |

Deductions + Net pay = Gross pay

The employees will receive the net pay; this amount will be shown in the cash book.

The employer has deducted amounts the employees owe to other people from the gross pay the employer owes to them. This is not the end of the story however; the employer also owes additional NI to HMRC, and pension contributions of its own to the trustees, over and above the amount of gross pay. The final payroll will be as follows.

| | | Deductions Employee | | | | Employer | Employer | Total |
|---|---|---|---|---|---|---|---|---|
| | PAYE | NI | Pension | Net pay | Gross pay | NI | Pension | payroll cost |
| | £ | £ | £ | £ | £ | £ | £ | £ |
| Anja | 550 | 250 | 150 | 2,050 | 3,000 | 310 | 200 | 3,510 |
| Mark | 500 | 230 | 135 | 1,885 | 2,750 | 265 | 180 | 3,195 |
| Dipak | 460 | 210 | 125 | 1,705 | 2,500 | 230 | 165 | 2,895 |
| | 1,510 | 690 | 410 | 5,640 | 8,250 | 805 | 545 | 9,600 |

Gross pay + Employer NI + Employer pension = Total payroll cost

The total payroll cost for Sunny Climes Ltd is £9,600. This is paid out as follows:

| | £ |
|---|---|
| Employees (net pay) | 5,640 |
| HMRC: Income tax PAYE | 1,510 |
| HMRC: Employee and employer NI (690 + 805) | 1,495 |
| Pension trustees: Employee and employer pension (410 + 545) | 955 |
| Total payroll cost | 9,600 |

### Interactive question 3: Payroll

Fantab Ltd has 10 employees who had gross pay of £190,000 per annum between them in 20X4. In that year, Fantab Ltd made net pay payments to employees of £129,200, and paid £20,900 to the pension trustees. Its total payroll cost was £220,400. How much did Fantab Ltd pay to HMRC in respect of NI and PAYE?

See **Answer** at the end of this chapter.

# 7 The journal

### Section overview

- The journal records transactions that are not recorded in any other book of original entry.

## 7.1 What is the journal used for?

The final book of original entry is the **journal**. This is the record of transactions which do not appear in any of the other books of original entry. **Non-current asset purchases are usually recorded via the journal.**

## Summary

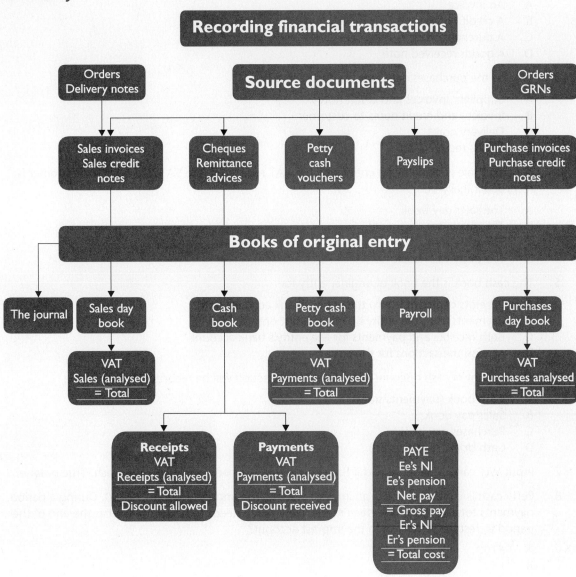

**Recording financial transactions**

**Source documents**

Orders / Delivery notes

Orders / GRNs

Sales invoices / Sales credit notes

Cheques / Remittance advices

Petty cash vouchers

Payslips

Purchase invoices / Purchase credit notes

**Books of original entry**

The journal

Sales day book

Cash book

Petty cash book

Payroll

Purchases day book

VAT
Sales (analysed)
= Total

VAT
Payments (analysed)
= Total

VAT
Purchases analysed
= Total

**Receipts**
VAT
Receipts (analysed)
= Total
Discount allowed

**Payments**
VAT
Payments (analysed)
= Total
Discount received

PAYE
Ee's NI
Ee's pension
Net pay
= Gross pay
Er's NI
Er's pension
= Total cost

CHAPTER 3

## Self-test

Answer the following questions.

1 Sales orders are source documents that are recorded in the sales day book. True or false?

2 When an entity returns goods to a supplier it will expect to receive from the supplier

   A   An invoice
   B   A credit note
   C   A purchase order
   D   A goods received note

3 What is the purchases day book used to record?

   A   Suppliers' invoices and credit notes
   B   Invoices and credit notes to customer
   C   Delivery notes
   D   Goods received notes

4 If a credit sale is made by an entity which is VAT registered, the VAT due from the customer is recorded initially in

   A   The sales day book
   B   The purchases day book
   C   The cash book
   D   The petty cash book

5 The cash book is the book of original entry for

   A   Receipts of amounts into the entity's bank account only
   B   Payments from the entity's bank account only
   C   Both receipts and payments for the entity's bank account
   D   All cash transactions for the entity

6 The amount of cash discount allowed on a transaction will be recorded initially in the

   A   Cash book (payments side)
   B   Sales day book
   C   Purchases day book
   D   Cash book (receipts side)

7 Input VAT cannot be reclaimed if the expenditure has been made via petty cash. True or false?

8 Petty cash is controlled under an imprest system. The imprest amount is £100. During a period, payments totalling £53 have been made. How much needs to be reimbursed at the end of the period to restore petty cash to the imprest account?

   A   £100
   B   £53
   C   £47
   D   £50

9 The cost of employer's NI is part of a company's

   A   Net pay
   B   Gross pay
   C   Gross wages and salaries cost
   D   Corporation tax charge

10 A transaction which does not involve payroll, cash or credit transactions is likely to be recorded in

   A   The cash book
   B   The petty cash book
   C   The sales day book
   D   The journal

Now, go back to the Learning Objectives in the Introduction. If you are satisfied you have achieved the objectives, please tick them off.

# Answers to Interactive questions

## Answer to Interactive question 1

Credit note; sales invoice

## Answer to Interactive question 2

(a) Cash book
(b) Sales day book
(c) Petty cash book
(d) Purchases day book
(e) Cash book
(f) Sales day book
(g) Purchases day book
(h) Cash book

## Answer to Interactive question 3

|  | £ |
|---|---|
| Total payroll cost | 220,400 |
| Employees (net pay) | (129,200) |
| Pension trustees | (20,900) |
| Amount paid to HMRC | 70,300 |

1   False. The sales invoice is recorded in the sales day book.

2   B   An invoice (A) is received in respect of the original purchase, after a purchase order (C) has been placed and a goods received note (D) has been created in respect of the delivery of goods.

3   A   Customers' invoices and credit notes (B) are recorded in the sales day book. Delivery notes and goods received notes (C and D) are not recorded directly in any day books.

4   A   VAT on credit sales is recorded in the sales day book initially (A), not the purchase day book (B) which relates to credit purchases, nor the cash book (C) which records the receipt from the customer when they settle the bill. The petty cash book (D) is not normally a book of original entry in respect of credit sales.

5   C   The cash book records *both* receipts *and* payments via the bank account. It does not record all cash transactions since the petty cash book records petty cash transactions.

6   D   Cash discount is allowed to customers, so it will be first recorded not when the invoice is recorded in the sales day book (B) but when cash is received from the customer. Discounts received would be recorded in the cash book (payments side) (A).

7   False. Petty cash books often have a column for VAT on small items of expenditure.

8   B   Under the imprest system, a reimbursement is made of the amount of the vouchers (or payments made) for the period.

9   C   The cost of employer's NI is added to gross pay (B) (which includes net pay (A)) to form the gross wages and salaries cost. Payroll taxes are not included in the company's corporation tax charge (D).

10  D   The journal records items which are not recorded in any other book of original entry.

# CHAPTER 4

# Ledger accounting and double entry

Introduction

Examination context

**Topic List**

# Introduction

## Learning objectives

Tick off

- Identify the sources of information for the preparation of accounting records and financial statements

- Record and account for transactions and events resulting in income, expenses, assets, liabilities and equity

- Prepare journals for nominal ledger entry

Specific syllabus learning outcomes are: 1c, d; 2d

## Syllabus links

The material in this chapter will be developed further in this paper, and then in the Professional Level module of Financial Accounting and Reporting.

## Examination context

Questions on the topics in this chapter will be set as multiple choice questions, some of which may involve calculations so that the correct answer can be selected. Very often double entry questions are phrased in terms of preparing a journal.

In the exam you may be required to:

- Identify the effect of debit and credit entries in ledger accounts for the elements of financial statements

- Specify the double entry needed to record particular transactions

- Identify how to post transactions to both the nominal and memorandum ledgers

- Identify entries in ledger accounts for VAT, payables and receivables

- Use ledger accounts to identify balancing figures

# 1 Ledger accounts

**Section overview**

- Ledger accounts summarise all the individual transactions listed in the books of original entry.
- Records should be kept in ledger accounts in chronological order, with cumulative totals built up.

## 1.1 Why do we need ledger accounts?

A business is continually making transactions, eg buying and selling. To prepare a statement of profit or loss and a statement of financial position on completion of every individual transaction would be a time consuming and cumbersome administrative task.

If a business records and **analyses** the transactions it makes, assets it acquires and liabilities it incurs then, when the time comes to prepare a statement of profit or loss and a statement of financial position, the relevant information can be taken from those records.

The **records of transactions, assets and liabilities** should be kept in the following ways.

- In **chronological order**, and **dated** so that transactions can be related to a particular period of time.

- Built up in **cumulative totals**.

  - Day by day (eg total sales on Monday, total sales on Tuesday)
  - Week by week
  - Month by month
  - Year by year

The first step in this process is to list all the transactions in various books of original entry, as we have seen. Now we will look at the method used to **analyse** these records: **ledger accounting** and **double entry**.

# 2 The nominal ledger

**Section overview**

- The nominal ledger is the accounting record which analyses all the entity's financial records.
- Ledger accounts for each type of transaction can take the form of a T account, the left hand side is the debit side, and the right hand side is the credit side.

## 2.1 What is the nominal ledger used for?

**Definition**

**Nominal ledger:** An accounting record which analyses the financial records of a business.

The nominal ledger contains details of assets, liabilities, capital, income and expenditure, and so profit and loss. It consists of a large number of different **ledger accounts**, each account having its own purpose or 'name' and an identity or code.

There may be various subdivisions, whether for convenience, ease of handling, confidentiality, security, or to meet the needs of computer software design. For example, the ledger may be split alphabetically, with different clerks responsible for sections A-F, G-M, N-R and S-Z. This can help to reduce fraud, as there would have to be collusion between the different section clerks.

Examples of ledger accounts in the nominal ledger include:

- Plant and machinery at cost (non-current asset)
- Motor vehicles at cost (non-current asset)
- Plant and machinery, provision for accumulated depreciation (deduction from non-current asset)
- Motor vehicles, provision for accumulated depreciation (deduction from non-current asset)
- Owner's capital (capital)
- Inventories – raw materials (current asset)
- Inventories – finished goods (current asset)
- Total trade receivables (current asset)
- Total trade payables (current liability)
- Wages and salaries (expense)
- Rent and local taxes (expense)
- Advertising expenses (expense)
- Bank charges (expense)
- Motor expenses (expense)
- Telephone expenses (expense)
- Sales (income)
- Total cash/bank overdraft (current asset/liability)

When it comes to drawing up the financial statements, the income and expense ledger accounts will together form the statement of profit or loss, while the asset, capital and liability ledger accounts go into the statement of financial position.

## 2.2 The format of a ledger account

If a ledger account were to be kept in an actual book, rather than as a computer record, it would look like this.

### ADVERTISING EXPENSES

| Date | Narrative | Ref. | £ | Date | Narrative | Ref. | £ |
|------|-----------|------|---|------|-----------|------|---|
| 20X6 | JFK Agency for quarter to 31 March | PL 348 | 2,500 | | | | |

There are two sides to the account, with an account heading on top. The lines form a 'T', so it is convenient to think in terms of **'T' accounts**.

- On top of the account is its name.
- There is a left hand, or **debit** side.
- There is a right hand, or **credit** side.

### NAME OF ACCOUNT

| | £ | | £ |
|---|---|---|---|
| Debit side | | Credit side | |

# 3 Double entry bookkeeping

**Section overview**

- The principle of double entry bookkeeping is that, for each transaction, every debit has a credit.

- Debit entries increase assets and expenses, and decrease liabilities, capital and income.

- Credit entries increase liabilities, capital and income, and decrease assets and expenses.

- A receipt of cash is a debit in the cash ledger account.

- A payment of cash is a credit in the cash ledger account.

- A credit sale is recorded as debit receivables (increase asset), credit sales (increase income).

- A credit purchase is recorded as debit purchases (increase expenses), credit payables (increase liabilities).

- Discount allowed to customers is credited to receivables along with payments received, and debited to a discount allowed ledger account.

- Discounts received from suppliers is debited to payables along with payments made, and credited to a discount received ledger account.

**Definition**

**Double entry bookkeeping:** Each transaction has an equal but opposite effect. Every accounting event must be entered in ledger accounts both as a debit and a credit.

## 3.1 Dual effect (duality concept)

**Double entry bookkeeping** is the method used to transfer totals from the **books of original entry** into the **nominal ledger**.

Central to this process is the idea that every transaction has two effects, the **dual effect** (also known as the **duality concept**). This feature is not something peculiar to business. If you were to purchase a car for £1,000 cash, for instance, you would be affected in two ways.

- You own a car worth £1,000.
- You have £1,000 less cash.

If instead you got a bank loan to make the purchase:

- You own a car worth £1,000.
- You owe the bank £1,000.

A month later if you pay a garage £50 to have the exhaust repaired:

- You have £50 less cash.
- You have incurred a repairs expense of £50.

**Ledger accounts**, with their debit and credit sides, are kept in a way which allows the two sided nature of every transaction to be recorded. This is known as **double entry bookkeeping**, because **every transaction is recorded twice in the ledger accounts**.

## 3.2 The rules of double entry bookkeeping

A **debit entry** will:

| | |
|---|---|
| • Increase an asset | • Decrease a liability |
| • Increase an expense | • Decrease capital |
| | • Decrease income |

A **credit entry** will:

- Decrease an asset
- Decrease an expense

- Increase a liability
- Increase capital
- Increase income

The basic rule, which must always be observed, is that **every financial transaction gives rise to two accounting entries, one a debit and the other a credit**. The total value of debit entries in the nominal ledger is therefore always equal to the total value of credit entries. Which account receives the credit entry and which receives the debit entry depends on the nature of the transaction.

- An **increase** in an **expense** (eg a purchase of stationery) or an **increase in an asset** (eg a purchase of office furniture) is a **debit**.

- An **increase** in **income** (eg a sale) or an **increase in a liability** (eg buying goods on credit) or **capital** is a **credit**.

- A **decrease** in an **asset** (eg making a cash payment) or a **decrease in an expense** is a **credit**.

- A **decrease** in a **liability** (eg paying a creditor) or **capital** or **income** is a **debit**.

In terms of 'T' accounts, for assets, liabilities and capital:

| ASSET | | LIABILITY | | CAPITAL | |
|---|---|---|---|---|---|
| £ | £ | £ | £ | £ | £ |
| DEBIT | CREDIT | DEBIT | CREDIT | DEBIT | CREDIT |
| Increase | Decrease | Decrease | Increase | Decrease | Increase |

For income and expenses, think about profit. Profit retained in the business increases capital. Income increases profit and expenses decrease profit.

| INCOME | | EXPENSE | |
|---|---|---|---|
| £ | £ | £ | £ |
| DEBIT | CREDIT | DEBIT | CREDIT |
| Decrease | Increase | Increase | Decrease |

## Interactive question 1: Debits and credits

Complete the following table relating to the transactions of a bookshop. (The first two are done for you.)

| (a) | Purchase of books on credit | | | |
|---|---|---|---|---|
| | • Payables increase | CREDIT | payables | (increase in liability) |
| | • Purchases increase | DEBIT | purchases | (increase in expense) |
| (b) | Purchase of cash register by cheque | | | |
| | • Own a cash register | DEBIT | non-current asset | (increase in asset) |
| | • Cash at bank decreases | CREDIT | cash at bank | (decrease in asset) |
| (c) | Payment received from a credit customer | | | |
| | • Receivables decrease | | | |
| | • Cash at bank increases | | | |
| (d) | Sell books for cash | | | |
| | • Revenue increases | | | |
| | • Cash at bank increases | | | |

See **Answer** at the end of this chapter.

## 3.3 Double entry for cash transactions

A good starting point is the cash account, ie the nominal ledger account in which receipts and payments of cash are recorded, or posted, from the book of original entry, the cash book.

- A cash **payment** is a **credit** entry in the cash account. Here **cash is decreasing**. Cash may be paid out, for example to pay an expense (such as insurance) or to purchase an asset (such as a machine). The matching debit entry is therefore made in the appropriate expense or asset account.

- A cash **receipt** is a **debit** entry in the cash account. Here **cash is increasing**. Cash might be received, for example, by a retailer who makes a cash sale. The credit entry would then be made in the revenue account (and the VAT account if relevant).

### Worked example: Cash transactions

In the cash book, the following transactions have been recorded (ignore VAT for now).

(a) A cash sale (ie a receipt) of £250
(b) Payment of a rent bill totalling £150
(c) Buy some goods for cash of £100
(d) Buy some shelves for cash of £200

How would these four transactions be entered (or 'posted') to the ledger accounts, and to which ledger accounts should they be posted? Remember each transaction will be posted twice, in accordance with double entry rules.

### Solution

(a) The two sides of the transaction are:

- £250 cash is received (debit cash account).
- Sales increase by £250 (credit sales account).

#### CASH ACCOUNT

| | £ | | £ |
|---|---|---|---|
| Sales a/c | 250 | | |

#### SALES ACCOUNT

| | £ | | £ |
|---|---|---|---|
| | | Cash a/c | 250 |

(The cash account entry is cross referenced to the sales account and vice versa. This enables a person looking at one of the ledger accounts to trace where the other half of the double entry is found.)

(b) The two sides of the transaction are:

- Cash is paid (credit entry in the cash asset account).
- Rent expense increases by £150 (debit entry in the rent expense account).

#### CASH ACCOUNT

| | £ | | £ |
|---|---|---|---|
| | | Rent a/c | 150 |

#### RENT ACCOUNT

| | £ | | £ |
|---|---|---|---|
| Cash a/c | 150 | | |

(c) The two sides of the transaction are:

- Cash is paid (credit entry in the cash asset account).
- Purchases increase by £100 (debit entry in the purchases expense account).

### CASH ACCOUNT

| | £ | | £ |
|---|---|---|---|
| | | Purchases a/c | 100 |

### PURCHASES ACCOUNT

| | £ | | £ |
|---|---|---|---|
| Cash a/c | 100 | | |

(d) The two sides of the transaction are:

- Cash is paid (credit cash account).
- Assets – in this case, shelves – increase by £200 (debit shelves account).

### CASH ACCOUNT

| | £ | | £ |
|---|---|---|---|
| | | Shelves a/c | 200 |

### SHELVES ACCOUNT

| | £ | | £ |
|---|---|---|---|
| Cash a/c | 200 | | |

If all four of these transactions related to the same business, the cash account of that business would end up looking as follows.

### CASH ACCOUNT

| | £ | | £ |
|---|---|---|---|
| Sales a/c | 250 | Rent a/c | 150 |
| | | Purchases a/c | 100 |
| | | Shelves a/c | 200 |

## 3.4 Double entry for credit transactions

Not all transactions are settled immediately. A business can purchase goods or non-current assets on credit terms, so that suppliers would be trade payables until settlement was made in cash. Equally, the business might grant customers credit terms, so they would then be trade receivables of the business. No entries can be made in the cash book when a credit transaction occurs, because no cash has been received or paid.

Instead of the cash account we use **receivables and payables accounts**. When a business acquires goods or services on credit, the credit entry is posted from the purchases day book to a 'trade payables' account instead of the cash account. The debit entry is posted to the expense or asset account, exactly as in the case of cash transactions. Similarly, when a sale is made to a credit customer, entries posted from the sales day book are a debit to the trade receivables account (instead of cash account), and a credit to the sales revenue account.

### 3.4.1 Double entry when credit transactions are entered into

**Worked example: Double entry for credit transactions**

Recorded in the sales day book and the purchases day book for a business are the following transactions.

(a)   The business sells goods on credit to Mr A for £2,000.
(b)   The business buys goods on credit from B Ltd for £100.

How and where are these transactions posted in the ledger accounts from the books of original entry?

**Solution**

(a)                                          TRADE RECEIVABLES (MR A)

| | £ | | £ |
|---|---|---|---|
| Sales a/c | 2,000 | | |

SALES ACCOUNT

| | £ | | £ |
|---|---|---|---|
| | | Trade receivables a/c (Mr A) | 2,000 |

(b)                                          TRADE PAYABLES (B LTD)

| | £ | | £ |
|---|---|---|---|
| | | Purchases a/c | 100 |

PURCHASES ACCOUNT

| | £ | | £ |
|---|---|---|---|
| Trade payables a/c (B Ltd) | 100 | | |

### 3.4.2 Double entry when cash is paid by customers or to suppliers

What happens when a credit transaction is eventually settled in cash? Suppose that, in the example above, the business paid £100 to B Ltd one month after the goods were acquired, recorded in the cash book. The two sides of this new transaction are:

(a)   Cash is paid (credit entry in the cash account).
(b)   The amount owing to trade payables is reduced (debit entry in the trade payables account).

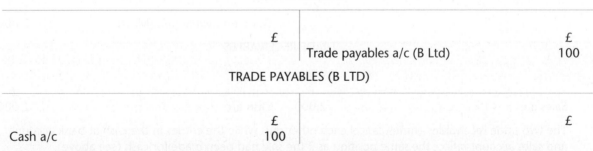

CASH ACCOUNT

| | £ | | £ |
|---|---|---|---|
| | | Trade payables a/c (B Ltd) | 100 |

TRADE PAYABLES (B LTD)

| | £ | | £ |
|---|---|---|---|
| Cash a/c | 100 | | |

If we now bring together the two parts of this example, the original purchase of goods on credit and the eventual settlement in cash, we find that the accounts appear as follows.

## CASH ACCOUNT

| | £ | | £ |
|---|---|---|---|
| | | Trade payables a/c (B Ltd) | 100 |

## PURCHASES ACCOUNT

| | £ | | £ |
|---|---|---|---|
| Trade payables a/c (B Ltd) | 100 | | |

## TRADE PAYABLES (B LTD)

| | £ | | £ |
|---|---|---|---|
| Cash a/c | 100 | Purchases a/c | 100 |

The two entries in trade payables cancel each other out, indicating that no money is owing to B Ltd. A cash account credit entry of £100 and a debit purchases account entry of £100 remain. These are the same as the entries used to record a **cash** purchase of £100. This is what we would expect: after the business has paid off its trade payables, it is in exactly the same position as if it had made a cash purchase, and the accounting records reflect this.

Similar reasoning applies when a customer settles a debt. In the example above, when Mr A pays his debt of £2,000 and it is recorded in the cash book, the two sides of the transaction are:

(a)   Cash is received (debit entry in the cash account).
(b)   The amount owed by trade receivables is reduced (credit entry in the trade receivables account).

## CASH ACCOUNT

| | £ | | £ |
|---|---|---|---|
| Trade receivables (Mr A) | 2,000 | | |

## TRADE RECEIVABLES (MR A)

| | £ | | £ |
|---|---|---|---|
| | | Cash a/c | 2,000 |

The accounts recording this sale to, and payment by, Mr A now appear as follows.

## CASH ACCOUNT

| | £ | | £ |
|---|---|---|---|
| Trade receivables (Mr A) | 2,000 | | |

## SALES ACCOUNT

| | £ | | £ |
|---|---|---|---|
| | | Trade receivables a/c (Mr A) | 2,000 |

## TRADE RECEIVABLES

| | £ | | £ |
|---|---|---|---|
| Sales a/c | 2,000 | Cash a/c | 2,000 |

The two trade receivables entries cancel each other out, while the entries in the cash at bank account and sales account reflect the same position as if the sale had been made for cash (see above).

### Interactive question 2: Debits and credits

Identify the debit and credit entries in the following transactions (ignore VAT).

(a)  Bought a machine on credit from A, cost £8,000.
(b)  Bought goods on credit from B, cost £500.
(c)  Sold goods on credit to C, value £1,200.
(d)  Paid D (a credit supplier) £300.
(e)  Collected £180 from E, a credit customer.
(f)  Paid net pay £4,000.
(g)  Received rent bill of £700 from landlord G.
(h)  Paid rent of £700 to landlord G.
(i)  Paid insurance premium £90.

See **Answer** at the end of this chapter.

## 3.4.3  Double entry for discounts

In Chapter 3 we saw how discounts allowed to customers and received from suppliers are recorded in a memorandum column of the cash book. This means that **neither the debit nor the credit entry is made in the cash account**; instead, the memorandum column is used to post the double entry to two nominal ledger accounts, as follows.

- Discounts allowed to customers

  DEBIT        Discounts allowed (administrative expense account)
  CREDIT      Trade receivables

The discount allowed reduces the balance owed by customers, so it is a **credit** in the receivables asset account. The other side of the entry is as a **debit** to the discount allowed expense account.

- Discounts received from suppliers

  DEBIT        Trade payables
  CREDIT      Discount received (other income account)

The discount received reduces the liability to suppliers, so it is a **debit** in the payables liability account. The other side of the entry is as a **credit** in the discount received income account.

### Interactive question 3: Ledger entries

Ron Knuckle set up a business selling fitness equipment. He put £7,000 of his own money into a business bank account (transaction A) and in his first period of trading, the following transactions occurred.

| Transaction | | £ |
| --- | --- | --- |
| B | Paid rent of shop for the period | 3,500 |
| C | Purchased equipment (inventories) on credit | 5,000 |
| D | Loan from bank | 1,000 |
| E | Purchase of shop fittings (for cash) | 2,000 |
| F | Sales of equipment: cash | 10,000 |
| G | Sales of equipment: on credit | 2,500 |
| H | Payments for trade payables (discount received £50) | 4,950 |
| I | Receipt from trade receivables (discount allowed £20) | 2,480 |
| J | Interest on loan (paid) | 100 |
| K | Other expenses (all paid in cash) | 1,900 |
| L | Drawings | 1,500 |

Ignore VAT.

Prepare the ledger accounts for Ron Knuckle by opening up the following accounts and completing them:

- Cash at bank
- Capital
- Loan
- Purchases
- Trade payables
- Rent
- Shop fittings

- Sales
- Trade receivables
- Discount received
- Discount allowed
- Loan interest
- Other expenses
- Drawings

See **Answer** at the end of this chapter.

# 4 The journal

## Section overview

- Journal entries have a particular format that you should use.

- Journals can be used to record any type of financial transaction, in which case the journal acts as the book of original entry for that transaction.

- Journals are particularly useful for recording internal transfers between ledger accounts.

## 4.1 What are journal entries used for?

The **journal** records transactions not recorded in any other book of original entry, such as credit purchases of **non-current assets**. In particular the **journal** keeps a record of **unusual movements between ledger accounts**. It is used to record any double entries made which do not arise from the other books of original entry, such as when errors are discovered and need to be corrected.

Whatever type of transaction is being recorded, the **format of a journal entry** is as follows.

| Date | Debit £ | Credit £ |
|---|---|---|
| Account to be debited | X | |
| Account to be credited | | X |

*Narrative to explain the transaction*

In due course, the ledger accounts will be written up to include the transactions listed in the journal.

A **narrative explanation** should accompany each journal entry. It is required for audit and control, to indicate the purpose and authority of every transaction which is not first recorded in a book of original entry.

## Worked example: Journal entries to record transactions

The following is a summary of the transactions of Hair by Fiona Middleton hairdressing business, of which Fiona is the sole owner.

| | |
|---|---|
| 1 January | Put in cash of £2,000 as capital |
| | Purchased brushes and combs for cash £50 |
| | Purchased hair driers from Gilroy Ltd on credit £150 |
| 30 January | Paid three months rent to 31 March £300 |
| | Collected and paid in takings £600 |
| 31 January | Gave Mrs Sullivan a perm, highlights etc on credit £80 |
| 31 January | Took out £100 for personal expenses |

Show the transactions by means of journal entries.

**Solution**

JOURNAL

|  |  |  | £ | £ |
|---|---|---|---|---|
| 1 January | DEBIT | Cash at bank | 2,000 | |
| | CREDIT | Fiona Middleton – capital account | | 2,000 |
| | *Initial capital introduced* | | | |
| 1 January | DEBIT | Brushes and combs account (non-current asset) | 50 | |
| | CREDIT | Cash at bank | | 50 |
| | *The purchase for cash of brushes and combs* | | | |
| 1 January | DEBIT | Hair dryer account (non-current asset) | 150 | |
| | CREDIT | Trade payables (Gilroy Ltd) | | 150 |
| | *The purchase on credit of hair driers as non-current assets* | | | |
| 30 January | DEBIT | Rent expense account | 300 | |
| | CREDIT | Cash at bank | | 300 |
| | *The payment of rent to 31 March* | | | |
| 30 January | DEBIT | Cash at bank | 600 | |
| | CREDIT | Sales revenue account | | 600 |
| | *Cash takings* | | | |
| 31 January | DEBIT | Trade receivables | 80 | |
| | CREDIT | Sales revenue account | | 80 |
| | *The provision of hair treatment on credit* | | | |
| 31 January | DEBIT | Drawings | 100 | |
| | CREDIT | Cash at bank | | 100 |
| | *Owner's drawings* | | | |

## 4.2 Journal entries to correct errors

Errors corrected by the journal must be **capable of correction by means of double entry** in the ledger accounts. In other words, the error must not have caused total debits and total credits to be unequal.

Special rules, covered in Chapter 6, apply to correcting errors which broke the rule of double entry.

# 5 The petty cash imprest system

**Section overview**

- The double entry for transactions recorded in the petty cash book works in the same way as the cash book.

## 5.1 Double entry for petty cash transactions

In Chapter 3, we saw how the petty cash book was used to operate the imprest system. It is now time to see how the **double entry** works.

A business starts with a cash float (imprest) on 1.3.20X7 of £250. This will be a payment from cash at bank to petty cash:

| DEBIT | Petty cash | £250 | |
|---|---|---|---|
| CREDIT | Cash at bank | | £250 |

Suppose five payments were made out of petty cash during March 20X7, none of which attracted VAT. The petty cash book might look as follows.

| Total receipts £ | Date | Narrative | Total payments £ | Postage £ | Travel £ |
|---|---|---|---|---|---|
| 250.00 | 1.3.X7 | Cash | | | |
| | 2.3.X7 | Stamps | 12.00 | 12.00 | |
| | 8.3.X7 | Stamps | 10.00 | 10.00 | |
| | 19.3.X7 | Travel | 16.00 | | 16.00 |
| | 23.3.X7 | Travel | 5.00 | | 5.00 |
| | 28.3.X7 | Stamps | 11.50 | 11.50 | |
| 250.00 | | | 54.50 | 33.50 | 21.00 |

At the end of each month (or at any other suitable interval) the total payments in the petty cash book are **posted** to nominal ledger accounts. This just means that the totals of the columns are entered as appropriate debit and credit entries in the ledger accounts. For March 20X7, £33.50 would be **debited** to the postage account and £21.00 to the travel account. The total payments of £54.50 are **credited** to the petty cash account. This completes the double entry.

| | | | £ | £ |
|---|---|---|---|---|
| DEBIT | Postage | | 33.50 | |
| DEBIT | Travel | | 21.00 | |
| CREDIT | Petty cash | | | 54.50 |

Next, the cash float needs to be topped up to the imprest amount by a payment of £54.50 from the main bank account:

| | | £ | £ |
|---|---|---|---|
| DEBIT | Petty cash | £54.50 | |
| CREDIT | Cash at bank | | £54.50 |

So double entry rules have been satisfied, and the petty cash book for the month of March 20X7 will look like this.

| Receipts £ | Date | Narrative | Payments £ | Postage £ | Travel £ |
|---|---|---|---|---|---|
| 250.00 | 1.3.X7 | Cash | | | |
| | 2.3.X7 | Stamps | 12.00 | 12.00 | |
| | 8.3.X7 | Stamps | 10.00 | 10.00 | |
| | 19.3.X7 | Travel | 16.00 | | 16.00 |
| | 23.3.X7 | Travel | 5.00 | | 5.00 |
| | 28.3.X7 | Stamps | 11.50 | 11.50 | |
| | 31.3.X7 | Balance c/d | 195.50 | | |
| 250.00 | | | 250.00 | 33.50 | 21.00 |
| 195.50 | 1.4.X7 | Balance b/d | | | |
| 54.50 | 1.4.X7 | Cash | | | |

The cash float is back up to (£195.50 + £54.50) = £250 imprest on 1.4.X7, ready for more payments to be made.

The petty cash account in the nominal ledger will be as follows.

PETTY CASH

| 20X7 | | £ | 20X7 | | £ |
|---|---|---|---|---|---|
| 1.3 | Cash | 250.00 | 31.3 | Payments | 54.50 |
| 1.4 | Cash | 54.50 | 1.4 | Balance c/d | 250.00 |
| | | 304.50 | | | 304.50 |
| 1.4 | Balance b/d | 250.00 | | | |

**Interactive question 4: Petty cash**

Summit Glazing operates an imprest petty cash system. The imprest amount is £150.00. At the end of the period the totals of the four analysis columns in the petty cash book were as follows.

| | £ |
|---|---|
| Column 1 | 23.12 |
| Column 2 | 6.74 |
| Column 3 | 12.90 |
| Column 4 | 28.50 |

How much cash is required to restore the imprest amount?

See **Answer** at the end of this chapter.

# 6 Day book analysis

**Section overview**

- When day books are analysed, totals are calculated for each column which are then posted to the ledger accounts that are relevant to that column.

## 6.1 How are day books posted?

In Chapter 3 we used the following example of four transactions in the sales day book.

SALES DAY BOOK

| Date | Invoice/credit note no. | Customer | Total £ | VAT £ | Boots £ | Shoes £ |
|---|---|---|---|---|---|---|
| 10.1.X0 | | | | | | |
| | I 247 | Jones & Co | 107.04 | 17.84 | 50.00 | 39.20 |
| | I 248 | Smith Co | 88.32 | 14.72 | 73.60 | – |
| | CN 004 | Alex & Co | (32.16) | (5.36) | – | (26.80) |
| | I 249 | Enor College | 1,291.68 | 215.28 | 800.30 | 276.10 |
| | | | 1,454.88 | 242.48 | 923.90 | 288.50 |

The business would open up a 'sale of shoes' account and a 'sale of boots' account as well as a VAT account and the trade receivables account. Then the sales day book totals would be **posted** to the nominal ledger accounts as follows.

| | | £ | £ |
|---|---|---|---|
| DEBIT | Trade receivables | 1,454.88 | |
| CREDIT | Sale of shoes account | | 288.50 |
| CREDIT | Sale of boots account | | 923.90 |
| CREDIT | VAT account | | 242.48 |

That is why the analysis of sales is kept. Exactly the same reasoning lies behind the analyses kept in the other books of original entry.

# 7 The receivables and payables ledgers

**Section overview**

- Individual ledger accounts for each credit customer (personal accounts) are maintained in the receivables ledger.

- A total receivables account is held in the nominal ledger, called the receivables control account.

- Individual ledger accounts for each credit supplier (personal accounts) are maintained in the payables ledger.

- A total payables account is held in the nominal ledger, called the payables control account.

## 7.1 Nominal ledger accounts and personal accounts

Nominal ledger accounts relate to types of income, expense, asset, capital and liability – rent, sales, trade receivables, payables and so on – rather than to the person to whom the money is paid or from whom it is received. However, there is also a need for **personal** accounts, most commonly for receivables and payables, and these are contained in the **receivables ledger** and **the payables ledger**. These are **memorandum accounts** only, in memorandum ledgers; they are **not** part of the double entry system. Instead summary **receivables control** and **payables control** accounts are kept in the nominal ledger.

Keeping each credit customer's account separately enables us to identify at any moment how much that customer owes us; similarly, the technique enables us to tell exactly how much we owe each credit supplier. Any disputes with customers or suppliers can thereby be more easily resolved.

## 7.2 Receivables ledger

The sales day book provides a chronological record of invoices and credit notes sent out by a business to credit customers. This might involve very large numbers of invoices/credit notes per day or per week. The same customer might appear in several different places in the sales day book, for sales made on credit at different times so a customer may owe money on several unpaid invoices. Similarly, the customer may make payments and take discounts at different times.

In addition to keeping a chronological record of invoices/credit notes and cash received/discount allowed, a business should also keep a record of how much money each **individual credit customer** owes, and what this total debt consists of. The need for a **personal account for each customer** is a practical one.

- A customer might ask how much they currently owe. Staff must be able to tell them.

- It is a common practice to send out **statements** to credit customers at the end of each month, showing how much they owe, and itemising new invoices or credit notes sent out and payments received during the month.

- The business managers will want to check the **credit position** of individual customers, and to ensure that no customer is exceeding their credit limit.

- Most important is the need to **match** payments received against debts owed. If a customer makes a payment, the business must be able to set off the payment against the customer's debt and establish how much he still owes on balance.

**Definition**

**Receivables ledger:** The memorandum ledger for customers' personal accounts. It is **not** part of the nominal ledger nor the double entry system, but double entry rules apply to the receivables ledger accounts.

Receivables ledger accounts are written up as follows.

- When invoices or credit notes are sent out, entries are made in the sales day book. Each one is then subsequently also entered in the relevant customer account in the receivables ledger: **invoices** on the **debit** side, and **credit notes** on the **credit** side.

- When receipts are debited in the cash book (cash/cheques etc received), each one is also entered in the **credit side** of the relevant customer account.

Each customer account is given a reference or code number, and it is that reference which appears in the **sales day book** and **cash book**.

Here is an example of how a receivables ledger account is laid out. The sales day book reference is SDB 48.

ENOR COLLEGE

| | | £ | | | A/c no: RL9 £ |
|---|---|---|---|---|---|
| | | | 10.1.X0 | Credit note SDB 48 (CN012) | 50.00 |
| Balance b/f | | 250.00 | 10.1.X0 | Cash CB 48 | 200.00 |
| 10.1.X0 | Sales SDB 48 (I 249) | 1,291.68 | Balance c/d | | 1,291.68 |
| | | 1,541.68 | | | 1,541.68 |
| 11.1.X0 | Balance b/d | 1,291.68 | | | |

## 7.3 Payables ledger

The payables ledger, like the receivables ledger, consists of a number of personal accounts. These are separate accounts for **each individual supplier**, and they enable a business to keep a continuous record of how much it owes each supplier at any time.

### Definition

**Payables ledger:** The memorandum ledger for suppliers' personal accounts. It is **not** part of the nominal ledger nor part of the double entry system, but double entry rules apply to the payables ledger accounts.

After entries are made in the purchases day book and cash book, they are also made in the relevant supplier account in the payables ledger. Entries are **posted** to the supplier's personal accounts in the payables ledger from the books of original entry (the purchases day book and the cash book).

Here is an example of how a payables ledger account is laid out.

COOK

| | | £ | | | A/c no: PL 31 £ |
|---|---|---|---|---|---|
| 15.3.X8 | Cash CB 48 | 100.00 | | Balance b/f | 200.00 |
| | Balance c/d | 421.60 | 15.3.X8 | Invoice I 4192 PDB 37 | 321.60 |
| | | 521.60 | | | 521.60 |
| | | | 16.3.X8 | Balance b/d | 421.60 |

## 7.4 Control accounts for the receivables and payables ledgers

Having personal accounts for every customer and supplier in the nominal ledger can become very unwieldy, so:

- **Details** of transactions are posted from the book of original entry using double entry principles to the memorandum **receivables and payables ledgers**.

- Only **totals** are posted from books of original entry to **nominal ledger** control accounts as part of the double entry system.

We shall return to control accounts in Chapter 6.

# 8 Accounting for discounts

**Section overview**

- Trade discount reduces the goods total amount on an invoice. It is not recorded separately anywhere in the accounting system.

- Cash discount is recorded only when it reduces the amount paid by the business (discount received) or received by it (discount allowed).

- Discount received from suppliers is recorded on the payments side of the cash book. It is debited to payables control and credited to discounts received (an income account).

- Discount allowed to customers is recorded on the receipts side of the cash book. It is debited to discounts allowed (an expense account) and credited to receivables control.

**Definition**

Discount: A reduction in the price of goods below the amount at which those goods would normally be sold to other customers.

There are two types of discount: trade discount and cash discount.

## 8.1 Trade discount

**Definition**

Trade discount: A reduction in the cost of goods, owing to the nature of the trading transaction. It usually results from buying goods in bulk. It is deducted from the list price of goods sold, to arrive at a final sales figure. **There is no separate ledger account for trade discount**.

### 8.1.1 Examples of trade discount

- A customer is quoted a price of £1 per unit for a particular item, but a lower price of 95p per unit if the item is bought in quantities of 100 units or more at a time. This is sometimes called **bulk discount**.

- An important customer or a regular customer is offered a discount on all the goods they buy, regardless of the size of each individual order, because the total volume of their purchases over time is so large.

## 8.2 Cash discount

**Definition**

Cash discount: A reduction in the amount payable in return for immediate payment in cash, or for payment within an agreed period. There are separate ledger accounts for cash discounts: one for discount allowed to customers, and one for discount received from suppliers.

For example, a supplier charges £1,000 for goods, but offers a discount of 5% if the goods are paid for immediately in cash.

## 8.3 Accounting for trade discount

A trade discount is a reduction in the amount of money initially demanded on an invoice.

- If a trade discount is received by a business for goods purchased from a supplier, the amount of money demanded from the business by the supplier will be net of discount (ie it will be the normal sales value less the discount).

- If a trade discount is given by a business for goods sold to a customer, the amount of money demanded of the customer by the business will be after deduction of the discount.

Trade discount should therefore be accounted for as follows.

- **Trade discounts received** should be **deducted from the gross cost of purchases** by the supplier. The cost of purchases in the payables ledger will be stated at gross cost minus discount, ie the invoiced amount.

- **Trade discounts allowed** should be **deducted from the gross sales price** by the business, so that revenue will be reported at invoice value net of trade discount, ie the invoiced amount.

## 8.4 Accounting for cash discount received

Whether to take advantage of a cash discount for prompt payment is a matter of **financing policy**.

### Worked example: Taking cash discount

If the business receives, say, £80 cash discount for paying a debt of £2,000 early, we account for this as follows:

- In the purchases account, we debit the invoiced price of £2,000, and the subsequent financing decision about accepting the cash discount is ignored. The credit is to trade payables.

- When we pay (£2,000 – £80) = £1,920 and take the discount, we **credit** cash and **debit** trade payables with £1,920.

- To account for the discount we **debit** trade payables £80, so eliminating the £2,000 debt entirely, and **credit** £80 to the discount received account (an income account).

### Interactive question 5: Discounts I

Soft Supplies Co recently purchased from Hard Imports Co 10 printers originally priced at £200 each. A 10% trade discount was negotiated together with a 5% cash discount if payment was made within 14 days. Calculate the following.

(a) The total of the trade discount
(b) The total of the cash discount

See **Answer** at the end of this chapter.

## 8.5 Accounting for cash discount allowed

The same principle is applied in accounting for cash discounts allowed to customers. Goods are sold at a trade price, and the offer of a discount on that price is a matter of financing policy for the business.

### Interactive question 6: Discounts II

You are required to prepare the statement of profit or loss of Seesaw Timber Merchants for the year ended 31 March 20X6, given the following information.

|  | £ |
|---|---|
| Purchases at gross cost | 120,000 |
| Trade discounts received | 4,000 |
| Cash discounts received | 1,500 |
| Cash sales | 34,000 |
| Credit sales at invoice price | 150,000 |
| Cash discounts allowed | 8,000 |
| Distribution costs | 32,000 |
| Administrative expenses | 40,000 |
| Drawings by owner, Tim Burr | 22,000 |

See **Answer** at the end of this chapter.

# 9 Accounting for VAT

### Section overview

- VAT on sales (output VAT) is debited to receivables as part of the posting from the sales day book and credited to the VAT liability account (it is owed to HMRC).

- VAT on purchases (input VAT) is debited to the VAT liability account (it is due from HMRC) and credited to payables as part of the posting from the purchases day book.

- The net amount of VAT owed to HMRC is paid to HMRC regularly.

## 9.1 What is VAT?

**VAT is an indirect tax on the supply of goods and services. Tax is collected at each transfer point in the chain from prime producer to final consumer.** Eventually, the consumer bears the tax in full and any tax paid earlier in the chain can be recovered by a registered trader who paid it.

### Worked example: VAT

A manufacturing company, A Ltd, purchases raw materials at a cost of £1,000 plus VAT at the standard rate of 20%. From the raw materials A Ltd makes finished products which it sells to a retail outlet, B plc, for £1,600 plus VAT at 20%. B plc sells the products to customers at a total price of £2,000 plus VAT at 20%. How much VAT is paid at each stage in the chain?

### Solution

|  | Value of goods sold £ | VAT 20% £ |
|---|---|---|
| Supply to A Ltd (A Ltd pays £200 VAT but recovers it) | 1,000 | 200 |
| Value added by A Ltd | 600 | |
| Sale to B plc (B plc pays £320 VAT but recovers it) | 1,600 | 320 |
| Value added by B plc | 400 | |
| Sale to 'consumers' (customers pay £400 VAT, and cannot recover it) | 2,000 | 400 |

## 9.2 How is VAT collected?

Although it is the final consumer who eventually bears the full VAT of £400, the sum is **collected and paid by the traders who make up the chain**, provided they are registered for VAT. Each trader must assume that his customer is the final consumer:

- He must collect and pay over VAT at the appropriate rate on the full sales value (known as **output tax**) of the goods sold.

- He is normally entitled to reclaim VAT paid on his own purchases of goods, expenses and non-current assets (known as **input tax**) and so makes a net payment to the HMRC equal to the tax on value added by himself.

In the example above, the supplier of raw materials collects from A Ltd output VAT of £200, all of which he pays over to HMRC. When A Ltd sells goods to B plc, output VAT is charged at the rate of 20% on £1,600 = £320. Only £120, however, is paid by A Ltd to HMRC, because the company is entitled to deduct input tax of £200 suffered on its own purchases. Similarly, B plc must charge its customers £400 in output VAT, but need only pay over to HMRC the net amount of £80 after deducting the £320 input VAT suffered on its purchase from A Ltd.

## 9.3 Registered and non-registered persons

**Traders whose sales (outputs) are below a certain level need not register for VAT** although they may do so voluntarily. Unregistered traders neither charge VAT on their outputs nor are entitled to reclaim VAT on their inputs. They are in the same position as a final consumer.

**All outputs of registered traders are either taxable or exempt.** Traders carrying on **exempt activities** (such as banks) cannot charge VAT on their outputs and consequently cannot reclaim VAT paid on their inputs.

Taxable outputs are chargeable at one of **three rates**.

- **Zero rate** (on printed books and newspapers for instance)
- **Reduced rate** (5% on domestic fuel)
- **Standard rate**: 20%

HMRC identifies supplies falling into each category. **Persons carrying on taxable activities** (even activities taxable at zero rate) **are entitled to reclaim VAT paid on their inputs.**

Some traders carry on a **mixture of taxable and exempt activities**. Such traders need to apportion the VAT suffered on inputs and **can usually only reclaim the proportion of input tax that relates to taxable outputs.**

Most traders account quarterly to HMRC for VAT.

- The most usual position is to have to pay the net balance to HMRC (when output tax exceeds input tax) ie HMRC is a payable.

- A trader who makes zero-rated supplies will have paid more input tax than it has received output tax, so will recover cash from HMRC, ie HMRC is a receivable.

## 9.4 Accounting for VAT

As a general principle the treatment of VAT in the trader's ledger accounts should reflect the trader's role as tax collector, so **VAT should not be included in income or in expenses, whether of a capital or a revenue nature**.

### 9.4.1 Irrecoverable VAT

Where the **trader suffers irrecoverable VAT** as a cost, as in the following cases, VAT should be included as an expense. (It cannot be claimed as input tax.)

- **Persons not registered** for VAT will suffer VAT on inputs as a cost. This will increase their expenses and the cost of any non-current assets they purchase.

- **Registered persons** who also carry on **exempted activities** may have a residue of input VAT which falls directly on them. In this situation the costs to which this residue applies will be inflated by the **irrecoverable VAT**.

- **Non-deductible inputs will be borne** by all traders.

  - VAT on **cars** purchased and used in the business is not reclaimable (VAT on a car acquired new for resale, ie by a car trader, is reclaimable).

  - VAT on **business entertaining** is not deductible as input tax other than VAT on entertaining staff.

Where VAT is not recoverable it must be regarded as part of the cost of the items purchased and included in the statement of profit or loss or statement of financial position as appropriate.

## 9.5 VAT and discounts

**VAT is charged on the goods or services total on an invoice (or credit note) net of both:**

- Trade discount
- Cash discount

This general principle is carried to the extent that where a discount is offered at the point of sale, VAT is charged on the amount net of the offered discount **even where it is subsequently not taken up**.

### Worked example: VAT and discounts

Matt sells usually sells goods at £130 each, he gives Anil a trade discount of £10 so he sells goods to Anil for £120. He also offers a cash discount of 5% for prompt payment. Matt is registered for VAT. This means that £120 × 5% = £6 cash discount is available.

How much output VAT should Matt include on Anil's invoice?

### Solution

If the discount had not been offered output VAT of £120 × 20% = £24.00 would be due. But because of the discount, Matt's sales invoice will show:

INVOICE

|  | £ |
| --- | --- |
| List price | 130.00 |
| Trade discount | (10.00) |
| Goods value | 120.00 |
| VAT (120 × 95% × 20%) | 22.80 |
| Invoice total | 142.80 |
| Cash discount available (£120 × 5%) | £6.00 |

If Anil takes up the discount, he need only pay £136.80 in full settlement (£142.80 – £6), but even if he does not take the discount, the amount of VAT is not adjusted.

## 9.6 VAT and irrecoverable debts

Most registered persons are obliged to record VAT when a supply is made or received (effectively when a sales invoice is raised or a purchase invoice recorded). This may have the effect that **output tax has to be paid to HMRC before it has all been received from customers**. If an amount due from a customer is subsequently written off as irrecoverable, the VAT element may not be recoverable from HMRC for some time after the sale.

## 9.7 Summary of accounting entries for VAT

In Chapter 3 we saw how VAT is initially recorded in the books of original entry. Let's summarise it now.

(a) **Sales revenue** shown in the statement of profit or loss must **exclude output VAT**. However trade receivables will **include** VAT, as they reflect the total amount due from customers. The sales day book is the book of original entry for VAT on credit sales.

The double entry posted from the sales day book for sales of £500,000 on credit is:

|  |  | £ | £ |
|---|---|---|---|
| DEBIT | Trade receivables a/c (including VAT, called **gross**) | 600,000 | |
| CREDIT | Sales a/c (excluding VAT, called **net**) | | 500,000 |
| | VAT a/c (20% × £500,000) – output tax | | 100,000 |

(b) **Expenses** shown in the statement of profit or loss must **exclude input VAT**. However, trade payables will **include** input VAT, as they reflect the total amount payable to suppliers. The purchases day book is the book of original entry for VAT on credit purchases. The double entry posted from the purchases day book for purchases of £400 is:

|  |  | £ | £ |
|---|---|---|---|
| DEBIT | Purchases expense (net) | 400 | |
| | VAT a/c (20% × £400) – input tax | 80 | |
| CREDIT | Trade payables (gross) | | 480 |

(c) Sales revenue received and expenses paid as cash transactions in the cash book or petty cash book must have the VAT recorded in these books of original entry, and then posted as above in (a) and (b).

(d) **Irrecoverable VAT** on expenses or non-current assets must be **included in the cost** of the expense or non-current asset in the statement of profit or loss or statement of financial position.

(e) The net amount due to HMRC should be included in **other payables** (or **other receivables**) in the statement of financial position.

## 9.8 Calculating VAT from a gross amount

If you are told that an amount **includes VAT** at 20% (a gross amount), you can calculate the VAT element by multiplying the gross amount by 20%/120% or 1/6. Therefore the net amount will always be 5/6 of the gross element.

### Worked example: VAT calculation

A sale of £200 attracts VAT at 20%, ie £40. The gross amount is £240. To get back to the VAT element:

£240 × 1/6 = £40

### Interactive question 7: VAT

Mussel is preparing financial statements for the year ended 31 May 20X9. Included in its statement of financial position as at 31 May 20X8 was a balance for VAT due from HMRC of £15,000.

Mussel's summary statement of profit or loss for the year to 31 May 20X9 is as follows.

|  | £'000 |
|---|---|
| Revenue (net) (all standard rated) | 500 |
| Purchases (net) (all standard rated) | (120) |
| Gross profit | 380 |
| Expenses (see note) | (280) |
| Net profit | 100 |

|  | £'000 |
|---|---|
| Note: expenses | |
| Wages and salaries (exempt of VAT) | 162 |
| Entertainment expenditure (£40 + irrecoverable VAT £8) | 48 |
| Other (net) (all standard rated at 20%) | 70 |
|  | 280 |

In respect of VAT payments of £5,000, £15,000 and £20,000 have been made in the year to HMRC and a repayment of £12,000 was received.

**Requirement**

What is the balance for VAT in the statement of financial position as at 31 May 20X9? Assume a 20% standard rate of VAT. (Hint: Use a T account for VAT.)

See **Answer** at the end of this chapter.

# 10 The use of Information Technology in modern accounting

**Section overview**

- The principles of accounting remain the same whether you are preparing accounts manually, or using an accountancy package.

- Accountancy packages are common place in most business.

- The advent of technology has had a significant effect on the accountancy profession, changing the nature of the type of work accountants do.

## 10.1 The use of IT in modern accounting

Most accounting systems are computerised and anyone training to be an accountant should be able to work with computerised systems. The most important point to remember is that the **principles** of computerised accounting are the same as those of **manual accounting**.

Most references to computerised accounting talk about accounting **packages**. This is a rather general term, but most of us can probably name the accounting package that we use at work. An accounting package consists of several accounting **modules**, eg receivables ledger, general ledger.

## 10.2 Accounting packages

Accounting functions retain the same names in computerised systems as in more traditional written records. Computerised accounting still uses the familiar ideas of day books, ledger accounts, double entry, trial balance and financial statements. The principles of working with computerised sales, purchase and general ledgers are exactly what would be expected in the manual methods they replace.

The only difference is that these various books of account have become invisible. Ledgers are now computer files which are held in a computer-readable form, ready to be called on.

## 10.3 Coding

Computers require vital information to be expressed in the form of codes. For example, general ledger accounts might be coded individually by means of a two-digit code.

00   Ordinary share capital
01   Share premium
05   Statement of profit or loss and other comprehensive income
15   Purchases
22   Receivables control account

41   Payables control account

42   Interest

43   Dividends

In the same way, individual accounts must be given a unique code number in the receivables ledger and payables ledger.

### 10.3.1   Example: coding

When an invoice is received from a supplier (example code 1234) for $3,000 for the purchase of raw materials, the transaction might be coded for input to the computer as:

| | General ledger | | Inventory | | |
|---|---|---|---|---|---|
| Supplier Code | Debit | Credit | Value | Code | Quantity |
| 1234 | 15 | 41 | $3,000 | 56742 | 150 |

Code 15 in our example represents purchases, and code 41 the payables control account. This single input could be used to update the payables ledger, the general ledger and the inventory ledger. The inventory code may enable further analysis to be carried out, perhaps allocating the cost to a particular department or product. Thus the needs of both financial accounting and cost accounting can be fulfilled at once.

## 10.4   Purchase and sales systems

The purchase (payables) and sales (receivables) systems will be the most important components of most company accounting systems.

### 10.4.1   Payables ledger system

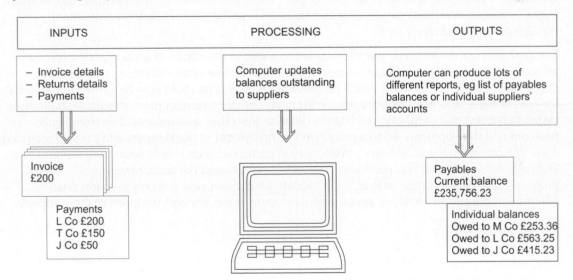

The payables ledger makes it possible for the business to keep track of what it owes each supplier.

### 10.4.2 Receivables ledger system

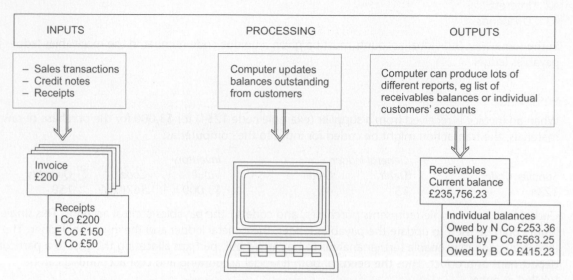

| INPUTS | PROCESSING | OUTPUTS |

Inputs:
- Sales transactions
- Credit notes
- Receipts

Invoice £200

Receipts
I Co £200
E Co £150
V Co £50

Processing:
Computer updates balances outstanding from customers

Outputs:
Computer can produce lots of different reports, eg list of receivables balances or individual customers' accounts

Receivables
Current balance
£235,756.23

Individual balances
Owed by N Co £253.36
Owed by P Co £563.25
Owed by B Co £415.23

The **receivables ledger** makes it possible to keep track of what is owed by each customer.

## 10.5 Effect of technology on the accounting profession

VisiCalc, the first spreadsheet programme for a computer was released in 1979. Prior to that, all spreadsheets were populated and calculated by hand. Changing one number in a spreadsheet necessitated the manual recalculating of the entire spreadsheet. Tasks that take seconds on an electronic spreadsheet, could take a bookkeeper days of painstaking calculations on a paper spreadsheet which might be spread over many large sheets and could take up the entire desk of an accountant, bookkeeper or accountancy clerk.

The increased use of electronic spreadsheets led to a shift in the nature of accountancy work. Fewer accountancy clerks and bookkeepers were required to complete labour intensive, but essentially low skilled calculations. The speed at which certain accountancy tasks could now be carried out meant that the cost of these tasks were reduced, thus making accountancy services more affordable. Businesses began to request more sophisticated financial analysis from their accountants. Therefore, while technological developments led to a reduction in employment of bookkeepers and accountancy clerks, it led to a growth in the accountancy profession, in particular, accountants with more sophisticated analytical skills than what was previously required. IT has allowed the accountancy profession to progress from 'bean counter' to that of the modern accountant who not only prepares financial information but can also analyse, advise, and participate in the strategic decisions of the company.

## Summary

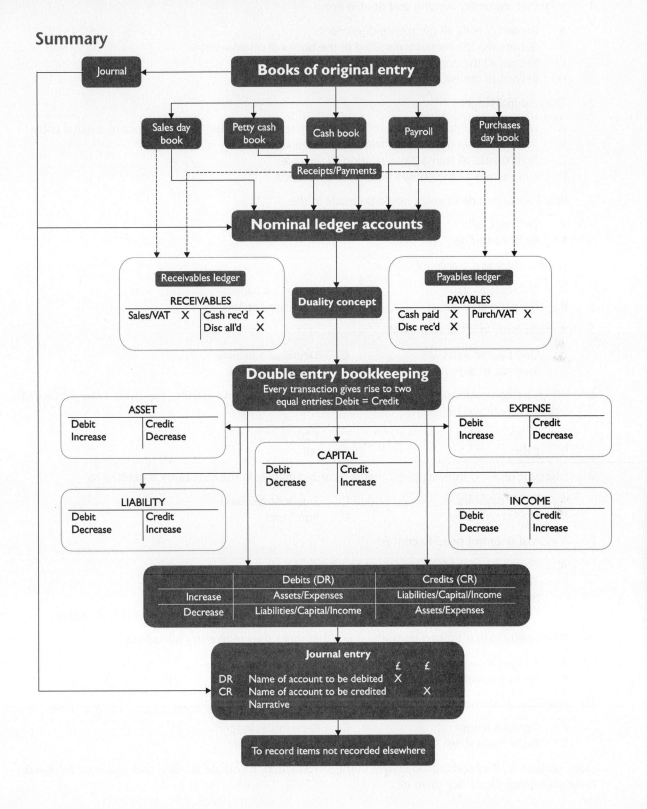

## Self-test

Answer the following questions.

1 Together ledger accounting and double entry

   A   Record directly all the source documents
   B   Summarise the transactions listed in the books of original entry
   C   Record all the entity's credit transactions
   D   Record all the entity's cash transactions

2 The nominal ledger

   A   Is the book of original entry for all transactions not recorded in other books of original entry
   B   Summarises all transactions relating to receivables
   C   Summarises all transactions relating to payables
   D   Summarises all the entity's financial transactions

3 In a T account a debit entry would be made in the

   A   Left hand side
   B   Right hand side

4 A debit entry in a T account will

   A   Decrease an asset         C   Increase a liability
   B   Decrease an expense    D   Decrease capital

5 A credit entry in a T account will

   A   Decrease an asset         C   Decrease a liability
   B   Increase an expense     D   Decrease capital

6 When a credit customer pays an invoice for £120 including VAT at 20%, the credit entry in the VAT ledger account will be

   A   £120               C   £20
   B   £100              D   Nil

7 Discount received from suppliers that is recorded initially in the cash book is debited to

   A   Trade payables        C   Discount received
   B   Trade receivables     D   Purchases

8 A journal does **not** need to contain

   A   The name of the ledger account to be debited
   B   The name of the ledger account to be credited
   C   Narrative
   D   The name of the book of original entry where the relevant source document is recorded

9 When petty cash is topped up to the imprest amount the credit entry is made to

   A   The petty cash book    C   The cash book
   B   Trade receivables     D   Trade payables

10 Individual customer accounts are kept in which ledger?

   A   Payables ledger       C   Receivables ledger
   B   Trade receivables     D   Nominal ledger

Now, go back to the Learning Objectives in the Introduction. If you are satisfied that you have achieved these objectives, please tick them off.

# Answers to Interactive questions

## Answer to Interactive question 1

(c)   Payment received from a credit customer

- Receivables decrease      CREDIT      Receivables      (decrease in asset)
- Cash at bank increases    DEBIT       Cash at bank     (increase in asset)

(d)   Sell books for cash

- Revenue increases         CREDIT      Sales            (increase in income)
- Cash at bank increases    DEBIT       Cash at bank     (increase in asset)

## Answer to Interactive question 2

|     |        |                                       | £     | £     |
|-----|--------|---------------------------------------|-------|-------|
| (a) | DEBIT  | Machine account (non-current asset)   | 8,000 |       |
|     | CREDIT | Trade payables                        |       | 8,000 |
| (b) | DEBIT  | Purchases account                     | 500   |       |
|     | CREDIT | Trade payables                        |       | 500   |
| (c) | DEBIT  | Trade receivables                     | 1,200 |       |
|     | CREDIT | Sales                                 |       | 1,200 |
| (d) | DEBIT  | Trade payables                        | 300   |       |
|     | CREDIT | Cash at bank                          |       | 300   |
| (e) | DEBIT  | Cash at bank                          | 180   |       |
|     | CREDIT | Trade receivables                     |       | 180   |
| (f) | DEBIT  | Wages account                         | 4,000 |       |
|     | CREDIT | Cash at bank                          |       | 4,000 |
| (g) | DEBIT  | Rent account                          | 700   |       |
|     | CREDIT | Trade payables                        |       | 700   |
| (h) | DEBIT  | Trade payables                        | 700   |       |
|     | CREDIT | Cash at bank                          |       | 700   |
| (i) | DEBIT  | Insurance expense                     | 90    |       |
|     | CREDIT | Cash at bank                          |       | 90    |

## Answer to Interactive question 3

In this answer we have calculated the balancing figure on the cash at bank account. We shall come back to this in Chapter 5. For now, just make sure that you completed all the necessary steps correctly.

### CASH AT BANK

|                            | £      |                                      | £      |
|----------------------------|--------|--------------------------------------|--------|
| Capital (A)                | 7,000  | Rent (B)                             | 3,500  |
| Bank loan (D)              | 1,000  | Shop fittings (E)                    | 2,000  |
| Sales (F)                  | 10,000 | Trade payables (H)                   | 4,950  |
| Trade receivables (I)      | 2,480  | Bank loan interest (J)               | 100    |
|                            |        | Other expenses (K)                   | 1,900  |
|                            |        | Drawings (L)                         | 1,500  |
|                            |        |                                      | 13,950 |
|                            |        | Balancing figure (the amount of cash |        |
|                            |        | left over after payments have been   |        |
|                            |        | made) – carried down                 | 6,530  |
|                            | 20,480 |                                      | 20,480 |
| Debit balance brought down | 6,530  |                                      |        |

## CAPITAL (RON KNUCKLE)

| | £ | | £ |
|---|---|---|---|
| | | Cash at bank (A) | 7,000 |

## BANK LOAN

| | £ | | £ |
|---|---|---|---|
| | | Cash at bank (D) | 1,000 |

## PURCHASES

| | £ | | £ |
|---|---|---|---|
| Trade payables (C) | 5,000 | | |

## TRADE PAYABLES

| | £ | | £ |
|---|---|---|---|
| Cash at bank (H) | 4,950 | Purchases (C) | 5,000 |
| Discount received (H) | 50 | | |
| | 5,000 | | 5,000 |

## RENT

| | £ | | £ |
|---|---|---|---|
| Cash at bank (B) | 3,500 | | |

## SHOP FITTINGS

| | £ | | £ |
|---|---|---|---|
| Cash at bank (E) | 2,000 | | |

## SALES

| | £ | | £ |
|---|---|---|---|
| | | Cash at bank (F) | 10,000 |
| | | Trade receivables (G) | 2,500 |

## TRADE RECEIVABLES

| | £ | | £ |
|---|---|---|---|
| Sales (G) | 2,500 | Cash at bank (I) | 2,480 |
| | | Discount allowed (I) | 20 |
| | 2,500 | | 2,500 |

## DISCOUNT RECEIVED

| | £ | | £ |
|---|---|---|---|
| | | Trade payables (H) | 50 |

## DISCOUNT ALLOWED

| | £ | | £ |
|---|---|---|---|
| Trade receivables (I) | 20 | | |

## BANK LOAN INTEREST

| | £ | | £ |
|---|---|---|---|
| Cash at bank (J) | 100 | | |

## OTHER EXPENSES

| | £ | | £ |
|---|---|---|---|
| Cash at bank (K) | 1,900 | | |

## DRAWINGS ACCOUNT

| | £ | | £ |
|---|---|---|---|
| Cash at bank (L) | 1,500 | | |

(a) If you want to make sure that this solution is complete, you should go through the transactions A to L and tick off each of them twice in the ledger accounts, once as a debit and once as a credit. When you have finished, all transactions in the 'T' account should be ticked, with only totals and the balancing figure in the cash at bank account left over.

(b) In fact, there is an easier way to check that the solution to this sort of problem does 'balance' properly, which we will see in Chapter 5.

(c) On asset, capital and liability accounts, the debit or credit balance represents the amount of the asset, capital or liability outstanding at the period end. For example, on the cash at bank account, debits exceed credits by £6,530 and so there is a balance on the credit side carried down to be a debit balance of cash in hand of £6,530. On the capital account, there is a credit balance of £7,000 and so the business owes Ron £7,000.

(d) The balances on the income and expense accounts represent the total of each type of income or expense for the period. For example, sales revenue for the period totals £12,500.

### Answer to Interactive question 4

£71.26. This is the total amount of cash that has been used.

### Answer to Interactive question 5

(a) £200 (£200 × 10 × 10%)
(b) £90 (£200 × 10 × 90% × 5%)

### Answer to Interactive question 6

SEESAW TIMBER MERCHANTS
STATEMENT OF PROFIT OR LOSS
FOR THE YEAR ENDED 31 MARCH 20X6

| | £ | £ |
|---|---|---|
| Revenue (150,000 + 34,000) | | 184,000 |
| Purchases (120,000 – 4,000) | | (116,000) |
| Gross profit | | 68,000 |
| Discounts received | | 1,500 |
| Expenses | | |
| Distribution costs | 32,000 | |
| Administrative expenses including discount allowed (40,000 + 8,000) | 48,000 | |
| | | (80,000) |
| Net loss transferred to the statement of financial position | | (10,500) |

## Answer to Interactive question 7

**VAT**

| | £ | | £ |
|---|---|---|---|
| Balance b/d | 15,000 | Output tax – (£500,000 × 20%) | 100,000 |
| Input tax – Purchases (£120,000 × 20%) | 24,000 | Cash received from HMRC | 12,000 |
| Input tax – Other expenses (£70,000 × 20%) | 14,000 | | |
| Cash paid to HMRC (5,000 + 15,000 + 20,000) | 40,000 | | |
| Balance c/d | 19,000 | | |
| | 112,000 | | 112,000 |
| | | Balance b/d | 19,000 |

Therefore there is a balance **owing to** HMRC of £19,000, which is shown on the statement of financial position as an **other payable**.

1   B   The nominal ledger contains summaries of both cash and credit transactions (C and D). Source documents are recorded directly in books of original entry, not the nominal ledger (A).

2   D   The nominal ledger contains summaries of transactions relating to both receivables and payables (B and C) as well as other transactions. Answer (A) describes the journal.

3   A   A credit entry is made in the right hand side.

4   D   Answers A, B and C all describe credit entries.

5   A   Answers B, C and D all describe debit entries.

6   D   The VAT is recorded in the VAT account when the invoice is first entered in the sales day book, not when the customer pays.

7   A   The double entry is debit trade payables, credit discount received (C). It has no effect on purchases (D) nor on trade receivables (B).

8   D   The journal is the book of original entry. Items A, B and C are all required in a journal entry, though narrative is often omitted when the journal is routine.

9   C   The double entry is debit petty cash (A), credit cash at bank. Trade receivables and payables (B and D) are unaffected.

10  C   The receivables ledger contains the individual customer accounts. The nominal ledger (D) contains the trade receivables account (B) which is the **total** of all the individual customer accounts. The payables ledger contains individual suppliers' accounts.

# CHAPTER 5

# Preparing basic financial statements

Introduction

Examination context

**Topic List**

Summary and Self-test

Answers to Interactive questions

Answers to Self-test

## Learning objectives

- Prepare a trial balance from accounting records and identify the uses of a trial balance ☐

- Prepare an extended trial balance ☐

- Prepare and present a statement of financial position, statement of profit or loss and statement of cash flows (or extracts therefrom) from the accounting records and trial balance in a format which satisfies the information requirements of the entity ☐

Specific syllabus learning outcomes are: 1f; 2c; 3c

## Syllabus links

The material in this chapter will be developed further in this paper, and then in the Professional Level module of Financial Accounting and Reporting.

## Examination context

Questions on the topics in this chapter will be set as multiple choice questions, some of which may involve calculations so that the correct answer can be selected.

In the exam you may be required to:

- Specify the nature of items in the statement of financial position: non-current and current assets, non-current and current liabilities, and capital

- Identify the correct balances on ledger accounts

- Identify how ledger account balances would appear in the trial balance

- Use a profit and loss ledger account to calculate gross profit or profit for the year

- Use the extended trial balance to calculate figures for basic financial statements

# 1 Balancing ledger accounts

### Section overview

- A ledger account is balanced by totalling both sides of the account, then subtracting the smaller amount from the larger one and inserting this as a balance on the side which had the smaller total. These balances are then extracted at the end of a reporting period for each nominal ledger account.

Look back at the Ron Knuckle's ledger accounts in the answer to Interactive question 3 in Chapter 4 to illustrate how the cash at bank account is balanced.

- First, the debits, and then the credits are totalled, giving two separate totals.

- The larger total is placed in the total columns on both the debit and credit side of the account.

- The smaller total is then subtracted from the larger total, and this amount is inserted as a balance on the side which had the smaller total.

At the end of a reporting period such as a month or a year, a balance is extracted for each nominal ledger account.

- All debits and credits, including opening balances, on the account are totalled.
- If total debits exceed total credits there is a **debit** balance on the account.
- If total credits exceed total debits the account has a **credit** balance.

In Ron Knuckle's ledger accounts, there was very little balancing to do

- Both trade payables and trade receivables balance off to zero.
- The cash at bank account has a debit balance of £6,530 (total debits exceed total credits).
- The total on the sales account is £12,500, which is a credit balance.

Otherwise, the accounts have only one entry each, so there is no totalling to do to arrive at the balance on each account.

# 2 The trial balance

### Section overview

- The balances at the end of a period on all the nominal ledger accounts are listed on a trial balance: debit balances appear in the debit column and credit balances in the credit column. When added up, the two columns should be equal.

- Extracting a trial balance serves as a check that certain types of error have not occurred in posting the accounts.

- The trial balance does not in itself detect errors of omission, commission or principle, nor compensating errors.

- An initial trial balance can be adjusted with journals using an extended trial balance to create a statement of profit or loss and statement of financial position.

### Definition

**Trial balance:** A list of nominal ledger balances shown in debit and credit columns, as a method of testing the accuracy of double entry bookkeeping. The trial balance is not part of the double entry system.

To draw up a trial balance, you need a set of ledger accounts. For the sake of convenience, we will continue to use Ron Knuckle's accounts, which we drew up in Chapter 4.

## 2.1 Listing ledger account balances in the trial balance

If double entry principles have been correctly applied throughout the period, total credit balances will equal total debit balances and so the totals will balance.

Here are the balances on Ron Knuckle's accounts.

|  | Debit £ | Credit £ |
|---|---:|---:|
| Cash at bank | 6,530 | |
| Capital | | 7,000 |
| Bank loan | | 1,000 |
| Purchases | 5,000 | |
| Trade payables | | 0 |
| Rent | 3,500 | |
| Shop fittings | 2,000 | |
| Sales | | 12,500 |
| Trade receivables | 0 | |
| Discount received | | 50 |
| Discount allowed | 20 | |
| Bank loan interest | 100 | |
| Other expenses | 1,900 | |
| Drawings | 1,500 | |
| | 20,550 | 20,550 |

It does not matter in what order the various accounts are listed in the trial balance.

## 2.2 What if the trial balance fails to balance?

If the two column totals on the trial balance are not equal, there must be an **error** in recording transactions in the ledger accounts, or in the addition of the trial balance.

Even if the trial balance balances, the following error types may still have arisen in the ledger accounts.

- **Omission errors**: a transaction is completely omitted, either in the nominal ledger, or the trial balance itself, so neither a debit nor a credit is made.

- **Commission errors**: a debit or credit is posted to the correct side of the nominal ledger, but to a **wrong account**. Eg, wages paid are debited to the rent account instead of the wages account.

- **Compensating errors**: one error is exactly cancelled by another error elsewhere.

- **Errors of principle**, such as cash from receivables being debited to trade receivables and credited to cash at bank instead of the other way round.

We shall come back to these errors, and what happens when the trial balance fails to balance, in Chapter 6.

## 2.3 Making adjustments after the trial balance is extracted

We often need to make adjustments after all ledger balances have been calculated and listed on the trial balance. **Adjustment journals** are needed for this.

## Worked example: Trial balance and adjustment journals

As at 31.3.20X7, a business, which is not registered for VAT, has the following nominal ledger balances.

| | Balance £ |
|---|---|
| Bank loan | 12,000 |
| Cash at bank | 11,700 |
| Capital | 13,000 |
| Rent | 1,880 |
| Trade payables | 11,200 |
| Purchases | 12,400 |
| Sales | 34,600 |
| Other payables | 1,620 |
| Trade receivables | 12,000 |
| Bank loan interest | 1,400 |
| Other expenses | 11,020 |
| Non-current assets | 22,020 |

On 31.3.X7 the business made the following transactions after the balances listed above had been calculated.

- Bought materials for £1,000, half for cash and half on credit
- Made sales of £1,040, £800 of which were on credit
- Paid wages to shop assistants of £260 in cash

Draw up a trial balance showing the balances as at the end of 31.3.X7.

## Solution

To draw up an **initial trial balance** we split the original balances into debit and credit balances. You need to use your knowledge of assets, capital, liabilities, expenses and income for this.

| | Debit £ | Credit £ |
|---|---|---|
| Bank loan | | 12,000 |
| Cash at bank | 11,700 | |
| Capital | | 13,000 |
| Rent | 1,880 | |
| Trade payables | | 11,200 |
| Purchases | 12,400 | |
| Sales | | 34,600 |
| Other payables | | 1,620 |
| Trade receivables | 12,000 | |
| Bank loan interest | 1,400 | |
| Other expenses | 11,020 | |
| Non-current assets | 22,020 | |
| | 72,420 | 72,420 |

Next prepare journals for the transactions on 31.3.X7.

| | | | £ | £ |
|---|---|---|---|---|
| (a) | DEBIT | Purchases | 1,000 | |
| | CREDIT | Cash at bank | | 500 |
| | | Trade payables | | 500 |
| (b) | DEBIT | Cash at bank | 240 | |
| | | Trade receivables | 800 | |
| | CREDIT | Sales | | 1,040 |
| (c) | DEBIT | Other expenses | 260 | |
| | CREDIT | Cash at bank | | 260 |

CHAPTER

5

Now we can produce the final trial balance

| | Debit £ | Credit £ |
|---|---|---|
| Bank loan | | 12,000 |
| Cash at bank (11,700 + 240 – 500 – 260) | 11,180 | |
| Capital | | 13,000 |
| Rent | 1,880 | |
| Trade payables (11,200 + 500) | | 11,700 |
| Purchases (12,400 + 1,000) | 13,400 | |
| Sales (34,600 + 1,040) | | 35,640 |
| Other payables | | 1,620 |
| Trade receivables (12,000 + 800) | 12,800 | |
| Bank loan interest | 1,400 | |
| Other expenses (11,020 + 260) | 11,280 | |
| Non-current assets | 22,020 | |
| | 73,960 | 73,960 |

## 2.4 The extended trial balance

An alternative way of presenting this information is to use an extended trial balance. This has debit and credit columns for the initial trial balance, plus debit and credit columns for adjustment journals. A revised trial balance is then created by cross-casting horizontally.

- To a **debit balance** in the TB, add debits and subtract credits from the adjustment columns. If the result is positive, insert it in the debit column of the revised trial balance. If it is negative, insert it in the credit column of the revised trial balance.

- To a **credit balance** in the TB, subtract debits and add credits. If the answer is positive, insert it in the credit column of the revised trial balance. If it is negative, insert it in the debit column of the revised trial balance.

| Ledger balance | Trial balance | | Adjustments | | Revised trial balance | |
|---|---|---|---|---|---|---|
| | Debit £ | Credit £ | Debit £ | Credit £ | Debit £ | Credit £ |
| Bank loan | | 12,000 | | | | 12,000 |
| Cash at bank | 11,700 | | 240 | 760* | 11,180 | |
| Capital | | 13,000 | | | | 13,000 |
| Rent | 1,880 | | | | 1,880 | |
| Trade payables | | 11,200 | | 500 | | 11,700 |
| Purchases | 12,400 | | 1,000 | | 13,400 | |
| Sales | | 34,600 | | 1,040 | | 35,640 |
| Other payables | | 1,620 | | | | 1,620 |
| Trade receivables | 12,000 | | 800 | | 12,800 | |
| Bank loan interest | 1,400 | | | | 1,400 | |
| Other expenses | 11,020 | | 260 | | 11,280 | |
| Non-current assets | 22,020 | | | | 22,020 | |
| | 72,420 | 72,420 | 2,300 | 2,300 | 73,960 | 73,960 |

\* 500 + 260

We shall see how a complete extended trial balance works later in this chapter.

# 3 Preparing the statement of profit or loss

**Section overview**

- To prepare the statement of profit or loss, all the income and expense account balances are transferred to a new ledger account in the nominal ledger, called the profit and loss ledger account. The balance on this account is the profit/(loss) for the period.

- The information summarised in the profit and loss ledger account is then transferred into the vertical statement of profit or loss format to show: revenue, cost of sales, gross profit, expenses and profit/(loss).

## 3.1 Preparing the profit or loss ledger account

The first step in preparing the statement of profit or loss is to create a new ledger account in the nominal ledger, called the **profit and loss ledger account**. To this account all the ledger account balances relating to the statement of profit or loss, both income and expense, are transferred. The profit and loss ledger account is part of the double entry system, so the basic rule of double entry still applies: every debit must have an equal and opposite credit entry.

The profit and loss ledger account contains the same information as the statement of profit or loss, and there are very few differences between the two. However, the statement of profit or loss lays the information out differently.

The first step is to **identify** the ledger accounts which relate to income and expenses. For Ron Knuckle, these accounts consist of purchases, rent, sales, discount allowed and received, bank loan interest, and other expenses.

Next, we transfer these balances to the profit and loss ledger account. For example, the balance on the purchases account is £5,000 DR. To transfer this balance, we write £5,000 on the credit side of the purchases account, and £5,000 on the debit side of the profit and loss ledger account. Now the balance on the purchases account has been moved to the profit and loss ledger account.

If we do the same thing with all the separate accounts of Ron Knuckle dealing with income and expenses, the result is as follows. (When we transfer or 'clear' these accounts to the profit and loss ledger account (P/L a/c) we double underline both sides of the ledger account we are transferring from to show that the balance is now zero.)

### PURCHASES

| | £ | | £ |
|---|---|---|---|
| Trade payables | 5,000 | P/L a/c | 5,000 |

### RENT

| | £ | | £ |
|---|---|---|---|
| Cash at bank | 3,500 | P/L a/c | 3,500 |

### SALES

| | £ | | £ |
|---|---|---|---|
| P/L a/c | 12,500 | Cash at bank | 10,000 |
| | | Trade receivables | 2,500 |
| | 12,500 | | 12,500 |

### DISCOUNT RECEIVED

| | £ | | £ |
|---|---|---|---|
| P/L a/c | 50 | Trade payables | 50 |

### DISCOUNT ALLOWED

| | £ | | £ |
|---|---|---|---|
| Trade receivables | 20 | P/L a/c | 20 |

### BANK LOAN INTEREST

| | £ | | £ |
|---|---|---|---|
| Cash at bank | 100 | P/L a/c | 100 |

### OTHER EXPENSES

| | £ | | £ |
|---|---|---|---|
| Cash at bank | 1,900 | P/L a/c | 1,900 |

| | £ | | £ |
|---|---|---|---|
| Purchases | 5,000 | Sales | 12,500 |
| Rent | 3,500 | Discount received | 50 |
| Discount allowed | 20 | | |
| Bank loan interest | 100 | | |
| Other expenses | 1,900 | | |
| **Profit for the period** | 2,030 | | |
| | 12,550 | | 12,550 |

The balance on the profit or loss ledger account is the profit for the period.

## 3.2 Preparing the statement of profit or loss

The items in the profit and loss ledger account are the same items that we need to draw up the statement of profit or loss.

- Sales and purchases are included in gross profit.
- All other income is added, and all other expenses are deducted, to arrive at profit for the period.

### Interactive question 1: Statement of profit or loss

Draw up Ron Knuckle's statement of profit or loss.

See **Answer** at the end of this chapter.

# 4 Preparing the statement of financial position

### Section overview

- To prepare the statement of financial position, the profit and loss ledger account balance is transferred to the capital ledger account.

- All the remaining balances (on the asset, capital and liabilities accounts) in the nominal ledger are then listed out in the vertical format statement of financial position to show: non-current and current assets (total assets), which are equal to capital plus non-current and current liabilities (total capital and liabilities).

## 4.1 Transferring profit/loss for the period to the capital account

The owner's capital comprises any cash introduced, plus any profits made by the business, less any drawings. At the stage we have now reached, these three elements are contained in different ledger accounts: cash introduced of £7,000 appears in the capital account; drawings of £1,500 appear in the drawings account; and the profit made by the business is represented by the £2,030 credit balance on the profit and loss account. To determine the closing capital balance we combine these in the **capital account**.

DRAWINGS

| | £ | | £ |
|---|---|---|---|
| Cash at bank | 1,500 | Capital a/c | 1,500 |

## PROFIT AND LOSS LEDGER ACCOUNT

| | £ | | £ |
|---|---|---|---|
| Purchases | 5,000 | Sales | 12,500 |
| Rent | 3,500 | Discount received | 50 |
| Bank loan interest | 100 | | |
| Other expenses | 1,900 | | |
| Discount allowed | 20 | | |
| Capital a/c | 2,030 | | |
| | 12,550 | | 12,550 |

## CAPITAL

| | £ | | £ |
|---|---|---|---|
| Drawings | 1,500 | Cash at bank | 7,000 |
| Balance c/d | 7,530 | P/L a/c | 2,030 |
| | 9,030 | | 9,030 |
| | | Balance b/d | 7,530 |

## 4.2 Preparing the statement of financial position

We now just have the cash, capital, bank loan, trade payables, non-current assets and trade receivables accounts.

These accounts represent assets, capital and liabilities of the business (not income and expenses) so their balances are **carried down** in the books of the business. This means that they become **opening balances** for the next reporting period.

The conventional method of ruling off a ledger account at the end of a reporting period and carrying down the balance to the next accounting period is illustrated by Ron Knuckle's bank loan account.

### BANK LOAN ACCOUNT

| | £ | | £ |
|---|---|---|---|
| Balance carried down (c/d) | 1,000 | Cash at bank | 1,000 |
| | | Balance brought down (b/d) | 1,000 |

Ron Knuckle therefore begins the new reporting period with a credit balance brought down of £1,000 on the loan account.

- A **credit balance brought down** denotes a liability.
- A **debit balance brought down** denotes an asset.

### Interactive question 2: Statement of financial position

Complete Ron Knuckle's simple statement of financial position.

See **Answer** at the end of this chapter.

# 5 Preparing basic financial statements

**Section overview**

- To prepare the statement of profit or loss and statement of financial position together, you need to follow through methodically the steps involved:

    - Calculate balances on all nominal ledger accounts

    - Prepare trial balance

    - Transfer income and expense balances to the profit and loss ledger account and calculate profit/(loss) for the period

    - Prepare statement of profit or loss

    - Transfer profit and loss ledger account and drawings balance to capital account

    - Prepare statement of financial position

We can now work through a full example of preparing a set of basic financial statements. This is by far the most important example in the Study Manual so far. It covers all the accounting steps from entering up ledger accounts to preparing the statement of profit or loss and statement of financial position. **You must try this example yourself first,** before carefully following through the solution.

## Worked example: Preparing financial statements

A business is established with capital of £2,000 paid by the owner into a business bank account, which has an overdraft facility. During the first year's trading, the following transactions occurred:

|  | £ |
|---|---|
| Purchases of goods for resale, on credit | 4,300 |
| Payments to suppliers | 3,600 |
| Sales, all on credit | 5,800 |
| Payments from customers | 3,200 |
| Non-current assets purchased for cash | 1,500 |
| Other expenses, all paid in cash | 900 |

Prepare ledgers accounts, a statement of profit or loss for the year and a statement of financial position as at the end of the year.

## Solution

The first thing to do is to open ledger accounts. The accounts needed are: cash at bank; capital; trade payables; purchases; non-current assets; sales; trade receivables; other expenses.

The next step is to perform the double entry bookkeeping for each transaction. Normally you would write them straight into the accounts, but to make this example easier to follow, they are listed below.

|  |  | Debit | Credit |
|---|---|---|---|
| (a) | Establishing business (£2,000) | Cash at bank | Capital |
| (b) | Credit purchases (£4,300) | Purchases | Trade payables |
| (c) | Payments to suppliers (£3,600) | Trade payables | Cash at bank |
| (d) | Credit sales (£5,800) | Trade receivables | Sales |
| (e) | Payments from customers (£3,200) | Cash at bank | Trade receivables |
| (f) | Non-current assets (£1,500) | Non-current assets | Cash at bank |
| (g) | Other (cash) expenses (£900) | Other expenses | Cash at bank |

So far, the ledger accounts will look like this.

## CASH AT BANK

| | £ | | £ |
|---|---|---|---|
| Capital | 2,000 | Trade payables | 3,600 |
| Trade receivables | 3,200 | Non-current assets | 1,500 |
| | | Other expenses | 900 |

## CAPITAL

| | £ | | £ |
|---|---|---|---|
| | | Cash at bank | 2,000 |

## TRADE PAYABLES

| | £ | | £ |
|---|---|---|---|
| Cash at bank | 3,600 | Purchases | 4,300 |

## PURCHASES

| | £ | | £ |
|---|---|---|---|
| Trade payables | 4,300 | | |

## NON-CURRENT ASSETS

| | £ | | £ |
|---|---|---|---|
| Cash at bank | 1,500 | | |

## SALES

| | £ | | £ |
|---|---|---|---|
| | | Trade receivables | 5,800 |

## TRADE RECEIVABLES

| | £ | | £ |
|---|---|---|---|
| Sales | 5,800 | Cash at bank | 3,200 |

## OTHER EXPENSES

| | £ | | £ |
|---|---|---|---|
| Cash at bank | 900 | | |

Next we balance the ledger accounts and draw up a trial balance to make sure the double entry is accurate.

| | Debit £ | Credit £ |
|---|---|---|
| Cash at bank | | 800 |
| Capital | | 2,000 |
| Trade payables | | 700 |
| Purchases | 4,300 | |
| Non-current assets | 1,500 | |
| Sales | | 5,800 |
| Trade receivables | 2,600 | |
| Other expenses | 900 | |
| | 9,300 | 9,300 |

Next the balances relating to income and expenses (ie sales, other income, purchases and other expenses) are cleared to a profit and loss ledger account. At this point, the ledger accounts will be as follows.

## CASH AT BANK

| | £ | | £ |
|---|---|---|---|
| Capital | 2,000 | Trade payables | 3,600 |
| Trade receivables | 3,200 | Non-current assets | 1,500 |
| Balance c/d | 800 | Other expenses | 900 |
| | 6,000 | | 6,000 |
| | | Balance b/d | 800* |

\* A credit balance b/d on the cash at bank ledger account means that this cash item is a liability, not an asset. This indicates a bank overdraft of £800.

## PROFIT AND LOSS LEDGER ACCOUNT

| | £ | | £ |
|---|---|---|---|
| Purchases account | 4,300 | Sales | 5,800 |
| Gross profit c/d | 1,500 | | |
| | 5,800 | | 5,800 |
| Other expenses | 900 | Gross profit b/d | 1,500 |
| Profit for the year (transferred to capital account) | 600 | | |
| | 1,500 | | 1,500 |

## CAPITAL

| | £ | | £ |
|---|---|---|---|
| Balance c/d | 2,600 | Cash at bank | 2,000 |
| | | P/L a/c (profit for the year) | 600 |
| | 2,600 | | 2,600 |
| | | Balance b/d | 2,600 |

## TRADE PAYABLES

| | £ | | £ |
|---|---|---|---|
| Cash at bank | 3,600 | Purchases | 4,300 |
| Balance c/d | 700 | | |
| | 4,300 | | 4,300 |
| | | Balance b/d | 700 |

## PURCHASES ACCOUNT

| | £ | | £ |
|---|---|---|---|
| Trade payables | 4,300 | P/L a/c | 4,300 |

## NON-CURRENT ASSETS

| | £ | | £ |
|---|---|---|---|
| Cash at bank | 1,500 | Balance c/d | 1,500 |
| Balance b/d | 1,500 | | |

## SALES

| | £ | | £ |
|---|---|---|---|
| P/L a/c | 5,800 | Trade receivables | 5,800 |

## TRADE RECEIVABLES

| | £ | | £ |
|---|---|---|---|
| Sales | 5,800 | Cash at bank | 3,200 |
| | | Balance c/d | 2,600 |
| | 5,800 | | 5,800 |
| Balance b/d | 2,600 | | |

| | £ | | £ |
|---|---|---|---|
| Cash at bank | 900 | P/L a/c | 900 |

The statement of profit or loss and statement of financial position are as follows.

**Statement of profit or loss**

| | £ |
|---|---|
| Sales | 5,800 |
| Cost of sales (purchases) | (4,300) |
| Gross profit | 1,500 |
| Expenses | (900) |
| Profit for the year | 600 |

**Statement of financial position**

| | £ | £ |
|---|---|---|
| *Assets* | | |
| Non-current assets | | 1,500 |
| Current assets | | |
| Trade receivables | | 2,600 |
| *Total assets* | | 4,100 |
| | | |
| *Capital and liabilities* | | |
| Capital | | |
| At start of period | 2,000 | |
| Profit for period | 600 | |
| At end of period | | 2,600 |
| Current liabilities | | |
| Bank overdraft | 800 | |
| Trade payables | 700 | |
| | | 1,500 |
| *Total capital and liabilities* | | 4,100 |

### Interactive question 3: Profit and loss ledger account

Polly had the following transactions in her first year of trading as a beauty therapist visiting clients at home.

| | |
|---|---|
| 1.1.X1 | Opened a bank account with £400. Took out bank loan for £5,000, and agreed an overdraft limit of the same amount |
| 1.1.X1 | Bought car for £2,500 cash. Insured it for £300 cash. Bought other equipment for £1,500, and consumable items for £500, both on credit |
| During year: | Charged customers £15,945, all on credit. |
| During year: | Purchased further consumables for £3,690 on credit, and diesel for car for £650 in cash. |
| During year: | Took £1,250 in cash from ATMs for herself |
| By end of year: | Received £12,935 from customers and paid £3,250 to suppliers |

Prepare Polly's ledger accounts including a profit and loss ledger account, and draw up a statement of profit or loss and statement of financial position in respect of her first year of trading.

See **Answer** at the end of this chapter.

# 6 The extended trial balance (ETB)

## Section overview

- We can prepare the statement of profit or loss and statement of financial position without a separate profit and loss ledger account if we use the extended trial balance (ETB).

- The ETB cross-casts from the trial balance and any adjusting journals straight to debit and credit columns for the statement of profit or loss (all income and expense items) and the statement of financial position (all asset, liability and capital items).

- If the entity has made a profit this is shown in the debit column for the statement of profit or loss, and in the credit column for the statement of financial position.

- If the entity has made a loss this is shown in the credit column for the statement of profit or loss, and in the debit column for the statement of financial position.

In Section 2.4 we saw how the extended trial balance (ETB) helped us to adjust an initial trial balance to create a revised one. The full way in which we use the ETB is to help us draw up a statement of profit or loss and statement of financial position, **without the need to create a profit and loss ledger account**.

## Worked example: Extended trial balance

Taking the revised trial balance from Section 2.4 and using it as the trial balance column of the ETB, we 'extend' it across so that:

- All the income and expense items are taken into the appropriate debit and credit columns of the statement of profit or loss.

- A profit for the year is calculated in the debit column of the statement of profit or loss.

- This profit for the year is inserted in the credit column of the statement of financial position to complete the double entry.

- All the other items are taken to the appropriate debit and credit columns of the statement of financial position. Note that we take the opening capital balance and the drawings balance straight from the trial balance to the statement of financial position.

- All columns are added up to ensure the double entry has been carried out properly.

- The statement of profit or loss and statement of financial position in IAS 1 format are prepared from the relevant columns of the ETB.

## Solution

| Ledger balance | Revised trial balance | | Statement of profit or loss | | Statement of financial position | |
|---|---|---|---|---|---|---|
| | Debit £ | Credit £ | Debit £ | Credit £ | Debit £ | Credit £ |
| Bank loan | | 12,000 | | | | 12,000 |
| Cash at bank | 11,180 | | | | 11,180 | |
| Capital | | 13,000 | | | | 13,000 |
| Rent | 1,880 | | 1,880 | | | |
| Trade payables | | 11,700 | | | | 11,700 |
| Purchases | 13,400 | | 13,400 | | | |
| Sales | | 35,640 | | 35,640 | | |
| Other payables | | 1,620 | | | | 1,620 |
| Trade receivables | 12,800 | | | | 12,800 | |
| Bank loan interest | 1,400 | | 1,400 | | | |
| Other expenses | 11,280 | | 11,280 | | | |
| Non-current assets | 22,020 | | | | 22,020 | |
| | | | 27,960 | 35,640 | 22,020 | |

| Ledger balance | Revised trial balance | | Statement of profit or loss | | Statement of financial position | |
|---|---|---|---|---|---|---|
| | Debit £ | Credit £ | Debit £ | Credit £ | Debit £ | Credit £ |
| Profit for the year | | | 7,680 | | | 7,680 |
| | 73,960 | 73,960 | 35,640 | 35,640 | 46,000 | 46,000 |

### Statement of profit or loss

| | £ | £ |
|---|---|---|
| Revenue | | 35,640 |
| Cost of sales | | |
| Purchases | | (13,400) |
| Gross profit | | 22,240 |
| Expenses | | |
| Other expenses | 11,280 | |
| Rent | 1,880 | |
| Finance costs (interest) | 1,400 | |
| | | (14,560) |
| Profit for the year | | 7,680 |

### Statement of financial position

| | £ | £ |
|---|---|---|
| Non-current assets | | 22,020 |
| Current assets | | |
| Trade receivables | 12,800 | |
| Cash at bank | 11,180 | |
| | | 23,980 |
| Total assets | | 46,000 |
| | | |
| Capital and liabilities | | |
| Opening capital | | 13,000 |
| Profit for year (from statement of profit or loss) | | 7,680 |
| Drawings | | 0 |
| Closing capital | | 20,680 |
| Non-current liabilities | | |
| Bank loan | | 12,000 |
| Current liabilities | | |
| Trade payables | 11,700 | |
| Other payables | 1,620 | |
| | | 13,320 |
| Total capital and liabilities | | 46,000 |

### Interactive question 4: Extended trial balance

Prepare an extended trial balance for Polly, for whom we prepared a statement of profit or loss and statement of financial position in Interactive question 3.

See **Answer** at the end of this chapter.

### Summary

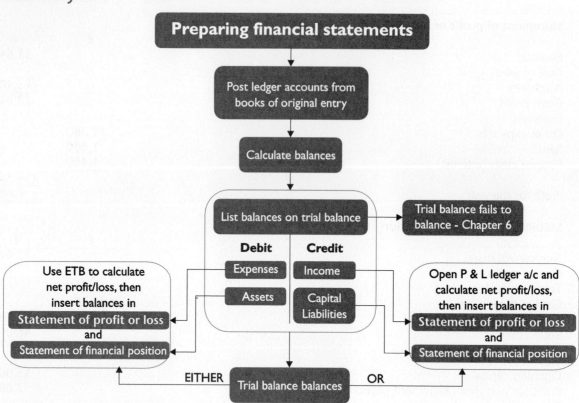

**Preparing financial statements**

Post ledger accounts from books of original entry

Calculate balances

List balances on trial balance

Trial balance fails to balance - Chapter 6

**Debit**

Expenses

Assets

**Credit**

Income

Capital
Liabilities

Use ETB to calculate net profit/loss, then insert balances in

Statement of profit or loss and

Statement of financial position

Open P & L ledger a/c and calculate net profit/loss, then insert balances in

Statement of profit or loss and

Statement of financial position

EITHER

Trial balance balances

OR

# Self-test

Answer the following questions.

1  In a period, sales are £140,000, purchases £75,000 and other expenses £25,000. What is the figure for profit for the period to be transferred to the capital account?

    A   £40,000
    B   £65,000
    C   £75,000
    D   £140,000

2  During March, Chan had the following items in the cash at bank account.

|  | £ |
|---|---|
| Balance at 1 March (overdrawn) | 500 |
| Receipts from receivables | 12,000 |
| Payments to payables | 7,000 |
| Payments for expenses | 3,000 |
| Cash drawn for own use | 1,200 |

What is the balance on Chan's cash at bank account on 31 March?

    A   Debit   £300
    B   Credit  £300
    C   Debit   £1,300
    D   Credit  £1,300

3  Which **three** of the following items will be listed as a credit balance on a trial balance?

    A   Trade payables
    B   Purchases
    C   Discounts received
    D   Sundry expenses
    E   Capital
    F   Drawings

4  Select whether the following balances will be in the debit or the credit columns of the trial balance.

|  | Debit | Credit |
|---|---|---|
| Machinery | ☐ | ☐ |
| Trade payables | ☐ | ☐ |
| Drawings | ☐ | ☐ |
| Discount allowed | ☐ | ☐ |
| Revenue | ☐ | ☐ |
| Discount received | ☐ | ☐ |
| Bank overdraft | ☐ | ☐ |
| Rental income | ☐ | ☐ |

5  When an error in a debit entry is cancelled out by an error in a credit entry, this is called

    A   A commission error
    B   A compensating error
    C   An omission error
    D   An error of principle

6    An error has led to Erica's trial balance failing to balance. This could have been caused by an error of commission.

☐ True

☐ False

7    The balance on Tim's loan account is £1,200. He has just realised that a £100 loan repayment that he made during the year was posted from the cash book to drawings. On the loan account line of the extended trial balance, adjusting for this mistake will mean:

A    A credit entry in the adjustments columns and a credit balance of £1,100 in the statement of financial position columns

B    A debit entry in the adjustments columns and a credit balance of £1,100 in the statement of financial position columns

C    A credit entry in the adjustments columns and a credit balance of £1,300 in the statement of financial position columns

D    A debit entry in the adjustments columns and a credit balance of £1,300 in the statement of financial position columns

8    Manny has a net loss of £400. This should be

A    Credited to the profit and loss ledger account and debited to the capital account
B    Debited to the profit and loss ledger account and credited to the capital account
C    Credited to the profit and loss ledger account and debited to the drawings account
D    Debited to the profit and loss ledger account and credited to the drawings account

9    At 31 December 20X6 Richard's total assets are £20,376 and his non-current liabilities are £10,000. If his current liabilities are £6,290 then his capital balance at 31 December 20X6 must be

A    £4,086
B    £16,666
C    £24,086
D    £36,666

10   The statement of profit or loss columns on Jude's ETB are £57,390 for the debit column and £84,928 for the credit column. What final entry does Jude need to make?

A    Credit £27,538 profit for the period
B    Credit £27,538 loss for the period
C    Debit £27,538 profit for the period
D    Debit £27,538 loss for the period

Now, go back to the Learning Objectives in the Introduction. If you are satisfied that you have achieved these objectives, please tick them off.

## Answer to Interactive question 1

RON KNUCKLE: STATEMENT OF PROFIT OR LOSS FOR FIRST TRADING PERIOD

|  | £ | £ |
|---|---:|---:|
| Revenue (= sales) |  | 12,500 |
| Cost of sales (= purchases) |  | (5,000) |
| Gross profit |  | 7,500 |
| Other income: discount received |  | 50 |
| Expenses |  |  |
| Rent | 3,500 |  |
| Discount allowed | 20 |  |
| Bank loan interest | 100 |  |
| Other expenses | 1,900 |  |
|  |  | (5,520) |
| Profit for the year (the balance on the profit and loss ledger account) |  | 2,030 |

## Answer to Interactive question 2

RON KNUCKLE

STATEMENT OF FINANCIAL POSITION AT END OF FIRST TRADING PERIOD

|  | £ |
|---|---:|
| *Assets* |  |
| Non-current assets | 2,000 |
| *Current assets* |  |
| Cash at bank | 6,530 |
| *Total assets* | 8,530 |
|  |  |
| *Capital and liabilities* |  |
| Owner's capital | 7,530 |
| *Non-current liabilities* |  |
| Bank loan | 1,000 |
| *Total capital and liabilities* | 8,530 |

## Answer to Interactive question 3

### CASH AT BANK

|  |  | £ |  |  | £ |
|---|---|---:|---|---|---:|
| 1.1.X1 | Capital | 400 | 1.1.X1 | Insurance | 300 |
| 1.1.X1 | Loan | 5,000 | 1.1.X1 | Non-current assets | 2,500 |
| 31.12.X1 | Trade receivables | 12,935 | 31.12.X1 | Car expenses | 650 |
|  |  |  | 31.12.X1 | Drawings | 1,250 |
|  |  |  | 31.12.X1 | Trade payables | 3,250 |
|  |  |  | 31.12.X1 | C/d | 10,385 |
|  |  | 18,335 |  |  | 18,335 |
| 31.12.X1 | B/d | 10,385 |  |  |  |

### CAPITAL

|  |  | £ |  |  | £ |
|---|---|---:|---|---|---:|
| 31.12.X1 | Drawings | 1,250 | 1.1.X1 | Cash at bank | 400 |
| 31.12.X1 | C/d | 9,955 | 31.12.X1 | P/L account | 10,805 |
|  |  | 11,205 |  |  | 11,205 |
|  |  |  | 31.12.X1 | B/d | 9,955 |

CHAPTER

5

## LOAN

| | | £ | | | £ |
|---|---|---|---|---|---|
| 31.12.X1 | C/d | 5,000 | 1.1.X1 | Cash at bank | 5,000 |
| | | 5,000 | | | 5,000 |
| | | | 31.12.X1 | B/d | 5,000 |

## NON-CURRENT ASSETS (NCA)

| | | £ | | | £ |
|---|---|---|---|---|---|
| 1.1.X1 | Cash at bank | 2,500 | 31.12.X1 | C/d | 4,000 |
| 1.1.X1 | Trade payables | 1,500 | | | |
| | | 4,000 | | | 4,000 |
| 31.12.X1 | B/d | 4,000 | | | |

## TRADE PAYABLES

| | | £ | | | £ |
|---|---|---|---|---|---|
| 31.12.X1 | Cash at bank | 3,250 | 1.1.X1 | NCA | 1,500 |
| 31.12.X1 | C/d | 2,440 | 1.1.X1 | Purchases | 500 |
| | | | 31.12.X1 | Purchases | 3,690 |
| | | 5,690 | | | 5,690 |
| | | | 31.12.X1 | B/d | 2,440 |

## INSURANCE

| | | £ | | | £ |
|---|---|---|---|---|---|
| 1.1.X1 | Cash at bank | 300 | 31.12.X1 | P/L account | 300 |
| | | 300 | | | 300 |

## CAR EXPENSES

| | | £ | | | £ |
|---|---|---|---|---|---|
| 31.12.X1 | Cash at bank | 650 | 31.12.X1 | P/L account | 650 |
| | | 650 | | | 650 |

## PURCHASES

| | | £ | | | £ |
|---|---|---|---|---|---|
| 1.1.X1 | Trade payables | 500 | 31.12.X1 | P/L account | 4,190 |
| 31.12.X1 | Trade payables | 3,690 | | | |
| | | 4,190 | | | 4,190 |

## SALES

| | | £ | | | £ |
|---|---|---|---|---|---|
| 31.12.X1 | P/L account | 15,945 | 31.12.X1 | Trade receivables | 15,945 |
| | | 15,945 | | | 15,945 |

## TRADE RECEIVABLES

| | | £ | | | £ |
|---|---|---|---|---|---|
| 31.12.X1 | Sales | 15,945 | 31.12.X1 | Cash at bank | 12,935 |
| | | | 31.12.X1 | C/d | 3,010 |
| | | 15,945 | | | 15,945 |
| 31.12.X1 | B/d | 3,010 | | | |

### DRAWINGS

|  |  | £ |  |  | £ |
|---|---|---|---|---|---|
| 31.12.X1 | Cash at bank | 1,250 | 31.12.X1 | Capital | 1,250 |
|  |  | 1,250 |  |  | 1,250 |

### PROFIT AND LOSS LEDGER ACCOUNT

|  |  | £ |  |  | £ |
|---|---|---|---|---|---|
| 31.12.X1 | Purchases | 4,190 | 31.12.X1 | Sales | 15,945 |
| 31.12.X1 | Car expenses | 650 |  |  |  |
| 31.12.X1 | Insurance | 300 |  |  |  |
| 31.12.X1 | Capital | 10,805 |  |  |  |
|  |  | 15,945 |  |  | 15,945 |

### POLLY: STATEMENT OF PROFIT OR LOSS FOR YEAR ENDED 31 DECEMBER 20X1

|  | £ |
|---|---|
| Revenue | 15,945 |
| Cost of sales |  |
| Purchases | (4,190) |
| Gross profit | 11,755 |
| Expenses |  |
| Car expenses | (650) |
| Insurance | (300) |
| Profit for the year | 10,805 |

### POLLY: STATEMENT OF FINANCIAL POSITION AS AT 31 DECEMBER 20X1

|  | £ | £ |
|---|---|---|
| Non-current assets |  | 4,000 |
| Current assets |  |  |
| Trade receivables | 3,010 |  |
| Cash at bank | 10,385 |  |
|  |  | 13,395 |
| Total assets |  | 17,395 |
| Capital and liabilities |  |  |
| Opening capital |  | 400 |
| Profit for year |  | 10,805 |
| Drawings |  | (1,250) |
| Closing capital |  | 9,955 |
| Non-current liabilities |  |  |
| Bank loan |  | 5,000 |
| Current liabilities |  |  |
| Trade payables |  | 2,440 |
| Total capital and liabilities |  | 17,395 |

## Answer to Interactive question 4

| Ledger balance | Trial balance | | Statement of profit or loss | | Statement of financial position | |
|---|---|---|---|---|---|---|
| | Debit £ | Credit £ | Debit £ | Credit £ | Debit £ | Credit £ |
| Cash at bank | 10,385 | | | | 10,385 | |
| Opening capital | | 400 | | | | 400 |
| Loan | | 5,000 | | | | 5,000 |
| Non-current assets | 4,000 | | | | 4,000 | |
| Trade payables | | 2,440 | | | | 2,440 |
| Insurance | 300 | | 300 | | | |
| Car expenses | 650 | | 650 | | | |
| Purchases | 4,190 | | 4,190 | | | |
| Sales | | 15,945 | | 15,945 | | |
| Trade receivables | 3,010 | | | | 3,010 | |
| Drawings | 1,250 | | | | 1,250 | |
| Profit for the year | | | 10,805 | | | 10,805 |
| | 23,785 | 23,785 | 15,945 | 15,945 | 18,645 | 18,645 |

## Answers to Self-test

**1 A**

PROFIT OR LOSS LEDGER ACCOUNT

| | £ | | £ |
|---|---|---|---|
| Purchases | 75,000 | Sales | 140,000 |
| Gross profit c/d | 65,000 | | |
| | 140,000 | | 140,000 |
| Other expenses | 25,000 | Gross profit b/d | 65,000 |
| Profit for the year – to capital a/c | 40,000 | | |
| | 65,000 | | 65,000 |

B is the **gross** profit figure, while C is the figure for purchases and D is the figure for sales.

**2 A**

CASH AT BANK

| | £ | | £ |
|---|---|---|---|
| Receivables | 12,000 | B/d | 500 |
| | | Payables | 7,000 |
| | | Expenses | 3,000 |
| | | Drawings | 1,200 |
| | | C/d | 300 |
| | 12,000 | | 12,000 |
| B/d | 300 | | |

**3 A, C, E** Purchases, sundry expenses and drawings are all debit balances.

**4**

| | Debit | Credit |
|---|---|---|
| Machinery | ✓ | |
| Trade payables | | ✓ |
| Drawings | ✓ | |
| Discount allowed | ✓ | |
| Revenue | | ✓ |
| Discount received | | ✓ |
| Bank overdraft | | ✓ |
| Rental income | | ✓ |

**5 B** A commission error (A) occurs when the double entry is complete, but the entries are made in the wrong account(s). An omission error (C) occurs when a transaction is completely omitted from the accounting records. An error of principle (D) occurs when the double entry is performed but the wrong treatment is applied to a transaction. With all four errors the trial balance will still balance.

**6** False. An error of commission does not lead to the trial balance failing to balance.

**7 B** The £100 payment was debited to drawings from cash. It needs to be credited to drawings and debited to the loan account, leading to a reduction in the loan balance on the statement of financial position to £1,100.

**8 A** A net loss is debited to the capital account, reducing the owner's interest in the business, and is credited to the profit and loss ledger account.

9    A    £20,376 – £10,000 – £6,290 = £4,086

10    C    The difference between the two columns is a debit, so this must appear in the debit column of the statement of profit or loss as a profit for the year; a credit entry would make it a loss for the year.

# CHAPTER 6

# Control accounts, errors and suspense accounts

Introduction

Examination context

**Topic List**

Summary and Self-test

Answers to Interactive questions

Answers to Self-test

# Introduction

## Learning objectives

- Prepare a trial balance from accounting records and identify the uses of a trial balance ☐

- Identify omissions and errors in accounting records and financial statements and demonstrate how the required adjustments will affect profits or losses ☐

- Correct omissions and errors in accounting records and financial statements using control account reconciliations and suspense accounts ☐

- Prepare an extended trial balance ☐

- Prepare journals for nominal ledger entry and to correct errors in draft financial statements ☐

Specific syllabus learning outcomes are: 1f; 2a, b, c, d

## Syllabus links

The accuracy of financial statements is the bedrock on which the rest of your studies for this paper, and for the Professional Level module of Financial Accounting and Reporting, are built.

## Examination context

Questions on the topics in this chapter will be set as multiple choice questions, some of which may involve calculations so that the correct answer can be selected. Very often double entry questions are phrased in terms of preparing a journal. In addition, the material covered in this chapter may also be examined as part of a long form question.

In the exam you may be required to:

- Identify distinctions between errors that cause trial balance imbalances and those that do not

- Identify a journal to correct errors

- Calculate a suspense account balance

- Identify the correct journal to clear a suspense account

- Identify the effects of correcting errors on draft gross or net profit

- Use the techniques of bank reconciliations to identify the correct cash at bank balance in the financial statements

- Use reconciliation techniques to identify the correct receivables and payables balances in the financial statements

# 1 What are control accounts?

### Section overview

- Control accounts in the nominal ledger for receivables and payables record **total** amounts in respect of all customers/suppliers.

- The memorandum receivables and payables ledgers record each transaction for individual customers and suppliers in their personal accounts. These are not part of the double entry system if control accounts are maintained.

- The total of all the balances in each memorandum ledger should equal the balance on the relevant control account.

In Chapter 4 when we looked at the memorandum receivables and payables ledgers (ie the ledgers containing personal accounts for customers and suppliers, which are not part of the nominal ledger double entry system) we briefly introduced the idea of **control accounts**.

### Definition

**Control account:** Nominal ledger account in which a record is kept of the total value of a number of similar individual items. Control accounts are used chiefly for trade receivables and payables.

- A **receivables control account** is a nominal ledger account in which records are kept of transactions involving all receivables in total. The balance on the receivables control account at any time will be the total amount due to the business from all its credit customers.

- A **payables control account** is a nominal ledger account in which records are kept of transactions involving all payables in total, and the balance on this account at any time will be the total amount owed by the business to all its credit suppliers.

Control accounts are also kept for wages and salaries, cash, VAT and non-current assets. The most important idea to remember, however, is that a control account is an account which keeps a total record for a collective item (eg receivables), which in reality consists of many individual items (eg individual trade receivables).

## 1.1 Control accounts (nominal ledger) and personal accounts (memorandum ledgers)

The amount owed by each credit customer is a balance on their personal account in the receivables ledger, which as we saw in Chapter 4 is a memorandum ledger only, outside the double entry system of the nominal ledger. The amount owed by all the credit customers together (ie all the trade receivables) is the balance on the **receivables control account**.

At any time the **balance on the receivables control account** should be **equal** to the **sum of the individual personal account balances** on the **receivables ledger**.

Most customers will have a **debit balance** on their personal account in the receivables ledger, as they owe the business money for goods/services supplied. Sometimes a customer may have a **credit balance**, perhaps because it has overpaid the business, or paid for goods and then returned some. While credit balances will show up on the receivables ledger balances quite clearly, the balance on the receivables control account in the nominal ledger is an aggregate balance and will always be a debit balance.

### Worked example: Receivables control account

A business has three trade receivables: A Arnold owes £80, B Bagshaw owes £310 and C Cloning owes £200.

*Receivables ledger personal accounts*

|  | £ |
|---|---|
| A Arnold | 80 |
| B Bagshaw | 310 |
| C Cloning | 200 |
|  | 590 |

The balance on the nominal ledger receivables control account should be the total, £590.

What has happened here is that three entries of £80, £310 and £200 were first entered into the sales day book. They were posted individually to the three personal accounts of Arnold, Bagshaw and Cloning in the receivables ledger, but these are not part of the double entry system.

Later, the **total** of £590 was posted from the sales day book to the nominal ledger, which is the double entry system:

|  |  | £ | £ |
|---|---|---|---|
| DEBIT | Receivables control account | 590 | |
| CREDIT | Sales | | 590 |

## 2 Operating control accounts

### Section overview

- Individual entries in receivables and payables ledgers are summarised and posted to relevant control accounts in the nominal ledger.

- For sales: debit receivables, credit sales & VAT.

- For receipts from customers and discount allowed: credit receivables, debit cash/discount allowed.

- For purchases: credit payables, debit purchases & VAT.

- For payments to suppliers and discount received: debit payables, credit cash/discount received.

- Other entries in receivables accounts: credit receivables, debit payables (contra with payables ledger); credit receivables, debit irrecoverable debts (debt written off); debit receivables, credit cash (customer's cheque dishonoured, or refund to customer).

- Other entries in payables accounts: credit payables, debit cash (refund from supplier); debit payables, credit receivables (contra with receivables ledger).

- The wages control account is used as a clearing account for all the postings from the payroll; at the end of each period the balance should be zero.

The two most important **control accounts** are those for **receivables** and **payables**. They are part of the double entry system; the receivables and payables ledger are memorandum ledgers only.

### 2.1 Accounting for receivables

Transactions involving receivables are accounted for by posting from books of original entry to both the personal accounts in the receivables ledger, and the receivables control account in the nominal ledger. Reference numbers are shown in the accounts to illustrate cross-referencing as follows:

- SDB refer to a sales day book page
- RL refer to a receivables ledger account
- NL refer to a nominal ledger account
- CB refer to a cash book page

## Worked example: Accounting for receivables

At 1 July 20X2, the Outer Business Company (not registered for VAT) had no trade receivables. During July, the following transactions affecting credit sales and customers occurred.

(a)   July 3: invoiced A Arnold for the sale on credit of hardware goods: £100

(b)   July 11: invoiced B Bagshaw for the sale on credit of electrical goods: £150

(c)   July 15: invoiced C Cloning for the sale on credit of hardware goods: £250

(d)   July 10: received payment from A Arnold of £90, in settlement of his debt in full, having taken a permitted cash discount of £10 for payment within seven days

(e)   July 18: received a payment of £72 from B Bagshaw in part settlement of £80 of his debt; a cash discount of £8 was allowed for payment within seven days of invoice

(f)   July 28: received a payment of £120 from C Cloning, who was unable to claim any discount

(g)   July 31: received notice that B Bagshaw had become insolvent, so no more payments could be expected from him. The balance of his debt was to be 'written off' as irrecoverable (£70)

Account numbers:

RL 4      A Arnold
RL 9      B Bagshaw
RL 13     C Cloning
NL 1      Cash at bank
NL 6      Receivables control account
NL 7      Discount allowed
NL 21     Sales: hardware
NL 22     Sales: electrical
NL 30     Irrecoverable debts expense

First we indicate in the sales day book where the column totals are to be posted, using the nominal ledger account code, and 'Dr' for debit and 'Cr' for credit. We also note where each invoice total is to be posted in the receivables ledger.

| | SALES DAY BOOK | | | | SDB 35 |
|---|---|---|---|---|---|
| Date 20X2 | Name | Receivables ledger ref | Total £ | Hardware £ | Electrical £ |
| July   3 | A Arnold | RL 4 Dr | 100.00 | 100.00 | |
| 11 | B Bagshaw | RL 9 Dr | 150.00 | | 150.00 |
| 15 | C Cloning | RL 13 Dr | 250.00 | 250.00 | |
| | | | 500.00 | 350.00 | 150.00 |
| | | | NL 6 DR | NL 21 CR | NL 22 CR |

Note: The personal accounts in the receivables ledger are usually debited on the day the invoices are sent out. The double entry in the nominal ledger accounts might be made at the end of each day, week or month; here it is made at the end of the month, by posting from the sales day book as follows.

| | | | £ | £ |
|---|---|---|---|---|
| DEBIT | NL 6 | Receivables control | 500 | |
| CREDIT | NL 21 | Sales: hardware | | 350 |
| | NL 22 | Sales: electrical | | 150 |

Next we do the same for the cash book. Remember that discounts allowed and received are recorded in the cash book as a book of original entry only; they are not included in the cross-cast total column.

CASH BOOK EXTRACT
RECEIPTS – JULY 20X2                                                    CB 23

| Date 20X2 | | Narrative | Receivable ledger ref | Total £ | Discount allowed £ | Receivables control £ |
|---|---|---|---|---|---|---|
| July | 10 | A Arnold | RL 4 CR | 90.00 | 10.00 | 90.00 |
| | 18 | B Bagshaw | RL 9 CR | 72.00 | 8.00 | 72.00 |
| | 28 | C Cloning | RL 13 CR | 120.00 | – | 120.00 |
| | | | | 282.00 | 18.00 | 282.00 |
| | | | | NL 1 DR | NL 6 CR | NL 6 CR |
| | | | | | NL 7 DR | |

**Note:** Posting discount allowed and cash separately to the receivables control account and to each receivables ledger personal account allows us to cross-check postings more easily.

At the end of July, the cash book is posted to the nominal ledger.

| | | | £ | £ |
|---|---|---|---|---|
| DEBIT | NL 1 | Cash at bank | 282.00 | |
| | NL 7 | Discount allowed | 18.00 | |
| CREDIT | NL 6 | Receivables control (282 + 18) | | 300.00 |

B Bagshaw's irrecoverable debt has to be removed from the nominal ledger account, via the journal, using a special nominal ledger expense account called **irrecoverable debt expense**. The credit entry will also be posted from the journal to B Bagshaw's personal account in the receivables ledger.

| | | | £ | £ |
|---|---|---|---|---|
| DEBIT | NL 30 | Irrecoverable debt expense | 70 | |
| CREDIT | NL 6 | Receivables control (RL 9) | | 70 |

The personal accounts in the receivables ledger are not part of the double entry system, but will look as follows after the postings from the sales day book, the cash book and the journal.

MEMORANDUM RECEIVABLES LEDGER
A ARNOLD                                                         A/c no: RL 4

| Date 20X2 | Narrative | Ref. | £ | Date 20X2 | Narrative | Ref. | £ |
|---|---|---|---|---|---|---|---|
| July 3 | Sales | SDB 35 | 100.00 | July 10 | Cash | CB 23 | 90.00 |
| | | | | | Discount | CB 23 | 10.00 |
| | | | 100.00 | | | | 100.00 |

B BAGSHAW                                                        A/c no: RL 9

| Date 20X2 | Narrative | Ref. | £ | Date 20X2 | Narrative | Ref. | £ |
|---|---|---|---|---|---|---|---|
| July 11 | Sales | SDB 35 | 150.00 | July 18 | Cash | CB 23 | 72.00 |
| | | | | | Discount | CB 23 | 8.00 |
| | | | | July 31 | Irrecoverable Debt | Jnl | 70.00 |
| | | | 150.00 | | | | 150.00 |

C CLONING                                                        A/c no: RL 13

| Date 20X2 | Narrative | Ref. | £ | Date 20X2 | Narrative | Ref. | £ |
|---|---|---|---|---|---|---|---|
| July 15 | Sales | SDB 35 | 250.00 | July 28 | Cash | CB 23 | 120.00 |
| | | | | July 31 | Balance | c/d | 130.00 |
| | | | 250.00 | | | | 250.00 |
| Aug 1 | Balance | b/d | 130.00 | | | | |

In the nominal ledger, the total accounting entries are made from the books of original entry to the ledger accounts at the end of the month.

NOMINAL LEDGER (EXTRACT)
RECEIVABLES CONTROL ACCOUNT

A/c no: NL 6

| Date 20X2 | Narrative | Ref. | £ | Date 20X2 | Narrative | Ref. | £ |
|---|---|---|---|---|---|---|---|
| July 31 | Sales | SDB 35 | 500.00 | July 31 | Cash | CB 23 | 282.00 |
| | | | | July 31 | Discount allowed | CB 23 | 18.00 |
| | | | | July 31 | Irrecoverable debt | Jnl | 70.00 |
| | | | | July 31 | Balance | c/d | 130.00 |
| | | | 500.00 | | | | 500.00 |
| Aug 1 | Balance | b/d | 130.00 | | | | |

So at 31 July the closing balance on the receivables control account (£130) is the same as the total of the individual balances on the personal accounts in the receivables ledger (£0 + £0 + £130).

The other nominal ledger accounts are written up as follows.

DISCOUNT ALLOWED

A/c no: NL 7

| Date 20X2 | Narrative | Ref. | £ | Date | Narrative | Ref. | £ |
|---|---|---|---|---|---|---|---|
| July 31 | Receivables | CB 23 | 18.00 | | | | |

CASH AT BANK ACCOUNT

A/c no: NL 1

| Date 20X2 | Narrative | Ref. | £ | Date | Narrative | Ref. | £ |
|---|---|---|---|---|---|---|---|
| July 31 | Cash received | CB 23 | 282.00 | | | | |

Note that discount allowed is **not** posted to the cash at bank account. It only affects the discount allowed and receivables control account.

SALES: HARDWARE

A/c no: NL 21

| Date | Narrative | Ref. | £ | Date 20X2 | Narrative | Ref. | £ |
|---|---|---|---|---|---|---|---|
| | | | | July 31 | Receivables | SDB 35 | 350.00 |

SALES: ELECTRICAL

A/c no: NL 22

| Date | Narrative | Ref. | £ | Date 20X2 | Narrative | Ref. | £ |
|---|---|---|---|---|---|---|---|
| | | | | July 31 | Receivables | SDB 35 | 150.00 |

IRRECOVERABLE DEBTS

A/c no: NL 30

| Date 20X2 | Narrative | Ref. | £ | Date | Narrative | Ref. | £ |
|---|---|---|---|---|---|---|---|
| July 31 | Receivables | Jnl | 70.00 | | | | |

The trial balance at 31 July 20X2 – for the nominal ledger only – is as follows.

TRIAL BALANCE

| | Debit £ | Credit £ |
|---|---|---|
| Cash (all receipts) | 282 | |
| Receivables | 130 | |
| Discount allowed | 18 | |
| Irrecoverable debts | 70 | |
| Sales: hardware | | 350 |
| Sales: electrical | | 150 |
| | 500 | 500 |

The trial balance is shown here to emphasise the point that a trial balance **includes** the balance on the control account, but **excludes** the balance on the personal accounts in the receivables ledger.

## 2.2 Accounting for payables

Refer back to revise the entries made in the purchases day book, the payables ledger personal accounts and the payables control account in the nominal ledger. Such entries are mirror images of the way we account for receivables, though there will be no irrecoverable debt entries in the payables accounts.

## 2.3 Entries in receivables/payables control accounts

Typical entries in the receivables and payables control accounts are set out below. The reference 'Jnl' indicates that the transaction is first entered in the journal before posting to the control account and other accounts indicated.

### Definitions

**Contra**: When a person or business is both a customer and a supplier, amounts owed by and owed to the person may be 'netted off' by means of a **contra**:

| | |
|---|---|
| DEBIT | Payables control account (and personal account in the payables ledger) |
| CREDIT | Receivables control account (and personal account in the receivables ledger) |

**Irrecoverable debt**: When a debt owed by a customer will never be paid, the total amount is removed from receivables:

| | |
|---|---|
| DEBIT | Irrecoverable debt expense |
| CREDIT | Receivables control account (and personal account in the receivables ledger) |

**Dishonoured cheque**: When a customer's cheque is paid into the business's bank but the customer's bank refuses to honour payment of it, it is 'written back' (the original entry is reversed) so as to remove the receipt of the cheque from the books and recreate the debt that has still not been paid:

| | |
|---|---|
| DEBIT | Receivables control account (and personal account in the receivables ledger) |
| CREDIT | Cash |

### RECEIVABLES CONTROL ACCOUNT

| | Ref. | £ | | Ref. | £ |
|---|---|---|---|---|---|
| Opening balance | b/d | 6,800 | Cash received | CB | 52,250 |
| Sales/VAT | SDB | 51,590 | Discounts allowed | CB | 1,250 |
| Dishonoured cheques from customers | Jnl | 1,000 | Contra with payables ledger | Jnl | 150 |
| Refunds paid to customers | CB | 110 | Irrecoverable debts | Jnl | 300 |
| | | | Balance | c/d | 5,550 |
| | | 59,500 | | | 59,500 |
| Balance | b/d | 5,550 | | | |

\* Sometimes customers overpay and are left with a credit balance on their personal accounts. This can be settled by the business refunding the overpayments in cash.

### PAYABLES CONTROL ACCOUNT

| | Ref. | £ | | Ref. | £ |
|---|---|---|---|---|---|
| Cash paid | CB | 29,840 | Opening balance | b/d | 8,230 |
| Discounts received | CB | 30 | Purchases/VAT | PDB | 30,940 |
| Contra with receivables ledger | Jnl | 150 | Refunds received from suppliers* | CB | 20 |
| Closing balance | c/d | 9,170 | | | |
| | | 39,190 | | | 39,190 |
| | | | Balance | b/d | 9,170 |

\* As with refunds to customers, so too the business may receive a refund in cash from a supplier regarding an overpayment.

As we saw above, posting from the journal to the receivables (or payables) ledgers and to the nominal ledger may be effected at the same time, as in the following example, where C Cloning has returned goods with a sales value of £50.

| Journal entry | Ref. | £ | £ |
|---|---|---|---|
| DEBIT     Sales: hardware | NL 21 | 50 | |
| CREDIT    Receivables control | NL 6 | | 50 |
| *C Cloning (personal account)* | *RL 13* | | *50* |
| Return of hardware goods | | | |

Here is an example of a journal recording the contra entry in respect of Perch Ltd.

| Journal entry | Ref. | DR £ | CR £ |
|---|---|---|---|
| DEBIT     Payables control | NL 14 | 150 | |
| CREDIT    Receivables control | NL 6 | | 150 |
| *Perch Ltd: payables ledger a/c* | *PL 82* | *150* | |
| *Perch Ltd: receivables ledger a/c* | *RL 49* | | *150* |

Contra between Perch Ltd's receivables and payables ledger accounts.

## Interactive question 1: Payables control account

A payables control account contains the following entries:

| | £ |
|---|---|
| Bank | 79,500 |
| Credit purchases | 83,200 |
| Discount received | 3,750 |
| Contra with receivables control account | 4,000 |
| Balance c/d at 31 December 20X8 | 12,920 |

There are no other entries in the account. What was the opening balance brought down at 1 January 20X8?

See **Answer** at the end of this chapter.

## Interactive question 2: Receivables control account

The total of the balances in a company's receivables ledger is £800 more than the debit balance on its receivables control account. Which one of the following errors could by itself account for the discrepancy?

A    The sales day book total column has been undercast by £800

B    Cash discounts totalling £800 have been omitted from the nominal ledger

C    One receivables ledger account with a credit balance of £800 has been treated as a debit balance in the list of balances

D    The cash receipts book has been undercast by £800

See **Answer** at the end of this chapter.

Figure 6.1 should help you now to see how the receivables ledger and receivables control account are used. Note that A overpaid by £20 in error, while B only paid part of what he owed.

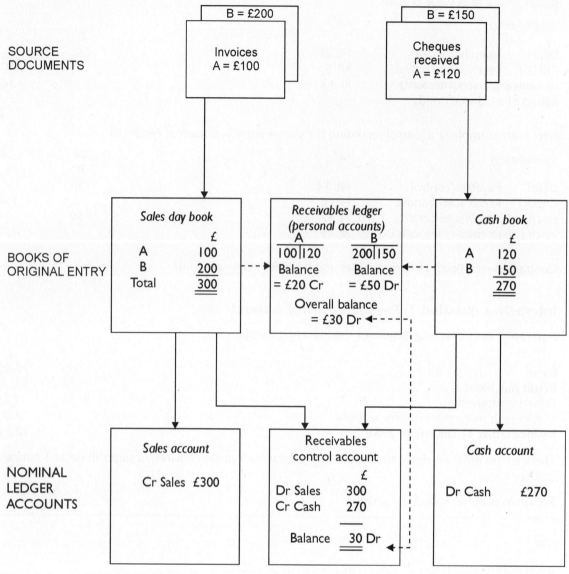

Figure 6.1 Accounting for receivables

The total of the balances on the receivables ledger (ie the personal account balances of A and B added up) equals the balance on the receivables control account.

## Interactive question 3: Receivables and payables control accounts

For Exports Co on 1 October 20X8 the receivables ledger balances were £8,024 debit and £57 credit, and the payables ledger balances on the same date were £6,235 credit and £105 debit. These balances have been checked and are correct.

For the year ended 30 September 20X9 the following particulars are available.

|  | £ |
|---|---|
| Sales | 62,514 |
| Purchases | 39,439 |
| Cash from credit customers | 55,212 |
| Cash to credit suppliers | 37,307 |
| Discount received | 1,475 |
| Discount allowed | 2,328 |
| Irrecoverable debts written off | 326 |
| Cash received in respect of debit balances in payables ledger (refunds from suppliers) | 105 |

|  | £ |
|---|---|
| Amount due from customer as shown by receivables ledger, offset against amount due to the same firm as shown by payables ledger (settlement by contra) | 434 |

What are the balances as at 30 September 20X9 on:

(a)   Receivables control account

(b)   Payables control account?

See **Answer** at the end of this chapter.

## 2.4   Accounting for wages: the wages control account

In Chapter 3 we looked at payroll as a book of original entry for the total costs of employing and paying staff. We now look at how payroll is accounted for in the nominal ledger, and how the wages control account is used:

- To maintain the accuracy of payroll double entry
- To identify errors in payroll double entry

### Worked example: Ledger accounting for payroll

The payroll looked at in Chapter 3 was as follows.

|  | PAYE | Deductions Ees' NI | Ees' pension | Net pay | Gross pay | Er's NI | Er's pension | Total payroll cost |
|---|---|---|---|---|---|---|---|---|
|  | £ | £ | £ | £ | £ | £ | £ | £ |
| Anja | 550 | 250 | 150 | 2,050 | 3,000 | 310 | 200 | 3,510 |
| Mark | 500 | 230 | 135 | 1,885 | 2,750 | 265 | 180 | 3,195 |
| Dipak | 460 | 210 | 125 | 1,705 | 2,500 | 230 | 165 | 2,895 |
|  | 1,510 | 690 | 410 | 5,640 | 8,250 | 805 | 545 | 9,600 |

When using the **wages control account** the objective is that at the end of the process the account balance clears to zero: it is a clearing account. This will affirm that the double entry has been made correctly, though compensating errors could still exist.

The first step is to account for net pay. Net pay is gross pay less deductions; we could debit it straight to the nominal ledger wages expense account, but instead we 'collect' all the entries in the wages control account:

|  |  | £ | £ |
|---|---|---|---|
| DEBIT | Wages control account | 5,640 |  |
| CREDIT | Cash at bank |  | 5,640 |
|  | *Payment of net pay to staff* |  |  |

The next step is to record those amounts which will be paid to outside agencies on behalf of employees. All employees' wages deductions have to be paid eventually to either HMRC or pension trustees, so at some point these will need to be credited to liability accounts – but where will the debit go to? Again, the answer is initially to the wages control account:

|  |  | £ | £ |
|---|---|---|---|
| DEBIT | Wages control account (1,510 + 690 + 410) | 2,610 | |
| CREDIT | HMRC (1,510 + 690) | | 2,200 |
| | Pension trustee | | 410 |
| | *Deductions from pay* | | |

Finally, we record the amounts which are payable to external agencies directly by the entity. The employers' NI and pension contributions also need to be credited to liability accounts – but where will the debit go to? Again, the answer is initially to the wages control account:

|  |  | £ | £ |
|---|---|---|---|
| DEBIT | Wages control account (805 + 545) | 1,350 | |
| CREDIT | HMRC | | 805 |
| | Pension trustee | | 545 |
| | *Additional employer costs* | | |

After these entries have been made the wages control account will look like this:

### WAGES CONTROL ACCOUNT

| | £ | | £ |
|---|---|---|---|
| Cash at bank (net pay) | 5,640 | Balance | 9,600 |
| HMRC (PAYE) | 1,510 | | |
| HMRC (Ees' NIC) | 690 | | |
| Pension trustee (Ees' pension) | 410 | | |
| HMRC (Er's NIC) | 805 | | |
| Pension trustee (Er's pension) | 545 | | |
| | 9,600 | | 9,600 |

The wages control account balance represents the total payroll cost to the business, which should be a debit in its wages expense account. Therefore, the final entry to bring the wages control account to zero is:

|  |  | £ | £ |
|---|---|---|---|
| DEBIT | Wages expense | 9,600 | |
| CREDIT | Wages control | | 9,600 |
| | *Total payroll costs for period* | | |

We could have omitted the wages control account entirely and just done one big journal as follows:

|  |  | £ | £ |
|---|---|---|---|
| DEBIT | Wages expense (gross pay + er's NI and er's pension) | 9,600 | |
| CREDIT | Cash at bank (net pay) | | 5,640 |
| | HMRC (PAYE + ees' NI + er's NI) | | 3,005 |
| | Pension trustee (ees' and er's) | | 955 |
| | *Total payroll costs for period* | | |

Many businesses use a wages control account so that the accuracy of the initial postings can be verified before making the final posting to wages expense.

# 3 The purpose of control accounts

**Section overview**

- Control accounts duplicate in summary form the individual entries in the memorandum ledgers: provide a check on the accuracy of postings; help to locate errors; provide an internal check; allow a total balance to be extracted quickly and easily; keep the number of nominal ledger accounts to a minimum.

- The receivables and payables ledger control accounts must be reconciled to the list of individual balances on the relevant memorandum ledger: strike a balance on all personal accounts; total the balances in the memorandum ledger; compare this total with the control account balance; identify reasons for failure to agree; prepare reconciliation statement; draw up correcting journals and post.

## 3.1 Why do we use control accounts?

- They help **check the accuracy** of entries made in the personal accounts. With hundreds of entries to make it is very easy to make a mistake posting entries. Figures can get **transposed**. Some entries might be **omitted** altogether, so that an invoice or a payment transaction does not appear in a personal account as it should. By performing (i) and (ii) below, it is possible to identify the fact that such errors have been made.

    (i) The receivables control account balance is compared with the total of individual balances on the personal accounts in the receivables ledger.

    (ii) The payables control account balance is compared with the total of individual balances on the personal accounts in the payables ledger.

- They help us **locate errors** in postings promptly. If a clerk fails to record an invoice or a payment in a personal account, or makes a transposition error, it would be difficult to locate the error or errors at the end of a year, say, given the number of transactions. By using the control account regularly, a comparison with the individual balances in the receivables or payables ledger can be made for every week or day of the month, and the error found much more quickly than if control accounts did not exist.

- They **provide an internal check** where there is a separation of clerical (bookkeeping) duties. The person posting entries to the control accounts will act as a check on the different person(s) whose job it is to post entries to the receivables and payables ledger accounts.

- They **provide total receivables and payables balances** more quickly for producing a trial balance or statement of financial position. A single balance on a control account is extracted more simply and quickly than individual balances in the receivables or payables ledger.

- They keep the number of accounts in the trial balance down to a **manageable size**, since the personal accounts are memorandum accounts only.

In computerised systems receivables and payables ledgers are often used without separate control accounts. In such systems, the receivables or payables ledger printouts produced by the computer constitute the list of individual balances as well as providing the total control account balance.

**Unless told otherwise in the exam, you should assume that a control account is part of the nominal ledger, with individual personal accounts kept in memorandum ledgers.**

## 3.2 Balancing and agreeing control accounts with the memorandum ledgers

The control accounts should be **balanced regularly** and the balance **agreed** with the sum of the individual customers' or suppliers' balances extracted from the receivables or payables ledgers respectively.

The balance on the control account **may not agree** with the sum of balances extracted, for one or more of the following reasons.

- The **total column in the book of original entry may be miscast** so an **incorrect amount** is **posted** to the control account (ie adding up incorrectly the total value of invoices, receipts or payments).

  Effect:

  – The nominal ledger debit and credit postings will balance, as both nominal ledger accounts will be incorrect.

  – The control account balance will not agree with the (correct) sum of individual balances extracted from the receivables ledger or payables ledger.

  Correction:

  – A journal entry must be made in the nominal ledger to correct the control account and the corresponding sales/VAT or expense/VAT accounts.

- An incorrect amount may be posted to an individual's personal account from the book of original entry to the memorandum ledger, eg a sale to C Cloning of £250 might be posted to his account as £520.

  Effect:

  – The nominal ledger would not be affected, as £250 would be correctly included in the total of the sales day book and posted.

  – The receivables ledger would be incorrect, since it contains a transposition error in recording £250 as £520. It is too high.

  – The two would not agree.

  Correction:

  – The sum of the memorandum ledger balances must be corrected, so in this case the total will decrease by £270. No entry in the nominal ledger is required.

- A transaction may be **recorded in the control account** and *not* in the **memorandum ledger**, or *vice versa*. This requires an entry in the ledger that has been missed out, which means a double entry posting if the control account has to be corrected, and a single entry if it is the individual's personal account in the memorandum ledger that is at fault.

- The list of balances extracted from the memorandum ledger may be **incorrectly extracted or miscast**. This would involve simply correcting the total of the balances.

### Worked example: Agreeing control account balance with the ledger

Reconciling the control account balance with the sum of the balances extracted from the receivables ledger should be done in two stages, though these stages can be completed simultaneously.

(1)  Correct the total of the balances extracted from the memorandum ledger. (The errors must be located first of course.)

|  | £ | £ |
|---|---|---|
| *Receivables ledger total* | | |
| Original total extracted | | 15,320 |
| Add difference arising from transposition error on | | |
| SDB posting of invoice (£95 written as £59) | | 36 |
| | | 15,356 |
| Less | | |
| Credit balance of £60 extracted as a debit balance (£60 × 2) | 120 | |
| Overcast of list of balances | 90 | |
| | | (210) |
| | | 15,146 |

(2) Bring down the balance on the control account, and adjust or post the account with correcting entries.

### RECEIVABLES CONTROL ACCOUNT

| | £ | | £ |
|---|---|---|---|
| Balance before adjustments | 15,091 | Cash book: posting omitted | 10 |
| Undercast of total invoices issued | | Credit note: Individual posting from SDB | |
| in sales day book | 100 | omitted from control account | 35 |
| | | Balance c/d (now in agreement | |
| | | with the corrected total of | |
| | | individual balances in (1)) | 15,146 |
| | 15,191 | | 15,191 |
| Balance b/d | 15,146 | | |

## Interactive question 4: Receivables control account

April Showers sells goods on credit to most of its customers and maintains a receivables control account. For the year to 30 October 20X3 the accountant discovers that the total of all personal accounts in the receivables ledger is £12,802, whereas the receivables control account balance is £12,550.

The following errors are discovered.

(a) Sales for the week ending 27 March 20X3 amounting to £850 had been omitted from the control account.

(b) A customer's debit balance of £300 had not been included in the list of balances.

(c) Cash received of £750 had been entered in a personal account as £570.

(d) Discount allowed totalling £100 had not been entered in the control account.

(e) A personal account debit balance had been undercast by £200.

(f) A contra item of £400 with the payables ledger had not been entered in the control account.

(g) An irrecoverable debt of £500 had not been entered in the control account.

(h) Cash received of £250 had been debited to a personal account.

(i) Discounts received of £50 had been debited to Bell's receivables ledger account.

(j) A Credit note for £200 had been omitted from the casting of the sales day book.

(k) Cash received of £80 had been credited to a personal account as £8.

(l) A cheque for £300 received from a customer and entered in the control account and personal account had been dishonoured by the bank, but no adjustment had been made in the control account.

### Requirements

(a) Prepare a corrected receivables control account, bringing down the amended balance as at 1 November 20X3.

(b) Prepare a statement showing the adjustments that are necessary to the list of personal account balances so that it reconciles with the amended receivables control account balance.

See **Answer** at the end of this chapter.

# 4 The cash at bank account, the cash book and the bank statement

## Section overview

- The cash at bank account in the nominal ledger is the control account for the cash book, although often they are one and the same.

- The cash at bank account, the cash book and the bank statement all reflect transactions through the business's bank account.

In many businesses, the **cash book** (comprising both receipts and payments) acts as both the book of original entry for all transactions affecting the bank account, and as the nominal ledger account for cash at bank.

Where there is a separate **cash at bank account** in the nominal ledger, making sure that its balance at the end of a period agrees with the balance carried down on the cash book at the same time is a useful accuracy and completion check.

In the case of cash at bank, there is another important control check: agreeing the **cash book balance** in the business's ledger accounts with the balance reported to it by the **bank statement**.

## 4.1 The cash book and the cash at bank account

So far in this Study Manual we have seen that:

- The **cash book** is the book of original entry for all transactions related to the company's bank account.

- The **cash at bank** account is the nominal ledger account (part of the double entry system) that is the permanent record of the business's bank transactions.

In some accounting systems the cash at bank account is posted only monthly or so from the cash book, with totals:

| | | | |
|---|---|---|---|
| DR | Cash at bank (with cash received) | CR | Corresponding income, asset, liability and capital accounts |
| CR | Cash at bank (with cash paid) | DR | Corresponding expense, asset, liability and capital accounts |

Once these postings have been made the business can be sure that its nominal ledger accounts are up to date, but in practice there is a lot of work involved in getting the cash book right before the postings can be made. This is because the cash book is essentially a record of what goes on in the business's bank account, and there are quite often discrepancies that need to be resolved, with the help of the bank statement.

In practice, it is common for the cash book to be treated as a ledger account in that balances are regularly extracted. The business always wants to know its cash balance, as this is a vital asset.

## 4.2 The bank statement

### Definition

**Bank statement:** A record of transactions on the business's bank account maintained by the bank in its own books.

### 4.2.1 Mirror image of the cash book

The bank statement is the mirror image of the cash book:

- Cash is an **asset** (a debit balance) in the business's ledger accounts. As far as the bank is concerned it owes the business money. Thus every item recorded as a debit in the business's books – a **positive bank balance, and any receipts of cash** – will be shown as a **credit on the bank statement**.

- When cash is a **liability** (a credit balance) in the business's books, as far as the bank is concerned it is owed money. Thus every credit entry in the business's books – a **negative bank balance, and any payments of cash** – will be shown as a **debit on the bank statement**.

### 4.2.2 Disagreement with the cash book

It is rare for the balance as shown on the bank statement to be the same as that on the cash book.

There are five common explanations for **differences between cash book and bank statement**.

- **Error.** Errors in calculation, or recording revenue and payments, may have been made in the business cash book, by the bank, or by both.

- **Unrecorded bank charges or bank interest.** The bank might charge interest or make charges for its services, which the customer is not informed about and so cannot record until the bank statement is received.

- **Automated payments and receipts.** Payments processed automatically by the banking system (direct debits and standing orders), and receipts processed automatically, may be shown on the bank statement, but not yet recorded in the cash book.

- **Dishonoured cheques.** When a customer sends in a cheque and it is banked, the business debits the cash book. However, it may be returned unpaid or 'dishonoured' by the customer's bank, usually because the customer has insufficient funds. The dishonour of the cheque will appear on the bank statement and will need to be 'written back' in the ledger accounts:

  | | | |
  |---|---|---|
  | DEBIT | Receivables | £X |
  | CREDIT | Cash at bank | £X |

- **Timing differences**

  - There may be some **cheques received**, recorded in the cash book and paid into the bank, but which have not yet been 'cleared' (paid by the bank) and added to the account by the bank. So although the business's records show that some cash has been added to the account, it has not yet been acknowledged by the bank – although it will be soon, once the cheque has cleared.

  - Similarly, the business might have made some **payments by cheque**, and reduced the balance in the cash book accordingly, but the person who receives the cheque might not bank it for a while. Even when it is banked, it takes a day or two for the bank to process it and for the money to be deducted from the account.

All these differences need to be identified and eradicated, using the **bank reconciliation** process.

# 5 The bank reconciliation

## Section overview

- The cash book needs to be regularly reconciled to the bank statement.

- The cash book and bank statement usually fail to agree because of: errors in the cash book or by the bank; bank charges and interest not entered in the cash book; automated payments and receipts not entered in the cash book; customers' cheques dishonoured or returned unpaid by the bank, not entered in the cash book; timing differences between the cash book and the bank statement (the cash book is usually more up-to-date: unpresented cheques and uncredited lodgements).

- Often correcting or additional entries are needed in the cash book as a result of the bank reconciliation; the bank statement then agrees/reconciles with the corrected cash book balance once timing differences are taken into account.

## Definition

**Bank reconciliation:** A comparison of a bank statement (sent monthly, weekly or even daily by the bank) with the cash book. Differences between the balance on the bank statement and the balance in the cash book should be identified and satisfactorily reconciled.

---

When doing a bank reconciliation, you will have to look for the following items on the bank statement and in the cash book.

(a) **Errors in the cash book**, such as transposition errors (eg writing £36 and £63) or cheques sent out but omitted from the cash book. The correct amount appears on the bank statement and the cash book must be updated.

(b) **Corrections and adjustments to the cash book**

    (i) Payments made into or from the bank account by way of debit card, standing order, direct debit or online transfer which have not yet been entered in the cash book.

    (ii) Bank interest and bank charges, not yet entered in the cash book.

    (iii) Dishonoured cheques not yet entered in the cash book.

(c) **Errors in the bank statement**, such as transposition errors, payments or receipts recorded twice or interest and fees deducted incorrectly. The correct amount appears in the cash book and the balance per the bank statement must be corrected.

(d) **Items reconciling the correct cash book balance to the bank statement (timing differences)**

    (i) Cheques paid out by the business and credited in the cash book which have not yet been presented to the bank, or 'cleared', and so do not yet appear on the bank statement. These are known as '**unpresented cheques**'.

    (ii) Cheques received by the business, paid into the bank and debited in the cash book, but which have not yet been cleared and entered in the bank account, and so do not yet appear on the bank statement. These are known as '**uncleared lodgements**'.

## Worked example: Bank reconciliation I

At 30 September 20X6, the balance in Wordsworth Co's cash book was £805.15 debit. A bank statement on 30 September 20X6 showed Wordsworth Co to be in credit at the bank by £1,112.30.

On investigation of the difference, it was established that:

(a)   The cash book had been undercast by £90.00 on the debit side.
(b)   Cheques paid in but not yet credited by the bank were £208.20.
(c)   Cheques drawn not yet presented to the bank were £425.35.

We need to show the correction to the cash book, then prepare a statement reconciling the balance per the bank statement to the balance per the cash book.

## Solution

(a)

|  | £ |
|---|---|
| Cash book balance brought forward | 805.15 |
| Add | |
| Correction of undercast | 90.00 |
| Corrected cash book balance | 895.15 |

(b)

|  | £ |
|---|---|
| Balance per bank statement | 1,112.30 |
| Add | |
| Uncleared lodgements | 208.20 |
|  | 1,320.50 |
| Less | |
| Unpresented cheques | (425.35) |
| Balance per corrected cash book | 895.15 |

---

## Worked example: Bank reconciliation II

At his year end of 30 June 20X0, Cook's cash book showed that he had an overdraft of £300 on his current account at the bank. A bank statement as at 30 June 20X0 showed that Cook has an overdraft of £35.

On checking the cash book and the bank statement you find the following.

(a)   Cheques drawn, amounting to £500, had been entered in the cash book but had not yet been presented.

(b)   Cheques received, amounting to £400, had been entered in the cash book, but had not yet been credited by the bank.

(c)   On instructions from Cook on 30 June 20X0 the bank had transferred £60 interest received on his savings account to his current account, but it only recorded the transfer on 5 July 20X0. This amount was credited in the cash book on 30 June 20X0.

(d)   Bank charges of £35 shown in the bank statement had not been entered in the cash book.

(e)   The payments side of the cash book had been undercast by £10.

(f)   Dividends received of £200 had been paid direct into the bank and not entered in the cash book.

(g)   A cheque for £50 from Sunil was recorded and banked on 24 June. This was returned unpaid on 30 June and then shown as a debit on the bank statement. No entry has been made in the cash book for the unpaid cheque.

(h)   A cheque issued to Jones for £25 was replaced when it was more than six months old, at which time it had become 'out of date' and the bank would have refused to pay it. It was entered again in the cash book, no other entry being made. Both cheques were included in the total of unpresented cheques shown above.

We need to make the appropriate adjustments in the cash book, then prepare a statement reconciling the amended balance with that shown in the bank statement.

## Solution

The errors to correct in the cash book are given in notes (c), (e), (f), (g) and (h) of the problem. Bank charges (note (d)) also call for an adjustment.

Item (c) is rather complicated. The transfer of interest from the deposit to the current account was given as an instruction to the bank on 30 June 20X0, probably because that is Cook's year end and he wants to make sure that all transactions are recorded. Since the correct entry should have been to debit the current account (and credit the deposit account) the correction in the cash book should be to debit the current account with $2 \times £60 = £120$ – ie to cancel out the incorrect credit entry in the cash book, and then to make the correct debit entry. However, the bank does not record the transfer until 5 July, and so it will not appear in the bank statement.

Item (h) also requires explanation. Two cheques have been paid to Jones, but one is now cancelled. Since the cash book is credited whenever a cheque is paid, it should be debited whenever a cheque is cancelled. The amount of unpresented cheques should be reduced by the amount of the cancelled cheque.

### CASH BOOK

| 20X0 | | £ | 20X0 | | £ |
|---|---|---|---|---|---|
| Jun 30 | Savings interest 60 × 2(c) | 120 | Jun 30 | Balance b/d | 300 |
| | Dividends paid direct | | | Bank charges (d) | 35 |
| | to bank (f) | 200 | | Correction of undercast (e) | 10 |
| | Cheque issued to Jones | | | Dishonoured cheque (g) | 50 |
| | cancelled (h) | 25 | | | |
| | Balance c/d | 50 | | | |
| | | 395 | | | 395 |

### BANK RECONCILIATION STATEMENT AT 30 JUNE 20X0

| | £ | £ |
|---|---|---|
| Balance per bank statement | | (35) |
| Add   Outstanding lodgements | 400 | |
| Savings interest not yet credited | 60 | |
| | | 460 |
| | | 425 |
| Less   Unpresented cheques | 500 | |
| Less cheque to Jones cancelled | (25) | |
| | | (475) |
| Balance per corrected cash book | | (50) |

In a bank reconciliation you should begin with the balance shown by the bank statement and end with the balance shown by the corrected cash book. This corrected cash book balance will appear in the statement of financial position as 'cash at bank'.

**In answering an exam question however, you should expect to work the other way round on occasion.**

---

### Interactive question 5: Bank reconciliation I

A bank reconciliation statement is being prepared. Using the table select the effect of each of the following on the closing balance shown by the bank statement of £388 in hand. (The closing balance shown by the cash book is £106 in hand.) Tick **one** box for each finding.

| | | Increase | Decrease | No effect |
|---|---|---|---|---|
| A | The bank has made a mistake in crediting the account with £110 belonging to another customer – an error not yet rectified. | ☐ | ☐ | ☐ |
| B | £120 received by the bank under a standing order arrangement has not been entered in the cash book. | ☐ | ☐ | ☐ |
| C | Cheques totalling £5,629 have been drawn, entered in the cash book and sent out to suppliers but they have not been presented for payment. | ☐ | ☐ | ☐ |
| D | Cheques totalling £5,577 have been received and entered in the cash book but not yet credited in the bank statements. | ☐ | ☐ | ☐ |

See **Answer** at the end of this chapter.

### Interactive question 6: Bank reconciliation II

Tilfer's bank statement shows £715 direct debits and £353 investment income not recorded in the cash book. The bank statement does not show a customer's cheque for £875 entered in the cash book on the last day of the reporting period. The cash book has a credit balance of £610.

What balance appears on the bank statement?

See **Answer** at the end of this chapter.

## 6  Types of error in accounting

### Section overview

- Errors can be classified as: errors of commission or omission, compensating errors, errors of principle and transposition errors.

- Many errors in the ledger accounts are detected during the control account reconciliation and bank reconciliation processes.

There are **five broad types of error** as follows.

- **Transposition** errors
- Errors of **omission**
- Errors of **principle**
- Errors of **commission**
- **Compensating errors**

Once an error has been detected, it needs to be put right.

- If the correction **involves a double entry** in the nominal ledger accounts, then it is recorded via an **entry** in the journal.

- When the error **breaks the rule of double entry**, then it is corrected via a journal entry using a **suspense account** to complete the double entry.

## 6.1 Transposition errors

### Definition

**Transposition errors:** When two digits in an amount are accidentally recorded the wrong way round.

- A sale is credited in the sales account as £6,843, but has been incorrectly debited in the receivables control account as £6,483. In consequence total debits will not equal to total credits: credits will exceed debits by 6,843 – 6,483 = 360. You can often detect a transposition error by checking whether the difference between debits and credits can be divided exactly by 9 (£360 ÷ 9 = £40).

## 6.2 Errors of omission

### Definition

**Error of omission:** Failing to record a transaction at all, or making a debit or credit entry, but not the corresponding double entry.

- A business receives an invoice from a supplier for £250, and the transaction is omitted from the books. As a result, both total debits **and** credits will be wrong by £250.

- A business receives an invoice from a supplier for £300, the payables control account is credited but no debit entry is made. In this case, the total credits would not equal total debits (because total debits are £300 less than they ought to be).

## 6.3 Errors of principle

### Definition

**Error of principle:** Making a double entry in the belief that the transaction is being entered in the correct accounts, but subsequently finding out that the accounting entry breaks the 'rules' of an accounting principle or concept. A typical example of such an error is to treat revenue expenditure incorrectly as capital expenditure.

- Machine repairs costing £150 (which should be treated as revenue expenditure) are debited to the cost of a non-current asset (capital expenditure). Although total debits still equal total credits, the repairs account is £150 understated and the cost of the non-current asset is £150 overstated.

- A business owner takes £280 cash out of the till for his personal use. The bookkeeper incorrectly debits sales by £280, when they should have debited drawings. This is an error of principle, so that drawings and sales are both understated by £280.

## 6.4 Errors of commission

### Definition

**Error of commission:** A mistake is made in recording transactions in the ledger accounts.

- **Putting a debit entry or a credit entry in the wrong account.** Telephone expenses of £540 are debited to the electricity expense account, an error of commission. Although total debits and credits balance, telephone expenses are understated by £540 and electricity expense is overstated by the same amount.

- **Casting errors (adding up).** Daily credit sales in the sales day book of £28,425 are incorrectly added up ('miscast') as £28,825. This amount is credited to sales and debited to receivables control. Although total debits and total credits are still equal, the nominal ledger is incorrect by £400. Note that if the correct individual entries are made in the receivables ledger, the total on the list of balances will be right, but it will not agree with the receivables control account balance.

## 6.5 Compensating errors

### Definition

Compensating errors: Errors which are, coincidentally, equal and opposite to one another.

---

**Compensating errors hide trial balance errors.**

- Administrative expenses of £2,822 are entered as £2,282 in the administrative expenses ledger account. At the same time, income of £8,931 is shown in the sales account as £8,391. Both debits and credits are £540 too low, and the mistake would not be apparent when the trial balance is cast.

# 7 Correcting errors

### Section overview
- Errors which have not caused an imbalance are corrected via journals.
- Errors which have broken the rules of double entry bookkeeping and result in the trial balance failing to balance can be corrected by (1) setting up a suspense account and then (2) clearing it with correcting journals.
- A suspense account may also be deliberately set up when a bookkeeper does not know where to put one side of an entry.
- Suspense accounts are always temporary and should never appear in financial statements; these should not be prepared until the errors have been corrected and the suspense account has been cleared.
- Some corrections of errors will result in adjustments to a draft profit calculated while there were still errors in the accounts.

Errors which leave total debits and credits in the ledger accounts in balance can be corrected just using **journal entries**.

Where errors mean that the trial balance does not balance, a **suspense account** has to be opened first, later cleared by a **journal entry**.

## 7.1 Journal entries

The journal requires a debit and an equal credit entry for each correction.

- If total debits equal total credits before a journal entry is made then they will still be equal after the journal entry is made, as would be the case if, for example, the original error was a debit wrongly posted as a credit and vice versa.
- If total debits and total credits are unequal before a journal entry is made, then they will still be unequal (by the same amount) after it is made.

### Worked example: Correcting errors with journal entries

A bookkeeper accidentally posts an invoice for £40 to the local property taxes account instead of to the electricity account. A trial balance is drawn up. Total debits are £40,000 and total credits are £40,000. A journal entry is made to correct the misposting error as follows.

| | | | |
|---|---|---|---|
| DEBIT | Electricity account | £40 | |
| CREDIT | Local property taxes account | | £40 |

*To correct a misposting of £40 from the local property taxes account to electricity account*

After the journal has been posted, total debits and credits will still be equal at £40,000.

Now suppose that, because of some error which has not yet been detected, total debits were originally £40,000 but total credits were £39,900. If the same journal correcting the £40 is put through, total debits will remain £40,000 and total credits will remain £39,900. Total debits were different by £100 **before** the journal, and they are still different by £100 **after** the journal.

---

This means that **journals alone can only be used to correct errors which require both a credit and (an equal) debit adjustment**.

In a question which requires a 'correcting journal'

- Work out **first** what the original entry was
- **Then** what the original entry should have been
- And **finally** what the correcting entry should be

### Interactive question 7: Journal entries

Write out the journal entries which would correct these errors.

(a) A business receives an invoice for £250 from a supplier which was omitted from the books entirely.

(b) Repairs worth £150 were incorrectly debited to the non-current asset (machinery) account instead of the repairs account.

(c) The bookkeeper of a business reduces cash sales by £280 because he was not sure what the £280 represented. In fact, it was drawings.

(d) Telephone expenses of £540 are incorrectly debited to the electricity account.

(e) A page in the sales day book has been added up to £28,425 instead of £28,825.

See **Answer** at the end of this chapter.

---

## 7.2 Suspense accounts

### Definition

Suspense account: An account showing a balance equal to the difference in a trial balance.

---

A suspense account is a **temporary** account which can be opened for the following reasons.

- A trial balance is drawn up which **does not balance** (ie total debits do not equal total credits).

- The bookkeeper of a business knows where to post one side of a transaction, **but does not know where to post the other side**. For example, a cash payment must obviously be credited to cash, but the bookkeeper may not know what the payment is for, and so will not know which account to debit. To complete the double entry, he debits suspense.

In both these cases, a **suspense account** is opened up until the problem is resolved.

## 7.3 Using a suspense account when the trial balance does not balance

When an error has occurred which results in an imbalance between total debits and total credits in the ledger accounts:

### Step 1
Open a suspense account with the amount of the imbalance

### Step 2
Use a journal entry to clear the suspense account and correct the error. It is good practice for the correcting side of the double entry to appear first in the journal, then the suspense account entry.

### Worked example: Suspense account

An accountant draws up a trial balance and finds that total debits exceed total credits by £162.

He knows that there is an error somewhere, but for the time being he opens a **suspense account** with a credit balance of £162. This serves two purposes.

- As the suspense account now exists, the accountant will not forget that there is an error (of £162) to be sorted out.

- Now that there is a credit of £162 in the suspense account, the trial balance balances.

When the cause of the £162 discrepancy is tracked down, it is corrected by means of a **journal entry**. Suppose the error was an omitted credit of £162 to the purchases account. The correcting journal entry is:

| | | | |
|---|---|---|---|
| CREDIT | Purchases | | £162 |
| DEBIT | Suspense a/c | £162 | |

*To close off suspense a/c and correct error of omission*

---

### Worked example: Suspense account and transposition error

Instead of entering the correct amount of £37,453 in the sales account, a bookkeeper entered £37,543 Trade receivables were posted correctly, so on the trial balance **credits exceeded debits** by £(37,543 − 37,453) = £90.

### Step 1
Equalise the total debits and credits by posting a **debit** of £90 to the suspense account.

### Step 2
Correcting journal entry: sales need to be reduced, and the suspense account needs to be cleared.

| | | | |
|---|---|---|---|
| DEBIT | Sales | £90 | |
| CREDIT | Suspense a/c | | £90 |

*To close off suspense a/c and correct transposition error*

---

## Worked example: Error of omission

A cheque payment of £250 was correctly credited to the cash account, but the bookkeeper omitted to debit the expense account. On the trial balance, credits exceeded debits by £250.

### Step 1

Debit £250 to the suspense account, to equalise the total debits and total credits.

### Step 2

Correcting journal entry: expenses need to be increased, and the suspense account cleared.

| | | | |
|---|---|---|---|
| DEBIT | Expense account | £250 | |
| CREDIT | Suspense a/c | | £250 |

*To close off suspense a/c and correct error of omission*

## Worked example: Error of commission

A cheque received for £460 is debited to cash but also debited to receivables control, instead of being credited.

The total debit balances now exceed the total credits by 2 × £460 = £920.

### Step 1

Make a credit entry of £920 in a suspense account, to equalise debits and credits.

### Step 2

Correcting journal entry: decrease trade receivables, and clear the suspense account.

| | | | |
|---|---|---|---|
| CREDIT | Trade receivables | | £920 |
| DEBIT | Suspense a/c | £920 | |

*To close off suspense a/c and correct error of commission*

## 7.4 Using a suspense account to complete the double entry

When a bookkeeper does not know where to post one side of a transaction, it can be temporarily recorded in a suspense account. A typical example is when the business receives cash through the post from a source which cannot be determined. The double entry in the accounts would be a debit in the cash book, and a credit to a suspense account.

## Worked example: Not knowing where to post a transaction

Windfall Garments banks a cheque for £620 from R J Beasley. The business has no idea who this person is, nor why he should be sending £620. The bookkeeper opens a suspense account:

| | | | |
|---|---|---|---|
| DEBIT | Cash | £620 | |
| CREDIT | Suspense a/c | | £620 |

It transpires that the cheque was in payment for a debt owed by the Haute Couture Corner Shop and paid out of the owner's personal bank account. The suspense account can now be cleared, as follows.

| | | | |
|---|---|---|---|
| CREDIT | Trade receivables | | £620 |
| DEBIT | Suspense a/c | £620 | |

## 7.5 Suspense accounts might contain several items

All errors and unidentifiable postings in a reporting period are merged together in the suspense account; until the cause of each error is discovered, the bookkeeper is unlikely to know exactly how many errors there are.

**An exam question might give you a suspense account balance, together with information to make corrections which will leave a nil balance on the suspense account and correct balances on the nominal ledger accounts.**

## 7.6 Suspense accounts are temporary

It must be stressed that a **suspense account should only be temporary**. Postings to a suspense account are only made when the bookkeeper doesn't know yet what to do, or when an error has occurred.

**There should be no suspense account when it comes to preparing the statement of profit or loss and statement of financial position. The suspense account should be cleared and all correcting entries made before the final financial statements are drawn up.**

## 7.7 Adjustment of profits for errors

Correcting errors can affect either the statement of financial position, the statement of profit or loss, or sometimes both. An error of omission corrected by debiting sales and crediting suspense with £90 meant that sales decreased, so gross profit was reduced by £90 as a result of the error being corrected.

If there are still errors to be corrected after the trial balance and initial statement of profit or loss and statement of financial position have been prepared, then corrections will alter those draft financial statements.

You may need to demonstrate how draft financial statements are affected by error corrections by calculating:

- How much gross or net profit is increased or reduced as a result of error correction
- The final gross or net profit after the error correction

### Interactive question 8: Errors

At T Down & Co year end, the trial balance contained a suspense account with a credit balance of £1,040.

Investigations revealed the following errors.

(i) A sale of goods on credit for £1,000 had been omitted from the sales account.

(ii) Delivery and installation costs of £240 on a new item of plant had been recorded as revenue expenditure in the distribution costs account.

(iii) Cash discount of £150 had been taken on paying a supplier, JW, even though the payment was made outside the time limit. JW is insisting that £150 is still payable.

(iv) A raw materials purchase of £350 had been recorded in the purchases account as £850, but the trade payables account was correctly written up.

(v) The purchases day book included a credit note for £230 as an invoice in the total column. The correct entry was made in the purchases account.

**Requirements**

(a) Prepare journal entries to correct **each** of the above errors. Narratives are **not** required.

(b) Open a suspense account and show the corrections to be made.

(c) Before the errors were corrected, T Down & Co's gross profit was calculated at £35,750 and the net profit for the year at £18,500. Calculate the revised gross and net profit figures after correction of the errors.

See **Answer** at the end of this chapter.

# 8 Correcting errors via the ETB

**Section overview**

- The journals which correct errors and make other adjustments can be put through the adjustments columns of the extended trial balance.

In Chapter 5 we saw how an extended trial balance made the preparation of the statement of profit or loss and statement of financial position easier and more clear-cut. The ETB is also useful when recording correcting journals made at the final stages of preparing financial statements, after the initial trial balance has been prepared. This is especially the case where a suspense account had to be used to make the trial balance agree.

As well as debit and credit columns for the TB, the statement of profit or loss and the statement of financial position, in a full ETB we include debit and credit columns for adjustments between the TB and the statement of profit or loss; we don't bother with a revised TB, as we initially used in Chapter 5. Instead the entries in the adjustment columns just get included in the cross-casting to the statement of profit or loss and statement of financial position columns.

**Worked example: Error correction on the ETB**

Handle extracted a trial balance and created a suspense account. He inserted the TB on his extended trial balance as follows:

| Ledger balance | Trial balance | | Adjustments | | Statement of profit or loss | | Statement of financial position | |
|---|---|---|---|---|---|---|---|---|
| | Debit | Credit | Debit | Credit | Debit | Credit | Debit | Credit |
| | £ | £ | £ | £ | £ | £ | £ | £ |
| Cash at bank | 5,415 | | | | | | | |
| Opening capital | | 10,000 | | | | | | |
| Loan | | 5,000 | | | | | | |
| Non-current assets | 30,000 | | | | | | | |
| Trade payables | | 18,689 | | | | | | |
| Expenses | 6,781 | | | | | | | |
| Purchases | 21,569 | | | | | | | |
| Sales | | 38,974 | | | | | | |
| Trade receivables | 9,445 | | | | | | | |
| Suspense | | 6,400 | | | | | | |
| Drawings | 5,853 | | | | | | | |
| Net profit | | | | | | | | |
| | 79,063 | 79,063 | | | | | | |

Handle has now discovered the following matters:

(a) An amount of £1,000 was credited on the bank statement in the year and entered in the cash book, but no other entry was made as the bookkeeper did not know what the receipt was in respect of. Handle tells you it was a payment on account from a major customer.

(b) A non-current asset was purchased on credit just before the year end, for £9,300. This was incorrectly entered in the trade payables account via a journal as £3,900, but the correct entry was made in non-current assets.

To correct these errors Handle uses the following journals:

| | | | £ | £ |
|---|---|---|---|---|
| (a) | CREDIT | Trade receivables | | 1,000 |
| | DEBIT | Suspense | 1,000 | |
| | | | | |
| (b) | CREDIT | Trade payables | | 5,400 |
| | DEBIT | Suspense | 5,400 | |

These are entered in the adjustments columns of the ETB, which is then cross-cast to produce Handle's statement of profit or loss and statement of financial position:

| Ledger balance | Trial balance | | Adjustments | | Statement of profit or loss | | Statement of financial position | |
|---|---|---|---|---|---|---|---|---|
| | Debit £ | Credit £ | Debit £ | Credit £ | Debit £ | Credit £ | Debit £ | Credit £ |
| Cash at bank | 5,415 | | | | | | 5,415 | |
| Opening capital | | 10,000 | | | | | | 10,000 |
| Loan | | 5,000 | | | | | | 5,000 |
| Non-current assets | 30,000 | | | | | | 30,000 | |
| Trade payables | | 18,689 | | 5,400 | | | | 24,089 |
| Expenses | 6,781 | | | | 6,781 | | | |
| Purchases | 21,569 | | | | 21,569 | | | |
| Sales | | 38,974 | | | | 38,974 | | |
| Trade receivables | 9,445 | | | 1,000 | | | 8,445 | |
| Suspense | | 6,400 | 6,400 | | | | | |
| Drawings | 5,853 | | | | | | 5,853 | |
| Net profit | | | | | 10,624 | | | 10,624 |
| | 79,063 | 79,063 | 6,400 | 6,400 | 38,974 | 38,974 | 49,713 | 49,713 |

No balance remains on the suspense account.

# Summary and Self-test

## Summary (1/2)

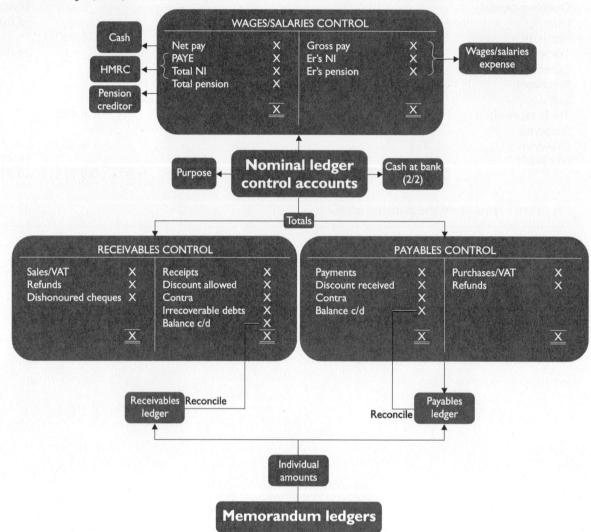

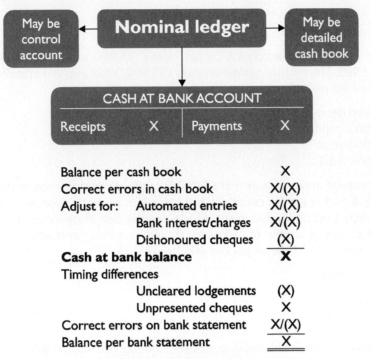

| CASH AT BANK ACCOUNT | | | |
|---|---|---|---|
| Receipts | X | Payments | X |

| | | |
|---|---|---|
| Balance per cash book | | X |
| Correct errors in cash book | | X/(X) |
| Adjust for: | Automated entries | X/(X) |
| | Bank interest/charges | X/(X) |
| | Dishonoured cheques | (X) |
| **Cash at bank balance** | | **X** |
| Timing differences | | |
| | Uncleared lodgements | (X) |
| | Unpresented cheques | X |
| Correct errors on bank statement | | X/(X) |
| Balance per bank statement | | X |

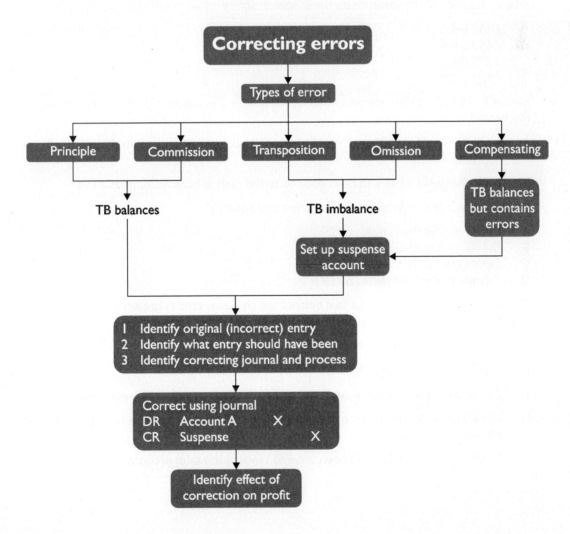

ICAEW

## Self-test

Answer the following questions.

1    On its receivables control account A Co has: sales £125,000, cash received £50,000, discounts allowed £2,000. The balance carried down is £95,000. What was the opening balance at the beginning of the period?

     A    £22,000 debit
     B    £22,000 credit
     C    £18,000 debit
     D    £20,000 debit

2    A bank statement shows a balance of £1,200 in credit. An examination of the statement shows a £500 cheque paid in per the cash book but not yet on the bank statement and a £1,250 cheque paid out but not yet on the statement. In addition the cash book shows the owner's correct calculation of savings interest of £50 which should have been received, but which is not on the statement. What is the balance per the cash book?

     A    £1,900 overdrawn
     B    £500 overdrawn
     C    £1,900 in hand
     D    £500 in hand

3    Sales of £460 have been debited to purchases, although the correct entry has been made to receivables control. The balance on the suspense account that needs to be set up is for:

     A    £460 debit
     B    £460 credit
     C    £920 debit
     D    £920 credit

4    Sutton & Co had a difference on its trial balance. After investigation the following errors were discovered.

     1    A sales invoice for £500 was mis-read by the clerk as £600 and entered as such into the ledger accounts.

     2    Bank charges of £145 had been debited to the cash at bank account as £154.

   How much was the original difference on the trial balance?

     A    Debits greater than credits by £9
     B    Debits greater than credits by £199
     C    Debits greater than credits by £299
     D    Credits greater than debits by £91

5    Gresham & Sons has drawn up a trial balance which shows credits greater than debits by £250. Which **two** of the following are possible explanations for this difference?

     A    Rent paid of £250 had been credited to the rent account

     B    The debit side of the trial balance had been undercast by £250

     C    Cash drawings of £125 had been debited to the cash and drawings accounts

     D    £250 paid for motor repairs had been debited to the motor vehicles (non-current assets) account

     E    A sales invoice for £250 had been entered twice in the sales account

6 The trial balance of Z Ltd as extracted from the books has a difference of £812, and this has been posted to the credit of a suspense account. Some errors, as set out below, have now been discovered.

1 The year end bank overdraft of £756 has been entered in the trial balance as a debit balance.

2 The total of discounts receivable for the last month of the year of £13,400 has been posted to the discounts receivable account as £14,300.

3 A purchase invoice totalling £2,015 has been correctly credited to the control account, but this amount has been debited to light and heat.

After correction of these errors, what is the remaining balance brought down on the suspense account?

A £1,815 DR
B £200 CR
C £956 CR
D £1,424 CR

7 On reconciling the purchases control account with the list of payables ledger balances, the accountant of Moore discovered that there were two reconciling items.

1 A purchase invoice from Polly totalling £158 had been entered on her account as £258, but was correctly entered in the purchases day book.

2 The purchases day book had been undercast by £100.

To complete the reconciliation, which of the following should happen?

| | | | £ | £ |
|---|---|---|---|---|
| A | DR | Purchases | 200 | |
| | CR | Payables ledger control account | | 200 |
| B | DR | Payables ledger control account | 100 | |
| | CR | Purchases | | 100 |
| | and reduce the amount shown as owed to Polly and the list of balances by £100 | | | |
| C | DR | Payables ledger control account | 200 | |
| | CR | Purchases | | 200 |
| | and reduce the amount shown as owed to Polly and the list of balances by £100 | | | |
| D | DR | Purchases | 100 | |
| | CR | Payables ledger control account | | 100 |
| | and reduce the amount shown as owed to Polly and the list of balances by £100 | | | |

8 Due to a fault in the company's computer software East Cowes Ltd's purchases day book was undercast by £8,800, and its sales day book was undercast by £3,800. In addition, debit balances of £580 had been omitted from the list of sales ledger balances, credit balances of £280 omitted from the list of payables ledger balances, and contras of £750 had not been entered anywhere in the books. After the correction of these errors East Cowes Ltd's profit will

A Decrease by £5,000
B Decrease by £4,700
C Decrease by £3,400
D Increase by £5,000

9   On 31 January 20X8 Randall's cash book for its current account showed a credit balance of £150 which did not agree with the bank statement balance. In performing the reconciliation the following points come to light.

|  | £ |
|---|---|
| *Not recorded in the cash book* |  |
| Bank charges | 36 |
| Transfer from savings account to current account | 500 |
| *Not recorded on the bank statement* |  |
| Unpresented cheques | 116 |
| Uncleared lodgements | 630 |

It was also discovered that the bank had debited Randall's account with a cheque for £400 in error. This should have been debited to Hopkirk's account.

What was the original balance on the bank statement?

A    £200 DR
B    £428 DR
C    £600 CR
D    £1,600 CR

10   A bank reconciliation statement for Worth Ltd at 31 December 20Y1 is in course of preparation. In the light of the information given below, compute the final balance shown by the cash book.

1    Overdrawn balance per bank statement is £1,019.

2    An amount of £250 credited in the bank statement under a standing order arrangement has not been entered in the cash book.

3    Cheques drawn and entered but not presented total £2,467.

4    Bank charges of £1,875 debited by the bank have not been entered in the cash book.

5    Cash and cheques received and entered but not credited in the bank statement total £4,986.

6    An uncorrected bank error has resulted in a cheque for £397 debited to Worth's account instead of to the account of the drawer.

The final balance shown by the cash book, after making all necessary corrections, should be

A    £6,831 DR
B    £3,141 DR
C    £1,897 DR
D    £228 DR

Now, go back to the Learning Objectives in the Introduction. If you are satisfied that you have achieved these objectives, please tick them off.

# Answers to Interactive questions

## Answer to Interactive question 1

PAYABLES CONTROL ACCOUNT

| | £ | | £ |
|---|---|---|---|
| Bank payments | 79,500 | Balance b/d (balancing figure) | 16,970 |
| Discount received | 3,750 | Purchases | 83,200 |
| Contra with receivables | 4,000 | | |
| Balance c/d | 12,920 | | |
| | 100,170 | | 100,170 |

## Answer to Interactive question 2

A  The total of sales invoices in the day book is debited to the control account. If the total is understated by £800, the debits in the control account will also be understated by £800. Options B and D would have the opposite effect: credit entries in the control account would be understated. Option C would lead to a discrepancy of 2 × £800 = £1,600.

## Answer to Interactive question 3

(a)                        RECEIVABLES CONTROL ACCOUNT

| 20X8 | | £ | 20X9 | | £ |
|---|---|---|---|---|---|
| Oct 1 | Balances b/d (8,024 – 57) | 7,967 | Sept 30 | Cash received from credit customers | 55,212 |
| 20X9 | | | | Discount allowed | 2,328 |
| Sept 30 | Sales | 62,514 | | Irrecoverable debts written off | 326 |
| | | | | Contra | 434 |
| | | | | Balance c/d | 12,181 |
| | | 70,481 | | | 70,481 |

(b)                        PAYABLES CONTROL ACCOUNT

| 20X8 | | £ | 20X8 | | £ |
|---|---|---|---|---|---|
| Sept 30 | Cash paid to credit suppliers | 37,307 | Oct 1 | Balance b/d (6,235 – 105) | 6,130 |
| | Discount received | 1,475 | 20X9 | | |
| | Contra | 434 | Sept 30 | Purchases | 39,439 |
| | Balance c/d | 6,458 | | Cash refund | 105 |
| | | 45,674 | | | 45,674 |

## Answer to Interactive question 4

(a)                        RECEIVABLES CONTROL ACCOUNT

| | £ | | £ |
|---|---|---|---|
| Uncorrected balance b/d | 12,550 | Discount omitted (d) | 100 |
| Sales omitted (a) | 850 | Contra entry omitted (f) | 400 |
| Bank: cheque dishonoured (l) | 300 | Irrecoverable debt omitted (g) | 500 |
| | | Credit note omitted (j) | 200 |
| | | Amended balance c/d | 12,500 |
| | 13,700 | | 13,700 |
| Balance b/d | 12,500 | | |

(b)   STATEMENT OF ADJUSTMENTS TO LIST OF BALANCES

|  | £ | £ |
|---|---|---|
| Original total of list of balances |  | 12,802 |
| Add   debit balance omitted (b) | 300 |  |
| debit balance undercast (e) | 200 |  |
|  |  | 500 |
|  |  | 13,302 |
| Less   transposition error (c): understatement of cash received | 180 |  |
| cash debited instead of credited (2 × £250) (h) | 500 |  |
| discounts received wrongly debited to Bell (i) | 50 |  |
| understatement of cash received (k) | 72 |  |
|  |  | (802) |
| Corrected total on list of balances |  | 12,500 |

## Answer to Interactive question 5

A    Decrease
B    No effect. Adjustment to cash book.
C    Decrease
D    Increase

CASH

|  | £ |  | £ |
|---|---|---|---|
| b/d | 106 | c/d | 226 |
| Standing order | 120 |  |  |
|  | 226 |  | 226 |

|  | £ |
|---|---|
| Balance per bank statement | 388 |
| Unpresented cheques | (5,629) |
| Uncleared lodgements | 5,577 |
| Bank error | (110) |
| Balance per cash account | 226 |

## Answer to Interactive question 6

|  | £ | £ |
|---|---|---|
| Balance per cash book |  | (610) |
| Items on statement, not in cash book |  |  |
| Direct debits | (715) |  |
| Investment income | 353 |  |
|  |  | (362) |
| Corrected balance per cash book |  | (972) |
| Item in cash book not on statement: |  |  |
| Customer's cheque (uncleared lodgements) |  | (875) |
| Balance per bank statement |  | (1,847) |

## Answer to Interactive question 7

(a)   DEBIT     Purchases                           £250
      CREDIT    Trade payables                               £250

      *A transaction previously omitted*

(b)   DEBIT     Repairs account                     £150
      CREDIT    Non-current asset (machinery) a/c            £150

      *The correction of an error of principle: repairs costs incorrectly added to non-current asset costs*

(c)  DEBIT        Drawings                                                  £280
     CREDIT       Sales                                                              £280

*An error of principle, in which sales were reduced to compensate for cash drawings not accounted for*

(d)  DEBIT        Telephone expense                                        £540
     CREDIT       Electricity expense                                                £540

*Correction of an error of commission: telephone expenses wrongly charged to the electricity account*

(e)  DEBIT        Trade receivables                                        £400
     CREDIT       Sales                                                              £400

*The correction of a casting error in the sales day book*
(£28,825 – £28,425 = £400)

## Answer to Interactive question 8

(a)

|       |        |                      | DR<br>£ | CR<br>£ |
|-------|--------|----------------------|---------|---------|
| (i)   | DEBIT  | Suspense a/c         | 1,000   |         |
|       | CREDIT | Sales                |         | 1,000   |
| (ii)  | DEBIT  | Non-current asset    | 240     |         |
|       | CREDIT | Distribution costs   |         | 240     |
| (iii) | DEBIT  | Discount received    | 150     |         |
|       | CREDIT | Trade payables       |         | 150     |
| (iv)  | DEBIT  | Suspense a/c         | 500     |         |
|       | CREDIT | Purchases            |         | 500     |
| (v)   | DEBIT  | Trade payables       | 460     |         |
|       | CREDIT | Suspense a/c         |         | 460     |

(b)

### SUSPENSE A/C

|               | £     |                      | £     |
|---------------|-------|----------------------|-------|
| (i)  Sales    | 1,000 | End of year balance  | 1,040 |
| (iv) Purchases| 500   | (vi) Trade payables  | 460   |
|               | 1,500 |                      | 1,500 |

(c)

|                                                    | £      |
|----------------------------------------------------|--------|
| Gross profit originally reported                   | 35,750 |
| Sales omitted (i)                                  | 1,000  |
| Incorrect recording of purchases (iv)              | 500    |
| Adjusted gross profit                              | 37,250 |
|                                                    |        |
| Net profit originally reported                     | 18,500 |
| Adjustments to gross profit £(37,250 – 35,750)     | 1,500  |
| Cash discount incorrectly taken (iii)              | (150)  |
| Non-current asset costs wrongly classified         | 240    |
| Adjusted net profit                                | 20,090 |

# Answers to Self-test

1   A                                    RECEIVABLES CONTROL

|  | £ |  | £ |
|---|---|---|---|
| Bal b/f (bal figure) | 22,000 | Cash | 50,000 |
| Sales | 125,000 | Discounts allowed | 2,000 |
|  |  | Bal c/f | 95,000 |
|  | 147,000 |  | 147,000 |

If you had answer B, you reversed the double entry and so produced a payables control account. In answer D, you omitted the discounts allowed figure; while in answer C you put discounts allowed on the debit instead of the credit side of the control account.

2   D

|  | £ | £ |
|---|---|---|
| Balance per bank statement |  | 1,200 |
| Add outstanding lodgements | 500 |  |
| deposit interest not yet credited | 50 | 550 |
|  |  | 1,750 |
| Less unpresented cheques |  | (1,250) |
| Balance per cash book |  | 500 |

3   D   Sales of £460 have been debited to accounts receivable and also £460 has been debited to purchases. Therefore the trial balance needs a credit of 2 × £460 = £920 to balance.

4   C   1   This error will not lead to a difference in the trial balance. Both receivables and sales will be overstated.

    2   The cash at the bank account has been debited (it should have been credited) with £154, bank charges debited with £145 therefore £299 more debits than credits.

5   B and E

|  | Should have | Have | Result |
|---|---|---|---|
| A | DR Rent £250<br>CR Bank £250 | CR Rent £250<br>CR Bank £250 | £500 more CRs than DRs |
| B | – | – | £250 more CRs than DRs |
| C | DR Drawings £125<br>CR Bank £125 | DR Bank £125<br>DR Drawings £125 | £250 more DRs than CRs |
| D | DR Repairs £250<br>CR Bank £250 | DR Non-current assets £250<br>CR Bank £250 | DRs = CRs (even though entry is wrong in principle) |
| E | DR Receivables £250<br>CR Sales £250 | DR Receivables £250<br>CR Sales £500 | £250 more CRs than DRs |

6   B                                    SUSPENSE

|  | £ |  | £ |
|---|---|---|---|
| Bank overdraft (2 × 756) | 1,512 | Opening balance | 812 |
| C/d (β) | 200 | Discounts | 900 |
|  | 1,712 |  | 1,712 |

7 D 1 As purchases day book entry is correct, subsequent double entry is correct. Personal account is incorrect.

    2 Double entry incorrect.

8 A

|  | Bookkeeping | Effect on profit £ |
|---|---|---|
| Undercast of purchase day book | DR Purchases | – 8,800 |
|  | CR Purchase ledger control account |  |
| Undercast of sales day book | DR Sales ledger control account |  |
|  | CR Sales | + 3,800 |
|  |  | – 5,000 |

Contras will not affect the profit for the year, whilst errors in the sales and purchase ledgers, not being part of the double entry system, cannot do so.

9 C

CASH AT BANK ACCOUNT

|  | £ |  | £ |
|---|---|---|---|
|  |  | Balance b/d | 150 |
| Transfer from savings a/c | 500 | Charges | 36 |
|  |  | Balance c/d | 314 |
|  | 500 |  | 500 |

|  | £ |
|---|---|
| Balance per cash book | 314 |
| Add unpresented cheques | 116 |
| Less uncleared lodgements | (630) |
| Less error by bank* | (400) |
| **Balance per bank statement** | **(600)** |

\* On the bank statement a debit is a payment **out of** the account.

10 C

|  | £ |
|---|---|
| Balance per bank statement | (1,019) o/d |
| Cheques not presented | (2,467) |
|  | (3,486) |
| Amount not credited | 4,986 |
|  | 1,500 |
| Bank error | 397 |
| Debit balance per cash book | 1,897 |

# CHAPTER 7

# Cost of sales and inventories

## Learning objectives

Tick off

- Record and account for transactions and events resulting in income, expenses, assets, liabilities and equity in accordance with the appropriate basis of accounting and the laws, regulations and accounting standards applicable to the financial statements ☐

- Prepare an extended trial balance ☐

- Identify the main components of a set of financial statements and specify their purpose and interrelationship ☐

- Prepare and present a statement of financial position, statement of profit or loss and statement of cash flows (or extracts therefrom) from the accounting records and trial balance in a format which satisfies the information requirements of the entity ☐

Specific syllabus learning outcomes are: 1d, 2c, 3a, 3c

## Syllabus links

The material in this chapter will be developed further in this paper, and then in the Financial Accounting and Financial Reporting papers later in the Professional stage.

## Examination context

Questions on the topics in this chapter will be set as multiple choice questions, some of which may involve calculations so that the correct answer can be selected. Very often double entry questions are phrased in terms of preparing a journal. In addition, the material covered in this chapter may also be examined as part of a long form question.

In the exam you may be required to:

- Identify the accounting principles behind cost of sales

- Specify the components of cost of sales in the statement of profit or loss

- Use margin and mark-up to calculate revenue or cost of sales

- Identify the accounting principles behind accounting for inventory

- Identify the purpose of an inventory count

- Specify what is included in the cost of inventory

- Identify the correct value for inventory using FIFO and AVCO

- Calculate net realisable values

- Use margin and mark-up to calculate closing inventory

- Identify how to account for drawings of inventory and for substantial losses of inventory

- Identify how to account for closing inventory in the ledger accounts and on the extended trial balance

- Calculate the figure in the statement of financial position for inventory

- Identify the effects of opening and closing inventory on gross and net profit in the statement of profit or loss

# 1 Cost of sales

The **cost of sales** is deducted from **revenue** in an entity's **statement of profit or loss**. Because it results in the **gross profit** it has long been regarded as a key figure in the financial statements.

### Definition

Cost of sales: Opening inventory + purchases + carriage inwards – closing inventory = cost of sales. This amount is then deducted from revenue to arise at the business's gross profit.

Inventory, both opening and closing, features in the statement of profit or loss whereas you might expect it to feature only in the statement of financial position, as an asset. How is this so?

## 1.1 Unsold goods at the end of a reporting period

Goods might be unsold at the end of a reporting period and so still be **held in inventory**. Under the **accrual concept**, the cost of these goods should not be included in cost of sales, instead it should be carried forward and matched against revenue in subsequent periods.

### Worked example: Closing inventory

The Umbrella Shop's financial year ends on 30 September each year. On 1 October 20X4 it had no goods in inventory. During the year to 30 September 20X5, it purchased 30,000 umbrellas costing £60,000 from umbrella suppliers. It resold the umbrellas for £5 each, and sales for the year amounted to £100,000 (20,000 umbrellas). At 30 September there were 10,000 unsold umbrellas left in inventory, valued at cost of £2 each.

**Requirement**

What was The Umbrella Shop's gross profit for the year?

### Solution

It purchased 30,000 umbrellas, but only sold 20,000. Purchase costs of £60,000 and sales of £100,000 do not relate to the same quantity of goods.

The gross profit for the year should be calculated by 'matching' the sales value of 20,000 umbrellas sold with the cost of those 20,000 umbrellas. The cost of sales in this example is therefore the cost of purchases minus the cost of goods in inventory at the year end.

| | | £ | £ |
|---|---|---|---|
| Sales (20,000 units at £5) | | | 100,000 |
| Purchases | 30,000 units at £2 | 60,000 | |
| Less closing inventory | (10,000) units at £2 | (20,000) | |
| Cost of sales | 20,000 units at £2 | | (40,000) |
| Gross profit | | | 60,000 |

## Worked example: Opening and closing inventory

In its next reporting period, 1 October 20X5 to 30 September 20X6, The Umbrella Shop purchased 40,000 umbrellas at a total cost of £95,000, and sold 45,000 umbrellas for £230,000. At 30 September 20X6 it had (10,000 + 40,000 – 45,000) = 5,000 umbrellas left in inventory, which together had cost £12,000.

### Requirement

What was The Umbrella Shop's gross profit for the second period?

### Solution

In this reporting period, it purchased 40,000 umbrellas to add to the 10,000 it already had in inventory at the start of the year. It sold 45,000, leaving 5,000 umbrellas in inventory at the year end. Once again, gross profit should be calculated by matching the value of 45,000 units of sales with the cost of those 45,000 units.

The cost of sales is the value of the 10,000 umbrellas in inventory at the beginning of the period, plus the cost of the 40,000 umbrellas purchased, less the cost of the 5,000 umbrellas in inventory at the period end.

|  |  | £ | £ |
|---|---|---|---|
| Sales (45,000 units) |  |  | 230,000 |
| Opening inventory* | 10,000 units at £2 | 20,000 |  |
| Add purchases | 40,000 units | 95,000 |  |
| Less closing inventory | (5,000) units | (12,000) |  |
| Cost of sales | 45,000 units |  | (103,000) |
| Gross profit |  |  | 127,000 |

\* Taken from the closing inventory value of the previous reporting period.

## 1.2 Cost of sales

|  | £ |
|---|---|
| Opening inventory value | X |
| Add cost of purchases (or, for a manufacturing company, the cost of production) | X |
| Add cost of carriage inwards (see below) | X |
| Less closing inventory value | (X) |
| Equals cost of sales | X |

In other words, to match 'sales' and 'cost of sales', it is necessary to adjust the cost of goods **purchased** or **manufactured** to allow for increases or reduction in inventory levels during the period.

## Interactive question 1: Gross profit

On 1 January 20X6, Grand Union Food Stores had goods in inventory valued at £6,000. During 20X6 its owner purchased supplies costing £50,000. Sales for the year to 31 December 20X6 amounted to £80,000. The cost of goods in inventory at 31 December 20X6 was £12,500.

### Requirement

Calculate the business's gross profit for the year.

See **Answer** at the end of this chapter.

## 1.3 Carriage inwards and outwards

'Carriage' refers to the **cost of transporting purchased goods** from the supplier to the premises of the business which has bought them. Someone has to pay for these delivery costs: sometimes the supplier pays (in which case the purchaser has no costs to record) and sometimes the purchaser pays. When the purchaser pays, the cost to the purchaser is **carriage inwards** when the goods are coming **into** the business, and **carriage outwards** when the goods are going **out** of the business.

- The **cost of carriage inwards** is added to the **cost of purchases**, and is therefore included in the calculation of cost of sales and gross profit.

- The **cost of carriage outwards** is a distribution cost deducted from gross profit in the **statement of profit or loss**.

### Worked example: Carriage inwards and carriage outwards

Gwyn Tring imports and resells clocks. He pays for the costs of delivering the clocks from his supplier in Switzerland to his shop, called Clickety Clocks, in Wales.

He resells clocks to other traders throughout the country, paying carriage costs for deliveries from his business premises to his customers.

On 1 July 20X5, he had clocks in inventory valued at £17,000. During the year to 30 June 20X6 he purchased more clocks for £75,000. Carriage inwards amounted to £2,000. Sales for the year were £162,100. Other business expenses amounted to £56,000, excluding carriage outwards which cost £2,500. The value of clocks in inventory at the year end was £15,400.

#### Requirement

Prepare the statement of profit or loss of Clickety Clocks for the year ended 30 June 20X6.

#### Solution

CLICKETY CLOCKS
STATEMENT OF PROFIT OR LOSS FOR THE YEAR ENDED 30 JUNE 20X6

|  | £ | £ |
|---|---|---|
| Revenue |  | 162,100 |
| Opening inventory | 17,000 |  |
| Purchases | 75,000 |  |
| Carriage inwards | 2,000 |  |
|  | 94,000 |  |
| Less closing inventory | (15,400) |  |
| Cost of sales |  | (78,600) |
| Gross profit |  | 83,500 |
| Carriage outwards | 2,500 |  |
| Other expenses | 56,000 |  |
|  |  | (58,500) |
| Net profit |  | 25,000 |

## 1.4 Inventory written off or written down

A trader might be unable to sell all the goods purchased, because before they can be sold they might:

- Be lost or stolen
- Be damaged and become worthless
- Become obsolete or out of fashion. These might be thrown away, or sold off at a low price

When goods are lost, stolen or thrown away as worthless, the business will make a loss on those goods because their 'sales value' will be nil.

Similarly, when goods lose value because they have become **obsolete** or out of fashion, the business will **make a loss** if their **net realisable value** is less than cost. For example, if goods which originally cost £500 are now obsolete and could only be sold for £150, the business would suffer a loss of £350.

If, at the end of a reporting period, a business still has goods in inventory which are either worthless or worth less than their original cost, the value of the inventories should be **written down** to:

- **Nothing**, if they are worthless, or
- Their **net realisable value**, if this is less than their original cost.

The cost of inventory written off or written down does not usually cause any problems in calculating the gross profit of a business, because the cost of sales already includes the cost of inventories written off or written down, as the following example shows.

### Worked example: Inventories written off and written down

Lucas Wagg ends his financial year on 31 March. At 1 April 20X5 he had goods in inventory valued at £8,800. During the year to 31 March 20X6, he purchased goods costing £48,000. Fashion goods which cost £2,100 were held in inventory at 31 March 20X6, and Lucas Wagg believes that these can only now be sold at a sale price of £400. Goods still held in inventory at 31 March 20X6 (including the fashion goods) had an original purchase cost of £7,600. Sales for the year were £81,400.

**Requirement**

Calculate Lucas Wagg's gross profit for the year ended 31 March 20X6.

### Solution

Initial calculation of closing inventory values:

|  | At cost £ | Realisable value £ | Amount written down £ |
|---|---|---|---|
| Fashion goods | 2,100 | 400 | 1,700 |
| Other goods (balancing figure) | 5,500 | | |
|  | 7,600 | | |

LUCAS WAGG
GROSS PROFIT FOR THE YEAR ENDED 31 MARCH 20X6

|  | £ | £ |
|---|---|---|
| Revenue | | 81,400 |
| Opening inventory | 8,800 | |
| Purchases | 48,000 | |
| Less closing inventory (400 + 5,500) | (5,900) | |
| Cost of sales | | (50,900) |
| Gross profit | | 30,500 |

By using the figure of £5,900 for closing inventories, the cost of sales automatically includes the inventory write-down of £1,700.

## 1.5 Inventory destroyed or stolen and subject to an insurance claim

Where a **material** amount of inventory has been stolen or destroyed, including their cost in gross profit will give a very distorted idea of the business's basic profitability:

- Purchases will include the cost of goods that could not be sold, so the accrual principle is broken, yet they are not in closing inventory either, so it will look as if the business's gross margin on sales has fallen catastrophically.

- There may be an amount of income as a result of an insurance claim, which cannot be included in cost of sales under the 'no offsetting' principle.

These problems are overcome by taking the cost of goods stolen or destroyed **out of purchases**, and including it under **expenses**. The insurance claim is treated as **other income** in calculating net profit; if it has not yet been received in the form **of cash** it is disclosed as **'other receivables'** on the statement of financial position.

## Worked example: Material amount of inventory stolen

Ethelberta had £15,000 of inventory as at 1 January 20X2. During the year to 31 December 20X2 she purchased inventory for £98,000, incurring carriage inwards of £150. She made sales of £150,000, incurring delivery costs to her customers of £2,400. At 31 December 20X2 she realises that she has inventory costing only £200 left; goods costing £18,000 have been stolen. The insurance company has agreed to pay her claim for 75% of the cost.

We shall prepare Ethelberta's statement of profit or loss on (a) the basis set out in Section 1.5 above, and compare this with (b) the alternative in Section 1.4.

### Solution

|  | (a) | | (b) | |
|---|---|---|---|---|
|  | £ | £ | £ | £ |
| Revenue |  | 150,000 |  | 150,000 |
| Opening inventory | 15,000 |  | 15,000 |  |
| Purchases | 98,000 |  | 98,000 |  |
| Carriage inwards | 150 |  | 150 |  |
| Inventory stolen | (18,000) |  | 0 |  |
| Closing inventory | (200) |  | (200) |  |
| Cost of sales |  | (94,950) |  | (112,950) |
| Gross profit |  | 55,050 |  | 37,050 |
| Other income (18,000 × 75%) |  | 13,500 |  | 13,500 |
| Cost of goods stolen |  | (18,000) |  | 0 |
| Distribution costs (carriage out) |  | (2,400) |  | (2,400) |
| Net profit |  | 48,150 |  | 48,150 |
| Gross profit margin (Gross profit/Revenue) |  | 36.7% |  | 24.7% |
| Net profit margin (Net profit/Revenue) |  | 32.1% |  | 32.1% |

Both treatments result in the same net profit. However, the treatment in (a) matches revenue with the cost of the goods that generated the revenue in gross profit, and also matches the cost of the goods stolen with the insurance receipt in respect of them in arriving at net profit. The treatment in (b) does not match revenue and expense so effectively.

## Interactive question 2: Insurance claim

Wasa lost inventory that cost £64,500 in a fire. The goods were insured for 60% of their cost.

**Requirement**

Prepare a journal to account for this in Wasa's books.

See **Answer** at the end of this chapter.

# 2 IAS 2 *Inventories* (FRS 102 s13)

## Section overview

- IAS 2 prescribes the accounting treatment for inventories
- Inventories are assets that are:
  - Held for sale in the ordinary course of business
  - In the process of production for such sale
  - In the form of materials or supplies to be consumed in the production process or in the rendering of services

## UK GAAP alert!

- The requirements of FRS 102 (UK GAAP) are the same as the IAS 2 requirements which you cover in the Accounting paper.

## 2.1 Objective and scope

The objective of IAS 2 *Inventories* is to prescribe the accounting treatment for inventories. In particular it provides guidance on the **determination of cost** and its subsequent recognition as an expense, including any write-down to **net realisable value**.

IAS 2 applies to all inventories except the following:

- Work in progress under construction contracts
- Financial instruments (eg shares, bonds)
- Biological assets

The treatment of the above are all outside the scope of the Accounting syllabus.

Certain inventories are exempt from the standard's measurement methods, ie those held by:

- Producers of agricultural, forest and mineral products
- Commodity-broker traders

## 2.2 Inventories

## Definition

Inventories. Assets:

- Held for sale in the ordinary course of business

- In the process of production for such sale

- In the form of materials or supplies to be consumed in the production process or in the rendering of services

Inventories can include:

- **Goods purchased and held for resale**
- **Finished goods**
- **Work in progress** being produced
- **Raw materials** awaiting use

# 3 Accounting for opening and closing inventories

**Section overview**

- In each reporting period, opening inventory is an expense in the statement of profit or loss:

  | | | |
  |---|---|---|
  | DEBIT | Cost of sales | £X |
  | CREDIT | Inventory account | £X |

- Closing inventory is deducted from cost of sales in the reporting period, so it can be carried forward and matched against the revenue it earns in the next period:

  | | | |
  |---|---|---|
  | DEBIT | Inventory account (statement of financial position) | £X |
  | CREDIT | Cost of sales | £X |

In order to calculate **gross profit** it is necessary to work out the **cost of sales**. To calculate the cost of sales the accruals principle necessitates determining values for **opening inventory** (ie inventory in hand at the beginning of the reporting period) and **closing inventory** (ie inventory in hand at the end of the reporting period). This allows us to carry forward the latter to the next accounting period where it will be matched with the income it earns.

The cost of sales figure in the statement of profit or loss is summarised as:

| | £ |
|---|---|
| Opening inventory | X |
| Plus purchases | X |
| Plus carriage inwards | X |
| Less closing inventory | (X) |
| Cost of sales | X |

However, writing down this formula hides three basic problems.

- How do you manage to get a **precise count** of inventories is held at any one time?

- Once counted, how do you **value** inventory?

- Assuming the inventory is given a value, how does the **double entry bookkeeping** for inventory work?

The purpose of this chapter is to answer all three of these questions. In order to make the presentation a little easier to follow, we shall take the last question first.

## 3.1 Ledger accounting for inventories

Purchases are introduced to the profit and loss ledger account via the following double entry:

| | | |
|---|---|---|
| DEBIT | Profit and loss ledger account | £X |
| CREDIT | Purchases account | £X |

But what about opening and closing inventories? How are their values accounted for in the double entry bookkeeping system? The answer is that an inventory account must be kept, but it is **only used at the end of a reporting period**, when the business counts and values inventory, in an **inventory count**.

(a) Once an inventory count is made and the business has a value for its closing inventory, the double entry is:

| | | |
|---|---|---|
| DEBIT | Inventory (asset) account | £X |
| CREDIT | Profit and loss ledger account | £X |

Rather than showing closing inventory as a 'plus' value in the statement of profit or loss (by adding it to revenue) it is shown as a 'minus' figure in arriving at **cost of sales**, as illustrated above. The debit balance on the closing inventory account represents a **current asset** in the statement of financial position.

(b) Closing inventory at the end of one period becomes opening inventory at the start of the next period. The inventory account remains unchanged, with a debit balance until the end of the next period. This value is now the opening inventory figure and is taken to the profit and loss ledger account:

| | | |
|---|---|---|
| DEBIT | Profit and loss ledger account | £X |
| CREDIT | Inventory account (opening inventory value) | £X |

## Worked example: Accounting for inventories

A business has opening capital of £2,000, represented entirely by inventory. During the first year's trading, when the owner took no drawings, the following transactions occurred.

| | £ |
|---|---|
| Purchases of goods for resale, on credit | 4,300 |
| Payments for trade payables | 3,600 |
| Sales, all on credit | 8,000 |
| Receipts from trade receivables | 3,200 |
| Non-current assets purchased for cash | 1,500 |
| Other expenses, all paid in cash | 900 |

All 'other expenses' relate to the current year.

Closing inventory is valued at £1,800.

**Requirement**

Prepare the ledger accounts, including a profit and loss ledger account, for the 12 month reporting period and a statement of financial position as at the end of the reporting period.

### CASH

| | £ | | £ |
|---|---|---|---|
| Trade receivables | 3,200 | Trade payables | 3,600 |
| Balance c/d | 2,800 | Non-current assets | 1,500 |
| | | Other expenses | 900 |
| | 6,000 | | 6,000 |
| | | Balance b/d | 2,800 |

### CAPITAL

| | £ | | £ |
|---|---|---|---|
| Balance c/d | 4,600 | Inventory | 2,000 |
| | | Profit and loss | 2,600 |
| | 4,600 | | 4,600 |
| | | Balance b/d | 4,600 |

### TRADE PAYABLES

| | £ | | £ |
|---|---|---|---|
| Cash | 3,600 | Purchases | 4,300 |
| Balance c/d | 700 | | |
| | 4,300 | | 4,300 |
| | | Balance b/d | 700 |

### PURCHASES

| | £ | | £ |
|---|---|---|---|
| Trade payables | 4,300 | Profit and loss | 4,300 |

## NON-CURRENT ASSETS

|  | £ |  | £ |
|---|---|---|---|
| Cash | 1,500 | Balance c/d | 1,500 |
| Balance b/d | 1,500 |  |  |

## SALES

|  | £ |  | £ |
|---|---|---|---|
| Profit and loss | 8,000 | Trade receivables | 8,000 |

## TRADE RECEIVABLES

|  | £ |  | £ |
|---|---|---|---|
| Sales | 8,000 | Cash | 3,200 |
|  |  | Balance c/d | 4,800 |
|  | 8,000 |  | 8,000 |
| Balance b/d | 4,800 |  |  |

## OTHER EXPENSES

|  | £ |  | £ |
|---|---|---|---|
| Cash | 900 | Profit and loss | 900 |

## INVENTORY

|  | £ |  | £ |
|---|---|---|---|
| Capital | 2,000 | Profit and loss (opening inventory) | 2,000 |
| Profit and loss (closing inventory) | 1,800 | Balance c/d (closing inventory) | 1,800 |
|  | 3,800 |  | 3,800 |
| Balance b/d | 1,800 |  |  |

## PROFIT AND LOSS LEDGER ACCOUNT

|  | £ |  | £ |
|---|---|---|---|
| Opening inventory (inventory a/c) | 2,000 | Sales | 8,000 |
| Purchases | 4,300 | Closing inventory (inventory a/c) | 1,800 |
| Gross profit c/d | 3,500 |  |  |
|  | 9,800 |  | 9,800 |
| Other expenses | 900 | Gross profit b/d | 3,500 |
| Net profit (transferred to capital account) | 2,600 |  |  |
|  | 3,500 |  | 3,500 |

## STATEMENT OF FINANCIAL POSITION AS AT THE END OF THE PERIOD

|  | £ | £ |
|---|---|---|
| ASSETS |  |  |
| *Non-current assets* |  | 1,500 |
| *Current assets* |  |  |
| Inventory | 1,800 |  |
| Trade receivables | 4,800 |  |
|  |  | 6,600 |
| *Total assets* |  | 8,100 |
| CAPITAL AND LIABILITIES |  |  |
| *Capital* |  |  |
| At start of period | 2,000 |  |
| Profit for period | 2,600 |  |
| At end of period |  | 4,600 |
| *Current liabilities* |  |  |
| Bank overdraft | 2,800 |  |
| Trade payables | 700 |  |
|  |  | 3,500 |
| *Total capital and liabilities* |  | 8,100 |

The closing debit balance on the inventory account is £1,800, which appears in the statement of financial position as a current asset.

The opening inventory of £2,000 was eliminated by transferring it as a debit balance to the profit and loss ledger account, ie:

DEBIT     Profit and loss ledger account (with value of opening inventory)
CREDIT    Inventory account (with value of opening inventory)

The debit in the profit and loss ledger account then increased the cost of sales, ie opening inventory is added to purchases in calculating cost of sales.

### Interactive question 3: Journals for inventory

In its nominal ledger Wickham plc had a balance on its inventory account at 1 July 20X2 of £23,490. At 30 June 20X3 it had inventory of £40,285.

Prepare a journal to record the situation as at the end of the reporting period in the nominal ledger of Wickham plc, in preparation for drawing up the statement of profit or loss and statement of financial position.

See **Answer** at the end of this chapter.

# 4 Inventories on the ETB

### Section overview

- The closing inventory is entered into both adjustment columns of the ETB for inventory. The debit is taken across to the statement of financial position; the credit is taken to the statement of profit or loss.

- Opening inventory is taken straight to the statement of profit or loss as a debit.

The closing inventory figure is generally accounted for after the initial trial balance has been extracted. Therefore, only opening inventory appears on the initial trial balance. An alternative way of incorporating the relevant figures is to use the ETB.

- Calculate the value of closing inventories (see below).

- Prepare the year-end journals for opening and closing inventories as usual (see above).

- Enter the journal for **closing inventory only** in the adjustments columns of the ETB using the inventories line. (There is a debit and a credit for the same amount on this line: the debit casts across to the statement of financial position, and the credit to the statement of profit or loss.)

- Include these adjustments in the ETB cross-cast to prepare the financial statements.

- Enter the journals for both opening and closing inventories in the ledger accounts.

In some ETBs there is no separate line for closing inventories, so the adjustment is made on the opening inventories line: this is the approach taken in the worked example that follows.

## Worked example: Inventories on the ETB

Sam's Music Shop trial balance as at 31 December 20X5 is as follows.

| Ledger balance | Trial balance | |
|---|---|---|
| | Debit £ | Credit £ |
| Cash at bank | | 5,123 |
| Opening capital | | 10,000 |
| Loan | | 12,000 |
| Non-current assets | 20,000 | |
| Trade payables | | 6,800 |
| Expenses | 12,785 | |
| Purchases | 18,425 | |
| Sales | | 38,745 |
| Trade receivables | 3,546 | |
| Inventories at 1.1.X5 | 8,754 | |
| Drawings | 9,158 | |
| | 72,668 | 72,668 |

Closing inventories at 31 December 20X5 cost £13,855.

**Requirement**

Complete Sam's ETB and calculate his net profit for the year.

### Solution

### Step 1

To account for closing inventories on the ETB prepare the year-end journal for closing inventory:

| | | £ | £ |
|---|---|---|---|
| DEBIT | Inventory (statement of financial position) | 13,855 | |
| CREDIT | Profit and loss ledger account | | 13,855 |
| | Recording closing inventory as an asset at the year end | | |

### Step 2

Enter this journal in the debit and credit adjustment columns on the ETB on the inventory ledger account line.

### Step 3

Cross-cast the ETB as follows:

- **Opening inventory** is recorded as a **debit** in the **statement of profit or loss**.

- The **debit** side of the **adjustment journal** is recorded as a **debit** in the **statement of financial position**.

- The **credit** side of the **adjustment journal** is recorded as a **credit** in the **statement of profit or loss**.

### Step 4

Prepare the financial statements.

### Step 5

Record both journals in the ledger accounts as usual.

Sam's ETB will be as follows:

| Ledger balance | Trial balance | | Adjustments | | Statement of profit or loss | | Statement of financial position | |
|---|---|---|---|---|---|---|---|---|
| | Debit £ | Credit £ | Debit £ | Credit £ | Debit £ | Credit £ | Debit £ | Credit £ |
| Cash at bank | | 5,123 | | | | | | 5,123 |
| Opening capital | | 10,000 | | | | | | 10,000 |
| Loan | | 12,000 | | | | | | 12,000 |
| Non-current assets | 20,000 | | | | | | 20,000 | |
| Trade payables | | 6,800 | | | | | | 6,800 |
| Expenses | 12,785 | | | | 12,785 | | | |
| Purchases | 18,425 | | | | 18,425 | | | |
| Sales | | 38,745 | | | | 38,745 | | |
| Trade receivables | 3,546 | | | | | | 3,546 | |
| Inventories | 8,754 | | 13,855 | 13,855 | 8,754 | 13,855 | 13,855 | |
| Drawings | 9,158 | | | | | | 9,158 | |
| Net profit | | | | | 12,636 | | | 12,636 |
| | 72,668 | 72,668 | 13,855 | 13,855 | 52,600 | 52,600 | 46,559 | 46,559 |

## SAM'S MUSIC SHOP – STATEMENT OF PROFIT OR LOSS FOR YEAR ENDED 31 DECEMBER 20X5

| | £ | £ |
|---|---|---|
| Revenue | | 38,745 |
| Cost of sales | | |
| Opening inventories | 8,754 | |
| Purchases | 18,425 | |
| Closing inventories | (13,855) | |
| Cost of sales | | (13,324) |
| Gross profit | | 25,421 |
| Expenses | | (12,785) |
| Net profit | | 12,636 |

## SAM'S MUSIC SHOP – STATEMENT OF FINANCIAL POSITION AS AT 31 DECEMBER 20X5

| ASSETS | £ | £ |
|---|---|---|
| *Non-current assets* | | 20,000 |
| *Current assets* | | |
| Inventories | 13,855 | |
| Trade receivables | 3,546 | |
| | | 17,401 |
| *Total assets* | | 37,401 |
| CAPITAL AND LIABILITIES | | |
| Opening capital | | 10,000 |
| Profit for year | | 12,636 |
| Drawings | | (9,158) |
| Closing capital | | 13,478 |
| *Non-current liabilities* | | |
| Bank loan | | 12,000 |
| *Current liabilities* | | |
| Trade payables | 6,800 | |
| Bank overdraft | 5,123 | |
| | | 11,923 |
| *Total capital and liabilities* | | 37,401 |

## 5 Counting inventories

**Section overview**

- The inventory count establishes quantities held in inventory at the end of the reporting period.

Business trading is a continuous activity, but financial statements must be drawn up at a particular date. In preparing a statement of financial position it is necessary to 'freeze' the activity of a business so as to determine its assets, capital and liabilities at that given moment. This includes establishing the quantities of inventories held.

In simple cases, when a business holds easily counted and relatively small amounts of inventory, quantities of inventories held at the date of the statement of financial position can be determined by physically counting them in an **inventory count**.

In more complicated cases, where a business holds considerable quantities of varied inventory, an alternative approach to establishing quantities is to maintain **continuous inventory records**. This means that a record is kept for every item of inventory, showing receipts and issues from the stores, and a running total. A few inventory items are counted each day to make sure the records are correct – this is called a 'continuous' count because it is spread out over the reporting period rather than completed in one count at a designated time.

Once the quantity of inventories is determined then a policy is required for **valuing individual items**.

## 6 Valuing inventories

**Section overview**

- Inventory is valued at the lower of (historical) cost of purchase, and net realisable value (NRV).
- NRV is the expected selling price less any costs to be incurred in achieving that sale.
- Cost comprises: purchase price, carriage, duties and conversion costs to bring item to its present location and condition.

### 6.1 Basic valuation: valuation at historical cost

There are **several methods** which, in theory, might be used for valuing items of inventory:

- At their **historical cost** (ie the cost at which they were originally bought)
- At their **expected selling price**
- At their expected selling price, less any costs still to be incurred in getting them ready for sale. This amount is referred to as inventory's **net realisable value** (NRV)
- At the amount it would cost to replace them (**replacement cost**)

The use of selling prices in inventory valuation is ruled out by the **realisation** concept because this would create a profit for the business before the inventory has been sold. **Using replacement costs** is problematic as these are very difficult to establish. The most obvious route then is to value them at **historical cost**. But what about **NRV**?

**Worked example: Valuing inventory at historical cost**

A trader buys two items of inventory, each costing £100. He can sell them for £140 each, but in the reporting period we shall consider, he has only sold one of them. The other is closing inventory.

Since only one item has been sold, you might think it is common sense that profit ought to be £40. But if closing inventory is valued at selling price, profit would be £80, ie profit would be taken on the closing inventory as well.

This would contradict the accounting concept of **realisation**, ie to claim a profit before the item has actually been sold.

| | £ | £ |
|---|---:|---:|
| Revenue | | 140 |
| Opening inventory | – | |
| Purchases (2 × £100) | 200 | |
| | 200 | |
| Less closing inventory (at selling price) | (140) | |
| Cost of sales | | ( 60) |
| Gross profit | | 80 |

The same objection **usually** applies to the use of NRV in inventory valuation. Suppose the item purchased for £100 requires £5 of further expenditure in getting it ready for sale and then selling it (eg £5 of processing costs and distribution costs). If its expected selling price is £140, its NRV is £(140 – 5) = £135. To value it at £135 in the statement of financial position would still be to anticipate a £35 profit.

**We are left with historical cost as the normal basis of inventory valuation.**

## 6.2 Basic valuation: lower of cost and NRV

The only time when (historical) cost is not used is when cost needs to be reduced to **NRV**.

### Worked example: Lower of cost and NRV

Suppose that the market in the above example slumps and the expected selling price is £90. The item's NRV is then £(90 – 5) = £85 and the business will make a loss of £15 (£100 – £85) on the item. Assets should not be overstated, so the so loss will be recognised by valuing the item in the statement of financial position at its NRV of £85.

**Inventory should be valued at the lower of cost and net realisable value.**

## 6.3 Applying the lower of cost and NRV

If a business has many inventory items on hand the comparison of cost and NRV should be carried out for each item separately. It is not sufficient to compare the total cost of all inventory items with their total NRV.

### Worked example: Valuing each inventory item separately

A company has four items of inventory at the end of its reporting period. Their cost and NRVs are as follows.

| Inventory item | Cost | NRV | Lower of cost / NRV |
|---|---:|---:|---:|
| | £ | £ | £ |
| 1 | 27 | 32 | 27 |
| 2 | 14 | 8 | 8 |
| 3 | 43 | 55 | 43 |
| 4 | 29 | 40 | 29 |
| | 113 | 135 | 107 |

It would be incorrect to compare total cost (£113) with total NRV (£135) and to state inventories at £113 in the statement of financial position. The company can foresee a loss of £6 on item 2 and this should be recognised immediately. If the four items are taken together in total the loss on item 2 is masked by the anticipated profits on the other items. By performing the cost/NRV comparison for each item separately the appropriate valuation of £107 can be derived. This is the value which should appear in the statement of financial position.

### Interactive question 4: Inventory valuation

The following figures relate to inventory held at the end of the reporting period.

|  | Item A | Item B | Item C |
| --- | --- | --- | --- |
| Cost | £20 | £9 | £14 |
| Selling price | £30 | £12 | £22 |
| Modification cost to enable sale | – | £2 | £8 |
| Marketing costs | £7 | £2 | £2 |
| Units held | 200 | 150 | 300 |

**Requirement**

Calculate the value of inventory for inclusion in the financial statements.

See **Answer** at the end of this chapter.

## 6.4 Determining the cost of inventory

Inventories may be:

- **Raw materials** or components bought from suppliers
- **Finished goods** which have been made by the business but not yet sold.
- **Part completed items** (this type of inventory is called **work in progress** or WIP).

### Definitions

**Cost of inventories:** All costs of purchase, of conversion (eg labour) and of other costs incurred in bringing the items to their present location and condition.

**Cost of purchase:** The purchase price, import duties and other non-recoverable taxes, transport, handling and other costs directly attributable to the acquisition of finished goods and materials.

### 6.4.1 What is included in the total cost of an item?

The total cost of an item includes all costs incurred in **bringing the item to its present location and condition**. This consists of

- The purchase cost of **raw materials**
- **Carriage**
- **Import taxes and duties**
- **Conversion costs**

### Definition

**Conversion costs:** Any costs involved in converting raw materials into final product, including labour, expenses directly related to the product and an appropriate share of production overheads (but not sales, administrative or general overheads).

### Worked example: Cost of manufactured goods

A business has the following details relating to production and sales for a reporting period:

Sales: 900 units at £600 each
1,000 units are produced with the following costs being incurred:
Opening inventory of raw materials: 200 units at £100 each
Purchases of raw materials: 1,050 units at £100 each
Closing inventory of raw materials: 250 units at £100 each

| | |
|---|---|
| Production wages | £150,000 |
| Production overheads | £100,000 |
| General administration, selling and distribution costs | £100,000 |

The **cost of production** should include an **appropriate share of production wages and production overheads**, but not **non-production expenses**.

The statement of profit or loss of this business for the reporting period is as follows:

| | £ | £ |
|---|---|---|
| Sales (900 units × £600) | | 540,000 |
| Cost of production (1,000 units) | | |
| *Raw materials* | | |
| Opening inventory (200 × £100) | 20,000 | |
| Purchases (1,050 × £100) | 105,000 | |
| Less closing inventory (250 × £100) | (25,000) | |
| Cost of raw materials used | 100,000 | |
| Production wages | 150,000 | |
| Production overheads | 100,000 | |
| Cost of production (1,000 units cost £350,000/1,000 = £350 each) | 350,000 | |
| Less closing inventory, finished goods (100 × £350) | (35,000) | |
| Cost of sales | | (315,000) |
| Gross profit | | 225,000 |
| General administration, selling and distribution costs | | (100,000) |
| Net profit | | 125,000 |

The cost of production is spread over the units produced. Any unsold units are valued at a figure that reflects a share of these costs. When the inventory is eventually sold, the production overheads associated with its manufacture will be thereby properly matched with the revenues earned.

---

### 6.4.2 What is the total cost of items left in inventory?

A business may be continually adding items to finished goods inventory, or purchasing a particular component. As each consignment is received from suppliers, or each finished goods batch is added to inventory, they are stored in the appropriate place, where they will be mingled with items already there. When the storekeeper issues items to production or to despatch they will simply pull out the nearest item to hand, which may have arrived in the latest consignment/batch, in an earlier consignment/batch or in several different consignments/batches.

There are several techniques which are used in practice to attribute a cost to inventory items; remember that actual materials, components and finished goods items can be issued in any order at all irrespective of when each one entered inventory.

## Definitions

**FIFO (first in, first out):** Items are used in the order in which they are received from suppliers, so oldest items are issued first. Inventory remaining is therefore the newer items.

**LIFO (last in, first out):** Items issued originally formed part of the most recent delivery, while oldest consignments remain in the bin. **This is disallowed under IASs.**

**AVCO (average cost):** As purchase prices can change with each new consignment received, the average value of an item is constantly changing. Each item at any moment is assumed to have been purchased at the average price of all the items together, so inventory remaining is therefore valued at the most recent average price.

**Standard cost:** All inventory items are valued at a pre determined cost. If this standard cost differs from prices actually paid during the period the difference is written off as a 'variance' in the statement of profit or loss.

**Replacement cost:** The cost of an inventory unit is assumed to be the amount it would cost now to replace it. This is often (but not necessarily) the unit cost of inventories purchased in the next consignment **following** the date of the statement of financial position.

**In the exam you can expect to use FIFO or AVCO for the valuation of inventory in the statement of financial position and the statement of profit or loss.**

## Worked example: FIFO and AVCO cost

To illustrate the various pricing methods, the following transactions will be used in each case.

TRANSACTIONS DURING MAY 20X7

|  | Quantity Units | Unit cost £ | Total cost £ |
|---|---|---|---|
| Opening balance 1 May | 100 | 2.00 | 200 |
| Receipts 3 May * | 400 | 2.10 | 840 |
| Issues 4 May ** | 200 |  |  |
| Receipts 9 May | 300 | 2.12 | 636 |
| Issues 11 May | 400 |  |  |
| Receipts 18 May | 100 | 2.40 | 240 |
| Issues 20 May | 100 |  |  |
| Closing balance 31 May | 200 |  |  |
|  |  |  | 1,916 |

*   Receipts mean goods are received into store.
**  Issues represent the issue of goods from store.

The problem is to put a valuation on the following.

(a)   The issues of materials
(b)   The closing inventory

### Requirement

How would issues and closing inventory be valued using each of the following in turn?

(a)   FIFO
(b)   AVCO

### Solution

(a)   **FIFO** assumes that materials are **issued out of inventory in the order in which they were delivered into inventory**, ie issues are priced at the cost of the earliest delivery remaining in inventory.

The cost of issues and the closing inventory value in the example, using FIFO, would be as follows.

| Date | Quantity Units | Value issued | Cost of issues £ | £ |
|---|---|---|---|---|
| 4 May | 200 | 100 at £2.00 | 200 | |
| | | 100 at £2.10 | 210 | |
| | | 200 | | 410 |
| 11 May | 400 | 300 at £2.10 | 630 | |
| | | 100 at £2.12 | 212 | |
| | | 400 | | 842 |
| 20 May | 100 | 100 at £2.12 | | 212 |
| | | | | 1,464 |
| Closing inventory value | 200 | 100 at £2.12 | 212 | |
| | | 100 at £2.40 | 240 | |
| | | 200 | | 452 |
| | | | | 1,916 |

Note that the cost of materials issued plus the value of closing inventory equals the cost of purchases plus the cost of opening inventory (£1,916).

(b) **AVCO** may be used in various ways in pricing inventory issues. The most common is the **cumulative weighted average pricing** method illustrated below.

- A weighted average price for all units in inventory is calculated. Issues are priced at this average cost, and the balance of inventory remaining has the same unit valuation.

- A new weighted average price is calculated whenever a new delivery of materials into store is received.

| Date | Received Units | Issued Units | Balance Units | Total inventory value £ | Unit cost £ | Price of issue £ |
|---|---|---|---|---|---|---|
| Opening inventory | | | 100 | 200 | 2.00 | |
| 3 May | 400 | | | 840 | 2.10 | |
| | | | 500 | 1,040 | 2.08 * | |
| 4 May | | 200 | | (416) | 2.08 ** | 416 |
| | | | 300 | 624 | 2.08 | |
| 9 May | 300 | | | 636 | 2.12 | |
| | | | 600 | 1,260 | 2.10 * | |
| 11 May | | 400 | | (840) | 2.10 ** | 840 |
| | | | 200 | 420 | 2.10 | |
| 18 May | 100 | | | 240 | 2.40 | |
| | | | 300 | 660 | 2.20 * | |
| 20 May | | 100 | | (220) | 2.20 ** | 220 |
| | | | | | | 1,476 |
| Closing inventory value | | | 200 | 440 | 2.20 | 440 |
| | | | | | | 1,916 |

\* A new unit cost of inventory is calculated whenever a new receipt of materials occurs.

\*\* Whenever inventories are issued, the unit value of the items issued is the current weighted average cost per unit at the time of the issue.

For this method too, the cost of materials issued plus the cost of closing inventory equals the cost of purchases plus the cost of opening inventory (£1,916).

## 6.5 Inventory valuations and profit

FIFO and AVCO each produced different costs, both of closing inventories and also of materials issues. Since raw material costs affect the cost of production, and the cost of production works through eventually into the cost of sales, it follows that **different methods of inventory valuation will provide different profit figures.**

## Worked example: Inventory valuations and profit

On 1 November 20X2 a company held 300 units of finished goods in inventory. These cost £3,600. During November 20X2 three batches of finished goods were received into store from the production department, as follows.

| Date | Units received | Production cost per unit |
|---|---|---|
| 10 November | 400 | £12.50 |
| 20 November | 400 | £14 |
| 25 November | 400 | £15 |

Finished goods sold during November were as follows.

| Date | Units sold | Sale price per unit |
|---|---|---|
| 14 November | 500 | £20 |
| 21 November | 500 | £20 |
| 28 November | 100 | £20 |
| | 1,100 | |

Identify the profit from selling inventory in November 20X2, applying the principles of:

(a)  FIFO
(b)  AVCO

Ignore administration, sales and distribution costs.

## Solution

(a)  **FIFO**

| Date | Issue costs | Issue cost £ | Closing inventory £ |
|---|---|---|---|
| 14 November | (300 units × £12) + (200 units × £12.50) | 6,100 | |
| 21 November | (200 units × £12.50) + (300 units × £14) | 6,700 | |
| 28 November | 100 units × £14 | 1,400 | |
| Closing inventory | 400 units × £15 | | 6,000 |
| | | 14,200 | 6,000 |

(b)  **AVCO**

| | Units | Unit cost £ | Balance in inventory £ | Total cost of issues £ | Closing inventory £ |
|---|---|---|---|---|---|
| 1 November Opening inventory | 300 | 12.000 | 3,600 | | |
| 10 November | 400 | 12.500 | 5,000 | | |
| | 700 | 12.286 | 8,600 | | |
| 14 November | (500) | 12.286 | (6,143) | 6,143 | |
| | 200 | 12.286 | 2,457 | | |
| 20 November | 400 | 14.000 | 5,600 | | |
| | 600 | 13.428 | 8,057 | | |
| 21 November | (500) | 13.428 | (6,714) | 6,714 | |
| | 100 | 13.428 | 1,343 | | |
| 25 November | 400 | 15.000 | 6,000 | | |
| | 500 | 14.686 | 7,343 | | |
| 28 November | (100) | 14.686 | (1,469) | 1,469 | |
| 30 November Closing inventory | 400 | 14.686 | 5,874 | 14,326 | 5,874 |

**Summary: profit**

|  | FIFO £ | AVCO £ |
|---|---|---|
| Opening inventory | 3,600 | 3,600 |
| Cost of production (400 × £12.50) + (400 × £14) + (400 × £15) | 16,600 | 16,600 |
| Closing inventory | (6,000) | (5,874) |
| Cost of sales | 14,200 | 14,326 |
| Sales (1,100 × £20) | 22,000 | 22,000 |
| Profit | 7,800 | 7,674 |

Different inventory valuations produce different cost of sales and profits figures. Here opening inventory values are the same, therefore the **difference in the amount of profit under each method is the same as the difference in the valuations of closing inventory**.

The profit differences are only temporary. The opening inventory in December 20X2 will be £6,000 or £5,874, depending on the inventory valuation used. Different opening inventory values will affect the cost of sales and profits in December, so that in the long run inequalities in cost of sales each month will even themselves out.

---

### Interactive question 5: FIFO

A firm has the following transactions with respect to its product R.

Year 1

Opening inventory: nil

Buys 10 units at £300 per unit
Buys 12 units at £250 per unit
Sells 8 units at £400 per unit
Buys 6 units at £200 per unit
Sells 12 units at £400 per unit

Year 2

Buys 10 units at £200 per unit
Sells 5 units at £400 per unit
Buys 12 units at £150 per unit
Sells 25 units at £400 per unit

**Requirement**

Using FIFO, calculate the following on an item by item basis for both year 1 and year 2.

- Closing inventory
- Sales
- Cost of sales
- Gross profit

See **Answer** at the end of this chapter.

---

# 7 Using mark-up/margin percentages to establish cost

### Section overview

- Mark-up is calculated on cost.
- Margin is calculated on sales.
- Margin and mark-up can help us to establish the cost of an item of inventory.

It is common to establish standard gross profit percentages in relation to cost to set the sales price:

- Inventory that cost £120 may be sold at a **margin** of 40%, so the sales value is £120 × 100/60 = £200, and the profit is £120 × 40/60 = £80.

- Inventory that cost £120 may be sold at a **mark-up** of 40% to reach a sales price of £168 (120 × 140/100).

These standard percentages can be set out as follows, using the above as an example:

| | Margin on sales (sales is the 100% figure) | | | Mark-up on cost (cost is the 100% figure) | | |
|---|---|---|---|---|---|---|
| | % | £ | | % | £ | |
| Sales | 100 | 200 | 120 × 100/60 | 140 | 168 | 120 × 140/100 |
| Cost | (60) | (120) | | (100) | 120 | |
| Gross profit | 40 | 80 | 120 × 40/60 | 40 | 48 | 120 × 40/100 |

**An exam question may ask you to use gross profit percentages in order to correct an error in recording inventory at the end of a reporting period.**

### Interactive question 6: Mark-up

A business has valued its inventory at £1,000, being the selling price of the items.

**Requirement**

What is the cost of closing inventory at cost assuming the business operates:

(a) On a margin of 25%?
(b) On a mark-up of 25%?

See **Answer** at the end of this chapter.

# 8 Writing off inventories, and inventory drawings

**Section overview**

- Provided inventory actually held is valued at the lower of cost and NRV, no inventory write-off entries are needed.

- When an owner draws out inventory: debit drawings, credit purchases.

Inventory held at the end of the reporting period may be faulty in some way, so it would appear that an amount needs to be written off. How do we account for this?

In fact, if the cost: NRV valuation method is followed, it is not necessary to write anything off inventory at the end of the reporting period as all damaged inventory would have been reduced down to its NRV when computing the value of closing inventory. It follows then that **we do not need to make any year-end accounting entries at all for inventory write-offs**: we simply include the appropriate low valuation of closing inventory in our year-end journal.

Note that **material loss of inventory during the reporting period** is accounted for by **reducing purchases** and increasing expenses in the statement of profit or loss. No entries are needed in the inventory account.

## 8.1 Inventory drawings

If an owner takes items of inventory from the business as drawings, we do not need to adjust opening or closing inventory at all. Instead we **reduce the purchases** figure in cost of sales with the cost of items withdrawn.

| DEBIT | Drawings | £X | |
|---|---|---|---|
| CREDIT | Purchases | | £X |

### Summary (1/2)

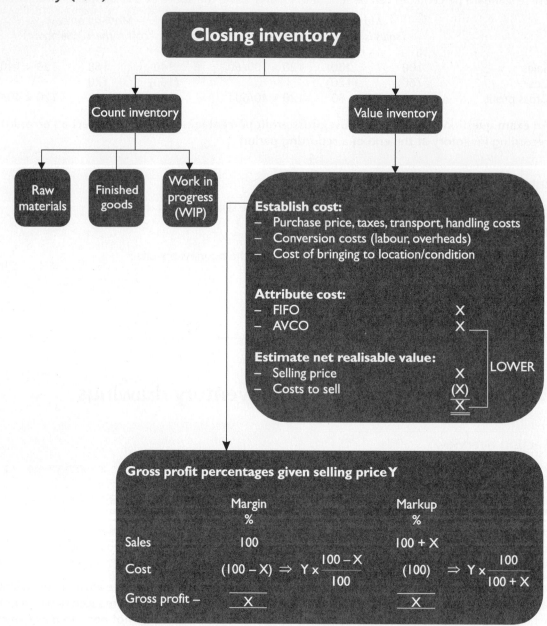

**Closing inventory**

Count inventory → Raw materials, Finished goods, Work in progress (WIP)

Value inventory →

**Establish cost:**
- Purchase price, taxes, transport, handling costs
- Conversion costs (labour, overheads)
- Cost of bringing to location/condition

**Attribute cost:**
- FIFO    X
- AVCO    X

**Estimate net realisable value:**
- Selling price    X
- Costs to sell    (X)
      X

LOWER

**Gross profit percentages given selling price Y**

|  | Margin % |  | Markup % |  |
|---|---|---|---|---|
| Sales | 100 |  | 100 + X |  |
| Cost | (100 − X) | $\Rightarrow Y \times \dfrac{100 - X}{100}$ | (100) | $\Rightarrow Y \times \dfrac{100}{100 + X}$ |
| Gross profit − | X |  | X |  |

ICAEW

# Summary (2/2)

**Accounting for inventories**

**Opening inventory:**

| | |
|---|---|
| DR | Cost of sales (income statement) |
| CR | Inventory account (Statement of financial position) |

**Closing inventory:**

| | |
|---|---|
| DR | Inventory account (statement of financial position) |
| CR | Cost of sales (income statement) |

## ETB

| | TB | | Adj | | IS | | SFP | |
|---|---|---|---|---|---|---|---|---|
| | DR | CR | DR | CR | DR | CR | DR | CR |
| **Inventory:** | | | | | | | | |
| – Opening | X | | | | | | | |
| – Closing | | | Y | Y | | | Y | |
| Cost of sales | | | | | X | Y | | |

## Self-test

Answer the following questions.

1 Which of the following is the correct calculation for cost of sales?

    A    Sales – purchases
    B    Opening inventory + purchases + closing inventory + carriage inwards
    C    Opening inventory + purchases – closing inventory + carriage inwards
    D    Sales – opening inventory - purchases + closing inventory – carriage inwards

2 Distinguish between carriage inwards and carriage outwards.

3 Cost of sales is £14,000. Purchases for the period are £14,000, carriage inwards is £1,000, carriage outwards is £1,500 and closing inventory is £13,000. What was the opening inventory figure?

    A    £10,500
    B    £11,500
    C    £12,000
    D    £13,000

4 Give three reasons why goods purchased might have to be written off.

5 Carlisle has the following inventory movements during May.

| | Units | £ per unit |
|---|---|---|
| Opening inventory | 40 | 9 |
| 2 May Goods in | 60 | 10 |
| 10 May Goods out | 50 | |
| 15 May Goods in | 70 | 11 |
| 18 May Goods out | 45 | |
| 24 May Goods in | 80 | 11 |

Assuming that the business values inventory on a FIFO basis, what will be the value of closing inventory at the end of the month?

    A    £1,615
    B    £1,655
    C    £1,700
    D    £1,705

6 A trader used the LIFO method to value inventory at the end of July at £3,110. Sales and purchases in July were as follows.

| Date | Purchases (units) | Sales (units) |
|---|---|---|
| 3 July | 100 at £20/unit | |
| 6 July | | 80 |
| 10 July | | 40 |
| 15 July | 50 at £22/unit | |
| 22 July | | 20 |
| 27 July | 80 at £25/unit | |

The opening inventory at 1 July was 50 units valued at £15 per unit. The trader needs to adopt the FIFO method.

What is the effect of this change on the trader's profit?

    A    £190 decrease
    B    £420 decrease
    C    £420 increase
    D    £190 increase

7 The inventory records for Simmons last month were as follows.

| Date | Purchases (units) | Sales (units) |
|---|---|---|
| 2 February | | 500 |
| 13 February | 800 | |
| 21 February | | 400 |
| 29 February | | 200 |

ICAEW

Opening inventory was 600 units valued at £12,000. Purchases in February were at £31.25 per unit.

The total cost of sales in February, using the AVCO method, is (to the nearest £):

A    £37,000
B    £28,000
C    £17,625
D    £22,000

8    What would be the effect on a business's profit of discovering that inventory with a cost of £1,250 and a net realisable value of £1,000 had been omitted from the inventory count at the end of the reporting period?

A    An increase of £1,250
B    An increase of £1,000
C    A decrease of £250
D    No effect

9    June Ltd has three lines of inventory at the end of its reporting period.

| | X | Y | Z |
|---|---|---|---|
| Original purchase price (per unit) | £1.50 | £6.50 | £5.00 |
| Estimated future selling price (per unit) | £4.25 | £8.00 | £3.50 |
| Selling and distribution costs (per unit) | £0.75 | £2.00 | £0.50 |
| Units in inventory | 100 | 200 | 250 |

At what value should inventory appear in the financial statements at the end of the reporting period?

A    £2,700
B    £2,325
C    £2,300
D    £2,100

10    Brecon manufactures cosmetics and toiletries. It has decided to repackage its puffer talc product in new covers, and discount the selling price.

The details of puffer talc are as follows.

| | Per item |
|---|---|
| Cost of manufacture | £2.50 |
| Repackaging cost to be incurred | £0.75 |
| Selling price | £3.00 |
| Discount on selling price | 10% |

At what amount should each item of puffer talc be included in inventory?

A    £3.00
B    £2.70
C    £2.25
D    £1.95

11    During the reporting period Malcolm took items with a selling price of £280 for his own use. He trades at a 40% mark-up and had a draft profit of £15,800 before making any adjustments for this matter. His final profit is

A    £15,520
B    £15,800
C    £15,600
D    £16,000

12 Percy Pilbeam is a book wholesaler. Commission of 4% on selling price is payable by Percy for each sale.

The following information is available in respect of total inventory of three of his most popular titles at the end of his reporting period.

|  | Cost £ | Selling price £ |
|---|---|---|
| Henry VIII – Shakespeare | 2,280 | 2,900 |
| Dissuasion – Jane Armstrong-Siddeley | 4,080 | 4,000 |
| Pilgrim's Painful Progress – John Bunion | 1,280 | 1,300 |

What is the total value of these inventories in Percy's statement of financial position?

A   £7,368
B   £7,400
C   £7,560
D   £7,640

13 Roberta Wickham decides to discount some of the slower-selling items in her music shop. These items at 31 March 20X0 are as follows.

| Item | Cost £ | Current price £ | Discount to be applied (% of current price) % |
|---|---|---|---|
| Liszt – To Port | 50 | 70 | 20 |
| Delius – Myth | 70 | 55 | 10 |
| Offenbach – Up the Wrong Tree | 150 | 225 | 10 |
| Bax – To the Wall | 30 | 35 | 50 |

What is the total inventory value of the above items at 31 March 20X0?

A   £267.00
B   £274.00
C   £300.00
D   £325.50

14 From the information below, calculate the value of Jock's closing inventory of foam liquid at 31 October 20X2 using each method of pricing the issue of materials to production.

Jock had 100 litres of foam liquid at 1 October 20X2, purchased at £3 per litre. During the month to 31 October 20X2 the following changes occurred.

|  | Date | Quantity (litres) | Cost per litre £ |
|---|---|---|---|
| Purchases | 7 October 20X2 | 200 | 2.50 |
|  | 14 October 20X2 | 300 | 3.00 |
|  | 21 October 20X2 | 50 | 4.00 |
|  | 28 October 20X2 | 100 | 3.50 |
|  |  | 650 |  |
|  |  |  |  |
| Issues | 4 October 20X2 | 80 |  |
|  | 11 October 20X2 | 70 |  |
|  | 18 October 20X2 | 250 |  |
|  | 25 October 20X2 | 200 |  |
|  |  | 600 |  |

Value of closing inventory:

FIFO basis                                    £ .....................................

AVCO basis                                  £ .....................................

Now, go back to the Learning Objectives in the Introduction. If you are satisfied that you have achieved these objectives, please tick them off.

## Answer to Interactive question 1

GRAND UNION FOOD STORES

STATEMENT OF PROFIT OR LOSS (EXTRACT) FOR THE YEAR ENDED 31 DECEMBER 20X6

|  | £ | £ |
|---|---|---|
| Revenue | | 80,000 |
| Opening inventories | 6,000 | |
| Add purchases | 50,000 | |
| Less closing inventories | (12,500) | |
| Cost of sales | | (43,500) |
| Gross profit | | 36,500 |

## Answer to Interactive question 2

|  |  | £ | £ |
|---|---|---|---|
| DEBIT | Expenses | 64,500 | |
| | Other receivables | 38,700 | |
| CREDIT | Purchases | | 64,500 |
| | Other income | | 38,700 |

## Answer to Interactive question 3

|  |  |  | £ | £ |
|---|---|---|---|---|
| 30.6.X3 | DEBIT | Profit and loss ledger account | 23,490 | |
| | CREDIT | Inventory (asset) | | 23,490 |
| | | *Clearing opening inventory to cost of sales* | | |
| 30.6.X3 | DEBIT | Inventory (asset) | 40,285 | |
| | CREDIT | Profit and loss ledger account | | 40,285 |
| | | *Recording closing inventory as an asset at the end of the reporting period* | | |

This journal could easily be amalgamated to debit the increase in inventory during the reporting period to the asset account, and to credit this to the profit and loss ledger account:

|  |  |  | £ | £ |
|---|---|---|---|---|
| 30.6.X3 | DEBIT | Inventory (asset) | 16,795 | |
| | CREDIT | Profit and loss ledger account | | 16,795 |
| | | *Recording closing inventory as an asset at the end of the reporting period, and as a deduction from the cost of sales* | | |

## Answer to Interactive question 4

| Item | Cost | NRV | Lower of cost/NRV Valuation | Quantity | Total value |
|---|---|---|---|---|---|
| | £ | £ | £ | units | £ |
| A (NRV: 30 – 7) | 20 | 23 | 20 | 200 | 4,000 |
| B (NRV: 12 – 2 – 2) | 9 | 8 | 8 | 150 | 1,200 |
| C (NRV: 22 – 8 – 2) | 14 | 12 | 12 | 300 | 3,600 |
| | | | | | 8,800 |

## Answer to Interactive question 5

### Year 1

| Purchases (units) | Sales (units) | Balance (units) | Unit cost £ | Inventory value £ | Cost of sales £ | Sales £ |
|---|---|---|---|---|---|---|
| 10 | | 10 | 300 | 3,000 | | |
| 12 | | 12 | 250 | 3,000 | | |
| | | 22 | | 6,000 | | |
| | 8 | (8) | 300 | (2,400) | 2,400 | 3,200 |
| | | 14 | | 3,600 | | |
| 6 | | 6 | 200 | 1,200 | | |
| | | 20 | | 4,800 | | |
| | 12 | (12) | | (3,100)* | 3,100 | 4,800 |
| | | 8 | | 1,700 | 5,500 | 8,000 |

* 2 @ £300 + 10 @ £250 = £3,100

### Year 2

| Purchases (units) | Sales (units) | Balance (units) | Unit cost £ | Inventory value £ | Cost of sales £ | Sales £ |
|---|---|---|---|---|---|---|
| B/f | | 8 | | 1,700 | | |
| 10 | | 10 | 200 | 2,000 | | |
| | | 18 | | 3,700 | | |
| | 5 | (5) * | | (1,100)* | 1,100 | 2,000 |
| | | 13 | | 2,600 | | |
| 12 | | 12 | 150 | 1,800 | | |
| | | 25 | | 4,400 | | |
| | 25 | (25) ** | | (4,400)** | 4,400 | 10,000 |
| | | 0 | | 0 | 5,500 | 12,000 |

\*   2 @ £250 + 3 @ £200 = £1,100
\*\* (3+10) @ £200 + 12 @ £150 = £4,400

### Statement of profit or loss

| Year 1 | £ | £ |
|---|---|---|
| Sales | | 8,000 |
| Opening inventory | 0 | |
| Purchases (3,000 + 3,000 + 1,200) | 7,200 | |
| Closing inventory | (1,700) | |
| Cost of sales | | (5,500) |
| Gross profit | | 2,500 |

| Year 2 | £ | £ |
|---|---|---|
| Sales | | 12,000 |
| Opening inventory | 1,700 | |
| Purchases (2,000 + 1,800) | 3,800 | |
| Closing inventory | 0 | |
| Cost of sales | | (5,500) |
| Gross profit | | 6,500 |

## Answer to Interactive question 6

(a)

|  | % | £ |
| --- | --- | --- |
| Sales | 100 | 1,000 |
| COS | (75) | (750) 1,000 × 75/100 |
| GP | 25 | 250 |

Inventory should be valued at £750 when a margin of 25% operates.

(b)

|  | % | £ |
| --- | --- | --- |
| Sales | 125 | 1,000 |
| COS | (100) | (800) 1,000 × 100/125 |
| GP | 25 | 200 |

Inventory should be valued at £800 when a mark-up of 25% operates.

1    C    Opening inventory + purchases − closing inventory + carriage inwards = cost of sales

2    Carriage inwards is paid on goods coming **into** the business and is added to the cost of purchases.

Carriage outwards is paid on goods going **out of** the business to customers and is charged to selling expenses.

3    C

| | £ |
|---|---:|
| Opening inventory value (balancing figure) | 12,000 |
| Add purchases (inc. carriage inwards) | 15,000 |
| | 27,000 |
| Less closing inventory | (13,000) |
| Cost of goods sold | 14,000 |

If you picked A, then you wrongly included carriage outwards in cost of goods sold. If you chose B, then you used the carriage outwards instead of the carriage inwards figure in your calculations. With D, you ignored carriage inwards and outwards altogether!

4   
- Goods are stolen or lost
- Goods are damaged
- Goods are obsolete

5    C    Closing inventory = 40 + 60 − 50 + 70 − 45 + 80 = <u>155 units</u>

Valued on a FIFO basis

| Date of purchase | Units | £ per unit | Total cost |
|---|---:|---:|---:|
| | | | £ |
| 24 May | 80 | 11 | 880 |
| 15 May | 70 | 11 | 770 |
| 2 May | 5 (β) | 10 | 50 |
| | 155 | | 1,700 |

6    D    Closing inventory = 50 + 100 + 50 + 80 − 80 − 40 − 20 = 140 units

Closing inventory under FIFO

| | £ |
|---|---:|
| 80 @ £25 = | 2,000 |
| 50 @ £22 = | 1,100 |
| 10 @ £20 = | 200 |
| | 3,300 |

So profit is (£3,110 − £3,300) = £190 more under FIFO

7    B    Closing inventory = 600 + 800 − 500 − 400 − 200 = <u>300 units</u>

Valued on an AVCO basis:

| Date of purchase | Units | £ per unit | Total cost |
|---|---:|---:|---:|
| | | | £ |
| Opening inventory | 600 | 20.00 | 12,000 |
| 2 Feb | (500) | 20.00 | (10,000) |
| | 100 | | 2000 |
| 13 Feb | 800 | 31.25 | 25,000 |
| | 900 | 30.00 | 27,000 |

| | £ |
|---|---:|
| Opening inventory | 12,000 |
| Purchases (800 × £31.25) | 25,000 |
| Closing inventory (300 × £30.00) | (9,000) |
| Cost of sales | 28,000 |

8    B    It should now be included in closing inventory at £1,000 (lower of cost and NRV). This will increase profit by £1,000.

9    D

|   |   | Lower of cost and NRV £ |
|---|---|---|
| X | At cost (100 × 1.50) | 150 |
| Y | At NRV (200 × (8.00 – 2.00)) | 1,200 |
| Z | At NRV (250 × (3.50 – 0.50)) | 750 |
|   |   | 2,100 |

10    D    Inventory valuation – Lower of

| | |
|---|---|
| – Cost | £2.50 |
| – Net realisable value (selling price less discount less repackaging cost) | £1.95 |

11    D

| | £ |
|---|---|
| Draft profit | 15,800 |
| Add back: drawings at cost £280 x 100/140 | 200 |
| | 16,000 |

12    A

| | Cost £ | NRV SP × 0.96 £ | Lower of cost and NRV £ |
|---|---|---|---|
| Shakespeare | 2,280 | 2,784 | 2,280 |
| Armstrong-Siddeley | 4,080 | 3,840 | 3,840 |
| Bunion | 1,280 | 1,248 | 1,248 |
| | | | 7,368 |

13    A

| | Cost £ | NRV SP ×(100 – disc) £ | Lower of cost and NRV £ |
|---|---|---|---|
| Liszt | 50.00 | 56.00 | 50.00 |
| Delius | 70.00 | 49.50 | 49.50 |
| Offenbach | 150.00 | 202.50 | 150.00 |
| Bax | 30.00 | 17.50 | 17.50 |
| | | | 267.00 |

14    At 31 October 20X2 Jock has 100 + 650 – 600 = 150 litres in inventory

**First in first out method (FIFO)**

| Quantity in inventory (litres) | Acquisition date | Cost per litre £ | Closing inventory value £ |
|---|---|---|---|
| 100 | 28 October | 3.50 | 350 |
| 50 | 21 October | 4.00 | 200 |
| 150 | | | 550 |

**Weighted average cost (AVCO)**

| Date | Quantity (litres) | Cost per litre | Value £ | Average cost per litre £ |
|---|---|---|---|---|
| Opening balance | 100 | 3.00 | 300 | 3.00 |
| 4 Oct Issue | (80) | 3.00 | (240) | |
| | 20 | | 60 | 3.00 |
| 7 Oct Purchase | 200 | 2.50 | 500 | |
| | 220 | | 560 | 2.55 |
| 11 Oct Issue | (70) | 2.55 | (178) | |
| | 150 | | 382 | 2.55 |
| 14 Oct Purchase | 300 | 3.00 | 900 | |
| | 450 | | 1,282 | 2.85 |
| 18 Oct Issue | (250) | 2.85 | (712) | |
| | 200 | | 570 | |
| 21 Oct Purchase | 50 | 4.00 | 200 | |
| | 250 | | 770 | 3.08 |
| 25 Oct Issue | (200) | 3.08 | (616) | |
| | 50 | | 154 | |
| 28 Oct Purchase | 100 | 3.50 | 350 | |
| | 150 | | 504 | 3.36 |

Closing inventory value = 150 litres @ £3.36 = £504

# CHAPTER 8

# Irrecoverable debts and allowances

Introduction

Examination context

**Topic List**

1 Irrecoverable debts

2 Allowances for receivables

3 Accounting for irrecoverable debts and receivables allowances

4 Irrecoverable debts and allowances on the ETB

Summary and Self-test

Answers to Interactive questions

Answers to Self-test

## Learning objectives

- Record and account for transactions and events resulting in income, expenses, assets, liabilities and equity in accordance with the appropriate basis of accounting and the laws, regulations and accounting standards applicable to the financial statements ☐

- Prepare an extended trial balance ☐

- Identify the main components of a set of financial statements and specify their purpose and interrelationship ☐

- Prepare and present a statement of financial position, statement of profit or loss and statement of cash flows (or extracts therefrom) from the accounting records and trial balance in a format which satisfies the information requirements of the entity ☐

Specific syllabus learning outcomes are: 1d, 2c, 3a, 3c

## Syllabus links

The material in this chapter will be developed further in this paper, and then in the Professional Level module of Financial Accounting and Reporting.

## Examination context

Questions on the topics in this chapter will be set as multiple choice questions, some of which may involve calculations so that the correct answer can be selected. Very often double entry questions are phrased in terms of preparing a journal. In addition, the material covered in this chapter may also be examined as part of a long form question.

In the exam you may be required to:

- Identify the accounting principles behind accounting for irrecoverable debts and allowances

- Identify journals for writing off irrecoverable debts, receiving cash in respect of debts previously written off, and setting up or adjusting specific allowances for receivables

- Calculate the figure in the statement of financial position figure for receivables

- Identify the statement of profit or loss figure for irrecoverable debts expense

- Identify the effects of irrecoverable debts and allowances for receivables on gross and profit for the period in the statement of profit or loss

- Specify how year-end irrecoverable debts and allowances for receivables are accounted for on the extended trial balance

# 1 Irrecoverable debts

**Section overview**

- Writing off an irrecoverable debt

  | DEBIT | Irrecoverable debts expense | £X | |
  |-------|------------------------------|----|----|
  | CREDIT | Trade receivables | | £X |

- Accounting for receipt of cash in respect of a debt previously written off:

  | DEBIT | Cash | £X | |
  |-------|------|----|----|
  | CREDIT | Irrecoverable debts expense | | £X |

- The fact that a customer's cheque is returned unpaid does not automatically mean the customer's debt should be written off.

Customers who buy goods on credit might fail to pay for them, perhaps out of dishonesty, or because they have gone bankrupt and cannot pay, or because there is a dispute between the parties about the amount payable.

For one reason or another, a business might decide to give up expecting payment of the debt and to **write it off**.

**Definitions**

**Irrecoverable debt:** A debt which is not expected to be paid.

**Writing off:** Charging the cost of the debt against the profit for the period.

## 1.1 Writing off irrecoverable debts

When a business decides that a particular debt will not be paid, the whole amount of the receivable in question is '**written off**' as an expense in the statement of profit or loss:

| DEBIT | Irrecoverable debts expense (statement of profit or loss) | £X | |
|-------|-----------------------------------------------------------|----|----|
| CREDIT | Trade receivables (statement of financial position) | | £X |

Irrecoverable debts written off are presented for as follows.

- **Sales** are shown at their final invoice value in the **statement of profit or loss**. The sale has been made, expense has been incurred making it and gross profit should be earned. The subsequent failure to collect the debt is a separate administrative matter.

- **Irrecoverable debts** expense is shown as an **administrative expense**.

- The receivable is removed from the receivables control account and ledger.

Suppose an invoice for services rendered to a customer for £300 is never going to be paid. The net effect of the way we account for this as follows:

|  | £ |
|--|---|
| Revenue (in the statement of profit or loss) | 300 |
| Irrecoverable debt written off (administrative expense) | (300) |
|  | 0 |

Overall however a loss is made on the transaction since the entity has incurred costs in rendering the service, and these will not be recovered. The business has also foregone the profit it could have made on the transaction in selling the good or service to a different customer.

When a debt is written off, the value of the receivable as a current asset is zero. It is no longer recognised as an asset because the business is unlikely to generate any benefits from it.

### 1.1.1 Irrecoverable debts written off and subsequently paid

An irrecoverable debt which has been written off might be unexpectedly paid.

Whether it is paid in the same reporting period or a subsequent one, the entry is

| DEBIT | Cash | £X | |
|---|---|---|---|
| CREDIT | Irrecoverable debts expense | | £X |

We do not need to credit receivables as this has already been done when the debt was initially written off.

### Worked example: Irrecoverable debt subsequently paid

We have the following information on Blacksmith's Forge for the year to 31 December 20X5.

| | £ |
|---|---|
| Inventory, 1 January 20X5 | 6,000 |
| Purchases | 122,000 |
| Inventory, 31 December 20X5 | 8,000 |
| Cash sales | 100,000 |
| Credit sales | 70,000 |
| Discounts allowed | 1,200 |
| Discounts received | 5,000 |
| Irrecoverable debts expense | 9,000 |
| Debts paid in 20X5 which were previously written off as irrecoverable in 20X4 | 2,000 |
| Other expenses | 31,800 |

We can prepare the statement of profit or loss as follows:

BLACKSMITH'S FORGE
STATEMENT OF PROFIT OR LOSS FOR THE YEAR ENDED 31.12.20X5

| | £ | £ |
|---|---|---|
| Sales (100,000 + 70,000) | | 170,000 |
| Opening inventory | 6,000 | |
| Purchases | 122,000 | |
| Less closing inventory | (8,000) | |
| Cost of sales | | (120,000) |
| Gross profit | | 50,000 |
| Add discounts received | | 5,000 |
| | | 55,000 |
| Expenses | | |
| Discounts allowed | 1,200 | |
| Irrecoverable debts expense (9,000 – 2,000) | 7,000 | |
| Other expenses | 31,800 | |
| | | (40,000) |
| Profit for the year | | 15,000 |

## 1.2 Dishonoured cheques and irrecoverable debts

We have seen that when a customer's cheque is dishonoured, we **debit trade receivables** (reinstating the debt) and **credit cash** (removing the 'receipt').

**In an exam question, unless you are specifically told otherwise, you should NOT automatically treat a dishonoured cheque as an irrecoverable debt.** Cheques may be dishonoured for administrative reasons that have nothing to do with a customer's actual inability to pay its debt, so do not presume that it will never be paid.

## 2 Allowances for receivables

Specific debts owed to the business are identified as certain never to be collected when irrecoverable debts are **written off**.

However, because of the risks involved in selling goods on credit, the business may conclude that some other specific debts have a risk of being irrecoverable. We call such balances '**doubtful receivables**'. We leave them as an asset on the statement of financial position, but create an **allowance** (a credit balance) which we set off against the receivable.

### Definition

**Allowance for receivables:** An amount in relation to specific debts that reduces the receivables asset to its prudent valuation in the statement of financial position. It is offset against trade receivables, which are shown at the net amount.

An allowance for receivables provides for potential irrecoverable debts, as a precaution by the business. The business will thereby be more likely to avoid claiming profits which subsequently fail to materialise because some specific debts turn out to be irrecoverable.

- When an allowance is first made, it is charged as an expense in the statement of profit or loss along with the irrecoverable debt expense for the period in which the allowance is created. The other side of the entry credits an account in the statement of financial position, the **allowance for receivables**. The double entry is:

  DEBIT     Irrecoverable debts expense (statement of profit or loss – administrative expense)    £X
  CREDIT   Allowance for receivables (statement of financial position)        £X

- When an allowance already exists, but is subsequently **increased**, the amount of the **increase** in allowance is **debited to irrecoverable debt expense**, and **credited to the allowance**.

- When an allowance already exists, but is subsequently **reduced**, the amount of the **decrease** in allowance is **credited** to **irrecoverable debt expense** in the statement of profit or loss for the period in which the reduction in allowance is made, and **debited to the allowance**.

### Worked example: Allowance for receivables 1

A business commences operations on 1 July 20X4, and in the twelve months to 30 June 20X5 makes credit sales of £300,000 and writes off irrecoverable debts of £6,000. Cash received from customers during the reporting period is £244,000.

|                                              | £         |
|----------------------------------------------|-----------|
| Credit sales during the reporting period     | 300,000   |
| Add receivables at 1 July 20X4               | 0         |
| Total debts owed to the business             | 300,000   |
| Less cash received from credit customers     | (244,000) |
|                                              | 56,000    |
| Less irrecoverable debts written off         | (6,000)   |
| Trade receivables outstanding at 30 June 20X5 | 50,000   |

Of these outstanding debts collection of an amount of £5,000 is doubtful.

The business accounts for its irrecoverable and doubtful debts as follows:

|        |                                          | £      | £     |
|--------|------------------------------------------|--------|-------|
| DEBIT  | Irrecoverable debts expense (£6,000 + £5,000) | 11,000 |       |
| CREDIT | Allowance for receivables                 |        | 5,000 |
|        | Trade receivables                         |        | 6,000 |

In the statement of financial position, the value of trade receivables (after the debt write-off, ie £50,000) must be shown with the allowance for receivables netted off.

|                                          | £       |
|------------------------------------------|---------|
| Total receivables at 30 June 20X5        | 50,000  |
| Less, allowance for receivables          | (5,000) |
| Amount in the statement of financial position | 45,000 |

## Worked example: Allowance for receivables 2

Corin Flake owns and runs the Aerobic Health Foods Shop. He commenced trading on 1 January 20X1, selling health foods to customers, most of whom make use of a credit facility that Corin offers. (Customers are allowed to purchase up to £200 of goods on credit but must repay a certain proportion of their outstanding debt every month.)

This credit system initially gives rise to a large number of irrecoverable debts, but experience helps Corin to control them by the third year. Corin Flake's results for his first three years of operations are as follows.

Year to 31 December 20X1
| Gross profit | £27,000 |
|---|---|
| Irrecoverable debts written off | £8,000 |
| Debts owed by customers as at 31 December 20X1 | £40,000 |
| Allowance for receivables | £1,000 |
| Other expenses | £20,000 |

Year to 31 December 20X2
| Gross profit | £45,000 |
|---|---|
| Irrecoverable debts written off | £10,000 |
| Debts owed by customers as at 31 December 20X2 | £50,000 |
| Allowance for receivables | £1,250 |
| Other expenses | £28,750 |

Year to 31 December 20X3
| Gross profit | £60,000 |
|---|---|
| Irrecoverable debts written off | £7,000 |
| Debts owed by customers as at 31 December 20X3 | £30,000 |
| Allowance for receivables | £800 |
| Other expenses | £32,850 |

### Requirement

For each of these three reporting periods, calculate the business's profit for the period, and state the value of trade receivables appearing in the statement of financial position as at 31 December.

## Solution

**AEROBIC HEALTH FOODS SHOP**
**STATEMENT OF PROFIT OR LOSS FOR THE YEARS ENDED 31 DECEMBER**

|  | 20X1 | | 20X2 | | 20X3 | |
|---|---|---|---|---|---|---|
|  | £ | £ | £ | £ | £ | £ |
| Gross profit | | 27,000 | | 45,000 | | 60,000 |
| Expenses: | | | | | | |
| Irrecoverable debts written off | 8,000 | | 10,000 | | 7,000 | |
| Increase/decrease in allowance for receivables* | 1,000 | | 250 | | (450) | |
| Other expenses | 20,000 | | 28,750 | | 32,850 | |
| | | (29,000) | | (39,000) | | (39,400) |
| Profit/(loss) for the year | | (2,000) | | 6,000 | | 20,600 |

\* We calculate the statement of profit or loss amount by:

- Preparing a T account for the allowance

- Carrying down the figure that we require at the end of each reporting period's statement of financial position

- Treating the balancing figure in the reporting period as the charge or the write back required in the statement of profit or loss for that reporting period.

### ALLOWANCE FOR RECEIVABLES

| | | £ | | | £ |
|---|---|---|---|---|---|
| 31.12.X1 | Balance c/d | 1,000 | 31.12.X1 | Irrecoverable debt expense | 1,000 |
| | | 1,000 | | | 1,000 |
| | | | 1.1.X2 | Balance b/d | 1,000 |
| 31.12.X2 | Balance c/d | 1,250 | 31.12.X2 | Irrecoverable debt expense (bal fig) | 250 |
| | | 1,250 | | | 1,250 |
| 31.12.X3 | Irrecoverable debt expense (bal fig) | 450 | 1.1.X3 | Balance b/d | 1,250 |
| 31.12.X3 | Balance c/d | 800 | | | |
| | | 1,250 | | | 1,250 |
| | | | 1.1.X4 | Balance b/d | 800 |

### VALUE OF TRADE RECEIVABLES IN THE STATEMENT OF FINANCIAL POSITION

| | As at 31.12.20X1 | As at 31.12.20X2 | As at 31.12.20X3 |
|---|---|---|---|
| | £ | £ | £ |
| Total value of receivables | 40,000 | 50,000 | 30,000 |
| Less allowance for receivables | (1,000) | (1,250) | (800) |
| Value in the statement of financial position | 39,000 | 48,750 | 29,200 |

# 3 Accounting for irrecoverable debts and receivables allowances

## Section overview

- The irrecoverable debts expense account will be debited with debts written off and with increases in allowances for receivables. It will be credited with amounts received in respect of debts written off, and with reductions in receivables allowances.

- The trade receivables account is only affected when it is credited when a debt is written off. It is unaffected by accounting entries related to the allowance for receivables.

## 3.1 Irrecoverable debts written off: ledger accounting entries

The double entry bookkeeping is split into two separate transactions. To recap:

- When it is decided that a particular debt will not be paid, the customer is no longer called an outstanding receivable, and becomes an irrecoverable debt.

  | | | |
  |---|---|---|
  | DEBIT | Irrecoverable debts expense account | £X |
  | CREDIT | Trade receivables | £X |

In the receivables ledger, personal accounts of the customers whose debts are irrecoverable will be credited off the ledger.

- At the end of the reporting period, the balance on the irrecoverable debt expense account is transferred to the profit and loss ledger account (like all other expense accounts).

  | | | |
  |---|---|---|
  | DEBIT | Profit and loss ledger account | £X |
  | CREDIT | Irrecoverable debts | £X |

- Where an irrecoverable debt is subsequently recovered, the accounting entries will be as follows.

  | | | |
  |---|---|---|
  | DEBIT | Cash | £X |
  | CREDIT | Irrecoverable debts expense account | £X |

### Interactive question 1: Irrecoverable debts written off

At 1 October 20X5 a business had total outstanding debts of £8,600. During the 12 month reporting period to 30 September 20X6 the following transactions took place.

(a) Credit sales £44,000.

(b) Payments from customers £49,000.

(c) Two debts, for £180 and £420, were declared irrecoverable and the customers are no longer purchasing goods from the company. These are to be written off.

**Requirement**

Prepare the trade receivables account and the irrecoverable debts account for the reporting period.

See **Answer** at the end of this chapter.

## 3.2 Allowance for receivables: ledger accounting entries

If particular customers are regarded as being less likely to pay but the debt is not seen as irrecoverable as such, the **trade receivables balance is completely untouched**. An allowance account is set up by the following entries:

| | | |
|---|---|---|
| DEBIT | Irrecoverable debts expense | £X |
| CREDIT | Allowance for receivables | £X |

When preparing the statement of financial position, the credit balance on the allowance account is deducted from the balance on the receivables account.

**In subsequent reporting periods**, the allowance will be adjusted as follows.

- Carry down the new allowance required in the allowance for receivables account.

- Calculate the charge or credit to the statement of profit or loss.

  - If the allowance has **risen**:

    | | | |
    |---|---|---|
    | CREDIT | Allowance for receivables | £X |
    | DEBIT | Irrecoverable debts expense | £X |

    with the amount of the increase.

  - If the allowance has **fallen**:

    | | | |
    |---|---|---|
    | DEBIT | Allowance for receivables | £X |
    | CREDIT | Irrecoverable debts expense | £X |

    with the amount of the decrease.

## Worked example: Accounting entries for allowance for receivables

Alex Gullible has total receivables outstanding at 31 December 20X2 of £28,000. He believes there is a chance that £280 of these balances may not be collected and wishes to make an appropriate allowance. Before now, he has not made any allowance for receivables at all.

On 31 December 20X3 his trade receivables are £40,000. He believes an allowance of £2,000 needs to be made against specific debts in the receivables ledger.

What accounting entries should Alex make on 31 December 20X2 and 31 December 20X3, and what figures for trade receivables will appear in his statements of financial position as at those dates?

## Solution

*At 31 December 20X2*

Alex will make the following entries:

| | | |
|---|---|---|
| DEBIT | Irrecoverable debts expense | £280 |
| CREDIT | Allowance for receivables | £280 |

In the statement of financial position receivables will appear as follows.

| | £ |
|---|---|
| Trade receivables | 28,000 |
| Less allowance for receivables | (280) |
| | 27,720 |

*At 31 December 20X3*

Following the procedure described above, Alex will calculate as follows.

### ALLOWANCE FOR RECEIVABLES

| | £ | | £ |
|---|---|---|---|
| Balance c/d (2) | 2,000 | Balance b/d (1) | 280 |
| | | Irrecoverable debts expense (3) | 1,720 |
| | 2,000 | | 2,000 |

So on completing step (3) he will make the following entries:

| | | |
|---|---|---|
| DEBIT | Irrecoverable debts expense | £1,720 |
| CREDIT | Allowance for receivables | £1,720 |

In the statement of financial position trade receivables will be shown as follows.

|  | £ |
|---|---|
| Trade receivables | 40,000 |
| Less allowance for receivables | (2,000) |
|  | 38,000 |

In practice, a statement of financial position would normally show only the net figure (£27,720 in 20X2, £38,000 in 20X3).

## Worked example: Accounting entries for specific allowance subsequently written off

Alex Gullible has doubts about a customer's ability to pay and makes an allowance for the whole of his debt of £3,000 at 31 December 20X4. During the year ended 31 December 20X5, the customer pays £2,000 and the balance of £1,000 is to be written off as irrecoverable. How is this accounted for during the year ended 31 December 20X5?

### Solution

The answer arises in three stages.

1   Set up the allowance
2   Receive cash and write off the balance
3   Write back allowance as a year end adjustment

ALLOWANCE FOR RECEIVABLES

|  | £ |  | £ |
|---|---|---|---|
| Irrecoverable debts | 3,000 | Specific allowance b/f | 3,000 |

RLCA (EXTRACT)

|  | £ |  | £ |
|---|---|---|---|
|  |  | Cash received | 2,000 |
|  |  | Irrecoverable debt | 1,000 |

IRRECOVERABLE DEBTS

|  | £ |  | £ |
|---|---|---|---|
| RLCA | 1,000 | Allowance for receivables | 3,000 |
| I/S | 2,000 |  |  |
|  | 3,000 |  | 3,000 |

So during the year ended 31 December 20X4, £3,000 is charged to the statement of profit or loss and during the year ended 31 December 20X5, £2,000 is recovered. This leaves a net charge for the two years of £1,000, the amount of the irrecoverable debt.

## Interactive question 2: Receivables allowance

Horace Goodrunning realises that his business will suffer an increase in customers not paying in the future and so he decides to make an allowance against those who are at greater risk at the end of each reporting period.

|  | Balance on receivables account | Balance at risk of default |
|---|---|---|
|  | £ | £ |
| Y/e 28.2.20X6 | 15,200 | 304 |
| Y/e 28.2.20X7 | 17,100 | 342 |
| Y/e 28.2.20X8 | 21,400 | 214 |

## Requirements

For each of the three reporting periods:

(a) What are the closing trade receivables and allowance for receivables balances?
(b) What charge is made to the statement of profit or loss?
(c) How would receivables appear in the statement of financial position?

See **Answer** at the end of this chapter.

# 4 Irrecoverable debts and allowances on the ETB

### Section overview

- An adjustment journal for writing off a debt debits the irrecoverable debts expense line and credits trade receivables. The debit increases the statement of profit or loss expense; the credit reduces trade receivables at the end of each reporting period.

- Adjustment journal for setting up or increasing a receivables allowance: debit irrecoverable debts, credit a receivables allowance line. The debit increases the statement of profit or loss expense; the credit sets up the allowance to be set against trade receivables in the statement of financial position.

So far we have looked at how irrecoverable debts and allowances are calculated then accounted for in the ledger accounts. Because decisions about irrecoverable debts and doubtful debts are usually made and accounted for after the initial trial balance has been extracted, a neater way of incorporating the relevant figures is to use the ETB.

- Calculate the amount of irrecoverable debts and the level of the allowance as usual

- Prepare the year end journals as usual

- Enter these journals in the adjustments columns of the ETB, opening new lines for irrecoverable debts expense and allowance for receivables if necessary

- Include these adjustments in the ETB cross-cast to prepare the financial statements

- Enter the journals in the ledger accounts as usual

### Worked example: Irrecoverable debts and allowances on the ETB

Lorraine runs a bookshop. She has extracted the following initial trial balance as at 31 December 20X9:

|  | DR £ | CR £ |
|---|---|---|
| Cash at bank | 4,391 | |
| Opening capital | | 20,000 |
| Loan | | 2,000 |
| Non-current assets | 30,000 | |
| Trade payables | | 9,642 |
| Irrecoverable debt expense | 50 | |
| Expenses | 3,896 | |
| Purchases | 42,875 | |
| Sales | | 96,475 |
| Trade receivables | 8,622 | |
| Allowance for receivables | | 350 |
| Drawings | 38,833 | |
| Suspense | | 200 |
| Profit for the year (to be determined) | ? | |
| | 128,667 | 128,667 |

She needs to take account of the following matters:

(a) As at the end of the reporting period there is a debt of £695 to be written off.

(b) Of the remaining receivables, Lorraine is concerned that one amount of £250 may prove difficult to recover, so wishes to make an allowance against it.

(c) During the reporting period, £200 was banked in respect of a debt which had been written off in the reporting period ended 31 December 20X8. The only entry in respect of this was in the cash at bank account.

Complete Lorraine's ETB to calculate her profit for the reporting period.

## Solution

| Ledger balance | Trial balance | | Adjustments | | Statement of profit or loss | | Statement of financial position | |
|---|---|---|---|---|---|---|---|---|
| | DR £ | CR £ | DR £ | CR £ | DR £ | CR £ | DR £ | CR £ |
| Cash at bank | 4,391 | | | | | | 4,391 | |
| Opening capital | | 20,000 | | | | | | 20,000 |
| Loan | | 2,000 | | | | | | 2,000 |
| Non-current assets | 30,000 | | | | | | 30,000 | |
| Trade payables | | 9,642 | | | | | | 9,642 |
| Irrecoverable debt expense | 50 | | 695 | 300 | 445 | | | |
| Expenses | 3,896 | | | | 3,896 | | | |
| Purchases | 42,875 | | | | 42,875 | | | |
| Sales | | 96,475 | | | | 96,475 | | |
| Trade receivables | 8,622 | | | 695 | | | 7,927 | |
| Allowance for receivables | | 350 | 100 | | | | | 250 |
| Drawings | 38,833 | | | | | | 38,833 | |
| Suspense | | 200 | 200 | | | | | |
| Profit for the period | | | | | 49,259 | | | 49,259 |
| | 128,667 | 128,667 | 995 | 995 | 96,475 | 96,475 | 81,151 | 81,151 |

The adjusting journals are as follows:

| | | | £ | £ |
|---|---|---|---|---|
| (a) | DEBIT | Irrecoverable debt expense | 695 | |
| | CREDIT | Trade receivables | | 695 |
| (b) | DEBIT | Allowance for receivables (350 – 250) | 100 | |
| | CREDIT | Irrecoverable debt expense | | 100 |
| (c) | DEBIT | Suspense a/c | 200 | |
| | CREDIT | Irrecoverable debt expense | | 200 |

## Summary

### Irrecoverable debts

**Write off:**
DR      Irrecoverable debts expense (income statement)
CR      Trade receivables (statement of financial position)

**Cash received re. debt written off:**
DR      Cash (statement of financial position)
CR      Irrecoverable debts expense (income statement)

### Doubtful debt

**Set up an allowance:**
DR      Irrecoverable debts expense (Income statement)
CR      Allowance for receivables (statement of financial position – net off trade receivables)

| ALLOWANCE FOR RECEIVABLES | | | |
|---|---|---|---|
| Decrease | X | Balance b/d | X |
| Balance c/d | X | Increase | X |
| | X | | X |

### ETB

| | Adj | | IS | | SFP | |
|---|---|---|---|---|---|---|
| | DR | CR | DR | CR | DR | CR |
| Irrecoverable debt expense | | | | | | |
|   – Write off debt | X | | X | | | |
|   – Increase allowance | Y | | Y | | | |
|   – Reduce allowance | | Z | | Z | | |
| Trade receivables | | X | | | | X |
| Allowance for receivables | Z | Y | | | Z | Y |

CHAPTER 8

## Self-test

Answer the following questions.

1   An irrecoverable debt arises in which of the following situations?

    A   A customer pays part of the account
    B   An invoice is in dispute
    C   The customer goes bankrupt
    D   A cheque received in settlement is dishonoured by the customer's bank

2   An allowance for receivables at the end of a reporting period of £4,000 is required. The allowance for receivables brought forward from the previous period is £2,000. What change is required this reporting period?

    A   Increase by £4,000
    B   Decrease by £4,000
    C   Increase by £2,000
    D   Decrease by £2,000

3   If a receivables allowance is increased, what is the effect on the statement of profit or loss?

4   What is the double entry to record an irrecoverable debt written off?

5   On 1 January 20X5 Plodd had a doubtful debt allowance of £1,000. During 20X5 he wrote off debts of £600 and was paid £80 by the liquidator of a company whose debts had been written off completely in 20X4. At the end of 20X5 it was decided to adjust the doubtful debts allowance to £900.

    What is the net expense for irrecoverable debts in the statement of profit or loss for 20X5?

    A   £420
    B   £580
    C   £620
    D   £780

6   Smith has receivables totalling £16,000 after writing off irrecoverable debts of £500, and he has an allowance for receivables brought forward of £2,000. He wishes to carry forward an allowance of £800.

    What will be the effect on profit of adjusting the allowance?

    A   £700 decrease
    B   £700 increase
    C   £1,200 decrease
    D   £1,200 increase

7   At 31 December 20X9 Folland's receivables totalled £120,000. Folland wishes to have an allowance against specific receivables of £3,600, which is 25% higher than it was before. During the year irrecoverable debts of £3,200 were written off and irrecoverable debts (written off three years previously) of £150 were recovered.

    What is the net charge for irrecoverable debts for the 12 month reporting period ended 31 December 20X9?

    A   £720
    B   £900
    C   £3,770
    D   £3,950

8 During the 12 month reporting period ended 31 December 20X8 Keele decreased its receivables allowance by £600. An irrecoverable debt written off in the previous reporting period amounting to £300 was recovered in 20X8.

If the profit of the reporting period **after** accounting for the above items is £5,000, what was it **before** accounting for them?

A £4,100
B £4,700
C £5,300
D £5,900

9 Bodkin had the following balances in its trial balance at 30 June 20X1.

|  | £ |
|---|---|
| Trade receivables | 70,000 |
| Irrecoverable debts expense | 500 |
| Allowance for receivables at 1 July 20X0 | 5,000 |

Bodkin wishes to carry forward at 30 June 20X1 an allowance equal to 10% of trade receivables.

What is the irrecoverable debts figure in the statement of profit or loss for the 12 month reporting period ended 30 June 20X1?

A Charge of £2,450
B Credit of £2,450
C Charge of £2,500
D Credit of £2,500

10 Wacko had a receivables allowance at 1 January 20X0 of £1,000. He calculates that at 31 December 20X0 a receivables allowance of £1,500 is required. In addition £2,000 of debts were written off during the reporting period, which includes £50 previously provided for.

How much should be included in Wacko's statement of profit or loss in relation to irrecoverable debts for the 12 month reporting period ended 31 December 20X0?

A £1,500
B £2,450
C £2,500
D £2,550

Now, go back to the Learning Objectives in the Introduction. If you are satisfied that you have achieved these objectives, please tick them off.

# Answers to Interactive questions

## Answer to Interactive question 1

### TRADE RECEIVABLES

| | £ | | £ |
|---|---|---|---|
| Opening balance b/fd | 8,600 | Cash | 49,000 |
| Sales | 44,000 | Irrecoverable debts expense (180 + 420) | 600 |
| | | Closing balance c/d | 3,000 |
| | 52,600 | | 52,600 |
| Opening balance b/d | 3,000 | | |

### IRRECOVERABLE DEBTS

| | £ | | £ |
|---|---|---|---|
| Receivables | 600 | P & L | 600 |
| | 600 | | 600 |

## Answer to Interactive question 2

The entries for the three reporting periods are shown below.

### TRADE RECEIVABLES (EXTRACT)

| | | £ | | £ |
|---|---|---|---|---|
| 28.2.20X6 | Balance | 15,200 | | |
| 28.2.20X7 | Balance | 17,100 | | |
| 28.2.20X8 | Balance | 21,400 | | |

### ALLOWANCE FOR RECEIVABLES

| | | £ | | | £ |
|---|---|---|---|---|---|
| 28.2.20X6 | Balance c/d | 304 | 28.2.20X6 | P & L account | 304 |
| | | 304 | | | 304 |
| 28.2.20X7 | Balance c/d | 342 | 1.3.20X6 | Balance b/d | 304 |
| | | | 28.2.20X7 | P & L account (bal fig) | 38 |
| | | 342 | | | 342 |
| 28.2.20X8 | P & L account (bal fig) | 128 | 1.3.20X7 | Balance b/d | 342 |
| 28.2.20X8 | Balance c/d | 214 | | | |
| | | 342 | | | |
| | | | | | 342 |
| | | | 1.3.20X8 | Balance b/d | 214 |

### PROFIT AND LOSS LEDGER ACCOUNT (EXTRACT)

| | | £ | | | £ |
|---|---|---|---|---|---|
| 28.2.20X6 | Allowance for receivables | 304 | | | |
| 28.2.20X7 | Allowance for receivables | 38 | | | |
| | | | 28.2.20X8 | Allowance for receivables | 128 |

### STATEMENT OF FINANCIAL POSITION: EXTRACT AS AT

| | 20X6 | 20X7 | 20X8 |
|---|---|---|---|
| | £ | £ | £ |
| *Current assets* | | | |
| Trade receivables | 15,200 | 17,100 | 21,400 |
| Less allowance for receivables | (304) | (342) | (214) |
| | 14,896 | 16,758 | 21,186 |

# Answers to Self-test

1  C  When a customer becomes bankrupt there is no money with which to settle the debt, so it must be regarded as being irrecoverable. A customer settling only part of an account, an invoice being in dispute and a cheque being dishonoured by the customer's bank (ie it being returned unpaid) may all be caused by administrative problems; further analysis of the situation will need to be done before concluding that the debt is irrecoverable.

2  C  The allowance in the statement of financial position needs to be increased by £2,000 to £4,000; this will be a charge in the statement of profit or loss.

3  The increase in the allowance is charged as an expense in the statement of profit or loss.

4  DEBIT   Irrecoverable debts account (expenses)
   CREDIT Trade accounts receivable

5  A

### ALLOWANCE FOR RECEIVABLES

|  | £ |  | £ |
|---|---|---|---|
| Irrecoverable debts | 100 | b/d | 1,000 |
| c/d | 900 |  |  |
|  | 1,000 |  | 1,000 |

### IRRECOVERABLE DEBTS EXPENSE

|  | £ |  | £ |
|---|---|---|---|
| Receivables | 600 | Cash | 80 |
|  |  | Allowance for receivables | 100 |
|  |  | Statement of profit or loss | 420 |
|  | 600 |  | 600 |

6  D

### ALLOWANCE FOR RECEIVABLES

|  | £ |  | £ |
|---|---|---|---|
| Irrecoverable debts expense | 1,200 | b/d | 2,000 |
| c/d | 800 |  |  |
|  | 2,000 |  | 2,000 |

7  C

### IRRECOVERABLE DEBTS EXPENSE

|  | £ |  | £ |
|---|---|---|---|
| Receivables | 3,200 | Cash | 150 |
| Allowance for receivables | 720 | Statement of profit or loss | 3,770 |
|  | 3,920 |  | 3,920 |

### ALLOWANCE FOR RECEIVABLES

|  | £ |  | £ |
|---|---|---|---|
| c/d | 3,600 | b/d (3,600 × 100/125) | 2,880 |
|  |  | Irrecoverable debts expense | 720 |
|  | 3,600 |  | 3,600 |

8  A

|  | £ |
|---|---|
| Profit before irrecoverable debts (balancing figure) | 4,100 |
| Add Decrease in allowance | 600 |
| Add Irrecoverable recovered | 300 |
| Profit after irrecoverable debts | 5,000 |

**9  C**

ALLOWANCE FOR RECEIVABLES

| | £ | | £ |
|---|---|---|---|
| | | b/d | 5,000 |
| c/d (10% × 70,000) | 7,000 | Irrecoverable debts expense | 2,000 |
| | 7,000 | | 7,000 |

IRRECOVERABLE DEBTS EXPENSE

| | £ | | £ |
|---|---|---|---|
| b/d | 500 | Statement of profit or loss charge | 2,500 |
| Allowance for receivables | 2,000 | | |
| | 2,500 | | 2,500 |

**10  C**

IRRECOVERABLE DEBTS EXPENSE

| | £ | | £ |
|---|---|---|---|
| Allowance for receivables | 500 | Statement of profit or loss charge | 2,500 |
| Receivables | 2,000 | | |
| | 2,500 | | 2,500 |

# CHAPTER 9

# Accruals and prepayments

Introduction

Examination context

**Topic List**

Summary and Self-test

Answers to Interactive questions

Answers to Self-test

# Introduction

## Learning objectives

- Record and account for transactions and events resulting in income, expenses, assets, liabilities and equity in accordance with the appropriate basis of accounting and the laws, regulations and accounting standards applicable to the financial statements ☐

- Prepare an extended trial balance ☐

- Identify the main components of a set of financial statements and specify their purpose and interrelationship ☐

- Prepare and present a statement of financial position, statement of profit or loss and statement of cash flows (or extracts therefrom) from the accounting records and trial balance in a format which satisfies the information requirements of the entity ☐

Specific syllabus learning outcomes are: 1d, 2c, 3a, 3c

## Syllabus links

The material in this chapter will be developed further in this paper, and then in the Professional Level module of Financial Accounting and Reporting.

## Examination context

Questions on the topics in this chapter will be set as multiple choice questions, some of which may involve calculations so that the correct answer can be selected. Very often double entry questions are phrased in terms of preparing a journal. In addition, the material covered in this chapter may also be examined as part of a long form question.

In the exam you may be required to:

- Identify the accounting principles behind accruals and prepayments

- Calculate figures in the statement of financial position for accruals and prepayments of expenditure

- Calculate figures in the statement of financial position for accrued and deferred income (arrears and advances)

- Identify the correct figures in the statement of profit or loss for income and expenses

- Identify the effects of accruals and prepayments of income and expenses on profit for the period in the statement of profit or loss

- Specify how year-end accruals and prepayments are accounted for on the extended trial balance

# 1 The principle behind accruals and prepayments

## Section overview

- The accrual principle requires that we match expenses with the revenue generated by them.

- We sometimes therefore need to carry forward actual expenditure to a subsequent period (a **prepayment**), or account for expenditure incurred before it is actually paid for (an **accrual**).

Gross profit should be calculated by **matching** revenue and cost of sales. Net profit should be calculated by charging the expenses which relate to that period. For example, in preparing the statement of profit or loss for a six month period, it would be appropriate to charge six months' expenses for rent, local property taxes, insurance and telephone costs, etc.

However, expenses may not actually be paid for during the period to which they relate.

## Worked example: Accrual principle

A business rents a shop for £20,000 per annum and pays the full annual rent on 1 April each year. If we calculate the profit of the business for six months to 30 June 20X7, the correct charge for rent in the statement of profit or loss is £10,000, even though the rent paid is £20,000 in that period. Similarly, the rent charge in the statement of profit or loss for the second six months of 20X7 is £10,000, even though no rent is actually paid in that period.

We use the **accrual principle** here to match expenses to the relevant time period.

## Definitions

Accruals (accrued expenses): Expenses which are charged against the profit for a particular period, even though they have not yet been paid for.

Prepayments (prepaid expenses): Expenses which have been paid in one reporting period, but are not charged against profit until a later period, because they relate to that later period.

The following examples clarify the principle involved, that **expenses should be matched against income in the period to which they relate**. Accruals and prepayments are the means by which we move charges into the correct reporting period.

- If we pay in this period for something which relates to the next reporting period, we use a **prepayment** to transfer that charge **forward** to the next period.

- If we have incurred an expense in this period which will not be paid for until the next period, we use an **accrual** to bring the charge **back** into this period.

# 2 Accruals

## Section overview

- To set up an accrual

| | | |
|---|---|---|
| DEBIT | Expense (statement of profit or loss) | £X |
| CREDIT | Accrual (liability on the statement of financial position) | £X |

## Worked example: Accruals 1

Horace Goodrunning ends his motor spares business's reporting period on 28 February each year. His telephone was installed on 1 April 20X6 and he receives his telephone bill quarterly at the end of each quarter. We need to calculate the telephone expense to be charged to the statement of profit or loss for the year ended 28 February 20X7.

Telephone expense for the three months ended:

| | £ |
|---|---|
| 30.6.20X6 | 23.50 |
| 30.9.20X6 | 27.20 |
| 31.12.20X6 | 33.40 |
| 31.3.20X7 | 36.00 |

All the bills were paid on the final day of each three-month period.

## Solution

As at 28 February 20X7, no telephone bill had been received in respect of 20X7 because it was not due for another month. However, the accrual principle means we cannot ignore the telephone expenses for January and February, and so an accrual of £24 is made, being two thirds of the final bill of £36.

The telephone expenses for the year ended 28 February 20X7 are as follows:

| | £ |
|---|---|
| 1 March – 31 March 20X6 (no telephone) | 0.00 |
| 1 April – 30 June 20X6 | 23.50 |
| 1 July – 30 September 20X6 | 27.20 |
| 1 October – 31 December 20X6 | 33.40 |
| 1 January – 28 February 20X7 (two months: £36 × 2/3)* | 24.00 |
| | 108.10 |

* The charge for the period 1 January – 28 February 20X7 is two thirds of the bill received on 31 March.

The accrual will also appear in the statement of financial position of the business as at 28 February 20X7, as a current liability. The journal to set this up is as follows:

| DEBIT | Electricity | £24 | |
|---|---|---|---|
| CREDIT | Accrual (current liability) | | £24 |

## Interactive question 1: Accruals I

Cleverley started in business as a paper plate and cup manufacturer on 1 January 20X2, preparing financial statements to 31 December 20X2. He is not registered for VAT. Electricity bills received were as follows.

| | 20X2 | 20X3 | 20X4 |
|---|---|---|---|
| | £ | £ | £ |
| 31 January | – | 491.52 | 753.24 |
| 30 April | 279.47 | 400.93 | 192.82 |
| 31 July | 663.80 | 700.94 | 706.20 |
| 31 October | 117.28 | 620.00 | 156.40 |

### Requirement

What should the electricity charge be for the year ended 31 December 20X2? Prepare a journal to record the accrual or prepayment as at 31 December 20X2.

See **Answer** at the end of this chapter.

# 3 Prepayments

### Section overview

- To set up a prepayment

    DEBIT      Prepayment (asset in the statement of financial position)      £X
    CREDIT    Expense (statement of profit or loss)                                              £X

### Worked example: Prepayments I

A business opens on 1 January 20X4 in a shop where the rent is £20,000 per year, payable quarterly in advance at the beginning of each three month period. Payments were made as follows.

|                            | £     |
|----------------------------|-------|
| 1 January 20X4             | 5,000 |
| 31 March 20X4              | 5,000 |
| 30 June 20X4               | 5,000 |
| 30 September 20X4          | 5,000 |
| 31 December 20X4           | 5,000 |

### Requirement

What will the rental charge be for the year ended 31 December 20X4?

### Solution

The total amount paid in the year is £25,000. The yearly rental, however, is only £20,000. The last payment was a prepayment as it is a payment in advance for the first three months of 20X5. The charge for 20X4 is therefore:

|                  | £       |
|------------------|---------|
| Paid in year     | 25,000  |
| Prepayment       | (5,000) |
|                  | 20,000  |

The double entry for this prepayment is:

| DEBIT    | Prepayments (current asset) | £5,000 |        |
|----------|-----------------------------|--------|--------|
| CREDIT   | Rent                        |        | £5,000 |

# 4 Accounting for accruals and prepayments

### Section overview

- Both accruals and prepayments are usually included as current liabilities/assets as they nearly always clear very soon after the end of the reporting period.

- In order not to double count accrued expenditure, or fail to account for prepaid expenditure at all, closing accruals and prepayments must be reversed at the start of the next reporting period:

    DEBIT    Accruals      £X            CREDIT    Expense           £X

    DEBIT    Expense        £X    CREDIT    Prepayment        £X

You can see from the double entry shown for both these examples that the other side of the entry is taken to the statement of financial position: an asset or a liability account that are needed only at the end of each reporting period.

- **Prepayments** are included in **current assets** in the statement of financial position as they represent money that has been paid out in advance of the expense being incurred. They usually clear within 12 months of the date of the statement of financial position. The balance on the prepayment ledger account is brought down as a debit balance at the beginning of the next period.

- **Accruals** are included in **current liabilities** as they represent liabilities which have been incurred but for which no invoice has yet been received. They nearly always clear soon after the end of the reporting period. The balance on the accruals account is brought down as a credit balance at the beginning of the next period.

| Transaction | DR | CR | Description |
| --- | --- | --- | --- |
| **Accrual** | Expense | Liability (accrual) | Expense incurred in period, not paid/recorded |
| **Prepayment** | Asset (prepayment) | (Reduction in) expense | Expense paid/recorded in period, not incurred until next period |

## 4.1 Reversing accruals and prepayments in new period

Prepayments and accruals must be **reversed** by an opening journal in the new period, otherwise the entity will charge itself twice for the same expense (accruals) *or* will never charge itself (prepayments).

| Transaction | DR | CR | Description |
| --- | --- | --- | --- |
| **Reverse accrual** | Accrual (opening credit balance on liability account) | Expense (new period) | Reversing accrual of expense set up in previous period |
| **Reverse prepayment** | Expense (new period) | Prepayment (opening debit balance on asset account) | Reversing prepayment of expense set up in previous period |

Once these **opening journals** are written up, the balance on the accruals and prepayments accounts will be zero. They will not be used again until the end of the new period.

Most accounting systems allow you to set up special journals called reversing journals which are flagged to automatically be reversed by the system after a specific date.

### 4.1.1 Reversing accruals

We shall use the electricity account from Interactive question 3 above, plus a new accrual ledger account, and see how the accrual is reversed at the beginning of the new period, then a new one is set up at its end.

ACCRUAL ACCOUNT

| | £ | | £ |
| --- | --- | --- | --- |
| *20X2* | | *20X2* | |
| 31.12 Balance c/d | 327.68 | 31.12 Electricity account | 327.68 |
| | 327.68 | | 327.68 |
| *20X3* | | *20X3* | |
| 1.1 Electricity account (accrual reversed) | 327.68 | 1.1 Balance b/d | 327.68 |

## ELECTRICITY ACCOUNT

| | | £ | | | £ |
|---|---|---|---|---|---|
| *20X2* | | | *20X2* | | |
| 30.4 | Cash | 279.47 | 31.12 | Statement of profit or loss | 1,388.23 |
| 31.7 | Cash | 663.80 | | | |
| 31.10 | Cash | 117.28 | | | |
| 31.12 | Accrual account | 327.68 | | | |
| | | 1,388.23 | | | 1,388.23 |
| *20X3* | | | *20X3* | | |
| 31.1 | Cash | 491.52 | 1.1 | Accrual reversed | 327.68 |
| 30.4 | Cash | 400.93 | 31.12 | Statement of profit or loss | 2,387.87 |
| 31.7 | Cash | 700.94 | | | |
| 31.10 | Cash | 620.00 | | | |
| 31.12 | Accrual account | 502.16 | | | |
| | | 2,715.55 | | | 2,715.55 |

The statement of profit or loss charge and accrual for 20X3 of £2,387.87 and £502.16 respectively can be checked as follows.

| Invoice paid | £ | Proportion charged in 20X3 | £ |
|---|---|---|---|
| 31.1.X3 | 491.52 | 1/3 | 163.84 |
| 30.4.X3 | 400.93 | all | 400.93 |
| 31.7.X3 | 700.94 | all | 700.94 |
| 31.10.X3 | 620.00 | all | 620.00 |
| 31.1.X4 | 753.24 | 2/3 | 502.16 |
| Charge to statement of profit or loss in 20X3 | | | 2,387.87 |

## 4.1.2 Reversing prepayments

Using the rent account from the prepayment worked example, the £5,000 rent prepaid in 20X4 will be reversed by an opening journal in the new period. The rent account will be added to by the payments in 20X5, and then reduced by a journal setting up the prepayment at the end of 20X5 in the same way.

### PREPAYMENT ACCOUNT

| | £ | | £ |
|---|---|---|---|
| *20X4* | | *20X4* | |
| 31.12 Rent a/c | 5,000.00 | 31.12 Balance c/d | 5,000.00 |
| | 5,000.00 | | 5,000.00 |
| *20X5* | | *20X5* | |
| 1.1 Balance b/d | 5,000.00 | 1.1 Rent a/c (prepayment reversed) | 5,000.00 |
| 31.12 Rent a/c | 5,000.00 | 31.12 Balance c/d | 5,000.00 |
| | 10,000.00 | | 10,000.00 |

### RENT

| | £ | | £ |
|---|---|---|---|
| *20X4* | | *20X4* | |
| In year Cash (5 payments) | 25,000.00 | 31.12 Prepayment a/c | 5,000.00 |
| | | 31.12 Statement of profit or loss | 20,000.00 |
| | 25,000.00 | | 25,000.00 |
| *20X5* | | *20X5* | |
| 1.1 Rent a/c (prepayment reversed) | 5,000.00 | 31.12 Prepayment a/c | 5,000.00 |
| In year Cash (5 payments) | 20,000.00 | 31.12 Statement of profit or loss | 20,000.00 |
| | 25,000.00 | | 25,000.00 |

## Interactive question 2: Accruals II

Ratsnuffer is a business dealing in pest control. Its owner, Roy Dent, employs a team of eight people who were paid £12,000 per annum each in the year to 31 December 20X5. At the start of 20X6 he raised salaries by 10% to £13,200 per annum each.

On 1 July 20X6, he hired a trainee at a salary of £8,400 per annum.

He pays his work force on the first working day of every month, one month in arrears, so that his employees receive their salary for January on the first working day in February, etc.

### Requirements

(a) Calculate the cost of salaries charged in Ratsnuffer's statement of profit or loss for the year ended 31 December 20X6.

(b) Calculate the amount actually paid in salaries during the year (ie the amount of cash received by the work force).

(c) State the amount of the accrual for salaries which will appear in Ratsnuffer's statement of financial position as at 31 December 20X6.

See **Answer** at the end of this chapter.

---

## Worked example: Prepayments 2

The Square Wheels Garage pays fire insurance annually in advance on 1 June each year. The firm's reporting period is the year ended 28 February. From the following record of insurance payments you are required to calculate the insurance charge to the statement of profit or loss for the 12 month reporting period ended 28 February 20X8.

*Insurance paid*

|  | £ |
|---|---|
| 1.6.20X6 | 600 |
| 1.6.20X7 | 700 |

### Solution

|  |  | £ |
|---|---|---|
| (a) | 3 months, 1 March – 31 May 20X7 (3/12 × £600) (opening prepayment) | 150 |
| (b) | 9 months, 1 June 20X7 – 28 February 20X8 (9/12 × £700) | 525 |
| | Insurance cost for the year to 28 February 20X8, charged to the statement of profit or loss | 675 |

At 28 February 20X8 there is a prepayment for insurance, covering the period 1 March – 31 May 20X8. This insurance premium was paid on 1 June 20X7, but only nine months worth of the annual cost is chargeable to the reporting period ended 28 February 20X8. The prepayment of (3/12 × £700) £175 as at 28 February 20X8 will appear as a current asset in the statement of financial position of the Square Wheels Garage.

In the same way, there was a prepayment of (3/12 × £600) £150 in the statement of financial position one year earlier as at 28 February 20X7.

*Summary*

|  | £ |
|---|---|
| Prepaid insurance premiums as at 28 February 20X7 | 150 |
| Add insurance premiums paid 1 June 20X7 | 700 |
| | 850 |
| Less insurance costs charged to the statement of profit or loss for the year ended 28 February 20X8 | (675) |
| Equals prepaid insurance premiums as at 28 February 20X8 (asset in statement of financial position) | 175 |

---

## Interactive question 3: Accruals and prepayments

The Batley Print Shop, which is not registered for VAT, rents a photocopying machine. It makes a quarterly payment as follows:

(a)   Three months rental in advance

(b)   A charge of 2 pence per copy made during the quarter just ended

The rental agreement began on 1 August 20X4. The first six quarterly bills were as follows.

| Bills dated | Rental | Cost of copies taken | Total |
|---|---|---|---|
| | £ | £ | £ |
| 1 August 20X4 | 2,100 | 0 | 2,100 |
| 1 November 20X4 | 2,100 | 1,500 | 3,600 |
| 1 February 20X5 | 2,100 | 1,400 | 3,500 |
| 1 May 20X5 | 2,100 | 1,800 | 3,900 |
| 1 August 20X5 | 2,700 | 1,650 | 4,350 |
| 1 November 20X5 | 2,700 | 1,950 | 4,650 |

The bills are paid promptly, as soon as they are received.

### Requirements

(a)   Calculate the charge for photocopying expenses for the year to 31 August 20X4 and the amount of prepayments and/or accrued charges as at that date.

(b)   Calculate the charge for photocopying expenses for the following year to 31 August 20X5, and the amount of prepayments and/or accrued charges as at that date.

See **Answer** at the end of this chapter.

---

## Worked example: Accruals 3

Mark opens a shop on 1 May 20X6 to sell camping equipment. The shop rent is £12,000 per annum, payable quarterly in arrears (with the first payment on 31 July 20X6). His reporting period ends on 31 December each year.

The rent ledger account as at 31 December 20X6 will record only two rental payments (on 31 July and 31 October) and there will be two months' accrued rental expenses for November and December 20X6 (£2,000), since the next rental payment is not due until 31 January 20X7.

The charge to the statement of profit or loss for the period to 31 December 20X6 will be for eight months' rent (May December inclusive), £8,000.

So far, the rent account appears as follows.

RENT ACCOUNT

| | | £ | | | £ |
|---|---|---|---|---|---|
| *20X6* | | | *20X6* | | |
| 31 July | Cash | 3,000 | | | |
| 31 Oct | Cash | 3,000 | 31 Dec | Statement of profit or loss | 8,000 |

To complete the picture, the accrual of £2,000 has to be put in, to bring the balance on the account up to the full charge for the year. At the beginning of the next year the accrual is reversed.

RENT ACCOUNT

| | | £ | | | £ |
|---|---|---|---|---|---|
| *20X6* | | | *20X6* | | |
| 31 July | Cash | 3,000 | | | |
| 31 Oct | Cash | 3,000 | | | |
| 31 Dec | Accruals | 2,000 | 31 Dec | Statement of profit or loss | 8,000 |
| | | 8,000 | | | 8,000 |
| | | | *20X7* | | |
| | | | 1 Jan | Accrual reversed | 2,000 |

The corresponding credit entry would be cash if rent is paid without the need for an invoice – eg with payment by standing order or direct debit at the bank. If there is always an invoice when rent becomes payable, the double entry would be:

DEBIT       Rent account                                    £2,000
CREDIT      Payables                                                      £2,000

Then when the rent is paid, the ledger entries would be:

DEBIT       Payables                                        £2,000
CREDIT      Cash                                                          £2,000

The rent account for the *next* year to 31 December 20X7, assuming no increase in rent in that year, would be as follows.

### RENT ACCOUNT

| 20X7 | | £ | 20X7 | | £ |
|---|---|---|---|---|---|
| 31 Jan | Cash | 3,000 | 1 Jan | Accrual reversed | 2,000 |
| 30 Apr | Cash | 3,000 | | | |
| 31 Jul | Cash | 3,000 | | | |
| 31 Oct | Cash | 3,000 | | | |
| 31 Dec | Accruals | 2,000 | 31 Dec | Statement of profit or loss | 12,000 |
| | | 14,000 | | | 14,000 |
| | | | 20X8 | | |
| | | | 1 Jan | Accrual reversed | 2,000 |

A full twelve months' rental charge is taken as an expense to the statement of profit or loss.

## Worked example: Prepayments 3

Terry Trunk commences business as a landscape gardener on 1 September 20X5. He immediately decides to join his local trade association, the Confederation of Luton Gardeners, for which the annual membership subscription is £180, payable annually in advance. He paid this amount on 1 September 20X5. In the following year he expects the subscription to rise by £12. Terry decides that his reporting period should end on 30 June each year.

In the first reporting period to 30 June 20X6 (10 months), a full year's membership will have been paid, but only ten twelfths of the subscription should be charged to the period (10/12 × £180 = £150). There is a prepayment of two months of membership subscription (ie 2/12 × £180 = £30).

The journal to set up the prepayment is as follows.

DEBIT       Prepayment account                              £30
CREDIT      Subscriptions account                                         £30

The balance on the subscriptions account (£150) should then be taken to the statement of profit or loss. The balance on the prepayment account will appear as a current asset in the statement of financial position as at 30 June 20X6, and will be reversed on 1 July 20X6.

### SUBSCRIPTIONS ACCOUNT

| 20X5 | | £ | 20X6 | | £ |
|---|---|---|---|---|---|
| 1 Sept | Cash | 180 | 30 Jun | Statement of profit or loss | 150 |
| | | | 30 Jun | Prepayment | 30 |
| | | 180 | | | 180 |
| 20X6 | | | | | |
| 1 Jul | Prepayment reversed | 30 | | | |

The subscription account for the next reporting period will be:

SUBSCRIPTIONS ACCOUNT

| | | £ | | | £ |
|---|---|---|---|---|---|
| *20X6* | | | *20X7* | | |
| 1 Jul | Prepayment reversed | 30 | 30 Jun | Statement of profit or loss (bal fig) | 190 |
| 1 Sept | Cash | 192 | 30 Jun | Prepayment (192 × 2/12) | 32 |
| | | 222 | | | 222 |
| *20X7* | | | | | |
| 1 Jul | Prepayment reversed | 32 | | | |

## Interactive question 4: Statement of profit or loss and statement of financial position

The Umbrella Shop has the following trial balance as at 30 September 20X8.

| | £ | £ |
|---|---|---|
| Sales | | 156,000 |
| Purchases | 65,000 | |
| Non-current assets | 200,000 | |
| Inventory at 1.10.X7 | 10,000 | |
| Cash at bank | 12,000 | |
| Trade receivables | 54,000 | |
| Trade payables | | 40,000 |
| Distribution costs | 10,000 | |
| Cash in hand | 2,000 | |
| Administrative expenses | 15,000 | |
| Finance costs | 5,000 | |
| Carriage inwards | 1,000 | |
| Carriage outwards | 2,000 | |
| Capital account at 1.10.X7 | | 180,000 |
| | 376,000 | 376,000 |

The following information is available:

(a) Closing inventory at 30.9.X8 is £13,000, after writing off damaged goods of £2,000.

(b) Included in administrative expenses is machinery rental of £6,000 covering the year to 31 December 20X8.

(c) A late invoice for £12,000 covering rent for the year ended 30 June 20X9 has not been included in the trial balance.

**Requirement**

Prepare a statement of profit or loss and statement of financial position for the year ended 30 September 20X8.

See **Answer** at the end of this chapter.

## Interactive question 5: Administrative expenses account

Xbat has posted £10,500 from its purchases day book to its administrative expenses ledger account during 20X2, and £250 direct from its cash book. At 31 December 20X2 the business estimates that the year-end accrual should be £100 less than the accrual brought forward, and the prepayment should be £150 less.

**Requirement**

What is the total cost of administrative expenses in the year ended 31 December 20X2?

See **Answer** at the end of this chapter.

# 5 The accrual principle and income

## Section overview

- The accrual principle also applies to income.

- Accrued income arises when receipt of income (such as rent or subscription) is in arrears at the year end.

- Deferred income arises when income has been received in advance at the end of the reporting period, so it needs to be carried forward and treated as income of the following reporting period.

- Accounting for accrued income

  | | | |
  |---|---|---|
  | DEBIT | Accrued income (asset in the statement of financial position) | £X |
  | CREDIT | Other income (statement of profit or loss) | | £X |

- Accounting for deferred income:

  | | | |
  |---|---|---|
  | DEBIT | Revenue or other income (statement of profit or loss) | £X |
  | CREDIT | Deferred income (liability in the statement of financial position) | | £X |

So far we have concentrated on accrued and prepaid expenses arising from the need to match expenses with the income to which they relate. It is also necessary sometimes to treat income in line with the accruals principle.

- Cash may be received in one period although the actual sale to which it relates occurs in the subsequent period. An example is a **deposit** (or **advance payment**, or **payment on account**) received from a customer on an item which will be delivered in the future. The deposit is banked but until the actual sale is recognised the cash should be treated as still being owing to the customer, not as income. This is known as **deferred income**, a **current liability** in the statement of financial position.

- Cash may be received in one period in relation to an event which arose in a previous period. An example is where a supplier makes a **refund** in relation to a purchase in a previous period. This is known as **accrued income**, a **current asset** on the statement of financial position.

The treatment is similar to accruals and prepayments of expenses:

- Calculate the amount of the deferred or accrued income.

- At the end of the reporting period, write up a journal which updates the relevant statement of profit or loss accounts, and which sets up the relevant asset and liability accounts.

- At the beginning of the next reporting period, reverse the double entry.

### Worked example: Deferred and accrued income

Sunrise Carpets sells floor coverings to the public. At the end of its 12 month reporting period,

31 December 20X4, it has recorded as sales £1,200 received from customers as deposits on carpets which are not due to be invoiced until February 20X5. In January 20X5 it records a £500 refund from one of its main suppliers as a result of exceeding the agreed level of custom during 20X4.

**Requirement**

Prepare journals:

(a) Recording these transactions in the ledger accounts for the reporting period ended 31 December 20X4.

(b) Recording these transactions in the ledger accounts for the reporting period ended 31 December 20X5.

## Solution

- The reversal of deferred income in 20X5 is not to a statement of profit or loss account but to trade receivables. This is because we are dealing with credit transactions: the full amount of the sale will be invoiced in February 20X5 (Debit Receivables, Credit Sales), so the deposit should be credited to trade receivables in the new reporting period in anticipation

- The full amount of purchases was originally invoiced by the supplier in 20X4, so the refund is treated as a deduction from what is owed to the supplier by being debited to trade payables in 20X5.

(a)

|  |  |  |  | £ | £ |
|---|---|---|---|---|---|
| 31.12.X4 | DEBIT | Sales | | 1,200 | |
| | CREDIT | Deferred income (liability) | | | 1,200 |
| | | *Deposits from customers* | | | |
| 31.12.X4 | DEBIT | Accrued income (asset) | | 500 | |
| | CREDIT | Purchases | | | 500 |
| | | *Refund from supplier* | | | |

(b)

|  |  |  |  | £ | £ |
|---|---|---|---|---|---|
| 1.1.X5 | DEBIT | Deferred income (liability) | | 1,200 | |
| | CREDIT | Trade receivables | | | 1,200 |
| | | *Reversal of deferred income* | | | |
| 1.1.X5 | DEBIT | Trade payables | | 500 | |
| | CREDIT | Accrued income (asset) | | | 500 |
| | | *Reversal of accrued income* | | | |

---

Most frequently this situation is seen in relation to subscriptions to clubs or associations, which do not generally maintain a receivables ledger and so just use cash accounting. Some members pay an annual subscription earlier than they need to (in **advance**), and others pay late (in **arrears**). At the end of the year there are bound to be amounts in arrears and amounts paid in advance, but the club will nevertheless need to make sure that the income figure it shows relates only to the actual reporting period. The treatment is as follows.

- Open a subscriptions receivable ledger account.

- Enter all the amounts you know eg annual income or cash received.

- Calculate the balancing figure – in an exam the balancing figure will be the amount you are looking for.

### SUBSCRIPTIONS RECEIVABLE

| | | | | |
|---|---|---|---|---|
| Opening arrears | X | Opening advances | X | |
| Annual income | X | Cash received in year | X | |
| | | Irrecoverable amounts | X | |
| Closing advances | X | Closing arrears | X | |
| | X | | X | |

C H A P T E R

9

### Interactive question 6: Accrued income

The Drones Club has a reporting period of 12 months to 30 June. Its annual subscription for the year ended 30 June 20X7 was £100, and this rose to £120 per annum for the year to 30 June 20X8. As at 1 July 20X6 the Club's members had paid £2,380 in advance, and were £4,840 in arrears. The Club only has 200 members, and there are no irrecoverable amounts. It received £23,620 in respect of subscriptions in the year to 30 June 20X7, and four members are known to be in arrears at 30 June 20X7.

Note: The Drones Club decided that from 1 July 20X6 they will no longer accept any part payment of subscriptions. This did not affect the collection of arrears.

#### Requirement

How many members have paid their subscriptions for the reporting period ended 30 June 20X8 in advance?

[Hint: Use the subscriptions receivable T account.]

See **Answer** at the end of this chapter.

You may also encounter deferred income/advances and accrued income/arrears in relation to rent receivable in the exam. Again, a single **rent receivable** ledger account is the best way to make the required calculations.

## 6 Accruals, prepayments, advances and arrears on the ETB

### Section overview

* An adjustment journal for accrued expenses on the ETB debits the expenses line and credits a new accrued line. The debit is added to the statement of profit or loss expense. The credit is a liability in the statement of financial position.

* Adjustment journal for prepaid expenses: debit new prepayments line, credit expenses line. The debit is an asset in the statement of financial position. The credit is deducted from the statement of profit or loss expense.

So far we have looked at how accruals and prepayments/advances and arrears are accounted for in the ledger accounts, using closing and opening journals. These are necessary to keep the ledger accounts up-to-date, but from the point of view of preparing the statement of profit or loss and statement of financial position the procedure can be rather cumbersome. This is because accruals, prepayments, advances and arrears at the period end are usually calculated and accounted for after the initial trial balance has been extracted. A neater way of incorporating the relevant figures is to use the ETB.

* We calculate the amounts of the accrued and prepaid expenses, and the deferred or accrued income, as usual.

* We prepare the period-end journals as usual.

* We enter these journals in the adjustments columns of the ETB, opening up lines in the statement of financial position column for accruals, prepayments, accrued income and deferred income as necessary.

* We include these adjustments in the ETB cross-cast to prepare the financial statements.

* We enter the closing journals in the ledger accounts as usual.

* We prepare and enter the opening journals.

## Worked example: Accruals and prepayments on the ETB

Jezebel makes and sells clothing to order. Her reporting period is the 12 months ended 31 December. She has extracted the following trial balance as at 31 December 20X1:

| | Debit £ | Credit £ |
|---|---:|---:|
| Cash at bank | 6,541 | |
| Opening capital | | 15,000 |
| Loan | | 8,000 |
| Non-current assets | 45,000 | |
| Trade payables | | 16,758 |
| Expenses | 10,877 | |
| Purchases | 62,975 | |
| Sales | | 157,632 |
| Other income | | 0 |
| Trade receivables | 22,854 | |
| Drawings | 49,143 | |
| | 197,390 | 197,390 |

She needs to take account of the following matters:

(a) Her quarterly power bills are £822. The last bill she paid was in respect of the quarter ending 31 October 20X1.

(b) Her annual rent bill of £2,970 was paid on 1 May 20X1 in respect of the year to 30 April 20X2.

(c) Sales include £350 received from cash customers in December in respect of items of clothing that Jezebel will complete in January 20X2.

(d) A royalty of £58 is due from a fashion magazine which used Jezebel's products in a fashion shoot. Jezebel wishes to account for this as other/accrued income rather than trade receivables.

We need to complete Jezebel's ETB to calculate her net profit for the reporting period.

## Solution

| Ledger balance | Trial balance | | Adjustments | | Statement of profit or loss | | Statement of financial position | |
|---|---:|---:|---:|---:|---:|---:|---:|---:|
| | Debit £ | Credit £ | Debit £ | Credit £ | Debit £ | Credit £ | Debit £ | Credit £ |
| Cash at bank | 6,541 | | | | | | 6,541 | |
| Opening capital | | 15,000 | | | | | | 15,000 |
| Loan | | 8,000 | | | | | | 8,000 |
| Non-current assets | 45,000 | | | | | | 45,000 | |
| Trade payables | | 16,758 | | | | | | 16,758 |
| Expenses (a),(b) | 10,877 | | 548 | 990 | 10,435 | | | |
| Purchases | 62,975 | | | | 62,975 | | | |
| Sales (c) | | 157,632 | 350 | | | 157,282 | | |
| Other income (d) | | | | 58 | | 58 | | |
| Trade receivables | 22,854 | | | | | | 22,854 | |
| Drawings | 49,143 | | | | | | 49,143 | |
| Accruals (822 x 2/3) (a) | | | | 548 | | | | 548 |
| Prepayments (2,970 x 4/12) (b) | | | 990 | | | | 990 | |
| Accrued income (d) | | | 58 | | | | 58 | |
| Deferred income (c) | | | | 350 | | | | 350 |
| Net profit | | | | | 83,930 | | | 83,930 |
| | 197,390 | 197,390 | 1,946 | 1,946 | 157,340 | 157,340 | 124,586 | 124,586 |

## Summary

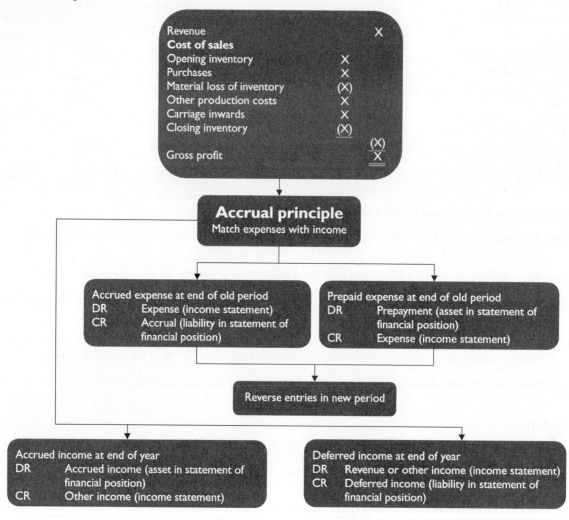

| Revenue | X |
|---|---|
| **Cost of sales** | |
| Opening inventory | X |
| Purchases | X |
| Material loss of inventory | (X) |
| Other production costs | X |
| Carriage inwards | X |
| Closing inventory | (X) |
| | (X) |
| Gross profit | X |

**Accrual principle**
Match expenses with income

Accrued expense at end of old period
DR          Expense (income statement)
CR          Accrual (liability in statement of
            financial position)

Prepaid expense at end of old period
DR          Prepayment (asset in statement of
            financial position)
CR          Expense (income statement)

Reverse entries in new period

Accrued income at end of year
DR          Accrued income (asset in statement of
            financial position)
CR          Other income (income statement)

Deferred income at end of year
DR          Revenue or other income (income statement)
CR          Deferred income (liability in statement of
            financial position)

### ETB

| | Adj | | IS | | SFP | |
|---|---|---|---|---|---|---|
| | DR | CR | DR | CR | DR | CR |
| Expense | A | B | A | B | | |
| Income | C | D | C | D | | |
| Accrual | | A | | | | A |
| Prepayment | B | | | | B | |
| Accrued income (arrears) | D | | | | D | |
| Deferred income (advances) | | C | | | | C |

## Self-test

Answer the following questions.

1   If a business has paid property tax of £1,000 for the year to 31 March 20X9, what is the prepayment in the financial statements for the 12 month reporting period ending on 31 December 20X8?

    A   £0
    B   £250
    C   £750
    D   £1,000

2   Rupa has the following balances in her ledger accounts.

|                    | £      |
|--------------------|--------|
| Purchases          | 75,000 |
| Carriage outwards  | 800    |
| Carriage inwards   | 1,000  |
| Discounts received | 2,000  |
| Opening inventory  | 10,000 |
| Closing inventory  | 12,000 |

What is Rupa's cost of sales?

    A   £72,000
    B   £73,000
    C   £74,000
    D   £74,800

3   On 5 May 20X8 Portals pays a rent bill of £1,800 for the eighteen months ended 30 June 20X9.

    What is the charge in the statement of profit or loss and the entry for rent in the statement of financial position in respect of the 12 month reporting period ended 31 March 20X9?

    A   £1,200 with prepayment of £300
    B   £1,200 with accrual of £600
    C   £1,500 with accrual of £300
    D   £1,500 with prepayment of £300

4   A firm made the following rent payments.

    £9,000 for the six months ended 31 March 20X6
    £12,000 for the six months ended 30 September 20X6
    £11,196 for the 12 months ended 30 September 20X7

    The charge to the statement of profit or loss for the 12 month reporting period ended 31 December 20X6 was

    A   £13,299
    B   £19,299
    C   £24,897
    D   £22,098

5   Elizabeth paid £2,500 for gas during the reporting period. At the beginning of the period she owed £500; at the end she owed £1,000.

    What charge should have appeared in her statement of profit or loss for that reporting period?

    A   £2,000
    B   £2,500
    C   £3,000
    D   £3,500

6    At the beginning of September Barney & Co were owed £200 in rent. At the end of September they were owed £400. £800 cash for rent was received during September.

What entry will be made in the statement of profit or loss for September for rent receivable?

A    Debit £600
B    Debit £1,000
C    Credit £600
D    Credit £1,000

Now, go back to the Learning Objectives in the Introduction. If you are satisfied that you have achieved these objectives, please tick them off.

# Answers to Interactive questions

## Answer to Interactive question 1

The three invoices received during 20X2 totalled £1,060.55, but this is not the full charge for the reporting period: the November and December electricity charge was not invoiced until the end of January 20X3. To show the correct charge for the reporting period, we **accrue** the charge for November and December based on January's bill. The charge for 20X2 is:

|  | £ |
|---|---|
| Paid in year | 1,060.55 |
| Accrual (2/3 × £491.52) | 327.68 |
|  | 1,388.23 |

The double entry for the accrual will be:

| DEBIT | Electricity account | £327.68 |  |
|---|---|---|---|
| CREDIT | Accruals |  | £327.68 |

## Answer to Interactive question 2

(a) Salaries charge in the statement of profit or loss year ended 31 December 20X6

|  | £ |
|---|---|
| Cost of 8 employees for a full year at £13,200 each | 105,600 |
| Cost of trainee for a half year (£8,400/2) | 4,200 |
|  | 109,800 |

(b) Salaries actually paid in 20X6

|  | £ |
|---|---|
| December 20X5 salaries paid in January (8 employees × £1,000 per month) | 8,000 |
| Salaries of 8 employees for January – November 20X6 paid in February – December | |
| (8 employees × £1,100 per month × 11 months) | 96,800 |
| Salary of trainee (for July – November paid in August – December: | |
| 5 months × £700 per month) | 3,500 |
| Salaries actually paid | 108,300 |

(c) Accrued salary as at 31 December 20X6

(ie costs charged in the Statement of profit or loss, but not yet paid)

|  | £ |
|---|---|
| 8 employees × 1 month × £1,100 per month | 8,800 |
| 1 trainee × 1 month × £700 per month | 700 |
|  | 9,500 |

Summary

|  | £ |
|---|---|
| Accrued salaries as at 1 January 20X6 (December 20X5 salaries) | 8,000 |
| Add salaries cost for 20X6 (Statement of profit or loss (a)) | 109,800 |
|  | 117,800 |
| Less salaries paid (b) | (108,300) |
| Equals accrued salaries as at 31 December 20X6 (liability in statement of financial position (c)) | 9,500 |

## SALARIES ACCOUNT

| 20X6 | £ | 20X6 | £ |
|---|---|---|---|
| Cash paid | 108,300 | 1.1 Accrual reversed | 8,000 |
| 31.12 Accrual | 9,500 | 31.12 Statement of profit or loss | 109,800 |
| | 117,800 | | 117,800 |

## Answer to Interactive question 3

(a) Year to 31 August 20X4

| | £ |
|---|---|
| One months' rental (1/3 × £2,100) * | 700 |
| Accrued copying charges (1/3 × £1,500) ** | 500 |
| Photocopying expense (Statement of profit or loss) | 1,200 |

\* From the quarterly bill dated 1 August 20X4
\*\* From the quarterly bill dated 1 November 20X4

There is a prepayment for 2 months' rental (2/3 × £2,100 = £1,400) as at 31 August 20X4, and an accrual for copying charges of £1,500/3 = £500

(b) Year to 31 August 20X5

| | £ | £ |
|---|---|---|
| Rental from 1 September 20X4 – 31 July 20X5 (11 months at £2,100 per quarter or £700 per month) | | 7,700 |
| Rental from 1 August – 31 August 20X5 (1/3 × £2,700) | | 900 |
| Rental charge for the year | | 8,600 |
| Copying charges: | | |
|     1 September – 31 October 20X4 (2/3 × £1,500) | 1,000 | |
|     1 November 20X4 – 31 January 20X5 | 1,400 | |
|     1 February – 30 April 20X5 | 1,800 | |
|     1 May – 31 July 20X5 | 1,650 | |
|     Accrued charges for August 20X5 (1/3 × £1,950) | 650 | |
| | | 6,500 |
| Photocopying expense (statement of profit or loss) | | 15,100 |

There is a prepayment for 2 months' rental (2/3 × £2,700 = £1,800) as at 31 August 20X5, and an accrual for copying charges of £1,950/3 = £650.

Summary of reporting period 1 September 20X4 – 31 August 20X5

| | Rental charges £ | Copying costs £ |
|---|---|---|
| Prepayment as at 31.8.20X4 (2/3 × £2,100) | 1,400 | |
| Accrued charge as at 31.8.20X4 | | (500) |
| Bills paid during the reporting period | | |
|     1 November 20X4 | 2,100 | 1,500 |
|     1 February 20X5 | 2,100 | 1,400 |
|     1 May 20X5 | 2,100 | 1,800 |
|     1 August 20X5 | 2,700 | 1,650 |
| Prepayment as at 31.8.20X5 (2/3 × £2,700) | (1,800) | |
| Accrued charge as at 31.8.20X5 | | 650 |
| Charge to the Statement of profit or loss for the reporting period | 8,600 | 6,500 |
| Items in the statement of financial position as at 31 August 20X5 | | |
|   Prepaid rental (current asset) | 1,800 | |
|   Accrued copying charge (current liability) | | 650 |

# Answer to Interactive question 4

THE UMBRELLA SHOP
STATEMENT OF PROFIT OR LOSS FOR THE YEAR ENDED 30 SEPTEMBER 20X8

|  | £ | £ |
|---|---|---|
| Sales |  | 156,000 |
| Opening inventory | 10,000 |  |
| Purchases | 65,000 |  |
| Carriage inwards | 1,000 |  |
| Closing inventory (W1) | (13,000) |  |
| Cost of sales |  | (63,000) |
| Gross profit |  | 93,000 |
|  |  |  |
| Distribution costs (10,000 + 2,000) | 12,000 |  |
| Administrative expenses (W2) | 16,500 |  |
| Finance costs | 5,000 |  |
|  |  | (33,500) |
| Net profit for the year |  | 59,500 |

THE UMBRELLA SHOP
STATEMENT OF FINANCIAL POSITION AS AT 30 SEPTEMBER 20X8

|  | £ | £ |
|---|---|---|
| **Assets** |  |  |
| *Non-current assets* |  | 200,000 |
|  |  |  |
| *Current assets* |  |  |
| Inventory (W1) | 13,000 |  |
| Trade receivables | 54,000 |  |
| Prepayments (W4) | 1,500 |  |
| Cash at bank and in hand (12,000 + 2,000) | 14,000 |  |
|  |  | 82,500 |
| **Total assets** |  | 282,500 |
| **Capital and liabilities** |  |  |
| *Owner's capital* |  |  |
| Balance brought forward | 180,000 |  |
| Profit for the year | 59,500 |  |
|  |  | 239,500 |
| *Current liabilities* |  |  |
| Trade payables | 40,000 |  |
| Accruals (W3) | 3,000 |  |
|  |  | 43,000 |
| **Total capital and liabilities** |  | 282,500 |

WORKINGS

(1) **Closing inventory**

As the figure of £13,000 is **after** writing off damaged goods, no further adjustments are necessary. Remember that you are crediting closing inventory to the statement of profit or loss and the corresponding debit is to the statement of financial position.

(2) **Administrative expenses**

|  | £ |
|---|---|
| Per trial balance | 15,000 |
| Add accrual (W3) | 3,000 |
| Less prepayment (W4) | (1,500) |
|  | 16,500 |

(3) **Accrual**

|  | £ |
|---|---:|
| Rent for year to 30 June 20X9 | 12,000 |
| Accrual for period to 30 September 20X8 ($^3/_{12} \times £12,000$) | 3,000 |

(4) **Prepayment**

|  | £ |
|---|---:|
| Machinery rental for the year to 31 December 20X8 | 6,000 |
| Prepayment for period 1 October to 31 December 20X8 ($^3/_{12} \times £6,000$) | 1,500 |

## Answer to Interactive question 5

### ADMINISTRATIVE EXPENSES

|  | £ |  | £ |
|---|---:|---|---:|
| Purchases day book | 10,500 |  |  |
| Cash book | 250 | Decrease in accruals | 100 |
| Decrease in prepayment | 150 | Statement of profit or loss | 10,800 |
|  | 10,900 |  | 10,900 |

## Answer to Interactive question 6

### SUBSCRIPTIONS RECEIVABLE

|  |  | £ |  |  | £ |
|---|---|---:|---|---|---:|
| 1.7.X6 | Arrears (accrued income reversed) | 4,840 | 1.7.X6 | Advances (deferred income reversed) | 2,380 |
| 30.6.X7 | Statement of profit or loss (200 × £100) | 20,000 | Year | Cash | 23,620 |
| 30.6.X7 | Advances (deferred income) bal fig | 1,560 | 30.6.X7 | Arrears (4 × £100) (accrued income) | 400 |
|  |  | 26,400 |  |  | 26,400 |

Advances total £1,560, which represents 13 members' payments (13 × £120 = £1,560).

1 B $^3/_{12}$ × £1,000 = £250

2 C

|  | £ |
|---|---|
| Opening inventory | 10,000 |
| Purchases | 75,000 |
| Carriage inwards | 1,000 |
| Less Closing inventory | (12,000) |
|  | 74,000 |

3 A

|  | £ |
|---|---|
| Statement of profit or loss 12/18 × 1,800 | 1,200 |
| Closing prepayment: 3/18 × 1,800 | 300 |

4 B

|  | £ |
|---|---|
| Statement of profit or loss: (3/6 × 9,000) + 12,000 + (3/12 × 11,196) | 19,299 |

5 C

|  | £ |
|---|---|
| Opening accrual | (500) |
| Cash paid | 2,500 |
| Closing accrual | 1,000 |
|  | 3,000 |

6 D

RENT RECEIVABLE

|  | £ |  | £ |
|---|---|---|---|
|  |  | Cash | 800 |
| Other receivables (reversal of opening accrued income) | 200 |  |  |
| Statement of profit or loss (bal fig) | 1,000 | Accrued income | 400 |
|  | 1,200 |  | 1,200 |

# CHAPTER 10

# Non-current assets and depreciation

Introduction

Examination context

**Topic List**

Summary and Self-test

Answers to Interactive questions

Answers to Self-test

## Learning objectives

Tick off

- Record and account for transactions and events resulting in income, expenses, assets, liabilities and equity in accordance with the appropriate basis of accounting and the laws, regulations and accounting standards applicable to the financial statements

- Prepare an extended trial balance

- Identify the main components of a set of financial statements and specify their purpose and interrelationship

- Prepare and present a statement of financial position, statement of profit or loss and statement of cash flows (or extracts therefrom) from the accounting records and trial balance in a format which satisfies the information requirements of the entity

Specific syllabus learning outcomes are: 1d, 2c, 3a, 3c

## Syllabus links

The material in this chapter will be developed further in this paper, and then in the Professional Level module of Financial Accounting and Reporting.

## Examination context

Questions on the topics in this chapter will be set as multiple choice questions, some of which may involve calculations so that the correct answer can be selected. Frequently double entry questions are expressed in terms of preparing a journal.

In the exam you may be required to:

- Identify the accounting principles behind accounting for non-current assets and depreciation

- Specify what is included in the cost of a non-current asset

- Use the straight line and reducing balance methods to calculate depreciation

- Calculate profits and losses on disposal of non-current assets, including part-exchange disposals

- Specify the effects of changing residual values, useful lives and depreciation methods on amounts in the statement of profit or loss and statement of financial position

- Identify how to account for non-current assets, depreciation and disposals in ledger accounts and the extended trial balance

- Calculate the figure in the statement of financial position for non-current assets, and the figures that appear in the non-current assets note

- Calculate the depreciation charge and the figure for profits or losses on disposals in the statement of profit or loss

- Identify the effects of depreciation and disposals on gross and net profit in the statement of profit or loss

- Specify the uses of the asset register

- Identify the accounting treatments of intangible assets, including goodwill and development expenditure

# 1 Non-current assets and depreciation (IAS 16) (FRS 102 s17)

**Section overview**

- Where an asset has a useful life that extends beyond one reporting period, the accrual principle apportions the value used in a period against the income it has helped to create. These are non-current assets

- The cost of a non-current asset includes: purchase price; delivery costs; taxes and duties; irrecoverable VAT; installation and assembly costs; professional fees; testing costs.

- Enhancement expenditure may be added to the cost subsequently.

- Part of an asset's cost may be settled by trading in an old asset in part-exchange.

- All assets except freehold land have a finite useful life.

- Many assets will have a residual value at the end of their useful lives.

- Depreciation allocates the asset's cost less its residual value over its useful life.

## 1.1 IAS 16 *Property, Plant and Equipment*

The objective of IAS 16 is to prescribe in relation to property, plant and equipment the accounting treatment for:

- The recognition of assets
- The determination of their carrying amounts
- The depreciation charges relating to them

This provides the users of financial statements with information about an entity's investment in its property, plant and equipment and changes in such investments.

IAS 16 should be followed when accounting for PPE *unless* another IAS or IFRS requires a **different** treatment, eg IFRS 5 *Non-current Assets Held for Sale and Discontinued Operations*.

**UK GAAP alert!**

There are no material differences between IAS 16 and FRS 102.

## 1.2 Cost of a non-current asset

The cost of a non-current asset includes **all amounts incurred to acquire the asset** and any amounts that can be **directly attributable** to **bringing the asset to the location and condition necessary for it to be capable of operating** in the way intended by management. With the exception of cars, where the VAT is not usually recoverable, the amount capitalised will **exclude** VAT.

**Directly attributable costs** include:

- Purchase price
- Delivery costs
- Stamp duty and import duties (and irrecoverable VAT on cars)
- Costs of preparing the site for installation and assembly of the asset
- Professional fees, such as legal and architects' fees
- Costs of testing whether the asset is functioning

Expenses such as general overhead costs, administration costs, training costs for staff, fuel in a vehicle on delivery and licence fees for operating the asset are **not** included as part of the total costs of the non-current asset.

The cost of **subsequent capital expenditure** on a non-current asset will be added to the cost of the asset, provided this expenditure **enhances** the benefits of the non-current asset or restores any benefits consumed. It is therefore called **enhancement expenditure**.

This means that costs of **major improvements** or a **major overhaul** may be capitalised. However, the costs of **repairs** that are carried out simply to **maintain existing performance** may **not** be capitalised: they will be treated as expenses of the reporting period in which the work is done, and charged in full as an expense in that period.

## 1.3 Paying for a non-current asset

A business might purchase a new non-current asset for **cash** or on **credit**, or it may hand over an old asset **in part-exchange**. This is common, for example, with motor vehicles. The supplier of the new asset agrees to take the old asset, and gives the buyer a reduction in the purchase price of the new asset. This reduction is the **part-exchange value of the old asset**.

### Worked example: Part-exchange

A business purchases a new delivery van, trading in an old van in part-exchange. The cost of the new van is £25,000 and the part-exchange value of the old van is £10,000, so the business will pay the van dealer £15,000.

Because paying for a new non-current asset is rarely straightforward, non-current asset purchases are usually recorded in the **journal** as the book of original entry.

## 1.4 Useful life

An asset may be seen as having a **physical life** and an **economic life**.

Most non-current assets suffer physical deterioration through usage and the passage of time. Although care and maintenance may succeed in extending the **physical life** of an asset, typically it will, eventually, reach a condition where the benefits have been exhausted.

However, a business may not wish to keep an asset until the end of its physical life. There may be a point when it becomes uneconomic to continue to use the asset even though there is still some physical life left. The **economic life** of the asset will be determined by such factors as technological progress and changes in demand.

### Definition

Useful life: The **estimated economic life** (rather than the potential physical life) of the non-current asset.

The only asset that is deemed to have an **unlimited useful life** is **freehold land**.

## 1.5 What is depreciation?

### Definition

Depreciation: The systematic allocation of the cost of an asset, less its residual value, over its useful life.

In determining the expenses for a period, it is important to include an amount to represent the consumption of non-current assets during that period (that is, **depreciation**).

To calculate the depreciation charge for a reporting period, the following factors are relevant:

- Asset cost (see section 1.2 above)
- Useful life (see section 1.4 above)
- Asset residual value

## 1.6 Residual value

At the end of a non-current asset's useful life the business will dispose of it and any expected amounts received represent its **residual value**. For instance, an asset that is expected to be sold for £500 at the end of its useful life has a residual value of £500. If it is unlikely to be a significant amount, a residual value of zero will be assumed. The cost of a non-current asset less its residual value represents the **total amount to be depreciated** over its estimated useful life (**its depreciable amount**).

Note. For exam purposes, always assume the residual value is zero unless told otherwise.

### Definition

Residual value: The estimated amount that the entity would currently obtain from disposing of the asset, after deducting estimated disposal costs.

### Interactive question 1: Depreciable amount

Arundel Enterprises purchased a new car for a sales representative. The invoice received contained the following information:

|  | £ |
|---|---|
| List price of the car | 18,720 |
| Deposit paid | (6,200) |
| Amount due | 12,520 |

It is estimated that the new car will have a useful life of three years and will have a residual value of £6,360.

Calculate the total amount to be depreciated in respect of the new car.

See **Answer** at the end of this chapter.

# 2 The objective of depreciation

### Section overview

- Depreciation arises from the application of the accrual principle. The method chosen should be applied consistently.

The depreciable amount is cost less residual value, and the useful life provides the time period over which the asset should be depreciated. So how much of this depreciable amount is charged against profits in each reporting period?

## 2.1 Accounting concepts and depreciation

**Consistency is important**. The depreciation basis or method selected should be applied consistently from period to period unless altered circumstances justify a change. When the basis *is* changed, the effect on current and future periods should be quantified and disclosed, and the reason for the change should be stated.

Various methods of allocating depreciation to reporting periods are available, but whichever is chosen must be applied **consistently** (as required by IAS 1: see Chapter 1), to ensure **comparability** from period to period. A change of basis is not allowed simply because of the profitability situation of the enterprise.

The need to depreciate non-current assets arises from the **accrual principle**. If money is expended in purchasing an asset then this amount must at some time be charged against profits. If the asset is one which contributes to an entity's revenue over a number of reporting periods it would be inappropriate to charge any single period (eg the period in which the asset was acquired) with the whole of the expenditure. Instead, some method must be found of spreading the cost of the asset over its useful life.

## 2.2 Common depreciation misconceptions

(a) It does not **reflect the fall in value of an asset over its life**.

(b) It is not 'setting aside money' to **replace the asset at the end of its useful life**. Even if the asset was not going to be replaced, its cost should still be allocated over its useful life.

# 3 Calculating depreciation

### Section overview

- Charge depreciation to statement of profit or loss, and set up an account in the statement of financial position called accumulated depreciation. When this is offset against the asset's cost account in the statement of financial position, we have its carrying amount.

- Depreciation may be calculated on the straight line basis:

$$\frac{\text{Asset cost} - \text{residual value}}{\text{Months of useful life}} = \text{Monthly depreciation charge}$$

- Reducing balance depreciation:

  Carrying amount × % to be applied = Annual depreciation charge.

- The depreciation method used should be applied consistently. A change in method may cause an increased charge.

- When there has been enhancement expenditure, this would usually be depreciated over the remaining useful life of the whole asset.

- The carrying amount of an asset should be reviewed and if there has been an impairment this impairment loss should be accounted for immediately.

- If there is a change in the estimate of the asset's useful life or residual value, this too will cause a change in the depreciation charge.

When a non-current asset is depreciated, two things must be accounted for.

(a) The **charge for depreciation** is a cost or expense of the reporting period in the statement of profit or loss.

(b) At the same time, the non-current asset is wearing out and being consumed, and so its **cost in the statement of financial position must be reduced** by the amount of depreciation charged. The value of the non-current asset in the statement of financial position will be its **carrying amount**.

### Definition

Carrying amount: Cost less accumulated depreciation.

The amount of depreciation deducted from the cost of a non-current asset to arrive at its **carrying amount** will build up (or 'accumulate') over time, as more depreciation is charged in each successive reporting period. This is called **accumulated depreciation**.

### Worked example: Accumulating depreciation on a non-current asset

If a non-current asset costing £40,000 has an expected useful life of four years and an estimated residual value of nil, it might be depreciated by £10,000 per annum.

|  | Depreciation charge for the year (income statement) (A) £ | Accumulated depreciation at end of year (B) £ | Cost of the asset (C) £ | Carrying amount at end of year (C − B) £ |
|---|---|---|---|---|
| At beginning of its life | – | – | 40,000 | 40,000 |
| Year 1 | 10,000 | 10,000 | 40,000 | 30,000 |
| Year 2 | 10,000 | 20,000 | 40,000 | 20,000 |
| Year 3 | 10,000 | 30,000 | 40,000 | 10,000 |
| Year 4 | 10,000 | 40,000 | 40,000 | 0 |
|  | 40,000 |  |  |  |

At the end of year 4, the full £40,000 of depreciation charges have been made in the statement of profit or loss of the four years. The carrying amount of the non-current asset is now nil.

## 3.1 Methods of depreciation

There are several different methods of depreciation. Of these, the ones which are relevant for *Accounting* are:

- Straight line method
- Reducing balance method

Remember that if an entity changes from one method to another this counts as a change in **accounting estimate**. There is no change in accounting policy, which remains: to **depreciate non-current assets**.

## 3.2 The straight line method of depreciation

### Definition

**Straight line depreciation:** The depreciable amount (cost less residual value) is charged in **equal instalments** to each reporting period over the expected useful life of the asset. (In this way, the carrying amount of the non-current asset declines at a steady rate, or in a 'straight line' over time.)

The **annual** depreciation charge is:

$$\frac{\text{Cost of asset minus residual value}}{\text{Expected useful life of the asset in years}}$$

The **monthly** depreciation charge is:

$$\frac{\text{Cost of asset} - \text{residual value}}{\text{Useful life in years} \times 12}$$

**Since straight line depreciation is charged monthly you should make the second, monthly, calculation in an exam.**

### Worked example: Straight line depreciation

(a) A non-current asset costing £24,000 with a useful life of 10 years and no residual value would be depreciated at the rate of:

$$\frac{£24,000}{10 \times 12} = £200 \text{ per month, or } £2,400 \text{ per annum.}$$

(b) A non-current asset costing £60,000 has a useful life of five years and a residual value of £6,000. The monthly depreciation charge using the straight line method is:

$$\frac{£(60,000 - 6,000)}{5 \times 12} = £900 \text{ per month, or £10,800 per annum}$$

The carrying amount of the non-current asset would be as follows:

|  | After 1 year £ | After 2 years £ | After 3 years £ | After 4 years £ | After 5 years £ |
|---|---|---|---|---|---|
| Cost of the asset | 60,000 | 60,000 | 60,000 | 60,000 | 60,000 |
| Accumulated depreciation | (10,800) | (21,600) | (32,400) | (43,200) | (54,000) |
| Carrying amount | 49,200 | 38,400 | 27,600 | 16,800 | 6,000 * |

\* ie its estimated residual value.

Since the straight line depreciation charge per annum is the same amount every 12 month reporting period, it is often convenient to state that depreciation is charged at the rate of x per cent per annum on the asset's depreciable amount. In the example in (a) above, the depreciation charge per annum is 10% of cost (ie 10% of £24,000 = £2,400). In (b), it is 20% of the depreciable amount (20% × (60,000 − 6,000) = £10,800)

The straight line method allocates the total depreciable amount in equal amounts between different reporting periods.

### Worked example: Monthly depreciation on the straight line

A business has a reporting period from 1 January to 31 December and purchases a non-current asset on 1 April 20X1, at a cost of £24,000. The expected life of the asset is four years, and its residual value is nil. What is the depreciation charge for the reporting period to 31 December 20X1?

### Solution

The monthly depreciation charge will be $\frac{£24,000}{4 \times 12}$ = £500 per month

Since the asset was acquired on 1 April 20X1, the business has only benefited from the use of the asset for 9 months instead of a full 12 months. We therefore charge depreciation in 20X1 of:

9 × £500 = £4,500

## 3.3 The reducing balance method of depreciation

### Definition

Reducing balance depreciation: The annual depreciation charge is a fixed percentage of the brought forward carrying amount of the asset.

**When calculating reducing balance depreciation in an exam you will NOT be concerned with the asset's residual value nor how to calculate the percentage: just the carrying amount and the reducing balance percentage given to you.**

The reducing balance method might be used to allocate a greater proportion of the total depreciable amount to the asset's earlier years and a lower proportion to its later years, as the benefits obtained by the business from using the asset decline over time.

## Worked example: Reducing balance method

A business purchases a non-current asset at a cost of £10,000 on 1 January 20X1, which it plans to keep for three years to 31 December 20X3. The business wishes to use the reducing balance method to depreciate the asset, and calculates that the rate of depreciation should be 40% of the reducing balance (carrying amount) of the asset.

The depreciation charge per annum and the carrying amount of the asset as at the end of each reporting period will be as follows.

|  | £ | Accumulated depreciation £ |  |
|---|---|---|---|
| Asset at cost | 10,000 |  |  |
| Depreciation in 20X1 (40%) | (4,000) | 4,000 |  |
| Carrying amount at end of 20X1 | 6,000 |  |  |
| Depreciation in 20X2 (40% of carrying amount 6,000) | (2,400) | 6,400 | (4,000 + 2,400) |
| Carrying amount at end of 20X2 | 3,600 |  |  |
| Depreciation in 20X3 (40% × 3,600) | (1,440) | 7,840 | (6,400 + 1,440) |
| Carrying amount at end of 20X3 | 2,160 |  |  |

The annual charge for reducing balance depreciation is higher in the earlier reporting periods of the asset's life, and lower in the later reporting periods (£4,000, £2,400 and £1,440 respectively).

The balance remaining at the end of the three year useful life of £2,160 is the estimated residual value which was taken into account when calculating that 40% reducing balance was appropriate.

**In an exam question, you will not have to calculate what amount of reducing balance depreciation should be charged monthly.**

## 3.4 Applying a depreciation method consistently

A business can choose which method of depreciation to apply to its non-current assets. Once this decision has been made it should be applied **consistently from reporting period to reporting period**.

A business can depreciate different categories of non-current assets in different ways. For example, if a business owns three cars, then each car would normally be depreciated in the same way (eg by the straight line method); but another category of non-current asset, say photocopiers, might be depreciated using a different method (eg by the reducing balance method).

## Interactive question 2: Depreciation

A lorry bought for a business cost £17,000 plus VAT at 20%. It is expected to last for five years and then to be sold for £2,000 plus VAT.

**Requirement**

Work out the depreciation to be charged each 12 month reporting period under:

(a)  The straight line method
(b)  The reducing balance method, using a rate of 35%

See **Answer** at the end of this chapter.

## 3.5 Depreciating enhancement expenditure

Where expenditure is incurred to **enhance** an asset after its initial purchase, this is added to the asset's cost and **depreciated over the asset's remaining useful life.**

Non-current assets and depreciation    261

C H A P T E R

10

## Worked example: Depreciating enhancement expenditure

Malcolm buys a building on 1.1.X0 for £200,000. On 1.1.X2 he adds an extension that cost £50,000.

Calculate the annual depreciation charge before and after the extension is built, on the basis of straight line depreciation over 10 years, with no residual value.

### Solution

Before extension: $\dfrac{£200,000}{10} = £20,000$ pa

After extension: $\dfrac{£200,000}{10} + \dfrac{£50,000}{8} = £26,250$

**In the exam you will not be required to depreciate enhancement expenditure using the reducing balance basis.**

## 3.6 Reviewing and changing the depreciation method

The depreciation method used and the carrying amount should **be reviewed annually** for appropriateness. If there are any changes in the expected pattern of use of the asset (and hence economic benefit), then the method used should be changed. The remaining carrying amount is depreciated under the new method, ie only current and future periods are affected.

## Worked example: Change in method of depreciation

Jakob Co purchased an asset for £100,000 on 1.1.X1. It had an estimated useful life of 5 years and it was depreciated using the reducing balance method at a rate of 40%. On 1.1.X3 it was decided to change the depreciation method to straight line. There was no change to the useful life, and no residual value is anticipated.

Show the depreciation charge for each year (to 31 December) of the asset's life.

### Solution

| Year | | Depreciation charge £ | Accumulated depreciation £ |
|---|---|---|---|
| 20X1 | £100,000 × 40% | 40,000 | 40,000 |
| 20X2 | £60,000 × 40% | 24,000 | 64,000 |
| 20X3 ⎫ | | 12,000 | 76,000 |
| 20X4 ⎬ $\dfrac{£100,000 - £64,000}{3 \text{ remaining years}}$ | | 12,000 | 88,000 |
| 20X5 ⎭ | | 12,000 | 100,000 |

## Interactive question 3: Change in depreciation method

Ford plc prepares its financial statements for the 12 month reporting period to 31 December each year. On 1 January 20X0 it bought a machine for £100,000 and depreciated it at 10% per annum on the reducing balance basis.

On 31 December 20X3, the machine will be included in Ford plc's financial statements at:

| | £ |
|---|---|
| Cost | 100,000 |
| Accumulated depreciation (10,000 + 9,000 + 8,100 + 7,290) | (34,390) |
| Carrying amount | 65,610 |

On 1 January 20X4, the company decided to change the basis of depreciation to straight line over a total life of nine years, ie five years remaining from 1 January 20X4. There is no residual value.

Calculate the revised annual depreciation charge.

See **Answer** at the end of this chapter.

## 3.7 Reviewing and changing carrying amount: fall in value (impairment loss)

When the value of a non-current asset falls to less than its carrying amount and the fall in value will not be recovered from future use of the asset, it is said to have suffered an **impairment loss** and should be **written down to its new value**. The statement of profit or loss charge for the impairment in the asset's value during the reporting period should be:

|  | £ |
|---|---|
| Carrying amount at the beginning of the period | X |
| Less reduced value (the new carrying amount at the end of the period) | (X) |
| Equals the charge for impairment in the asset's value in the period (**impairment loss**) | X |

### Worked example: Impairment loss

A business purchased a building on 1 January 20X1 at a cost of £100,000. The building had a 20 year life. On 31 December 20X5 the business decides that since property prices have fallen sharply and future trading prospects are poor, the building is now worth only £60,000, and the value of the asset should be reduced accordingly in the financial statements of the business for the 12 month reporting period ended 31 December 20X5.

The building was being depreciated over 20 years, at the rate of 5% per annum on cost.

Before the asset is reduced in value, the annual depreciation charge is:

$$\frac{£100,000}{20 \text{ years}} = £5,000 \text{ per annum}$$

This will be charged in 20X1, 20X2, 20X3, 20X4 **and** 20X5.

As at 31 December 20X5 the accumulated depreciation is thus £25,000 and the carrying amount of the building is £75,000, which is £15,000 more than the new asset value. This £15,000 should be written off as an impairment loss in 20X5, so that the total charge in 20X5 is:

|  | £ |
|---|---|
| 'Normal' depreciation charge in 20X5 | 5,000 |
| Impairment loss recognised in 20X5 | 15,000 |
| Charge against profit in 20X5 | 20,000 |

An alternative method of calculation is as follows:

|  | £ |
|---|---|
| Carrying amount of the building in 31 December 20X4 £(100,000 – 20,000) | 80,000 |
| Revised asset value at end of 20X5 | (60,000) |
| Charge against profit in 20X5 | 20,000 |

The building has a further life of 15 years, and its value is now £60,000. From 20X6 to 20Y0, the annual charge for depreciation will be:

$$\frac{£60,000}{15 \text{ years}} = £4,000 \text{ per annum}$$

## 3.8 Reviewing and changing useful life or residual value

The depreciation charge on a non-current asset depends not only on the asset's cost but also on **residual value** and its **estimated useful life**. These should also be reviewed and changed if they are no longer appropriate.

## Worked example: Change in useful life

A business purchased a non-current asset costing £12,000 with an estimated useful life of four years and no residual value. **If it used the straight line method of depreciation**, it would make an annual depreciation charge of 25% of £12,000 = £3,000.

The business decides after two years that the useful life of the asset has been underestimated, and it still has five more years in use to come, making its total life seven years.

For the first two years, the asset is depreciated by £3,000 per annum, so that its carrying amount after two years is £(12,000 – 6,000) = £6,000. If the remaining life of the asset is now revised to five more years, the remaining amount to be depreciated (£6,000) is spread over the remaining useful life, giving an annual depreciation charge for the final 5 years of:

$$\frac{\text{Carrying amount at time of change}}{\text{Revised useful life}}$$

$$= \frac{£6,000}{5 \text{ years}} = £1,200 \text{ per year}$$

## Interactive question 4: Change in residual value

An asset had a cost of £1,000, an estimated useful life of 10 years and a residual value of £200. At the start of year 3 a review shows its remaining useful life was unchanged but the residual value was reduced to nil.

Calculate the depreciation charge for each of years 1 to 3 on the straight line basis.

See **Answer** at the end of this chapter.

When an impairment loss is recognised (see 3.7 above), the asset's remaining useful life and residual value should also be reviewed and possibly revised (if straight line depreciation is being used). The reducing balance percentage rate should be revised if relevant.

## Interactive question 5: Impairment

On 1 January 20X1 Tiger buys a non-current asset for £120,000, with an estimated useful life of 20 years and no residual value. Tiger depreciates its non-current assets on a straight line basis. Its reporting period is the 12 months ended 31 December.

On 31 December 20X3 the asset will be included in the statement of financial position as follows:

|  | £ |
|---|---|
| Non-current asset at cost | 120,000 |
| Accumulated depreciation (3 × (£120,000 ÷ 20)) | (18,000) |
| Carrying amount | 102,000 |

### Requirements

Consider each of these alternatives separately.

(a)  On 1 January 20X4 the remaining useful life is revised to 15 years from that date.

Calculate the revised annual depreciation charge.

(b)  On 1 January 20X4 the remaining useful life is revised to 10 years from that date. An impairment review shows that the value is £95,000 as at 1 January 20X4.

Show how the impairment loss would be recorded and calculate the revised annual depreciation charge.

See **Answer** at the end of this chapter.

# 4 Accounting for depreciation

**Section overview**

- Accounting for depreciation:

  | | | |
  |---|---|---|
  | DEBIT | Depreciation expense (statement of profit or loss) | £X |
  | CREDIT | Accumulated depreciation (statement of financial position) | £X |

**Definition**

**Accumulated depreciation:** The total amount of the asset's depreciation amount that has been allocated to reporting periods to date.

## 4.1 Accounting for depreciation

There are two basic aspects of accounting for depreciation to remember.

(a) A **depreciation charge** is made in the statement of profit or loss in each reporting period for every depreciable non-current asset. Nearly all non-current assets are depreciable, the most important exception being freehold land.

(b) The total **accumulated depreciation** on a non-current asset builds up as the asset gets older. The total accumulated depreciation is always getting larger, until the non-current asset is fully depreciated.

Accounting for depreciation is as follows.

- Set up an accumulated depreciation account for each separate category of non-current asset, for example plant and machinery, land and buildings, fixtures and fittings, motor vehicles.

- With the depreciation charge for the period:

  | | | |
  |---|---|---|
  | DEBIT | Depreciation expense (statement of profit or loss) | £X |
  | CREDIT | Accumulated depreciation account (statement of financial position) | £X |

- The balance on the accumulated depreciation account is the total accumulated depreciation. This is always a credit balance brought forward in the ledger account.

- **The non-current asset cost accounts are unaffected by depreciation.**

- In the statement of financial position, the balance on the **accumulated depreciation** account is set against the **non-current asset cost accounts** to derive the **carrying amount** of the non-current assets.

This is how the non-current asset cost, accumulated depreciation and depreciation charge accounts might appear in a trial balance:

| | | DR £ | CR £ |
|---|---|---|---|
| Freehold building | – cost | 2,000,000 | |
| Freehold building | – accumulated depreciation (£20,000 current reporting period) | | 500,000 |
| Motor vehicles | – cost | 70,000 | |
| Motor vehicles | – accumulated depreciation (£15,000 current reporting period) | | 40,000 |
| Office equipment | – cost | 25,000 | |
| Office equipment | – accumulated depreciation (£3,000 current reporting period) | | 15,000 |
| Depreciation expense | (20,000 + 15,000 + 3,000) | 38,000 | |

They would be shown at the following carrying amounts in the statement of financial position:

*Non-current assets*

| | |
|---|---|
| Freehold building | 1,500,000 |
| Motor vehicles | 30,000 |
| Office equipment | 10,000 |

In the statement of profit or loss the depreciation charge would be included partly in administrative expenses and partly in distribution costs:

| | |
|---|---|
| Administrative expenses (20,000 + 3,000) | 23,000 |
| Distribution costs | 15,000 |
| | 38,000 |

## Worked example: Accounting for depreciation I

Brian Box set up his own computer software business on 1 March 20X6. He purchased a computer system on credit from a manufacturer for £16,000. The system has an expected life of three years and a residual value of £2,500. Using the straight line method of depreciation, the non-current asset account, accumulated depreciation account and statement of profit or loss (extract) and statement of financial position (extract) would be as follows, for each of the next three reporting periods ending 28 February 20X7, 20X8 and 20X9.

### NON-CURRENT ASSET: COMPUTER EQUIPMENT COST

| Date | | £ | Date | | £ |
|---|---|---|---|---|---|
| 1.3.X6 | Trade payables | 16,000 | 28.2.X7 | Balance c/d | 16,000 |
| 1.3.X7 | Balance b/d | 16,000 | 28.2.X8 | Balance c/d | 16,000 |
| 1.3.X8 | Balance b/d | 16,000 | 28.2.X9 | Balance c/d | 16,000 |
| 1.3.X9 | Balance b/d | 16,000 | | | |

The annual depreciation charge is $\dfrac{£(16,000 - 2,500)}{3 \text{ years}} = £4,500$ pa

### ACCUMULATED DEPRECIATION

| Date | | £ | Date | | £ |
|---|---|---|---|---|---|
| 28.2.X7 | Balance c/d | 4,500 | 28.2.X7 | Statement of profit or loss | 4,500 |
| 28.2.X8 | Balance c/d | 9,000 | 1.3.X7 | Balance b/d | 4,500 |
| | | | 28.2.X8 | Statement of profit or loss | 4,500 |
| | | 9,000 | | | 9,000 |
| 28.2.X9 | Balance c/d | 13,500 | 1.3.X8 | Balance b/d | 9,000 |
| | | | 28.2.X9 | Statement of profit or loss | 4,500 |
| | | 13,500 | | | 13,500 |
| | | | 1.3.X9 | Balance b/d | 13,500 |

At the end of three reporting periods, the asset is fully depreciated down to its residual value (£16,000 − £13,500 = £2,500). If it continues to be used by Brian Box, it will not be depreciated any further (unless its estimated residual value is reduced).

STATEMENT OF PROFIT OR LOSS (EXTRACT)

| Year ending: | | £ |
|---|---|---|
| 28 Feb 20X7 | Depreciation expense | 4,500 |
| 28 Feb 20X8 | Depreciation expense | 4,500 |
| 28 Feb 20X9 | Depreciation expense | 4,500 |

STATEMENT OF FINANCIAL POSITION (EXTRACT) AS AT 28 FEBRUARY

| | 20X7 £ | 20X8 £ | 20X9 £ |
|---|---|---|---|
| Computer equipment at cost | 16,000 | 16,000 | 16,000 |
| Less accumulated depreciation | (4,500) | (9,000) | (13,500) |
| Carrying amount | 11,500 | 7,000 | 2,500 |

In theory, the non-current asset is now at the end of its useful life. However, until it is sold off or scrapped, the asset will still appear in the statement of financial position at cost (less accumulated depreciation) and it should remain in the ledger accounts for computer equipment until disposal.

## Worked example: Accounting for depreciation II

Brian Box prospers in his computer software business, and before long he purchases a car for himself, and later one for his chief assistant Bill Ockhead. Relevant data is as follows.

| | Date of purchase | Cost | Estimated life | Estimated residual value |
|---|---|---|---|---|
| Brian Box car | 1 June 20X6 | £20,000 | 3 years | £2,000 |
| Bill Ockhead car | 1 June 20X7 | £15,500 | 3 years | £2,000 |

The straight line method of depreciation is to be used.

Prepare the vehicles account and vehicles accumulated depreciation account for the reporting periods to 28 February 20X7 and 20X8.

Calculate the carrying amount of the vehicles as at 28 February 20X8.

### Solution

(a) (i)

Brian Box car    Monthly depreciation $= \dfrac{£(20,000 - 2,000)}{3 \times 12} =$    £500 pm

Depreciation 1 June 20X6 – 28 February 20X7 (9 × £500)    £4,500
1 March 20X7 – 28 February 20X8 (12 × £500)    £6,000

(ii)

Bill Ockhead car    Monthly depreciation $= \dfrac{£(15,500 - 2,000)}{3 \times 12} =$    £375 pm

Depreciation 1 June 20X7 – 28 February 20X8 (9 × £375)    £3,375

(b)                                    MOTOR VEHICLES

| Date | | £ | Date | | £ |
|---|---|---|---|---|---|
| 1 Jun 20X6 | Payables (or cash) (car purchase) | 20,000 | 28 Feb 20X7 | Balance c/d | 20,000 |
| 1 Mar 20X7 | Balance b/d | 20,000 | | | |
| 1 Jun 20X7 | Payables (or cash) (car purchase) | 15,500 | 28 Feb 20X8 | Balance c/d | 35,500 |
| | | 35,500 | | | 35,500 |
| 1 Mar 20X8 | Balance b/d | 35,500 | | | |

| Date | | £ | Date | | £ |
|---|---|---|---|---|---|
| 28 Feb 20X7 | Balance c/d | 4,500 | 28 Feb 20X7 | Statement of profit or loss | 4,500 |
| | | | 1 Mar 20X7 | Balance b/d | 4,500 |
| 28 Feb 20X8 | Balance c/d | 13,875 | 28 Feb 20X8 | Statement of profit or loss (6,000+3,375) | 9,375 |
| | | 13,875 | | | 13,875 |
| | | | 1 Mar 20X8 | Balance b/d | 13,875 |

STATEMENT OF FINANCIAL POSITION (WORKINGS) AS AT 28 FEBRUARY 20X8

| | Brian Box car £ | £ | Bill Ockhead car £ | £ | Total £ |
|---|---|---|---|---|---|
| Asset at cost | | 20,000 | | 15,500 | 35,500 |
| Accumulated depreciation | | | | | |
| Year to 28 Feb 20X7 | 4,500 | | – | | |
| Year to 28 Feb 20X8 | 6,000 | | 3,375 | | |
| | | (10,500) | | (3,375) | (13,875) |
| Carrying amount | | 9,500 | | 12,125 | 21,625 |

## 4.2 Depreciation on the ETB

Because the final depreciation calculation is usually accounted for after the initial trial balance has been extracted, the only figure for accumulated depreciation on the initial trial balance is the one for the balance brought forward. We can incorporate the relevant figures using the ETB.

- Calculate the amount of depreciation to be charged

- Prepare the year-end journal to record depreciation expense (and impairment loss if relevant)

- Enter the journal in the adjustments columns of the ETB using the accumulated depreciation line plus a line for depreciation expense

- Include these adjustments in the ETB cross-cast to prepare the financial statements

- Enter the journals for depreciation in the ledger accounts and bring down the balance on the accumulated depreciation account.

# 5 Non-current asset disposals

**Section overview**

- A disposal account is used to calculate the profit or loss on disposal of an asset, which is the amount by which the sales proceeds of the asset differs from its carrying amount at the date of disposal.

- Accounting for disposals:

  | | | | |
  |---|---|---|---|
  | DEBIT | Disposal account with asset's carrying amount | £X | |
  | CREDIT | Disposal account with sales proceeds | | £X |
  | DEBIT | Cash with proceeds | £X | |
  | DEBIT | Accumulated depreciation | £X | |
  | CREDIT | Asset cost | | £X |

- When an old asset has been attributed an NRV when given in part-exchange for a new one, the part-exchange value is accounted for as the old asset's disposal proceeds.

Non-current assets might be sold off at some stage during their life, either when their useful life is over or before then.

Whenever a business sells something, it will make a profit or a loss. When non-current assets are disposed of, there will be **a profit or loss on disposal**. As it is a capital item being sold, the profit or loss will be **capital income** or a **capital expense**. Profits are shown as other income, and losses are reported as administrative expenses or distribution costs in the statement of profit or loss of the business, not as part of gross profit. They are commonly referred to as '**profit (or loss) on disposal of non-current assets**'.

## 5.1 The principles behind calculating the profit or loss on disposal

The profit or loss on the disposal of a non-current asset is the difference between:

- The **carrying amount** of the asset at the time of its sale, and
- Its **net disposal proceeds**, the value received less any costs of making the sale.

A **profit** is made when the net disposal proceeds **exceed** the carrying amount. A **loss** is made when the net disposal proceeds are **less** than the carrying amount.

### Worked example: Disposal of a non-current asset I

A business purchased a non-current asset on 1 January 20X1 for £25,000. It had an estimated life of six years and an estimated residual value of £7,000 and is depreciated on the straight line basis. The asset was sold after three years on 1 January 20X4 to another trader who paid £17,500 for it.

What was the profit or loss on disposal?

### Solution

$$\text{Annual depreciation} = \frac{£(25,000 - 7,000)}{6 \text{ years}} = £3,000 \text{ per annum}$$

|  | £ |
|---|---:|
| Cost of asset | 25,000 |
| Less accumulated depreciation (3 × £3,000) | (9,000) |
| Carrying amount at date of disposal | 16,000 |
| Disposal proceeds | 17,500 |
| Profit on disposal | 1,500 |

This profit will be shown in the statement of profit or loss as an item of **other income**, added to the gross profit to arrive at net profit.

### Worked example: Disposal of a non-current asset II

A business purchased a machine on 1 July 20X1 for £39,000. The machine had an estimated residual value of £3,000 and a life of eight years. The machine was sold for £18,600 on 31 December 20X4. To make the sale, the business had to incur dismantling costs and costs of transporting the machine to the buyer's premises of £1,200.

The business uses the straight line method of depreciation. What was the profit or loss on disposal of the machine?

### Solution

$$\text{Depreciation expense} \quad \frac{£(35,000 - 3,000)}{8 \text{ years}} = £375 \text{ per month, and } £4,500 \text{ per annum}$$

In 20X1 only six months depreciation was charged, because the asset was purchased six months into the reporting period.

| | £ | £ |
|---|---:|---:|
| Non-current asset at cost | | 39,000 |
| Depreciation in 20X1 (6 × £375) | 2,250 | |
| 20X2, 20X3 and 20X4 (3 × £4,500) | 13,500 | |
| Accumulated depreciation | | (15,750) |
| Carrying amount at date of disposal | | 23,250 |
| Disposal proceeds | 18,600 | |
| Costs incurred in making the sale | (1,200) | |
| Net disposal proceeds | | (17,400) |
| Loss on disposal | | (5,850) |

This loss will be shown as part of administrative expenses in the statement of profit or loss of the business. It is a capital expense, not a trading loss, and it should not therefore be part of the calculation of gross profit.

## 5.2 Accounting for non-current asset disposals

We record the disposal of non-current assets in a **disposals ledger account**.

(a) The following items appear in the disposals account:

    (i) The value of the asset (at cost)
    (ii) The accumulated depreciation up to the date of sale
    (iii) The disposal proceeds, if any

(b) The profit or loss on disposal is the difference between:

    (i) The disposal proceeds and
    (ii) The carrying amount of the asset at the time of disposal.

(c) The ledger accounting entries are as follows.

    (i) DEBIT     Disposal account     £X
        CREDIT   Non-current asset cost account     £X

    with the **cost** of the asset disposed of (the cost of the asset is removed from the statement of financial position).

    (ii) DEBIT    Accumulated depreciation account     £X
        CREDIT   Disposal account     £X

    with the **accumulated depreciation** on the asset as at the date of sale (the accumulated depreciation on the asset is removed from the statement of financial position).

    (iii) DEBIT   Cash book (or receivables)     £X
         CREDIT   Disposal account     £X

    with the **disposal proceeds** of the asset.

The balance on the disposal account is the profit or loss on disposal and the corresponding double entry is recorded in the profit and loss ledger account itself, ie in the statement of profit or loss.

### Worked example: Accounting for the disposal of non-current assets

A business has £110,000 worth of machinery at cost. Its policy is to depreciate at 20% per annum straight line. The total accumulated depreciation now stands at £70,000. The business sells for £19,000 a machine which it purchased exactly two years ago for £30,000.

Show the relevant ledger entries.

**Solution**

### MACHINERY – COST

| | £ | | £ |
|---|---|---|---|
| Balance b/d | 110,000 | Disposals | 30,000 |
| | | Balance c/d | 80,000 |
| | 110,000 | | 110,000 |
| Balance b/d | 80,000 | | |

### MACHINERY – ACCUMULATED DEPRECIATION

| | £ | | £ |
|---|---|---|---|
| Disposals (20% of £30,000 for 2 years) | 12,000 | Balance b/d | 70,000 |
| Balance c/d | 58,000 | | |
| | 70,000 | | 70,000 |
| | | Balance b/d | 58,000 |

### DISPOSAL ACCOUNT

| | £ | | £ |
|---|---|---|---|
| Machinery – cost | 30,000 | Machinery – accumulated depreciation | 12,000 |
| Statement of profit or loss (profit on sale) | 1,000 | Cash | 19,000 |
| | 31,000 | | 31,000 |

*Check:*

| | £ |
|---|---|
| Asset at cost | 30,000 |
| Accumulated depreciation at time of sale | (12,000) |
| Carrying amount at time of sale | 18,000 |
| Disposal proceeds | 19,000 |
| Profit on disposal | 1,000 |

## 5.3 Accounting for disposals of non-current assets given in part-exchange

Quite often a business does not receive cash for the asset, but instead get a 'part-exchange' or 'trade-in value' for it against the cost of a new asset. Instead of disposal proceeds being received in the form of cash or promised in the form of a receivable, use the **part exchange value** given to the asset by the other party as its **disposal value**.

### Worked example: Accounting for part-exchange disposals I

Asset A, costing £20,000 is acquired by a business for £12,000 cash, plus its old Asset B. The part-exchange value attributed to Asset B is £20,000 – £12,000 = £8,000. This amount must be compared with Asset B's carrying amount in order to establish the profit or loss on Asset B's disposal.

Asset B cost £15,000 and has had £4,000 depreciation charged in respect of it, so its carrying amount at the date of the part-exchange disposal is £11,000. The business has made a loss of £11,000 – £8,000 = £3,000 on Asset B's disposal.

The £8,000 part-exchange value must be included in the cost of Asset A, along with the £12,000 cash handed over.

(a)

| | | £ | £ |
|---|---|---|---|
| DEBIT | Asset A cost | 20,000 | |
| CREDIT | Cash | | 12,000 |
| CREDIT | Disposal account (Asset B's part-exchange value) | | 8,000 |

*Being the acquisition of Asset A for cash and part-exchange of Asset B*

(b)

| | | £ | £ |
|---|---|---|---|
| DEBIT | Asset B accumulated depreciation | 4,000 | |
| CREDIT | Disposal account (Asset B) | | 4,000 |
| DEBIT | Disposal account (Asset B) | 15,000 | |
| CREDIT | Asset B cost account | | 15,000 |

*Being the removal of Asset B from the ledger accounts*

(c)

| | | £ | £ |
|---|---|---|---|
| DEBIT | Statement of profit or loss | 3,000 | |
| CREDIT | Disposal account | | 3,000 |

*Being the loss on disposal of Asset B (8,000 – (15,000 – 4,000))*

### DISPOSALS ACCOUNT

| | £ | | £ |
|---|---|---|---|
| Asset B cost (b) | 15,000 | Disposal proceeds (part exchange value) (a) | 8,000 |
| | | Asset B accumulated depreciation (b) | 4,000 |
| | | Statement of profit or loss (c) | 3,000 |
| | 15,000 | | 15,000 |

## Worked example: Accounting for part-exchange disposals II

A business trades in an asset that cost £30,000 two years ago for a new asset that costs £60,000. A cheque for £41,000 was also handed over in full settlement. Assets are depreciated on the straight line basis over five years. What are the relevant ledger account entries?

### Solution

### MACHINERY ACCOUNT

| | £ | | £ |
|---|---|---|---|
| Balance b/d | 30,000 | Disposals | 30,000 |
| Cash | 41,000 | Balance c/d | 60,000 |
| Disposals | | | |
| (part exchange value £ (60,000 – 41,000)) | 19,000 | | |
| | 90,000 | | 90,000 |
| Balance b/d | 60,000 | | |

The new asset is recorded in the non-current asset account at cost £(41,000 + 19,000) = £60,000.

### MACHINERY ACCUMULATED DEPRECIATION

| | £ | | £ |
|---|---|---|---|
| Disposals (20% of £30,000 for 2 years) | 12,000 | Balance b/d | 12,000 |

### DISPOSALS

| | £ | | £ |
|---|---|---|---|
| Cost | 30,000 | Accumulated depreciation | 12,000 |
| Statement of profit or loss (profit on sale) | 1,000 | Cost – part-exchange value | 19,000 |
| | 31,000 | | 31,000 |

## Interactive question 6: Non-current asset ledger accounts

A business purchased two machines on 1 January 20X5 at a cost of £15,000 each. Each had an estimated life of five years and a nil residual value. The straight line method of depreciation is used.

Owing to an unforeseen slump in market demand for its end product, the business decided to reduce its output, and switch to making other products instead. On 31 March 20X7, one machine was sold (on credit) to a buyer for £8,000.

Later in the reporting period, however, it was decided to abandon production altogether, and the second machine was sold on 1 December 20X7 for £2,500 cash.

Prepare the machinery account, accumulated depreciation of machinery account and disposal account for the 12 month reporting period to 31 December 20X7 to determine the profit or loss on disposal of each machine.

See **Answer** at the end of this chapter.

## 5.4 Accounting for non-current assets on the ETB

Earlier we saw how depreciation is accounted for on the ETB. We can now draw together a comprehensive example of entries on the ETB in respect of non-current assets, made after the extraction of an initial trial balance.

### Worked example: Non-current assets on the ETB

Rodrigo's initial trial balance as at 31 December 20X0 is as follows.

| Ledger balance | Trial balance Debit £ | Credit £ |
|---|---:|---:|
| Current assets | 87,420 | |
| Capital at 1.1.X0 | | 100,000 |
| Freehold land and buildings – cost at 1.1.X0 | 100,000 | |
| Freehold land and buildings – accumulated depreciation at 1.1.X0 | | 15,000 |
| Plant and equipment – cost at 1.1.X0 | 45,000 | |
| Plant and equipment – accumulated depreciation at 1.1.X0 | | 18,750 |
| Motor vehicles – cost at 1.1.X0 | 25,000 | |
| Motor vehicles – accumulated depreciation at 1.1.X0 | | 14,650 |
| Current liabilities | | 15,420 |
| Expenses | 5,830 | |
| Purchases | 58,740 | |
| Sales | | 205,640 |
| Drawings | 47,670 | |
| Suspense | | 200 |
| | 369,660 | 369,660 |

The following matters have now been discovered:

(a) On 1 January 20X0 Rodrigo disposed of an item of plant that had cost £10,000 and on which £1,250 depreciation had been charged. He received a cheque for £7,950. The only accounting entry made was to debit cash.

(b) On 1 January 20X0 he also traded in a car that had cost £8,000 and on which £4,500 depreciation had been charged for a new car costing £13,300. He handed over a cheque in addition for £7,750. The only entry with regard to this transaction was in the cash book.

(c) With regard to the assets held at 31 December 20X0, depreciation on the freehold building of £5,000, on plant and equipment of £5,290, and on motor vehicles of £6,900, is to be charged.

**Requirement**

Prepare Rodrigo's year-end journals as at 31 December 20X0 in respect of these matters, and complete the ETB.

## Solution

### (a)

| | | £ | £ |
|---|---|---|---|
| DEBIT | Suspense | 7,950 | |
| CREDIT | Disposal – plant | | 7,950 |
| DEBIT | Plant and equipment – accumulated depreciation | 1,250 | |
| | Disposal – plant (carrying amount) | 8,750 | |
| CREDIT | Plant and equipment – cost | | 10,000 |

*Being the correct recording of cash received on disposal of plant, and the removal of the asset's cost and accumulated depreciation*

### (b)

| | | £ | £ |
|---|---|---|---|
| DEBIT | Motor vehicles – cost | 13,300 | |
| CREDIT | Suspense | | 7,750 |
| | Disposal – car given in part exchange (13,300 – 7,750) | | 5,550 |

*Being the correct recording of purchase of a new car for £13,300*

| | | £ | £ |
|---|---|---|---|
| DEBIT | Motor vehicles – accumulated depreciation | 4,500 | |
| | Disposal – car given in part exchange (carrying amount) | 3,500 | |
| CREDIT | Motor vehicles – cost | | 8,000 |

*Being the removal of the cost and accumulated depreciation in relation to a car, given in part exchange for a new one*

### (c)

| | | £ | £ |
|---|---|---|---|
| DEBIT | Expenses (depreciation) | 17,190 | |
| CREDIT | Freehold land and buildings – accumulated depreciation | | 5,000 |
| | Plant and equipment – accumulated depreciation | | 5,290 |
| | Motor vehicles – accumulated depreciation | | 6,900 |

*Being the depreciation charge for the reporting period*

| Ledger balance | Trial balance | | Adjustments | | Statement of profit or loss | | Statement of financial position | |
|---|---|---|---|---|---|---|---|---|
| | Debit £ | Credit £ | Debit £ | Credit £ | Debit £ | Credit £ | Debit £ | Credit £ |
| Current assets | 87,420 | | | | | | 87,420 | |
| Capital at 1.1.X0 | | 100,000 | | | | | | 100,000 |
| Freehold land and buildings – cost | 100,000 | | | | | | 100,000 | |
| Freehold land and buildings – accumulated depreciation | | 15,000 | | 5,000 | | | | 20,000 |
| Plant and equipment – cost | 45,000 | | | 10,000 | | | 35,000 | |
| Plant and equipment – accumulated depreciation | | 18,750 | 1,250 | 5,290 | | | | 22,790 |
| Motor vehicles – cost | 25,000 | | 13,300 | 8,000 | | | 30,300 | |
| Motor vehicles – accumulated depreciation | | 14,650 | 4,500 | 6,900 | | | | 17,050 |
| Current liabilities | | 15,420 | | | | | | 15,420 |
| Expenses | 5,830 | | 17,190 | | 23,020 | | | |
| Purchases | 58,740 | | | | 58,740 | | | |
| Sales | | 205,640 | | | | 205,640 | | |
| Drawings | 47,670 | | | | | | 47,670 | |
| Suspense | | 200 | 7,950 | 7,750 | | | | |
| Disposal – plant | | | 8,750 | 7,950 | 800 | | | |
| Disposal – car | | | 3,500 | 5,550 | | 2,050 | | |
| Net profit | | | | | 125,130 | | | 125,130 |
| | 369,660 | 369,660 | 56,440 | 56,440 | 207,690 | 207,690 | 300,390 | 300,390 |

ICAEW

# 6 The asset register

## Section overview

- The asset register lists out all the details of each non-current asset. Its tables should reconcile to the ledger account for non-current assets in the nominal ledger.

## Definition

**Asset register:** A listing of all non-current assets owned by the organisation, broken down by department, location or asset type, and containing non-financial information (such as chassis numbers and security codes) as well as financial information.

An asset register is maintained primarily for internal control purposes. It shows an organisation's investment in capital equipment in financial terms, and allows the business to trace from its ledger accounts for non-current assets to individual assets.

## 6.1 Data kept in an asset register

Details about **each non-current** asset include the following.

- The internal reference number (for physical identification purposes)
- Manufacturer's serial number (for maintenance purposes)
- Description of asset
- Location of asset
- Department which uses the asset
- Purchase date (for calculation of depreciation)
- Cost, and any enhancement expenditure
- Depreciation method and estimated useful life (for calculation of depreciation)
- Carrying amount

It is good practice to 'reconcile' or agree the net carrying amounts of all the assets on the asset register with the net carrying amount of non-current assets recorded in the nominal ledger:

|                                                                 | £    |
|-----------------------------------------------------------------|------|
| Assets at cost (from the non-current asset cost ledger account) | X    |
| Accumulated depreciation (from the ledger account)              | (X)  |
| Total of carrying amounts listed in the asset register          | X̲    |

Any difference should be investigated and corrected. These usually arise from computational errors or from items being taken out of the asset register with no equivalent change being made in ledger accounts, or *vice versa*, for instance because:

- Assets have been stolen, damaged or scrapped (for nil proceeds).
- Assets are obsolete.
- There are new assets, not yet recorded in the register.
- There have been enhancements not yet recorded in the register.
- There are errors in the register.

C
H
A
P
T
E
R

10

# 7 Intangible non-current assets

**Section overview**

- Purchased goodwill may appear as an asset in a company's statement of financial position. It represents the amount paid for a business in excess of what its net assets are worth.

- Some development costs are capitalised on the statement of financial position.

- Intangible non-current assets should be subject to reviews for impairment of their value.

Not all assets held for the long term can be touched; some are **intangible**.

## 7.1 Goodwill

If a business has **goodwill** it means that the market value of the business as a going concern is greater than the book value of its assets less its liabilities.

Goodwill is created by good relationships between a business and its customers, for example:

- By building up a **reputation** (by word of mouth perhaps) for high quality products or high standards of service

- By responding promptly and helpfully to queries and complaints from **customers**

- Through the **personality** of the staff, their **attitudes** to customers and their **skills**

Although the value of goodwill to a business might be extremely significant it **is not usually valued** in the financial statements.

For example, the welcoming smiles of shop staff may contribute more to a supermarket's profits than the fact that a new electronic cash register has recently been acquired; even so, whereas the cash register will be recorded in the ledger accounts as a non-current asset, the value of staff would be ignored for accounting purposes.

- Goodwill is inherent in the business but it has not been directly paid for, so **valuation** is difficult.

- Goodwill changes from day to day. One act of bad customer relations might damage goodwill and one act of good relations might improve it. Staff with a favourable personality might retire or leave, to be replaced by staff who need time to become established. Since goodwill is continually changing in value, it cannot **reliably** be recorded in the accounts.

## 7.2 Purchased goodwill

The exception to the general rule that goodwill has no objective valuation arises when an existing business is purchased. The buyer has to pay for not only its non-current assets and inventories (and perhaps take over its payables and receivables too) but also for its goodwill. This is why the **purchase consideration** for most businesses is **more than the value of their net assets.**

**Worked example: Goodwill**

Tony Tycoon purchases Clive Dunwell's business for £30,000. Clive's business has total assets less liabilities of £25,000, all of which are taken over by Tony. Tony will be paying (£30,000 – £25,000) = £5,000 **more** for the business than its net assets are worth, because he is purchasing the **goodwill** of the business too. The statement of financial position of Tony's business when it begins operations (assuming that he does not change the value of what he has acquired) will be as follows:

TONY TYCOON
STATEMENT OF FINANCIAL POSITION AS AT THE START OF BUSINESS

| | £ |
|---|---|
| Intangible non-current asset: goodwill | 5,000 |
| Other net assets acquired | 25,000 |
| Net assets | 30,000 |
| | |
| Capital | 30,000 |

Purchased goodwill is shown in this statement of financial position because it has been directly paid for. It has no tangible substance, and so it is an **intangible non-current asset**.

## Definition

**Purchased goodwill:** The excess of the purchase consideration paid for a business over the fair value of the individual assets and liabilities acquired.

## 7.3 Accounting for purchased goodwill

Purchased goodwill is a premium paid for the acquisition of a business as a going concern: it is often referred to as a 'premium on acquisition'. A purchaser pays such a premium because they believe that the true value of the business includes goodwill, which has value in addition to its tangible net assets.

Goodwill continually changes. A business cannot last forever on its past reputation; it must create new goodwill as time goes on.

If the goodwill loses some or all of its value, it is deemed to have become 'impaired'. Its value in the statement of financial position is then written down by the amount of the impairment and the **impairment loss** is charged against the profit of the period.

Goodwill should be treated as an **intangible non-current asset**. It is kept at cost in the statement of financial position subject to an **annual review for impairment**. It is **not** depreciated.

## 7.4 How is the value of purchased goodwill decided?

The value of the goodwill is a matter for the purchaser and seller to agree upon in fixing the purchase consideration. However, two methods of valuation are worth mentioning here.

(a) The seller and buyer agree on a price without specifically quantifying the goodwill. The purchased goodwill will then be the difference between the price agreed and the value of the net assets in the books of the **new business**.

(b) The calculation of goodwill may precede fixing the purchase consideration and may become a central element of negotiation. There are many ways of arriving at a value for goodwill and most of them are related to the profit record of the business in question. For instance, they may agree to value goodwill as 2 × profit of the previous reporting period, or a similar calculation.

Goodwill shown by the purchaser in their accounts will be the difference between the purchase consideration and **their own valuation** of the tangible net assets acquired. If A values his tangible net assets at £40,000 and goodwill is agreed at £21,000 then B agrees to pay £61,000 for the business. When setting up accounts for the asset acquired, B may value the tangible net assets at only £38,000, so the goodwill in B's books will be £61,000 – £38,000 = £23,000.

We shall come back to goodwill in Chapter 15.

### Interactive question 7: Goodwill

Toad goes into business with £10,000 capital and agrees to buy Thrush's shop for £6,500. Thrush's recent financial statements show total assets less liabilities of £3,500, which Toad values at £4,000.

**Requirement**

Prepare the statement of financial position of Toad's business at the following times.

(a)  Before he purchases Thrush's business
(b)  After the purchase

See **Answer** at the end of this chapter.

## 7.5 Development costs

Large companies spend significant amounts of money on development activities from which they hope to generate revenues in future periods. These amounts are credited to cash or payables and debited to an account for development expenditure. The accounting problem is **how to treat the debit balance on the development cost account** at the date of the statement of financial position.

There are two possibilities.

- The debit balance may be classified as an **expense** and transferred to the statement of profit or loss. This is referred to as '**writing off**' the expenditure. The argument here is that it is an expense just like rent or wages and its accounting treatment should be the same.

- The debit balance may be classified as an **asset** and included in the statement of financial position. This is referred to as 'capitalising' or 'carrying forward' or 'deferring' the expenditure. This argument is based on the **accrual principle**. If development activity eventually leads to new or improved products which generate income, the costs should be carried forward to be matched against that income in future reporting periods.

  When development expenditure is carried forward as an asset the accounting entries are:

  | | | |
  |---|---|---|
  | DEBIT | Non-current assets | £X |
  | CREDIT | Cash/payables | £X |

The cost of this non-current asset will need to be allocated to the statement of profit or loss as it is matched against the income it helps to generate. This process is essentially the same as for depreciation of tangible non-current assets, but it is called **amortisation**.

## 7.6 Other intangible assets

A business may have other types of intangible asset:

- **Patents** on ideas or designs that the business has developed or bought. These are used to generate income over many reporting periods. They are valued at cost and are subject to amortisation in line with the business's policy, and to regular impairment reviews, which may result in an impairment loss.

- **Investments held for the long term**. The valuation of these falls outside the scope of the *Accounting* syllabus.

# 8 The non-current assets note to the statement of financial position

**Section overview**

- The non-current assets note to the statement of financial position provides the details behind the single figure for tangible non-current assets in the statement of financial position.

There is usually a detailed note to the financial statements in respect of **property, plant and equipment**, with just the summarised figure in the statement of financial position. For each class of property, plant and equipment the note shows:

- Cost and accumulated depreciation brought forward
- Additions during the reporting period
- Disposals during the reporting period, and the related accumulated depreciation
- Depreciation charge for the reporting period
- Closing balance carried forward

Note that disposal proceeds, and gains/losses on disposal, do **not** appear in the non-current assets note.

**Worked example: The non-current assets note**

We prepared Rodrigo's ETB earlier in this chapter. We can now prepare his non-current assets (property, plant and equipment) note from his ETB as follows.

|  | Freehold land and buildings £ | Plant and equipment £ | Motor vehicles £ | Total £ |
|---|---|---|---|---|
| *Cost* |  |  |  |  |
| At 1.1.X0 | 100,000 | 45,000 | 25,000 | 170,000 |
| Additions |  |  | 13,300 | 13,300 |
| Disposals |  | (10,000) | (8,000) | (18,000) |
| At 31.12.X0 | 100,000 | 35,000 | 30,300 | 165,300 |
| *Accumulated depreciation* |  |  |  |  |
| At 1.1.X0 | 15,000 | 18,750 | 14,650 | 48,400 |
| Charge for the reporting period | 5,000 | 5,290 | 6,900 | 17,190 |
| Disposals |  | (1,250) | (4,500) | (5,750) |
| At 31.12.X0 | 20,000 | 22,790 | 17,050 | 59,840 |
| *Carrying amount* |  |  |  |  |
| At 1.1.X0 | 85,000 | 26,250 | 10,350 | 121,600 |
| At 31.12.X0 | 80,000 | 12,210 | 13,250 | 105,460 |

On Rodrigo's statement of financial position at 31 December 20X0 there will just be a single figure, for 'Property, plant and equipment', of £105,460.

## Summary (1/2)

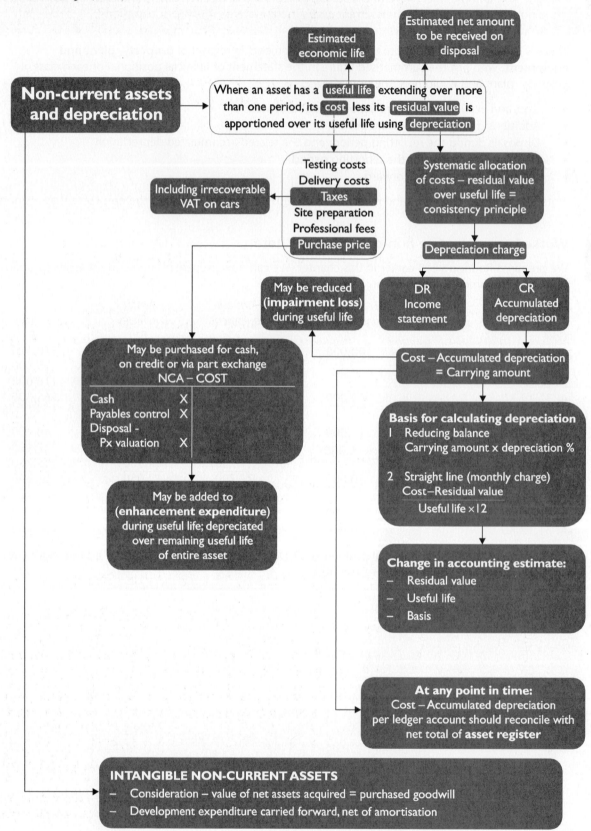

**Estimated economic life**

**Estimated net amount to be received on disposal**

**Non-current assets and depreciation**

Where an asset has a useful life extending over more than one period, its cost less its residual value is apportioned over its useful life using depreciation

Testing costs
Delivery costs
**Taxes**
Site preparation
Professional fees
Purchase price

**Including irrecoverable VAT on cars**

Systematic allocation of costs – residual value over useful life = consistency principle

Depreciation charge

**May be reduced (impairment loss) during useful life**

DR
Income statement

CR
Accumulated depreciation

May be purchased for cash, on credit or via part exchange
NCA – COST

| | |
|---|---|
| Cash | X |
| Payables control | X |
| Disposal - | |
| Px valuation | X |

Cost – Accumulated depreciation = Carrying amount

**Basis for calculating depreciation**
1 Reducing balance
Carrying amount x depreciation %

2 Straight line (monthly charge)
$$\frac{Cost - Residual\ value}{Useful\ life \times 12}$$

May be added to **(enhancement expenditure)** during useful life; depreciated over remaining useful life of entire asset

**Change in accounting estimate:**
– Residual value
– Useful life
– Basis

**At any point in time:**
Cost – Accumulated depreciation per ledger account should reconcile with net total of **asset register**

**INTANGIBLE NON-CURRENT ASSETS**
– Consideration – value of net assets acquired = purchased goodwill
– Development expenditure carried forward, net of amortisation

## Summary (2/2)

### Accounting for non-current assets

**1 Acquire asset**

| DR | Cost | X | |
|----|------|---|---|
| CR | Cash/payables/disposal | | X |

**2 Depreciate asset**

| DR | Depreciation charge | X | |
|----|---------------------|---|---|
| CR | Accumulated depreciation | | X |

**3 Dispose of asset**

| DISPOSAL | | | |
|----------|---|---|---|
| Cost | X | Accumulated depreciation | X |
| | | Cash/payables/ Px valuation | X |
| IS (profit) | X | IS (loss) | X |
| | X | | X |

### NON-CURRENT ASSETS (PPE) NOTE TO STATEMENT OF FINANCIAL POSITION

| | Land and buildings £ | Plant and equipment £ | Motor vehicles £ | Total £ |
|---|---|---|---|---|
| **Cost** | | | | |
| B/d | X | X | X | X |
| Additions | X | X | X | X |
| Disposals | (X) | (X) | (X) | (X) |
| C/d | X | X | X | X |
| **Accumulated depreciation** | | | | |
| B/d | X | X | X | X |
| Charge for year | X | X | X | X |
| Disposals | (X) | (X) | (X) | (X) |
| C/d | X | X | X | X |
| **Carrying amount** | | | | |
| B/d | X | X | X | X |
| C/d | X | X | X | X |

# Self-test

Answer the following questions.

1 Materials purchased and used by P & Co for repairs to office buildings have been included in the draft financial statements as purchases.

The necessary amendment will

   A   Increase gross profit with no effect on net profit
   B   Increase gross profit and reduce net profit
   C   Have no effect on either gross profit or net profit
   D   Reduce gross profit and increase net profit

2 Marcellus acquired new premises at a cost of £250,000 on 1 January 20X1. Marcellus paid the following further costs during the year ended 31 December 20X1.

| | £ |
|---|---|
| Costs of initial adaptation | 13,900 |
| Legal costs relating to purchase | 1,200 |
| Monthly cleaning contract | 9,600 |
| Office furniture | 6,500 |

What amount should appear as the cost of premises in the company's statement of financial position at 31 December 20X1?

   A   £250,000
   B   £263,900
   C   £265,100
   D   £271,600

3 Why is depreciation provided on non-current assets?

   A   To ensure that sufficient funds are available to replace the assets
   B   To show the assets at replacement cost on the statement of financial position
   C   To spread the cost of the assets over their useful lives
   D   To show the fall in market value of the assets in the statement of profit or loss

4 ABC, whose reporting period is the 12 months ended 31 December, has provided depreciation monthly at the rate of 10% per annum on cost on a piece of plant bought on 1 September 20X0 costing £15,000. The depreciation method was changed from straight line to 10% reducing balance at the end of 20X3.

The depreciation charge on this asset for 20X5 was

   A   £1,500
   B   £945
   C   £900
   D   £889

5 A business with a reporting period of the 12 months ended 30 June buys a non-current asset on 1 July 20X3 for £200,000. Depreciation is charged at 15% per annum on the reducing balance basis. On 30 June 20X5 the asset was sold for £54,800.

What was the loss on sale of the asset?

   A   £89,700
   B   £85,200
   C   £68,025
   D   £55,200

6   In the year ended 31 December 20X7 B traded in for £6,860 a vehicle costing £12,000 on 1 November 20X5 against the cost (£9,600) of a replacement vehicle. The balance due for the new vehicle has been paid in cash and debited to the cost of vehicles account, no other entries relating to the transaction having been made.

What net adjustment is required to the company's cost of vehicles account as a result of this transaction?

A   £9,600 DR
B   £12,000 CR
C   £6,800 DR
D   £5,140 CR

7   A business acquired a car on 1 October 20X5 for £117,000 and has depreciated it on a reducing balance basis at 20% per annum. On 30 September 20X7 the car was sold for £58,000.

What is the loss on disposal of the car in the financial statements for the 12 month reporting period to 30 September 20X7?

A   £14,560
B   £14,800
C   £16,880
D   £29,360

8   A business buys a machine on 1 January 20X1 for £10,000 and depreciates it at 10% per annum straight line. At the end of 20X2 the machine's remaining useful life is reassessed at six years remaining and it is now believed that the machine has a residual value of £500.

What is the depreciation charge for the third year of the machine's use?

A   £950
B   £1,250
C   £1,267
D   £1,350

9   The following information relates to the disposal of two machines by Paddock.

|                          | Machine 1 £ | Machine 2 £ |
| ------------------------ | ----------- | ----------- |
| Cost                     | 120,000     | 140,000     |
| Disposal proceeds        | 90,000      | 80,000      |
| Profit/(loss) on disposal | 30,000     | (40,000)    |

What was the total carrying amount of both machines sold at the date of disposal?

A   £100,000
B   £160,000
C   £180,000
D   £240,000

10  On 1 June 20X1 Quandry bought a non-current asset for £50,000 which had an estimated useful life of 10 years and a residual value of £2,000. Quandry depreciates its non-current assets on a straight line basis. Quandry's reporting period is the 12 months ended 31 December.

On 1 January 20X4 the asset's remaining useful life is revised to eight years from that date with no residual value. An impairment review at that date shows that the recoverable amount of the asset is considered to be only £25,000.

What is the total depreciation and impairment loss charge for this asset in 20X4?

A   £3,125
B   £12,400
C   £15,725
D   £18,000

Now, go back to the Learning Objectives in the Introduction. If you are satisfied that you have achieved these objectives, please tick them off.

# Answers to Interactive questions

## Answer to Interactive question 1

|  | £ |
|---|---|
| Cost | 18,720 |
| Less Estimated residual value | (6,360) |
| Total amount to be depreciated | 12,360 |

The deposit represents part of the payment for the new vehicle and is not relevant in calculating the depreciable amount of the new car.

## Answer to Interactive question 2

(a) Under the straight line method, depreciation for each of the five years is:

$$\text{Annual depreciation} = \frac{£(17,000 - 2,000)}{5} = £3,000$$

Remember that VAT on lorries is recoverable; it is only in respect of cars that it is irrecoverable.

(b) Under the reducing balance method, depreciation for each of the five years is as follows:

| Year | Depreciation |  | £ |
|---|---|---|---|
| 1 | 35% × £17,000 | = | 5,950 |
| 2 | 35% × (£17,000 − £5,950) = 35% × £11,050 | = | 3,868 |
| 3 | 35% × (£11,050 − £3,868) = 35% × £7,182 | = | 2,514 |
| 4 | 35% × (£7,182 − £2,514) = 35% × £4,668 | = | 1,634 |
| 5 | 35% × (£4,668 − £1,634) = 35% × £3,034 | = | 1,062 |

## Answer to Interactive question 3

$$\text{New annual charge from 20X4} = \frac{£65,610}{5 \text{ years}} = £13,122 \text{ per annum}$$

## Answer to Interactive question 4

|  | Year 1 £ | Year 2 £ | Year 3 £ |
|---|---|---|---|
| Cost | 1,000 | 1,000 | 1,000 |
| Accumulated depreciation | (80) | (160) | (265) |
| Carrying amount | 920 | 840 | 735 |
| Charge for the year (W) | 80 | 80 | 105 |

WORKING

|  |  |  |
|---|---|---|
| $\dfrac{1,000 - 200}{10}$ | $\dfrac{1,000 - 200}{10}$ | $\dfrac{840}{8}$ |

ICAEW

## Answer to Interactive question 5

(a) Revised annual depreciation charge

$$\text{Revised annual charge} = \frac{\text{Carrying amount at revision} - \text{Residual value}}{\text{Revised remaining life}}$$

$$= \frac{£102,000}{15}$$

$$= \underline{£6,800} \text{ per annum}$$

(b) Impairment loss and revised annual depreciation charge

| | £ |
|---|---|
| 31 December 20X4 | |
| Impairment loss (102,000 – 95,000) | 7,000 |
| Annual charge $\dfrac{£95,000}{10}$ | 9,500 |
| Total statement of profit or loss charge in 20X4 | = $\underline{16,500}$ |

## Answer to Interactive question 6

### MACHINERY ACCOUNT

| | | £ | | | £ |
|---|---|---|---|---|---|
| *20X7* | | | *20X7* | | |
| 1 Jan | Balance b/d (2 × £15,000) | 30,000 | 31 Mar | Disposal of machinery account | 15,000 |
| | | | 1 Dec | Disposal of machinery account | 15,000 |
| | | $\underline{30,000}$ | | | $\underline{30,000}$ |

### MACHINERY – ACCUMULATED DEPRECIATION

| | | £ | | | £ |
|---|---|---|---|---|---|
| *20X7* | | | *20X7* | | |
| 31 Mar | Disposal account (W1) | 6,750 | | | |
| | | | 1 Jan | Balance b/d ($24 \times \dfrac{30,000}{5 \times 12}$) | 12,000 |
| 1 Dec | Disposal account (W2) | 8,750 | 31 Mar | Charge to disposal $\dfrac{15,000}{60} \times 3$ | 750 |
| | | | 1 Dec | Charge to disposal $\dfrac{15,000}{60} \times 11$ | 2,750 |
| | | $\underline{15,500}$ | | | $\underline{15,500}$ |

### WORKING

1   Depreciation at date of disposal = (15,000/60) × 27 = £6,750
2   Depreciation at date of disposal = (15,000/60) × 35 = £8,750

### DISPOSAL ACCOUNT

| | | £ | | | £ |
|---|---|---|---|---|---|
| *20X7* | | | *20X7* | | |
| 31 Mar | Machinery | 15,000 | 31 Mar | Receivables (proceeds) | 8,000 |
| | | | 31 Mar | Accumulated depreciation | 6,750 |
| | | | 31 Mar | Loss on disposal | 250 |
| 1 Dec | Machinery | 15,000 | 1 Dec | Cash (proceeds) | 2,500 |
| | | | 1 Dec | Accumulated depreciation | 8,750 |
| | | | 31 Dec | Loss on disposal | 3,750 |
| | | $\underline{30,000}$ | | | $\underline{30,000}$ |

## Answer to Interactive question 7

(a) Toad's statement of financial position before the purchase is:

|  | £ |
|---|---:|
| Cash | 10,000 |
| Capital | 10,000 |

(b) Thrush's valuation of the assets to be acquired is irrelevant to Toad, who sees the situation thus:

|  | £ |
|---|---:|
| Consideration (cash to be paid) | 6,500 |
| Less total assets less liabilities acquired (at Toad's valuation) | (4,000) |
| Difference (purchased goodwill) | 2,500 |

Toad must put through the following journal on acquisition, opening up a goodwill ledger account.

|  |  | £ | £ |
|---|---|---:|---:|
| DEBIT | Assets/liabilities (shop) | 4,000 | |
| DEBIT | Goodwill | 2,500 | |
| CREDIT | Cash | | 6,500 |

Toad's statement of financial position immediately after the purchase is therefore:

|  | £ |
|---|---:|
| Goodwill | 2,500 |
| Assets/liabilities acquired in shop | 4,000 |
| Cash (£10,000 – £6,500) | 3,500 |
|  | 10,000 |
| Capital | 10,000 |

(Normally one would have more detail as to the breakdown of the assets and liabilities, but this is not relevant here. The main point is that the assets/liabilities acquired are tangible whereas the goodwill is not.)

This question highlights the difference between 'internally generated' goodwill, which (as in Thrush's case above) is not shown in the books and 'purchased' goodwill, which is. The purchased goodwill in this case is simply Thrush's internally generated goodwill, which has changed hands, bought by Toad at the consideration shown in Toad's accounts.

# Answers to Self-test

1   A   To correct reduce purchases (increase to GP and NP), increase repairs (decrease NP, no effect on GP).

The decrease and increase to NP cancel out. Overall effect on GP is an increase.

2   C

|  | £ |
|---|---|
| Purchase price | 250,000 |
| Adaptation | 13,900 |
| Legal costs | 1,200 |
|  | 265,100 |

3   C   Depreciation spreads (cost – residual value) over useful life

4   C

|  | £ |
|---|---|
| Cost | 15,000 |
| Accumulated depreciation to 31 December 20X3 ($\frac{15,000}{120} \times 40$) | (5,000) |
| Carrying amount at date of change | 10,000 |
| Depreciation for 20X4 (10,000 × 10%) | (1,000) |
|  | 9,000 |
| Depreciation for 20X5 @ 10% | 900 |

5   A

|  | £ |
|---|---|
| Cost 1 July 20X3 | 200,000 |
| Depreciation to 30 June 20X4 | (30,000) |
|  | 170,000 |
| Depreciation to 30 June 20X5 | (25,500) |
|  | 144,500 |
| Less Proceeds | (54,800) |
| Loss on sale | 89,700 |

6   D

|  | £ |
|---|---|
| Debit with trade in allowance (to get to total cost of new vehicle of £9,600) | 6,860 DR |
| Credit with cost of old vehicle (to remove cost of old vehicle) | (12,000) CR |
| Net adjustment | (5,140) CR |

7   C

|  | £ |
|---|---|
| Cost 1 October 20X5 | 117,000 |
| Depreciation to 30 September 20X6 | (23,400) |
|  | 93,600 |
| Depreciation to 30 September 20X7 | (18,720) |
|  | 74,880 |
| Loss on sale (58,000 – 74,880) | 16,880 |

**8    B**

|  |  | £ |
|---|---|---:|
| Cost |  | 10,000 |
| Depreciation | 20X1 (10% × 10,000) | (1,000) |
|  |  | 9,000 |
|  | 20X2 (10% × 10,000) | (1,000) |
| Carrying amount at end 20X2 |  | 8,000 |

Depreciation charge for 20X3 ($\frac{8,000-500}{6}$)          1,250

**9    C**

|  | Machine 1 | Machine 2 | Total |
|---|---:|---:|---:|
|  | £ | £ | £ |
| Disposal proceeds | 90,000 | 80,000 |  |
| Carrying amount (β) | (60,000) | (120,000) | (180,000) |
| Profit/(loss) on disposal | 30,000 | (40,000) |  |

**10    C**

|  | £ |
|---|---:|
| Cost | 50,000 |
| Accumulated depreciation to 31 December 20X3 $\frac{50,000-2,000}{120} \times 31$ | (12,400) |
| Carrying amount at 31 December 20X3 | 37,600 |
| Impairment loss (37,600 – 25,000) | 12,600 |
| Annual charge (25,000 ÷ 8) | 3,125 |
|  | 15,725 |

# CHAPTER 11

# Company financial statements

Introduction

Examination context

**Topic List**

Summary and Self-test

Answers to Interactive questions

Answers to Self-test

### Learning objectives

- Record and account for transactions and events resulting in income, expenses, assets, liabilities and equity in accordance with the appropriate basis of accounting and the laws, regulations and accounting standards applicable to the financial statements

- Record and account for changes in the ownership structure and ownership interests in an entity

- Prepare an extended trial balance

- Identify the main components of a set of financial statements and specify their purpose and interrelationship

- Prepare and present a statement of financial position and statement of profit or loss (or extracts therefrom) from the accounting records and trial balance in a format which satisfies the information requirements of the entity

Specific syllabus learning outcomes are: 1d, e, 2c, 3a

### Syllabus links

The material in this chapter will be developed further in the Professional Level module of Financial Accounting and Reporting.

### Examination context

Questions on the topics in this chapter will be set as multiple choice questions, some of which may involve calculations so that the correct answer can be selected. Very often double entry questions are phrased in terms of preparing a journal. In addition, the material covered in this chapter may also be examined as part of a long form question.

In the exam you may be required to:

- Specify the unique features of company financial statements: equity (share capital and reserves), provisions and tax

- Specify the distinctions between equity shares, and redeemable and irredeemable preference shares

- Identify how to account for issues of shares and payment of dividends

- Identify how loans should be split into their current and non-current liability categories for the statement of financial position

- Identify how to account for tax, including under-provisions and over-provisions

# 1 The nature of a limited company

**Section overview**

- Companies are legally separate from their owners, so the presentation of owners' capital is particularly important.

- A company's initial capital is divided into shares which have a par or 'nominal' value, and an issue value that can exceed that amount.

- A private company may not issue securities (shares and loan stock) to the public at large. A public company may do so, either through a public listing or otherwise.

- Particular features of company accounting relate to: owners' capital (equity); debt capital; provisions; tax.

Limited companies are the most common form of private sector business organisation. Businesses that are not limited companies tend to be small in size, or provide specialised professional services, such as firms of accountants or solicitors.

A company has a **separate legal existence**, independent of its owner(s). It can enter contracts in its own name, it can sue or be sued, and it is liable to the tax authorities for tax on the profits that it earns. The profits available to the owners of a company are profits **after** deducting taxation.

Because a company has this legal identity, separate from its owners, the way it raises capital from its owners, and is accountable to its owners for the capital that it holds, is more formalised than for sole traders or partnerships.

## 1.1 Share capital and shareholders

A company's **initial capital** is divided into units of equal size, known as **shares**, issued to individuals or companies, called **shareholders**. The total capital raised is referred to as **equity share capital**.

Ownership of a share entitles the shareholder to receive payment of a share of profit, or **dividend**.

By law, shares must have a **par value** (the Companies Act 2006 calls this the 'nominal value'), which can be any amount, for example 1p, 5p, 10p, 25p, 50p, £1 and so on. However, all shares of the same type ('class') have the same par value. For example, £100,000 par value of share capital might be represented by 100,000 shares of £1 each, or 200,000 shares of 50p each, or 1,000,000 shares of 10p each, and so on. It is possible to have differing classes of share which carry different rights for their owners.

The par value of shares will rarely bear any relationship to either:

- The **issue price** at which the share was originally issued by the company, to raise capital; or

- The **current market value** of the share if the shares of the company are traded on a stock market.

The original **issue price of a share matters to a company** because it is the amount of cash raised for each share issued. A company will often issue shares at above ('at a premium to') par value. For example, a company with shares of £1 might issue shares at £1.50 per share when the company is first incorporated, then make a further issue of shares some years later at, say, £2 each, and then a further issue some time after that at, say, £3.50 each.

The **current market value of a share** has no bearing on company financial statements at all, because this is the price at which an existing shareholding is sold by one person (not the company) to another person (not the company). Such transactions do not give rise to anything that has to be recorded in the company's accounting records.

## 1.2 Public and private companies

Companies are either public or private companies.

- A **public company** has 'plc' in its name. A public company may offer its securities (shares and loan stock such as bonds) for sale to persons who are unrelated to the company ('the public'), but is subject to stricter regulation than private companies. In particular, a public company must have issued capital of at least £50,000. Before it can trade, at least £12,500 plus the whole of any premium on issue must have been received as cash. Effectively this means that a public limited company must have net assets (assets less liabilities) of at least £12,500. Note that all companies whose shares are traded on a stock market must be 'plcs', but not all plcs have their shares traded on a stock market.

- A **private company** ends its name with 'Limited' or 'Ltd'. A private company is any company that is not a public company. Private companies cannot offer their securities for sale to the public at large. There is no minimum level of net assets.

## 1.3 Accounting for companies

Companies have distinctive characteristics to be accounted for. The following are examinable in *Accounting:*

- Equity (owners' capital comprising share capital, retained earnings and other reserves), rights issues and bonus issues
- Forms of debt capital (non-current liabilities)
- Provisions
- Tax on profits
- Dividends

# 2 Equity: share capital

**Section overview**

- Share capital can be split into:
    - Equity shares (no entitlement to a set amount of dividend)
    - Irredeemable preference shares (set entitlement to dividends)
- Redeemable preference shares are entitled to a set amount of dividend but are treated as non-current liabilities (debt capital).
- The figure for called-up share capital at par value appears on the statement of financial position. This may be less than the figure for issued share capital. If an amount of called-up capital is unpaid, this is treated as an 'other receivable'.
- Of the issue price, any excess or 'premium' received over par value is credited to share premium (a reserve or 'other component of equity').

## 2.1 Equity shares and preference shares

Companies often have just one class of share, ordinary shares, which are referred to in the Companies Act 2006 as '**equity share capital**' because each share represents an equal interest in the ownership of the company. (Occasionally, a company might have two classes of equity or ordinary share, usually known as 'A ordinary' and 'B ordinary' shares. Most public companies in the UK, however, have just one class of equity share.)

A company might also issue **preference shares**, which entitle their holders to a dividend out of profits (preference dividend) **before** equity shareholders are entitled to any equity dividend.

Once the preference dividend has been paid, the remaining profit 'belongs' to the equity shareholders. However, the directors will usually decide to retain some profits (**retained earnings**) within the company, and the equity dividend will be an amount declared by the directors as being appropriate and affordable.

## 2.2 Issued and called-up share capital

The **issued share capital** of a company (also known as its **allotted share capital**) is the par value of the shares that have actually been issued to shareholders.

If a company issues shares but 'calls up' the issue amounts in instalments, instead of raising cash immediately, it then has **called-up share capital** that is less than its issued share capital.

### Worked example: Called-up share capital

A company issues 100,000 shares of £1 at par value, but only calls up 75p per share as a first instalment. The issued share capital is £100,000, but the called-up share capital is only £75,000. The figure in the statement of financial position will be £75,000.

**In a company's statement of financial position, the figure for share capital is the called-up share capital.**

On the face of the company's statement of financial position, or in a note, called-up equity share capital and irredeemable preference share capital at par value are shown separately.

STATEMENT OF FINANCIAL POSITION (EXTRACT)

|  | £'000 |
|---|---|
| *Equity* |  |
| Share capital: equity shares of 50p each  (81.5m shares) | 40,750 |
| Share capital: 6% irredeemable preference shares of £1 (9m shares) | 9,000 |
|  | 49,750 |

If a company has called-up share capital, but is waiting for payment from some shareholders, it has **paid up capital** of less than its called-up capital.

### Worked example: Paid up capital

A company issues one million shares of £1 at par, and asks for payment in full on issue, but it is still owed £5,000 by shareholders who have yet to pay what they owe. The called-up share capital is £1,000,000, but the paid up share capital is only £995,000. In the statement of financial position, the **share capital** (a credit balance) is the called-up share capital of £1,000,000, and the unpaid capital of £5,000 is shown as an '**other receivable**' (a debit balance).

## 2.3 Irredeemable and redeemable preference shares

- Only preference shares which the company is not entitled to buy back or redeem at some stage in the future, known as **irredeemable preference shares**, are treated as **share capital**.

- Preference shares which the company is entitled to buy back from its shareholders or 'redeem' at some future time are called **redeemable preference shares**, treated as **non-current liabilities (debt capital)**.

**In an exam question it will be specified whether preference shares are redeemable or irredeemable.**

## 2.4 Accounting for share capital

- When shares are issued at their **par value** and they are **fully paid**:

|  | £ | £ |
|---|---|---|
| DEBIT  Cash | X |  |
| CREDIT  Share capital (par value) |  | X |

- When shares are issued at a **premium to their par value**, and the full amount is paid:

|  | | £ | £ |
|---|---|---|---|
| DEBIT | Cash | X | |
| CREDIT | Share capital (par value) | | X |
|  | Share premium (excess over par value) | | X |

- When shares are issued at their par value but an amount remains **uncalled** by the company

|  | | £ | £ |
|---|---|---|---|
| DEBIT | Cash | X | |
| CREDIT | Share capital (called-up amount of issued shares) | | X |

- When shares are issued and called-up at their par value but an amount remains **unpaid**:

|  | | £ | £ |
|---|---|---|---|
| DEBIT | Cash | X | |
|  | Other receivables (unpaid capital) | X | |
| CREDIT | Share capital (par value) | | X |

# 3 Equity: retained earnings and other reserves

**Section overview**

- Retained earnings: built up with each reporting period's profits, depleted by dividends and losses. Amounts may also be transferred to or from other reserves, or reclassified as share capital in a bonus issue.

- Share premium: set up with premium over par value of issued share capital (equity and irredeemable preference shares). The account may be reduced by a bonus issue.

- General reserve: created by a transfer from retained earnings.

Share capital is shown in the statement of financial position at its called-up value. Any other amounts attributable to owners (equity shareholders) are shown separately as **reserves** (referred to in IAS 1 as either 'retained earnings' or 'other components of equity').

A company might have a number of different reserves, each set up for a different purpose, including the following which are examinable in *Accounting*:

- Retained earnings
- Share premium
- General reserve

## 3.1 Retained earnings

**Definition**

**Retained earnings:** A reserve used to accumulate the company's retained earnings.

Retained earnings comprise the income (profits and gains less losses) that the company retains within the business, ie income that has not been paid out as dividends or transferred to any other reserve.

The retained earnings ledger account would look like this (note that if there was a loss this would be debited to the ledger account):

| | £ | | £ |
|---|---|---|---|
| Dividends of the period | X | Balance b/d (opening statement of financial position) | X |
| Transfers to general reserve | X | Profit for the reporting period (from statement of profit or loss) | X |
| Balance c/d (closing statement of financial position) | <u>X</u> | | |
| | <u>X</u> | | <u>X</u> |

We shall look at the transfer to general reserve shortly.

The balance carried down on the retained earnings ledger account represents the company's **accumulated profits and losses over time** out of which it may, if it wishes, pay dividends to its shareholders in the future.

## 3.2 Share premium

The Companies Act 2006 prohibits shares from being issued at a price below ('at a discount to') their par value. Commonly they are issued at a **price above par value**. When this happens, the excess of the issue price above the par value is added to a share premium reserve.

### Worked example: Share premium

A company issues 1 million 50p equity shares at a price of £4.20 per share for cash.

The shares are issued at a premium of £3.70 (£4.20 – £0.50) above their par value, and the share issue should be recorded in the ledger accounts as follows.

| | | £ | £ |
|---|---|---|---|
| DEBIT: | Cash | 4,200,000 | |
| CREDIT: | Share capital: equity shares of 50p | | 500,000 |
| | Share premium | | 3,700,000 |

There are tight legal restrictions on the use of the share premium reserve. **Dividends** cannot be paid out from it, but it may be reclassified as share capital via a **bonus issue**, as we shall see shortly.

## 3.3 General reserve

A company might hold retained earnings that it has no intention of distributing to owners as a dividend at any time in the future in a **general reserve** rather than in retained earnings. This is a decision that the company makes in line with its constitution. Unless there is a specific rule in the constitution, general reserves remain distributable as dividends.

A company might have other reserves in its financial statements. It is sufficient for you to know at this stage that such reserves might exist, without needing to know why and how they are used.

# 4 Dividends

## Section overview

- An equity (or ordinary) share entitles its holder to dividends which vary in amount depending on the performance and policy of the company.

- A preference share entitles the holder to a fixed dividend, whose payment takes priority over that of ordinary share dividends.

**Equity dividends:**

The dividend to be paid to the shareholders is decided by the board of directors. The dividend rate can be expressed in a number of different ways.

## Worked example: Equity dividends I

It can be quoted in terms of the pence amount each share receives, for example, the equity share information may appear in the trial balance as follows:

| | £ | £ |
|---|---|---|
| Ordinary share capital (£1 per share) | | 400,000 |

The company paid an equity dividend of 5p per share.

This means that the dividend paid amounts to £20,000. This is calculated by multiplying 400,000 shares by 5p.

### Nominal value of shares

The nominal value of a share is an arbitrary value given to that unit. It is a base value, which does not change and therefore it differs from the market value of the share. If the market value of a share is higher than its nominal value, the difference is accounted for in the share premium account.

It is very important, therefore, that you note the nominal value of the share, as this will affect the number of shares in issue, and therefore your calculation of dividends and bonus issues. £1 is the most common nominal value but it can be more or less than this.

- If the nominal value of shares is £1, and the value of the ordinary share capital account is £500,000, that means there are 500,000 ordinary shares in issue (£500,000 ÷ £1).

- If the nominal value of the shares was £2, and the value of the ordinary share capital account was £500,000, that means there are 250,000 ordinary shares in issue (£500,000 ÷ £2).

- If the nominal value of shares is 50p, and the value of the ordinary share capital account is £500,000, that means there are 1,000,000 ordinary shares in issue (£500,000 ÷ £0.50).

## Worked example: Equity dividends II

If the nominal value of the share was 50p, and the value of the equity share capital remained at £400,000 (from e.g. 1), the trial balance would appear as follows:

| | £ | £ |
|---|---|---|
| Ordinary share capital (50p per share) | | 400,000 |

The payment of an equity dividend of 5p per share dividend would now result in a total dividend of £40,000. This is because there are actually 800,000 50p shares in issue.

### Preference dividends:

A company may also issue preference shares, which entitle the holders to a dividend out of profits (preference dividend) before the equity (ordinary) shareholders are entitled to any equity dividend.

Preference shares are often expressed as follows:

| | £ | £ |
|---|---|---|
| 7% £1 irredeemable preference shares | | 100,000 |

This means that the preference dividend to be paid will be £7,000. (£100,000 × 7%).

**Calculating the dividends from retained earnings:**

Retained earnings comprise the income (profits and gains less losses) that the company retains within the business, i.e. income that has not been paid out as dividends or transferred to any other reserve.

In some cases, you may be expected to calculate the dividends paid during the period without any information regarding the dividend rate to be paid. Instead, you need to understand the composition of the retained earnings account.

## Worked example: Dividends and retained earnings

The retained earnings of a company at 1 January 20X5 was £800,000. The retained earnings at 31 December 20X5 is £1,140,000. The profit for the year is £370,000. What was the total dividend paid during the year?

### Solution

The total dividend paid during the year is £30,000

*Working*

| Retained earnings | | | | |
|---|---|---|---|---|
| | £ | | | £ |
| Dividends (bal. fig.) | 30,000 | B/fwd | | 800,000 |
| C/fwd | 1,140,000 | Profit for the year | | 370,000 |
| | 1,170,000 | | | 1,170,000 |

# 5 Rights issues and bonus issues of shares

## Section overview

- A rights issue of shares is made to existing owners in proportion to their shareholdings.

- Amounts from retained earnings and share premium may be reclassified as share capital in a bonus issue:

| | | £ | £ |
|---|---|---|---|
| DR | Share premium | X | |
| | Retained earnings | X | |
| CR | Share capital | | X |

## 5.1 Rights issues of shares

Large share issues to raise new cash are often in the form of a rights issue.

## Definition

**Rights issue:** New shares are offered to existing owners in proportion to their existing shareholding, usually at a discount to the current market price.

For example, a company with 20 million shares in issue decides to raise more cash by issuing 5 million new shares. It can offer the new shares to existing owners in a '1 for 4' rights issue: each existing owner is offered one new share for every four currently held (20 million/5 million = 4).

## Interactive question 1: Rights issue

The statement of financial position of Omnibus plc contains the following information.

| | £'000 |
|---|---|
| **ASSETS** | |
| Non-current assets | 18,600 |
| Current assets | 2,900 |
| Total assets | 21,500 |
| **EQUITY AND LIABILITIES** | |
| *Equity* | |
| Share capital: equity shares of 20p each | 6,000 |
| Share premium | 5,700 |
| Retained earnings | 7,000 |
| *Total equity* | 18,700 |
| *Total liabilities* | 2,800 |
| *Total equity and liabilities* | 21,500 |

The company decides to make a 1 for 3 rights issue for cash, fully paid, at a price of £1.80 per share.

**Requirement**

What are the balances for (a) current assets, (b) share capital and (c) share premium after the rights issue?

See **Answer** at the end of this chapter.

## 5.2 Bonus issues of shares

### Definition

**Bonus issue** (or **capitalisation issue** or **scrip issue**): An issue of fully paid shares to existing owners, free of charge, in proportion to their existing shareholdings.

**A bonus issue does not involve any cash inflow for the company**. The company converts some of its reserves (share premium **or** retained earnings **or** both) into new fully-paid share capital issued at its par value. The double entry for the **par value** of the bonus shares issued is:

DEBIT      Share premium OR retained earnings (OR both)
CREDIT    Share capital

The balance on share premium cannot (by law) be paid to owners as dividends. There are only a few transactions that can ever reduce share premium. One of these is a **bonus issue** of shares.

**In an exam you should assume that a company uses the share premium account as fully as it can before using retained earnings, unless told otherwise.**

### Worked example: Bonus issue

A company has the following statement of financial position.

| | £'000 |
|---|---|
| **ASSETS** | 30,000 |
| **EQUITY AND LIABILITIES** | |
| *Equity* | |
| Share capital: equity shares of £1 each | 5,000 |
| Share premium | 1,300 |
| Retained earnings | 9,700 |

| | |
|---|---|
| *Total equity* | 16,000 |
| *Total liabilities* | 14,000 |
| *Total equity and liabilities* | 30,000 |

The company decides to make a 2 for 5 bonus issue of shares.

The company is issuing (£5m/5 × 2) = 2,000,000 new shares of £1 each to its owners, in proportion to their existing shareholdings. It will:

| | | £ | £ |
|---|---|---|---|
| DEBIT | Share premium (total balance of the share premium reserve) | 1,300,000 | |
| DEBIT | Retained earnings (remainder) | 700,000 | |
| CREDIT | Share capital | | 2,000,000 |

The statement of financial position after the issue shows no change in assets or liabilities, but equity has changed, as follows.

| | £'000 |
|---|---|
| **ASSETS** | 30,000 |
| **EQUITY AND LIABILITIES** | |
| *Equity* | |
| Share capital: equity shares of £1 each (£5m + £2m) | 7,000 |
| Share premium (£1.3m – £1.3m) | 0 |
| Retained earnings (£9.7m – £0.7m) | 9,000 |
| *Total equity* | 16,000 |
| *Total liabilities* | 14,000 |
| *Total equity and liabilities* | 30,000 |

## Interactive question 2: Bonus issue

The statement of financial position of Canvat plc at 31 December 20X1 is as follows:

| | £'000 |
|---|---|
| **ASSETS** | 2,000 |
| **EQUITY AND LIABILITIES** | |
| *Equity* | |
| Share capital: 800,000 50p equity shares | 400 |
| Share premium | 500 |
| Retained earnings | 300 |
| *Total equity* | 1,200 |
| *Total liabilities* | 800 |
| *Total equity and liabilities* | 2,000 |

The directors decide to make a 1 for 5 bonus issue, followed by a 1 for 3 rights issue at £1.60 per share.

Show the revised statement of financial position of Canvat plc after both share issues have taken place.

See **Answer** at the end of this chapter.

**Calculating the dividends from retained earnings where there has been a bonus issue during the year:**

If there is no share premium account, or you are specifically told to use the retained earnings account for the issue of bonus shares, you should understand how this transaction will affect the calculation of dividends from the retained earnings account.

### Worked example: Bonus issue, dividends and retained earnings

Using the information from the Worked Example on page 297, suppose that the company held £100,000 equity shares of £1 each. During the year the company decided to make a 1 for 10 bonus issue of shares from the retained earnings account. Calculate the dividends paid during the year.

## Solution

The total dividend paid during the year is £20,000

WORKINGS

(1)

**Share capital**

|  | £ |  | £ |
|---|---|---|---|
|  |  | B/fwd | 100,000 |
| C/fwd | 110,000 | Bonus issue | 10,000 |
|  | 110,000 |  | 110,000 |

(2)

**Retained earnings**

|  | £ |  | £ |
|---|---|---|---|
| Bonus issue | 10,000 | B/fwd | 800,000 |
| Dividends (bal. fig.) | 20,000 | Profit for the year | 370,000 |
| C/fwd | 1,140,000 |  |  |
|  | 1,170,000 |  | 1,170,000 |

# 6 Non-current liabilities (debt capital)

**Section overview**

- Non-current liabilities comprise debt securities (debentures, loan stock and bonds), plus bank loans and redeemable preference shares.

- Interest on non-current liabilities is a contractual obligation and must be accrued for in the calculation of profit before tax.

- Any amounts that are repayable in less than 12 months must be classified as current liabilities. The balance is treated as non-current liabilities: long-term borrowings.

A company is a legal person so when it borrows it is solely liable for the debt (a sole trader and partners are personally liable for loans to their businesses).

A company may borrow directly from a bank or it may borrow in the form of **debt securities** (loan stock, debenture loans or bonds). These securities are normally issued as certificates, each with a par value, in return for cash (the loan principal). The certificate's owner is legally entitled to interest on its par value, and is entitled to repayment of the principal 'at maturity', ie when the loan period reaches its end at a specifiable future date. This is known as redemption. It is a contractual obligation to pay interest on debt securities.

Debt securities are similar in concept to any other type of loan. Unless they are due to reach maturity within 12 months, they are included in **non-current liabilities** in the statement of financial position. Any amount due for redemption within 12 months is shown under **current liabilities**. Interest is part of **finance costs** in the statement of profit or loss; unpaid interest at the statement of financial position date is shown as **other payables**.

## 6.1 Accounting for non-current liabilities

On issue of debt:

| DEBIT | Cash | £X |  |
|---|---|---|---|
| CREDIT | Non-current liabilities |  | £X |

On repayment of debt:

| DEBIT | Non-current liabilities | £X |  |
|---|---|---|---|
| CREDIT | Cash |  | £X |

Remember that:

- Any **redeemable preference shares** in issue will also be treated as liabilities (either current or non-current) rather than equity

- Any debt that is due for repayment in less than 12 months after the statement of financial position date is reclassified from non-current to **current liabilities**.

# 7 Provisions

### Section overview

- Provisions are liabilities that can only be measured using estimation, so they are disclosed separately from other liabilities.

- IAS 37 *Provisions, Contingent Liabilities and Contingent Assets* provides guidance on when provisions and contingencies should be recognised and if so, at what amount.

**Provisions** are liabilities of a company that are shown separately from other liabilities because the amount of a provision can be measured only by using a substantial degree of estimation.

IAS 37 aims to ensure that:

- **Appropriate recognition criteria and measurement bases are applied** to provisions, contingent assets and contingent liabilities.

- **Sufficient information is disclosed** in the notes to the financial statements to enable users to understand their nature, timing and amount.

### UK GAAP alert!

There are no significant differences in the treatment of provisions under UK GAAP.

### Definitions

A **provision**: is a liability of uncertain timing or amount.

A **liability**: is a present obligation of the entity arising from past events, the settlement of which is expected to result in an outflow from the entity of resources embodying economic benefits.

Note that while this definition in IAS 37 means that provisions are viewed as a sub-class of liabilities, a provision differs from an actual accrual for, say, gas supplies, where it is known that there will be one gas bill, to be paid X weeks after the end of the reporting period for roughly £Y.

An example is a **provision for claims under warranty**, where a manufacturer agrees to make good any deficiencies in a product becoming apparent within, say, 12 months of the date of sale. It is known that warranty claims will arise but the precise number, value and timing are unknown. So judgement has to be used in deciding how much the **warranty provision** should be for. Provisions may be included as current or non-current liabilities, depending on the circumstances.

### Worked example: Provision

A company sells a product with a two-year warranty. The company estimates that 5% of warranties will be invoked, at a cost of £15,000.

The journal entries would be as follows:

| | £ | £ |
|---|---|---|
| DEBIT: Expense (statement of profit or loss) | 15,000 | |
| CREDIT: Current liability (statement of financial position) | | 15,000 |

The following year, due to a change in material used, the company estimated that only 3% or warranties would be invoked, at a cost of £9,000.

The journal entries would be as follows:

|  | £ | £ |
|---|---|---|
| CREDIT: Expense (statement of profit or loss) |  | 6,000 |
| DEBIT: Current liability (statement of financial position) | 6,000 |  |

# 8 Tax

## Section overview

- Any tax due on profits is the company's liability and therefore must be shown:
    - As a deduction in the statement of profit or loss
    - As a payable in the statement of financial position.

- Any over-provision or under-provision in previous reporting periods is credited/debited in the current reporting period's statement of profit or loss.

A company as a separate legal entity is liable to pay tax on its profits to HMRC itself: the liability is not that of its owners'. Tax is therefore treated as a **deduction from profit**. Any outstanding liability for unpaid tax is shown as a **liability** on the statement of financial position (**tax payable**), either current or non-current depending on the circumstances.

## 8.1 Accounting for tax

Different methods of accounting for tax (excluding VAT) can be used, but in this Study Manual a single tax payable ledger account is used for both the expense in the statement of profit or loss and the liability in the statement of financial position.

When a tax liability arises and is identified, the double entry to record it is:

| DEBIT | Tax expense (statement of profit or loss) | £X |  |
|---|---|---|---|
| CREDIT | Tax payable account |  | £X |

When a tax payment is made:

| DEBIT | Tax payable account | £X |  |
|---|---|---|---|
| CREDIT | Cash |  | £X |

At the end of the reporting period, any balance on the tax payable account is carried down. Usually this is a credit balance and is shown as 'Tax payable' under current liabilities on the statement of financial position.

## Worked example: Tax I

Hardwork plc has estimated that £90,000 is payable in tax on the profits earned in the year ended 31 December 20X1. None of this tax has been paid by the date of the statement of financial position.

The tax will be accounted for as follows:

### TAX PAYABLE ACCOUNT

| 20X1 | £ | 20X1 | £ |
|---|---|---|---|
| Balance c/d | 90,000 | Tax expense (statement of profit or loss) | 90,000 |
|  | 90,000 |  | 90,000 |
|  |  | 20X2 |  |
|  |  | Balance b/d | 90,000 |

Since a company's statement of profit or loss is usually prepared before the tax due is finally agreed with HMRC, the expense in the statement of profit or loss is an estimate. It nearly always proves to be too high (**over-provision**) or too low (**under-provision**). Instead of going back to the financial statements for the reporting period and changing them:

- Any **over-provision** from the previous reporting period **reduces the tax expense for the subsequent reporting period.**

- Any **under-provision** from the previous reporting period **increases the tax expense for the subsequent reporting period.**

### Worked example: Tax II

In the year to 31 December 20X2, Hardwork plc has a credit balance brought down on its tax payable account of £90,000 (1). It agrees with HMRC that the tax due on 20X1's profits is £87,000, which it pays in February 20X2 (2). Its over-provision for 20X1 is therefore £3,000 (3). It estimates that its tax due on 20X2's profits should be £100,000 (4).

Hardwork plc's net tax expense in the statement of profit or loss for the year to 31 December 20X2 will be £100,000 (4) less the over-provision of £3,000 (1) in the previous reporting period, ie £97,000. Its statement of financial position current liability is £100,000 (5).

The ledger account is as follows.

### TAX PAYABLE ACCOUNT

| 20X2 | £ | 20X2 | £ |
|---|---|---|---|
| Cash (2) | 87,000 | Balance b/d (1) | 90,000 |
| Statement of profit or loss: over-provision | | Statement of profit or loss: charge for | |
| 20X1 (3) | 3,000 | 20X2 (4) | 100,000 |
| Balance c/d (5) | 100,000 | | |
| | 190,000 | | 190,000 |
| | | 20X3 | |
| | | Balance b/d: Tax payable | 100,000 |

Note that any balance owed to HMRC in respect of VAT or PAYE/NIC is disclosed as **other payables**, not as **tax payable**.

# 9 Revenue

### Section overview

- Revenue includes credit and cash sales (net of trade discounts), refunds and VAT.
- Revenue should be recognised when it is probably that future economic benefits will flow to the entity and these benefits can be measured reliably.
- Revenue is income arising in the ordinary course of an entity's activities.

Revenue includes both credit and cash sales, net of trade discount, refunds and VAT. Cash discounts allowed to customers are **not** deducted when arriving at the revenue figure (these are normally shown as administrative expenses).

IAS 18 *Revenue* prescribes the accounting treatment of revenue recognition in common types of transaction. It states that in general terms revenue should be recognised:

- When it is **probable that future economic benefits will flow to the entity** and
- These benefits can be **measured reliably.**

Revenue should be measured at the fair value of the consideration received or receivable.

IAS 18 applies to:

- Sale of goods (manufactured items and items purchased for resale).

- The rendering of services (which typically involves the performance by the entity of a contractually agreed task over an agreed period of time).

- The use by others of entity assets yielding interest, royalties and dividends.

Income is defined in the IASB's *Conceptual Framework* as 'increases in economic benefits in the form of inflows or enhancements of assets or decreases of liabilities that result in increases in equity.' **Revenue is simply income arising in the ordinary course of an entity's activities** and it may be referred to as:

- Sales
- Turnover
- Interest
- Dividends
- Royalties

### Definition

**Revenue:** The gross inflow of economic benefits during the period arising in the course of the ordinary activities of an entity when those flows result in increases in equity, other than increases relating to contributions from equity participants.

### UK GAAP alert!

There are no significant differences between FRS 102 and IAS 18.

## 10 The regulatory framework for company financial statements

### Section overview

- Extensive regulation covers the content and format of company financial statements, and the methods used to prepare some, if not all, of the figures.

- Prescribed formats enable users to find information and to make comparisons more easily.

- Statement of profit or loss should usually cover a reporting period of 12 months. Both the statement of profit or loss and the statement of financial position must be clearly named and dated.

Company financial statements prepared for **external** publication are extensively regulated to protect investors who use information to make economic decisions, especially when comparing different companies. **Published financial statements** are therefore prepared on the same basis by all companies so investors can make meaningful comparisons. Rules and regulations are applied to:

- **Content:** what information the financial statements should contain, and what supporting information should go with them

- **Accounting concepts:** how figures should be prepared

- **Presentation:** how the financial statements should be presented

The main sources of accounting regulations for companies are:

- Accounting standards (IASs and IFRSs);
- Legislation, in particular the Companies Act 2006.

In this Study Manual we have already covered most of what you need to know at this stage of your studies regarding the content, concepts and presentation of financial statements prepared under IASs. We now need to draw it all together into the **IAS 1 formats** for the statement of profit or loss and statement of financial position and IAS 8 *Accounting Policies, Changes in Accounting Estimates and Errors.*

**UK GAAP alert!**

The formats of financial statements for unlisted companies under UK GAAP are specified by the Companies Act 2006 and are covered in Chapter 14.

## 10.1 Why does IAS 1 include formats?

The purpose of setting out formats for a statement of profit or loss and statement of financial position is to make it easier for the users of financial statements:

- To **find the items they are particularly interested in:** companies are prevented from using complex layouts and formats that make the financial statements more difficult to understand

- To **make comparisons of the results of different companies**, or between the results of the same company from one reporting period to the next.

It is for this second reason that IAS 1 requires **comparative figures for the previous reporting period to be shown**, as well as the figures for the reporting period being reported. In some cases a statement of financial position from an even earlier reporting period may be required as well.

## 10.2 Structure and content of financial statements

- On each statement of financial position and statement of profit or loss, the following information needs to be prominently displayed:

  - **Name** of the company

  - **Date of the statement of financial position/reporting period covered** – financial statements should not normally cover reporting periods longer than 12 months

- The statement of financial position must distinguish between **current and non-current assets** and **current and non-current liabilities**. Current items are to be settled within 12 months of the date of the statement of financial position.

- In the **accounting policies note** to the financial statements the entity must disclose the **measurement basis** used in their preparation (historical cost or net realisable value, for instance), and the other **accounting policies** used that are relevant to an understanding of the financial statements.

## 10.3 IAS 8 *Accounting Policies, Changes in Accounting Estimates and Errors*

**UK GAAP alert!**

- The requirements of FRS 102 are the same the IAS 8 requirements which you cover in the Accounting paper.

IAS 8 prescribes the criteria for selecting and changing accounting policies, together with the accounting treatment and disclosure of changes in accounting policies, changes in accounting estimates and correction of errors.

The application of IAS 8 enhances the relevance, faithful representation and comparability by ensuring that:

- Information is available about the accounting policies adopted by different entities.

- Different entities adopt a common approach to the distinction between a change in accounting policy and a change in an accounting estimate.

- The scope for accounting policy changes is constrained.

- Changes in accounting policies, changes in accounting estimates and corrections of errors are dealt with in a comparable manner by different entities.

## 10.4 Ethics as an issue for regulators

As discussed in Chapter 1, trust in the financial information produced by accountants is essential. How to ensure that information is reliable and fit for purpose is therefore a key concern of regulators and government. One of the ways in which this trust can be achieved is by ensuring that the individuals involved in the production of the material are acting with integrity, which can be defined as acting in a straightforward and honest manner.

Professional bodies can instil integrity in their members through their leadership, policies, the information and training they provide, and the ethical standards which members are expected to adhere to.

The overall regulatory framework within a country or market can be very complex and needs to be underpinned by ethical values. The process also needs to be:

- Honest and truthful
- Transparent and adaptable
- Legally compliant
- Consistent

While the development of policy and guidance can be useful in achieving this, a rules-based approach can also devalue the requirements on the individuals to act ethically, as the emphasis can shift to keeping within the letter or the law, rather than the spirit of it.

# Summary and Self-test

## Summary

**Statement of financial position
Accounting implications**

**Limited companies**

**Statement of profit or loss
Accounting implications**

Tax liability

Called up share capital (NV)
Share premium (premium)
Other receivables (unpaid shares)

Bonus issue
DR    Share premium        X
CR    Equity shares          X

Separate legal entity
Equity and reserves
– Equity (ordinary) shares
– Irredeemable preference shares
– Share premium
– Retained earnings
– General and other reserves

Debt capital (non-current liabilities)
– Loan stock
– Redeemable preference shares
– Long-term bank loans
Provisions (current liabilities)
– Warranty provisions

Tax charge + over/under
provision in the IS

| | |
|---|---|
| B/d | X |
| Profit | X |
| Loss | (X) |
| Reserve transfers | X/(X) |
| Dividends | (X) |
| C/d | X |

Interest/dividends
= Finance costs in IS

**IAS 1 formats**

Satisfy qualitative characteristics of
– Comparability (comparative year's figures required)
– Understandability

# Self-test

Answer the following questions.

1 A company's assets and liabilities at the beginning and end of a reporting period were as follows.

|  | Beginning £ | End £ |
|---|---|---|
| Non-current assets (carrying amount) | 85,000 | 150,000 |
| Current assets | 120,000 | 110,000 |
| Equity shares of £1 | 100,000 | 125,000 |
| Share premium | 5,000 | 10,000 |
| Retained earnings | 50,000 | 67,000 |
| Trade and other payables | 30,000 | 40,000 |
| Tax payable | 20,000 | 18,000 |

During the reporting period the company issued a further 25,000 shares at £1.20 each. £22,000 for tax expense was shown in the statement of profit or loss.

The company's profit before tax for the reporting period was

A £17,000

B £20,000

C £27,000

D £39,000

2 You are supplied with the following extract from Niton plc's statements of financial position at 31 January 20X9 and 20X8.

|  | 31 January 20X9 £m | 31 January 20X8 £m |
|---|---|---|
| Equity shares of £1 each | 120 | 100 |
| Share premium | 260 | 220 |

Notes

(1) On 1 July 20X8 there was a 1 for 10 bonus issue
(2) On 30 September 20X8 there was a rights issue
(3) There are no other reserve balances

What was the total amount received from the issue of shares for the year ended 31 January 20X9?

A £10m

B £20m

C £50m

D £60m

3 The figure for equity in the IAS 1 statement of financial position is represented by

A Called-up share capital plus share premium
B Total assets less current liabilities
C Paid share capital plus retained earnings
D Total assets less total liabilities

4 Which of the following would cause a company's profit for the period to increase?

A Issue of 100,000 £1 equity shares at £1.02

B Discount allowed of £255

C Disposal for £8,500 of a fork-lift truck which originally cost £15,000 and has a carrying amount of £9,250

D Receipt of £25 in respect of a receivable previously written off as irrecoverable

5  Which **two** of the following transactions could affect a company's retained earnings for the reporting period?

    A    Rights issue of shares
    B    Transfer to the general reserve
    C    Purchase of land
    D    Repayment of debentures at their par value
    E    Increase of tax due

6  Raymond plc issues 135,000 equity shares with a par value of £3 each at a price of £5 each for cash.

Which of the following sets of entries would be made to record this transaction?

    A    Credit Bank £675,000, Debit Share capital £405,000, Debit Share premium £270,000
    B    Debit Bank £675,000, Credit Share capital £135,000, Credit Share premium £540,000
    C    Debit Bank £675,000, Credit Share capital £405,000, Credit Share premium £270,000
    D    Credit Bank £675,000, Debit Share capital £135,000, Debit Share premium £540,000

7  The following information is available in relation to the tax figures to be included in the financial statements of Godshill plc.

|  | 31 December 20X7 £ | 31 December 20X6 £ |
|---|---|---|
| Tax payable | 271,500 | 237,600 |
| Statement of profit or loss tax expense | 269,700 | 219,800 |

What is the total tax paid during the year ended 31 December 20X7?

    A    £185,900
    B    £235,800
    C    £237,600
    D    £269,700

8  If tax is under-provided in the statement of profit or loss for 20X7, in the following year's statement of profit or loss the effect will be:

    A    A reduction in profit for the reporting period
    B    An increase in profit for the reporting period
    C    A reduction in gross profit
    D    An increase in gross profit

Now, go back to the Learning Objectives in the Introduction. If you are satisfied that you have achieved these objectives, please tick them off.

# Answers to Interactive questions

## Answer to Interactive question 1

There are 30 million shares of 20p in issue (£6 million/20p per share). A 1 for 3 rights issue involves an issue of 30 million/3 = 10 million shares at £1.80, to raise cash of £18 million. The issued share capital goes up by 10 million shares at 20p each, £2m. The share premium on the issue is £1.80 − 20p = £1.60 per share, or £16 million in total.

| | £'000 |
|---|---|
| **ASSETS** | |
| *Non-current assets* | 18,600 |
| *Current assets (2.9m+18m) (a)* | 20,900 |
| *Total assets* | 39,500 |
| | |
| **EQUITY AND LIABILITIES** | |
| *Equity* | |
| Share capital: equity shares of 20p each ((6m/3) + 6m) (b) | 8,000 |
| Share premium ((6m/(0.2 × 3)) × £1.60) + 5.7m) (c) | 21,700 |
| Retained earnings | 7,000 |
| *Total equity* | 36,700 |
| *Total liabilities* | 2,800 |
| *Total equity and liabilities* | 39,500 |

## Answer to Interactive question 2

### Canvat plc: statement of financial position at 31 December 20X1

| | £'000 |
|---|---|
| **TOTAL ASSETS** (2m + (320,000 × 1.60)) | 2,512 |
| | |
| **EQUITY AND LIABILITIES** | |
| *Equity* | |
| Share capital (400 + 80 + 160) | 640 |
| Share premium (500 + 352 – 80) | 772 |
| Retained earnings | 300 |
| *Total equity* | 1,712 |
| *Total liabilities* | 800 |
| *Total equity and liabilities* | 2,512 |

The bonus issue is of 800,000/5 = 160,000 50p shares:

| DEBIT | Share premium | £80,000 | |
|---|---|---|---|
| CREDIT | Share capital | | £80,000 |

The rights issue is of (800,000 + 160,000)/3 = 320,000 50p shares at £1.60 each, ie £512,000:

| | | £ | £ |
|---|---|---|---|
| DEBIT | Cash | 512,000 | |
| CREDIT | Share capital (320,000 × 50p) | | 160,000 |
| | Share premium (320,000 × (1.60 – 0.50)) | | 352,000 |

The ledger accounts are as follows:

### SHARE CAPITAL

| | Number | £ | | Number | £ |
|---|---|---|---|---|---|
| Balance c/d | 1,280,000 | 640,000 | Balance b/d | 800,000 | 400,000 |
| | | | 1 for 5 bonus issue | 160,000 | 80,000 |
| | | | 1 for 3 rights issue | 320,000 | 160,000 |
| | 1,280,000 | 640,000 | | 1,280,000 | 640,000 |

## SHARE PREMIUM

| | £ | | £ |
|---|---|---|---|
| Bonus issue | 80,000 | Balance b/d | 500,000 |
| Balance c/d | 772,000 | Rights issue: cash | 352,000 |
| | 852,000 | | 852,000 |

## RETAINED EARNINGS

| | £ | | £ |
|---|---|---|---|
| Balance c/d | 300,000 | Balance b/d | 300,000 |

**1**    D

|  | £ |
|---|---|
| Opening net assets (85,000 + 120,000 – 30,000 – 20,000) or (100 + 5 + 50) | 155,000 |
| Closing net assets (150,000 + 110,000 – 40,000 – 18,000) | 202,000 |
| Increase in net assets | 47,000 |
| Less proceeds of share issue (25,000 × £1.20) | (30,000) |
| Retained profit for reporting period (67,000 – 50,000) | 17,000 |
| Add tax charged | 22,000 |
| Profit before tax | 39,000 |

**2**    D

**SHARE CAPITAL**

| | £m | | £m |
|---|---|---|---|
| | | b/d | 100 |
| | | Bonus issue (100 ÷10) | 10 |
| c/d | 120 | Rights issue (β) | 10 |
| | 120 | | 120 |

**SHARE PREMIUM**

| | £m | | £m |
|---|---|---|---|
| Bonus issue | 10 | b/d | 220 |
| c/d | 260 | Rights issue (β) | 50 |
| | 270 | | 270 |

Therefore, the rights issue was of 10,000,000 shares at a premium of £5 per share. Total raised was £60,000,000.

**3**    D    Total equity = share capital and reserves = net assets (assets less liabilities).

**4**    D    The premium on the issue of shares must be credited to share premium. Discount allowed to suppliers is an expense that decreases profits. The disposal of the truck results in a loss which reduces profit. Reduction in irrecoverable debts expense increases profits.

**5**    B and E

| | | | | | |
|---|---|---|---|---|---|
| A | DR | Cash | CR | Share capital/share premium |
| B | DR | Retained earnings | CR | General reserve |
| C | DR | Non-current assets | CR | Cash |
| D | DR | Debentures | CR | Cash |
| E | DR | Statement of profit or loss (tax expense) | CR | Tax payable |

**6**    C    Cash raised is 135,000 × £5 = £675,000, which is debited to cash at bank. The credit to share capital is 135,000 × £3 par value = £405,000, while the credit to share premium is 135,000 × £2 = £270,000.

**7**    B    TAX PAYABLE

| | £ | | £ |
|---|---|---|---|
| Paid (β) | 235,800 | b/d | 237,600 |
| c/d | 271,500 | Statement of profit or loss | 269,700 |
| | 507,300 | | 507,300 |

**8**    A    A previous reporting period's under-provision means an additional expense in the current reporting period's statement of profit or loss. This has no effect on gross profit; it is profit for this reporting period that is reduced.

# CHAPTER 12

# Company financial statements under IFRS

Introduction

Examination context

**Topic List**

    1   The statement of profit or loss (IAS 1)

    2   The statement of financial position (IAS 1)

    3   Applying the IAS 1 formats

Summary and Self-test

Technical reference

Answers to Self-test

# Introduction

## Learning objectives

- Prepare and present a statement of financial position and statement of profit or loss (or extracts therefrom) from the accounting records and trial balance in a format which satisfies the information requirements of the entity

Specific syllabus learning outcomes are: 1d, e, 2c, 3a

## Syllabus links

The material in this chapter will be developed further in the Professional Level module of Financial Accounting and Reporting. The focus of this chapter is the preparation of company financial statements under IFRS only. UK GAAP financial statements are prepared in chapter 14.

## Examination context

40% of the assessment will be the preparation of single company financial statements. In the assessment you will be asked to produce either a statement of profit or loss and statement of financial position, or a statement of cash flows. You will be given an extract from a TB or some draft financial statements, with additional information and be required to complete calculations in order to fill in a pro-forma template.

In the online exam all expenses / losses in the statement of profit or loss must be included as negative numbers, i.e. with a minus sign in front or in brackets.

The calculations and workings will include aspects from other chapters, as the preparation of the accounts will bring together knowledge from most parts of the syllabus.

You may also be examined on the contents of this chapter by multiple choice questions, which may involve calculations so that the correct answer can be selected. Very often double entry questions are phrased in terms of preparing a journal.

In the exam you may be required to:

- Identify how expenses should be categorised into cost of sales, administrative expenses, distribution costs and finance costs

- Specify the requirements of IAS 1 in relation to company financial statements

# 1 The statement of profit or loss (IAS 1)

**Section overview**

- The statement of profit or loss must show balances as set out in the IAS 1 format, including gross profit, profit before tax and (post-tax) profit for the reporting period.

The IAS 1 **statement of profit or loss functional format** to be learned is shown in the example below (Ducat plc). This includes the minimum disclosure requirements of IAS 1. The main requirement is that **all items of income and expense recognised in a period shall be included in profit or loss**.

Note that the statement of profit or loss stops at profit (or loss) for the reporting period.

**The presentation of the final retained earnings figure for the reporting period, as seen in the statement of financial position, is beyond the scope of** *Accounting*, **as it is presented in a separate statement which is not examinable, called the statement of changes in equity (SCE).**

**Worked example: Statement of profit or loss**

Ducat plc's statement of profit or loss is presented below.

DUCAT PLC
STATEMENT OF PROFIT OR LOSS FOR THE YEAR ENDED 31 DECEMBER 20X3

|  | £ |
|---|---:|
| Revenue | 623,000 |
| Cost of sales | (414,000) |
| Gross profit | 209,000 |
| Other income | 26,000 |
| Distribution costs | (73,000) |
| Administrative expenses | (32,000) |
| Finance costs | (15,000) |
| Profit before tax | 115,000 |
| Tax expense | (35,000) |
| Profit for the period | 80,000 |

## 1.1 Cost of sales, distribution costs and administrative expenses

The allocation of expenses to each of these three headings calls for judgement. In practice the rules are not rigid. IAS 1 states that an entity shall present an analysis of expenses using a classification based on either the nature of expenses or their functions within the entity, whichever provides information that is reliable and more relevant. The format and classification used here is the **functional** one. Additional disclosures on the nature of expenses, including depreciation and amortisation, are required.

For the *Accounting* exam you should expect to make the following classifications.

| Cost of sales | Distribution costs | Administrative expenses |
|---|---|---|
| Purchases plus carriage inwards adjusted for opening and closing inventory, and any substantial losses of inventory.<br><br>In a manufacturing company wages of production staff, and maintenance and depreciation expenses of production non-current assets, plus losses on their disposal, are also included. | Wages etc of marketing and distribution staff.<br><br>Sales commission<br><br>Distribution expenses such as vehicle running costs and carriage outwards.<br><br>Depreciation of motor vehicles used for distribution, and marketing costs such as advertising and promotion, and any loss on disposal of such assets.<br><br>Depreciation of other non-current assets used by distribution operations and any loss on disposal of such assets.<br><br>The cost of advertising and selling activities, since these are a part of distributing goods and services to customers. | Wages of administrative staff.<br><br>Depreciation of non-current assets used by non-production and non-distribution operations, and any loss on disposal of such assets.<br><br>Amortisation of intangible assets.<br><br>Cash discount allowed to customers.<br><br>Expense of substantial loss of inventory<br><br>Irrecoverable debts expense |

## 1.2 Other income

Income other than income classified as revenue should be shown separately. Examples of other income include:

- Dividends received on investments
- Interest received on savings
- Rent received from property
- Discounts received from suppliers
- Insurance claim proceeds
- Profits on disposal of non-current assets

## 1.3 Finance costs

- Interest payable on bank loans and overdrafts
- Interest on debt securities

# 2 The statement of financial position (IAS 1)

**Section overview**

- The statement of financial position is split between total assets and total equity plus liabilities.
- Both assets and liabilities must show the current/non-current split.

The IAS 1 statement of financial position format is as follows.

DUCAT PLC
STATEMENT OF FINANCIAL POSITION AS AT 31 DECEMBER 20X3

|  | £ | £ |
|---|---:|---:|
| **ASSETS** | | |
| *Non-current assets* | | |
| Property, plant and equipment | | 427,000 |
| Goodwill | | 15,000 |
| Other intangible assets | | 110,000 |
| | | 552,000 |
| *Current assets* | | |
| Inventories | 51,000 | |
| Trade and other receivables | 102,000 | |
| Other current assets (eg prepayments) | 20,000 | |
| Cash and cash equivalents | 33,000 | |
| | | 206,000 |
| *Total assets* | | 758,000 |
| **EQUITY AND LIABILITIES** | | |
| *Equity* | | |
| Share capital: £1 equity shares | | 150,000 |
| Share capital: 10% £1 irredeemable preference shares | | 20,000 |
| Reserves: share premium | | 125,000 |
| Reserves: retained earnings | | 161,000 |
| Reserves: general | | 65,000 |
| *Total equity* | | 521,000 |
| *Non-current liabilities* | | |
| Long-term borrowings | | 158,000 |
| *Current liabilities* | | |
| Trade and other payables (including accruals) | 36,000 | |
| Short-term borrowings | 22,000 | |
| Provisions | 10,000 | |
| Current tax payable | 11,000 | |
| | | 79,000 |
| *Total equity and liabilities* | | 758,000 |

Points to note

- All tangible assets (including land and buildings) are combined under the heading 'property, plant and equipment'. The user would refer to the non-current assets note, as covered in Chapter 10, for detail.

- Trade receivables and any other receivables (including VAT due) are combined as 'trade and other receivables'; prepayments are included in the heading 'other current assets'. The allowance for receivables is set off here.

- Cash in hand and at bank are combined as 'cash and cash equivalents'.

- Any long-term liabilities such as bank loans or debt securities that are not repayable within 12 months are combined as 'long-term borrowings' under 'non-current liabilities'. Redeemable preference shares would be included here.

- There are detailed disclosure requirements for share capital in IAS 1, in particular of the issued, fully paid and partly paid share capital, and of the par value. The figure included in the statement of financial position is the called-up share capital, both paid and unpaid.

- Bank overdrafts, which are technically repayable on demand, are called 'short-term borrowings'. They are not offset against any cash and cash equivalent asset balances.

- Trade payables and other payables (including VAT, PAYE/NIC and sales commission owed, interest payable and accruals) are combined as 'trade and other payables'.

- Current amounts of tax payable are each shown as a separate item under current liabilities.

# 3 Applying the IAS 1 formats

## Section overview

- To apply the IAS 1 formats:

  - Extract a trial balance

  - Draw up adjustment journals

  - Complete the ETB

  - Gather the ledger accounts together appropriately regarding the statement of profit or loss cost of sales, administrative expenses and distribution cost headings

  - Complete the formats for statement of profit or loss and statement of financial position

The formats we use here are adapted from IAS 1. The Standard sets out a minimum requirement for what should appear on the face of the statement of financial position, although additional items are allowed to make the information more relevant. No set order of items is presented in IAS 1; entities are encouraged to adapt the order and the descriptions to enhance **relevance**, though in practice **comparability** encourages similar entities to adopt similar presentations.

Where a single figure or 'line item' appears in the statement of financial position, the company must disclose further sub-classifications in the notes in a manner that is appropriate to its operations.

## Worked example: Preparing IAS 1 format financial statements

To draw together everything we have covered so far we shall work through a full example of how to use the ETB to prepare an IAS 1 format statement of profit or loss and statement of financial position.

The chief accountant of Format plc has extracted the following trial balance from the ledger as at 31 December 20X2.

FORMAT PLC
TRIAL BALANCE AS AT 31 DECEMBER 20X2

|  | £'000 | £'000 |
|---|---|---|
| Issued equity shares of £1 |  | 800 |
| 10% irredeemable preference shares of £1 each |  | 200 |
| Trade receivables and trade payables | 1,820 | 1,866 |
| Bank | 80 |  |
| Inventory at 1.1.X2 | 1,950 |  |
| 6% debentures |  | 1,000 |
| Sales |  | 9,500 |
| Rental income |  | 200 |
| Debenture interest (six months to 30.6.X2) | 30 |  |
| Administration and general expenses, excluding salaries | 650 |  |
| Administration salaries | 275 |  |
| Distribution expenses | 616 |  |
| Purchases | 5,125 |  |
| Salaries associated with manufacture of goods | 300 |  |
| Carriage inwards | 100 |  |
| Property costs | 300 |  |
| Retained earnings |  | 1,100 |
| Freehold land, at cost | 2,120 |  |
| Fixtures and fittings, at cost | 2,000 |  |
| Accumulated depreciation, fixtures and fittings |  | 900 |
| Allowance for irrecoverable debts |  | 100 |
| Goodwill | 300 |  |
|  | 15,666 | 15,666 |

The following items have yet to be dealt with.

1. An inventory count has revealed the closing inventory figure to be £2,020,000.

2. The company depreciates fixtures and fittings at 20% straight line cost.

3. An impairment review has shown that 10% should be written off goodwill. The charge should be to administrative expenses.

4. The credit controller has said that a debt of £15,000 should be written off as irrecoverable, and the allowance for receivables should be increased to £200,000.

5. The tax due on profits for the year is estimated at £750,000.

6. The allocation of expenditure between cost of sales, distribution costs and administrative expenses should be as follows.

|  | Distribution % | Administrative % |
|---|---|---|
| Property costs | 25 | 75 |
| Depreciation | 50 | 50 |

7. The debentures are repayable in full in ten years time. Interest is paid in two equal instalments per annum.

**Requirement**

Prepare year-end journals and an ETB for Format plc, and present a statement of profit or loss for Format plc for the year ended 31 December 20X2 and a statement of financial position as at that date.

NB: In the online exam all expenses / losses in the statement of profit or loss must be included as negative numbers, i.e. with a minus sign in front or in brackets.

## Solution

The year-end journals to be put through in the adjustments column are as follows:

|  |  | £'000 | £'000 |
|---|---|---|---|
| **1** |  |  |  |
| DEBIT | Closing inventory (statement of financial position) | 2,020 |  |
| CREDIT | Closing inventory (statement of profit or loss) |  | 2,020 |
| **2 and 6** |  |  |  |
| DEBIT | Administrative expenses | 200 |  |
|  | Distribution costs | 200 |  |
| CREDIT | Fixtures and fittings – accumulated depreciation (2,000 × 20%) |  | 400 |
| **3** |  |  |  |
| DEBIT | Administrative expenses | 30 |  |
| CREDIT | Goodwill (300 × 10%) |  | 30 |
| **4** |  |  |  |
| DEBIT | Administrative expenses | 115 |  |
| CREDIT | Trade receivables |  | 15 |
|  | Allowance for irrecoverable debts (200 – 100) |  | 100 |
| **5** |  |  |  |
| DEBIT | Tax expense (statement of profit or loss) | 750 |  |
| CREDIT | Tax payable (statement of financial position) |  | 750 |
| **6** |  |  |  |
| DEBIT | Administrative expenses (300 × 0.75) | 225 |  |
|  | Distribution costs (300 × 0.25) | 75 |  |
| CREDIT | Property costs |  | 300 |
| **7** |  |  |  |
| DEBIT | Debenture interest | 30 |  |
| CREDIT | Trade and other payables |  | 30 |

The extended trial balance is as follows:

| | Trial balance Debit £'000 | Trial balance Credit £'000 | Adjustments Debit £'000 | Adjustments Credit £'000 | Statement of profit or loss Debit £'000 | Statement of profit or loss Credit £'000 | Statement of financial position Debit £'000 | Statement of financial position Credit £'000 |
|---|---|---|---|---|---|---|---|---|
| £1 equity shares | | 800 | | | | | | 800 |
| 10% £1 irredeemable preference shares | | 200 | | | | | | 200 |
| Trade receivables | 1,820 | | | 15 | | | 1,805 | |
| Trade payables | | 1,866 | | 30 | | | | 1,896 |
| Bank | 80 | | | | | | 80 | |
| Inventory | 1,950 | | 2,020 | 2,020 | 1,950 | 2,020 | 2,020 | |
| 6% debentures | | 1,000 | | | | | | 1,000 |
| Sales | | 9,500 | | | | 9,500 | | |
| Rental income | | 200 | | | | 200 | | |
| Debenture interest | 30 | | 30 | | 60 | | | |
| Administrative expenses | 650 | | 570* | | 1,220 | | | |
| Administration salaries | 275 | | | | 275 | | | |
| Distribution expenses | 616 | | 275** | | 891 | | | |
| Purchases | 5,125 | | | | 5,125 | | | |
| Manufacturing salaries | 300 | | | | 300 | | | |
| Carriage inwards | 100 | | | | 100 | | | |
| Property costs | 300 | | | 300 | | | | |
| Retained earnings | | 1,100 | | | | | | 1,100 |
| Freehold land – cost | 2,120 | | | | | | 2,120 | |
| Fixtures and fittings – cost | 2,000 | | | | | | 2,000 | |
| F&F – accumulated depreciation | | 900 | | 400 | | | | 1,300 |
| Allowance for irrecoverable debts | | 100 | | 100 | | | | 200 |
| Goodwill | 300 | | | 30 | | | 270 | |
| Tax | | | 750 | 750 | 750 | | | 750 |
| Profit | | | | | 1,049 | | | 1,049 |
| | 15,666 | 15,666 | 3,645 | 3,645 | 11,720 | 11,720 | 8,295 | 8,295 |

\*   200 (Jnl 2) + 30 (Jnl 3) + 115 (Jnl 4) + 225 (Jnl 6) = 570
\*\*   200 (Jnl 2) + 75 (Jnl 6) = 275

FORMAT PLC
STATEMENT OF PROFIT OR LOSS FOR THE YEAR ENDED 31 DECEMBER 20X2

| | £'000 |
|---|---|
| Revenue | 9,500 |
| Cost of sales (W1) | (5,455) |
| Gross profit | 4,045 |
| Other income | 200 |
| Administrative expenses (W1) | (1,495) |
| Distribution costs (W1) | (891) |
| Finance costs | (60) |
| Profit before tax | 1,799 |
| Tax expense | (750) |
| Profit for the period | 1,049 |

FORMAT PLC
STATEMENT OF FINANCIAL POSITION AS AT 31 DECEMBER 20X2

|  | £'000 | £'000 |
|---|---|---|
| **ASSETS** | | |
| *Non-current assets* | | |
| Property, plant and equipment (W3) | | 2,820 |
| Goodwill | | 270 |
| | | 3,090 |
| *Current assets* | | |
| Inventories | 2,020 | |
| Trade and other receivables (1,805 – 200 allowance) | 1,605 | |
| Cash and cash equivalents | 80 | |
| | | 3,705 |
| *Total assets* | | 6,795 |
| **EQUITY AND LIABILITIES** | | |
| *Equity* | | |
| Equity share capital: £1 equity shares | | 800 |
| Preference share capital: 10% £1 shares | | 200 |
| Retained earnings (W2) | | 2,149 |
| *Total equity* | | 3,149 |
| *Non-current liabilities* | | |
| Long-term borrowings: 6% debentures | | 1,000 |
| *Current liabilities* | | |
| Trade and other payables | 1,896 | |
| Tax payable | 750 | |
| | | 2,646 |
| *Total equity and liabilities* | | 6,795 |

WORKINGS

(1) **Analysis of expenses**

|  | Cost of sales £'000 | Distribution costs £'000 | Admin expenses £'000 |
|---|---|---|---|
| Opening inventory | 1,950 | | |
| Administrative expenses | | | 1,220 |
| Salaries | 300 | | 275 |
| Distribution costs | | 891 | |
| Purchases | 5,125 | | |
| Carriage inwards | 100 | | |
| Closing inventory | (2,020) | | |
| | 5,455 | 891 | 1,495 |

(2) **Retained earnings**

|  | £'000 |  | £'000 |
|---|---|---|---|
| | | Balance b/d | 1,100 |
| | | Profit for the period (statement of profit or loss) | 1,049 |
| Balance c/d | 2,149 | | |
| | 2,149 | | 2,149 |

### (3) Property, plant and equipment note

| | Freehold land £'000 | Fixtures and fittings £'000 | Total £'000 |
|---|---|---|---|
| **Cost** | | | |
| At 1.1.X2 | 2,120 | 2,000 | 4,120 |
| Additions | | | |
| Disposals | | | |
| At 31.12.X2 | 2,120 | 2,000 | 4,120 |
| **Accumulated depreciation** | | | |
| At 1.1.X2 | | 900 | 900 |
| Charge for the year (£2,000 × 20%) | | 400 | 400 |
| Disposals | | | |
| At 31.12.X2 | | 1,300 | 1,300 |
| **Carrying amount** | | | |
| At 1.1.X2 | 2,120 | 1,100 | 3,220 |
| At 31.12.X2 | 2,120 | 700 | 2,820 |

## Summary

**IAS 1 formats**

### Statement of profit or loss for the reporting period

|  | £'000 |
|---|---|
| Revenue | 623,000 |
| Cost of sales | (414,000) |
| Gross profit | 209,000 |
| Other income | 26,000 |
| Distribution costs | (73,000) |
| Administrative expenses | (32,000) |
| Finance costs | (15,000) |
| Profit before tax | 115,000 |
| Tax expense | (35,000) |
| Profit for period | 80,000 |

### Statement of financial position at the reporting period end

|  | £ | £ |
|---|---|---|
| **ASSETS** | | |
| **Non-current assets** | | |
| Property, plant and equipment | | 427,000 |
| Goodwill | | 15,000 |
| Intangible assets | | 110,000 |
| | | 552,000 |
| **Current assets** | | |
| Inventories | 51,000 | |
| Trade and other receivables | 102,000 | |
| Prepayments | 20,000 | |
| Cash and cash equivalents | 33,000 | |
| | | 206,000 |
| **Total assets** | | 758,000 |
| **EQUITY AND LIABILITIES** | | |
| **Equity** | | |
| Equity share capital: £1 equity shares | | 150,000 |
| Preference share capital: 10% £1 irredeemable preference shares | | 90,000 |
| Share premium | | 55,000 |
| General reserve | | 65,000 |
| Retained earnings | | 161,000 |
| **Total equity** | | 521,000 |
| **Non-current liabilities** | | |
| Long-term borrowings | | 158,000 |
| **Current liabilities** | | |
| Trade and other payables | 29,000 | |
| Short-term borrowings | 22,000 | |
| Accruals | 5,000 | |
| Provisions | 10,000 | |
| Tax payable | 13,000 | |
| | | 79,000 |
| **Total equity and liabilities** | | 758,000 |

**Satisfy qualitative characteristics of**
- Comparability
- Relevance and verifiability

**Accounting powers**
- Relevant IASs are mandatory
- Where no relevant IAS, apply judgement in line with Conceptual Framework
- Applied consistently

CHAPTER

12

## Self-test

Answer the following question.

1   Mince plc is preparing its financial statements for the year ended 30 September 20X6, having prepared an initial trial balance. The initial trial balance shows the following balances:

|  | £ |
|---|---|
| Administrative expenses paid (including rent) | 32,874 |
| Discounts allowed (to be included in administrative expenses) | 1,085 |
| Prepayment of rent at 1 October 20X5 | 2,894 |

On 31 August 20X6 Mince plc paid its quarterly rent in advance of £5,400. In Mince plc's statement of profit or loss the figure for administrative expenses will be:

A   £31,453
B   £32,495
C   £32,874
D   £33,253

2   Which THREE of the following would be included in current liabilities in a company's financial statements?

A   Allowance for receivables
B   Bank overdraft
C   Tax payable
D   Share capital
E   Provisions

3   A company has a balance of £2,500 (debit) on its tax account at 31 December 20X6 relating to the tax payable on the 20X5 profits. The company's estimated tax liability for the year to 31 December 20X6 is £15,000.

The tax charge in the statement of profit or loss for the year ended 31 December 20X6 is:

A   £2,500
B   £12,500
C   £15,000
D   £17,500

Now, go back to the Learning Objectives in the Introduction. If you are satisfied that you have achieved these objectives, please tick them off.

## 1 Structure and content of company financial statements

- Comparative figures for the previous reporting period must be shown.

  IAS 1 para 38

- Name of the company, and the date of the statement of financial position or the reporting period covered, must be prominently displayed.

  IAS 1 para 51

- Financial statements should not normally cover reporting periods longer than one year.

  IAS 1 para 36

- The statement of financial position must distinguish between current and non-current assets and current and non-current liabilities. Current items are to be settled within 12 months of the date of the statement of financial position.

  IAS 1 paras 60 and 61

- Share capital and reserves disclosures.

  IAS 1 para 79

- Minimum requirements and adaptation of format of statement of financial position; additional disclosures.

  IAS 1 paras 54, 55, 57, 77

- All items of income and expense recognised in a reporting period shall be included in profit or loss; minimum disclosure requirements are set out.

  IAS 1 paras 81, 82 and 88

- An entity shall present an analysis of expenses using a classification based on either the nature of expenses or their function within the entity, which provides information which is more reliable and relevant. Additional disclosures on the nature of expenses, including depreciation and amortisation, are required.

  IAS 1 paras 99, 103 and 104

- A note must disclose the measurement bases used in preparing the financial statements, and other accounting policies that are relevant to an understanding of them.

  IAS 1 para 117

## 2 Format of statement of profit or loss and statement of financial position

- Formats, including statement of profit or loss in functional format.

  IAS 1 IG6

  IAS 1 para 39

## 3 Additional comparative information

- When an entity applies an accounting policy retrospectively, makes a retrospective restatement of items in its financial statements or reclassifies items in its financial statements, an additional statement of financial position as at the beginning of the earliest comparative period must be presented.

1   D   The opening prepayment of rent of £2,894 needs to be debited to administrative expenses, and the closing prepayment of £5,400 × 2/3 = £3,600 needs to be credited. Total administrative expenses will therefore be £32,874 + £1,085 + £2,894 – £3,600 = £33,253.

2   B, C, E

Share capital is equity in the statement of financial position. Allowance for receivables is shown as a deduction from receivables under current assets.

3   D

|  | £ |
| --- | --- |
| Current year | 15,000 |
| Underprovision in previous year | 2,500 |
| Tax expense in statement of profit or loss | 17,500 |

# CHAPTER 13

# Statement of cash flows

# Introduction

## Learning objectives

- Prepare and present a statement of cash flows (or extracts therefrom) from the accounting records and trial balance in a format which satisfies the information requirements of the entity

Specific syllabus learning outcome is: 3c

## Syllabus links

The material in this chapter will be developed further in the Professional Level module of Financial Accounting and Reporting.

This is the first time that you will have come across a statement of cash flows in your studies. However, as you will see in the rest of the chapter, most of the information needed to produce a statement of cash flows is contained in the statement of profit or loss and statement of financial position, both of which you will be familiar with from your studies so far.

## Examination context

40% of the assessment will be the preparation of single company financial statements. In the assessment you will be asked to produce either a statement of profit or loss and statement of financial position, or a statement of cash flows. You will be given an extract from a TB or some draft financial statements, with additional information and be required to complete calculations in order to fill in a pro-forma template.

The calculations and workings will include aspects from other chapters, as the preparation of the accounts will bring together knowledge from most parts of the syllabus.

You may also be examined on the contents of this chapter by multiple choice questions, which may involve calculations so that the correct answer can be selected. Very often double entry questions are phrased in terms of preparing a journal.

In the exam you may be required to:

- Prepare extracts from a cash flow statement

- Calculate the cash flow from operating activities

# 1 Statement of cash flows (IAS 7)

> ## Section overview
>
> - The statement of cash flows shows movements in cash and cash equivalents.
> - Both listed and unlisted companies are required to produce a statement of cash flows.
> - The statement of cash flows is a useful addition to the financial statements because accounting profit is not the only indicator of performance.
> - The statement of cash flows concentrates on the sources and uses of cash and is a useful indicator of liquidity and solvency.

## 1.1 IAS 7 *Statement of Cash Flows* (FRS 102 s.7)

The objective of IAS 7 *Statement of Cash Flows* is to provide *historical* information about changes in cash and cash equivalents, classifying **cash flows** between operating, investing and financing activities. This will provide information to users of financial statements about the entity's **ability to generate cash and cash equivalents**, as well as indicating the cash needs of the entity.

IAS 7 sets out the structure of a statement of cash flows and it sets the minimum level of disclosure. In the assessment you may be asked to prepare a statement of cash flows in a pro-forma template. You will be provided with financial information, usually in the form of draft financial statements, and you will be given some additional information about transactions that you need to make adjustments for in order to insert the numbers into the pro-forma.

### UK GAAP alert!

The format of the statement of cash flows under FRS 102 is the same as the IFRS format.

Entities eligible for disclosure exemptions under FRS 102 are also exempt from the preparation of a statement of cash flows

## 1.2 Purpose of IAS 7

IAS 7 begins with the following statement.

'Information about the cash flows of an entity is useful in providing users of financial statements with a basis to assess the ability of the entity to generate cash and cash equivalents and the needs of the entity to utilise those cash flows.'

It has been argued that 'profit' does not always give a useful or meaningful picture of a company's operations. Readers of a company's financial statements might even be misled by a reported profit figure. Consider the following examples.

(a) Shareholders might believe that if a company makes a profit after tax of, say, £100,000 then this is the amount which it could afford to pay as a dividend. Unless the company has sufficient cash available to stay in business and also to pay a dividend, the shareholders' expectations would be wrong.

(b) Employees might believe that if a company makes profits, it can afford to pay higher wages next year. This opinion may not be correct: the ability to pay wages depends on the availability of cash.

(c) Cash is the lifeblood of the business. Survival of a business entity depends not so much on profits as on its ability to pay its debts when they fall due. Such payments might include 'profit and loss' items such as material purchases, wages, interest and taxation etc, but also capital payments for new non-current assets and the repayment of loan capital when this falls due (for example, on the redemption of debentures).

From these examples, it is clear that a company's future performance and prospects depend not so much on the 'profits' earned in a period, but more realistically on liquidity or cash flows.

The statement of cash flows should be used **in conjunction** with the rest of the financial statements. Users can gain further appreciation of:

- The change in net assets

- The entity's financial position (liquidity and solvency)

- The entity's ability to adapt to changing circumstances and opportunities by affecting the amount and timing of cash flows

Statements of cash flows **enhance comparability** as they are not affected by differing accounting policies used for the same type of transactions or events.

Cash flow information of a historical nature can be used as an indicator of the amount, timing and certainty of future cash flows. Past forecast cash flow information can be **checked for accuracy** as actual figures emerge. The relationship between profit and net cash flow and the impact of changing prices can be analysed over time.

## 1.3 Scope

IAS 7 requires all entities to include a statement of cash flows as an integral part of their financial statement.

All types of entity can provide useful information about cash flows as the need for cash is universal, whatever the nature of their revenue-producing activities.

### Definitions

Cash flows: These are inflows and outflows of cash and cash equivalents.

Cash: Comprises cash on hand and demand deposits.

Cash equivalents: Short-term, highly liquid investments that are readily convertible to known amounts of cash and which are subject to an insignificant risk of changes in value (maturity of three months or less from the date of acquisition).

# 2 Format of the statement of cash flows

### Section overview

- The statement of cash flows summarises all movements of cash into and out of the business during the accounting period. The cash inflows and outflows are classified under the following headings:

    - **Operating activities**: These are primarily derived from the principal revenue-producing activities of the entity and other activities that are not investing or financing activities.

    - **Investing activities**: These are the cash flows derived from acquisition and disposal of non-current assets and other investments not included in cash equivalents.

    - **Financing activities**: These are activities that result in changes in the size and composition of the equity capital and borrowings of the entity.

    The total cash flows for each heading are totalled to give the net inflow or outflow of cash and cash equivalents for the period.

## 2.1 Cash flows from operating activities

IAS 7 defines operating activities as the principal revenue producing activities of the entity and other activities that are not investing or financing activities. This is an indication of how well the entity can generate enough cash flows to maintain its operations and meet its debts without relying on external finance.

Cash flows from operating activities can consist of:

- Cash receipts from the sale of goods and the rendering of services
- Cash receipts from royalties, fees, commissions and other revenue
- Cash payments to suppliers for goods and services
- Cash payments to and on behalf of employees

Cash flows from interest paid and income taxes paid are also dealt with here.

IAS 7 allows two possible layouts for **cash generated from operations**

- The **indirect** method
- The **direct** method

The **direct method is preferred by IAS 7** but is not compulsory. In practical terms the indirect method is likely to be easier and less time consuming to prepare and is more likely to be examined. **In the exam you should use the indirect method unless the question specifies otherwise.**

## 2.2 Direct method

Using the direct method, cash generated from operations would be analysed as follows and shown as a note to the statement of cash flows:

Gross operating cash flows for the year ended December 20X4

|  | £ |
|---|---|
| Cash received from customers | X |
| Cash payments to suppliers | (X) |
| Cash payments to and on behalf of employees | (X) |
| Cash generated from operations | X |

The reasons for certain items being added and others being deducted is very straightforward with this method – cash inflows are added and cash outflows are deducted. Entities are encouraged to use this method as it provides information that is not available under the indirect method which may be useful in estimating future cash flows.

## 2.3 Indirect method

Using the indirect method, cash generated from operations is calculated by performing a reconciliation between:

- Profit before tax as reported in the statement of profit or loss
- Cash generated from operations

This reconciliation is produced as follows:

| Reconciliation of profit/loss before tax to cash generated from operations for the year ended 31 December 20X7 | |
|---|---|
|  | £ |
| Profit/(loss) before tax | X |
| Finance cost | X |
| Investment income | (X) |
| Depreciation charge | X |
| Amortisation charge | X |
| Loss/(profit) on disposal of non-current assets | X/(X) |
| (Increase)/decrease in inventories | (X)/X |
| (Increase)/decrease in trade and other receivables | (X)/X |
| (Increase)/decrease in prepayments | (X)/X |
| Increase/(decrease) in trade and other payables | (X)/X |
| Increase/(decrease) in accruals | (X)/X |
| Increase/(decrease) in provisions | (X)/X |
| **Cash generated from operations** | X |

| | |
|---|---|
| Tax paid | (X) |
| Interest paid | (X) |
| **Net cash from/used in operating activities** | X |

## 2.4 Explanation

Cash flows from operating activities also include payments and refunds of income tax unless they can be specifically identified with investing or financing activities. Corporation tax payments relate to profits from operations and so they are a cash flow from operating activities.

It is important to understand why certain items are added and others subtracted. Note the following points.

(a) Depreciation is not a cash expense, but is deducted in arriving at the profit figure in the statement of profit or loss. It makes sense, therefore, to eliminate it by adding it back.

(b) By the same logic, a loss on a disposal of a non-current asset (arising through underprovision of depreciation) needs to be added back and a profit on disposal needs to be deducted.

(c) An increase in inventory means less cash – you have spent cash on buying inventory.

(d) An increase in receivables means receivables have not paid as much, therefore less cash.

(e) If we pay off payables, causing the figure to decrease, again we have less cash.

(f) In your exam you should use parentheses to denote a negative number eg -1,250 should be written as (1,250).

### Worked example: Cash flows from operating activities

Quest Plc has profit before tax for the year to 31 December 20X6 of £850, after charging £650 for depreciation and making a profit on sale of a car of £120.

The statement of financial position for the year shows the following entries:

| | 20X6 | 20X5 |
|---|---|---|
| Inventories | 586 | 763 |
| Trade and other receivables | 1,021 | 589 |
| Trade and other payables | 443 | 1,431 |

**Requirement**

Calculate the net cash from operating activities

**Solution**

| | £ |
|---|---|
| Profit before tax | 850 |
| Depreciation (add) | 650 |
| Gain on sale of property, plant and equipment (deduct) | (120) |
| Movement in inventories (add a decrease) | 177 |
| Movement in trade receivables (deduct an increase) | (432) |
| Movement in trade payables (deduct a decrease) | (988) |
| Net cash from operating activities | 137 |

### Worked example: Direct method

Hail plc commenced trading on 1 January 20X7 following a share issue which raised £35,000. During the year the company entered into the following transactions:

- Purchases from suppliers were £19,500, of which £2,550 was unpaid at the year end.
- Wages and salaries amounted to £10,500, of which £750 was unpaid at the year end.
- Sales revenue was £29,400, including £900 receivables at the year end.

## Solution

Cash generated from operations would be calculated and disclosed as follows:

**Gross operating cash flows for the year ended 31 December 20X7**

| | £ |
|---|---:|
| Cash received from customers (29,400 – 900) | 28,500 |
| Cash paid to suppliers and employees | (26,700) (W) |
| Cash generated from operations | 1,800 |

WORKING

| | £ |
|---|---:|
| Cash paid to suppliers (19,500 – 2,550) | 16,950 |
| Cash paid to and on behalf of employees (10,500 – 750) | 9,750 |
| Cash paid to suppliers and employees | 26,700 |

## 2.5 Payments of interest and income tax

The **adjustments** in the statement of cash flows to '**cash generated from operations**' to arrive at '**net cash from operating activities**' consist of **payments of interest and income tax**.

A similar method can be used to calculate the cash flows for interest paid and income tax paid. For each item, the information available might be:

- Opening balance at the start of the period (opening statement of financial position)
- Statement of profit or loss (the amount of the item, as reported)
- Closing balance at the end of the period (closing statement of financial position)

The cash flow is a balancing figure obtained from these three figures.

A T account can be used as a working.

### Worked example: Interest paid

A company's financial statements show the following information:

| | At 1 Jan 20X2 £ | At 31 Dec 20X2 £ | For the year 20X2 £ |
|---|---:|---:|---:|
| Interest payable | 54,000 | 63,000 | |
| Interest charge | | | 240,000 |

Interest paid is calculated as follows.

INTEREST PAID

| | £ | | £ |
|---|---:|---|---:|
| **Cash payment** (balancing figure) | **231,000** | Balance b/d | 54,000 |
| Balance c/d | 63,000 | Statement of profit or loss | 240,000 |
| | 294,000 | | 294,000 |

Alternatively, this could be calculated as follows:

(54,000 + 240,000 – 63,000) = £231,000

A similar technique can be used to calculate payments of income tax in the year. The taxation payment refers to payments of **income** tax, not to payments of sales tax (VAT) or tax paid by employees.

The opening and closing statements of financial position will show a liability for income tax. The income tax charge for the year is shown in the statement of profit or loss. The figure for income taxes paid during the year is derived as a balancing figure.

### Interactive question 1: Income tax

A company had a liability for income tax at 31 December 20X6 of £940,000 and a liability for income tax at 31 December 20X7 of £1,125,000. The income tax charge for the year to 31 December 20X7 was £1,270,000. What amount of income tax was paid during the year?

INCOME TAX PAID

| | £ | | £ |
|---|---|---|---|
| | | | |

See **Answer** at the end of this chapter.

## 2.6 Investing activities

Cash flows from investing activities are calculated separately in the statement of cash flows in order to identify the extent to which expenditures have been made on resources intended to generate future income and cash flows. These are the acquisition and disposal of long-term assets and other investments not included in cash equivalents.

This could include the following items:

- Cash payments to acquire property, plant and equipment, intangibles and other non-current assets, including those relating to capitalised development costs and self-constructed property, plant and equipment

- Cash receipts from sales of property, plant and equipment, intangibles and other non-current assets

- Cash payments to acquire equity or debt of other entities

- Cash receipts from sales of equity or debt of other entities

- Interest received

- Dividends received

### Cash receipts from sales of property, plant and equipment

A T account can be used for calculating the cash receipts from sales of property, plant and equipment (PPE). The company's accounts will include the amount of any profit or loss on disposal. A note to the accounts on non-current assets will show the cost and the accumulated depreciation for property, plant and equipment disposed of during the year. The cash received from the sale is the balancing figure in the T account.

PROPERTY, PLANT AND EQUIPMENT – DISPOSAL ACCOUNT

| | £ | | £ |
|---|---|---|---|
| Cost/valuation of asset disposed of | X | Accumulated depreciation | X |
| Profit on disposal | X | Loss on disposal | X |
| | | **Cash received** (balancing figure) | X |
| | X | | X |

### Worked example: Cash receipts from sale of PPE

A company's statement of financial position as at the beginning and the end of the year showed the following.

**Property, plant and equipment**

| | £ |
|---|---|
| Cost | |
| At 1 January 20X7 | 760,000 |
| Disposals | (240,000) |
| At 31 December 20X7 | 520,000 |
| | |
| Depreciation | |
| At 1 January 20X7 | 270,000 |
| Disposals | (180,000) |
| Charge for year | 50,000 |
| At 31 December 20X7 | 140,000 |
| | |
| Carrying amount | |
| At 31 December 20X7 | 380,000 |
| At 31 December 20X6 | 490,000 |

The property, plant and equipment was disposed of at a loss of £7,000. What was the cash flow from the disposal?

### Solution

The balancing figure can be obtained by constructing a disposal of property, plant and equipment account as a working.

#### PROPERTY, PLANT AND EQUIPMENT – DISPOSAL ACCOUNT

| | £ | | £ |
|---|---|---|---|
| Cost | 240,000 | Accumulated depreciation | 180,000 |
| | | Loss on disposal | 7,000 |
| | | Cash received (balancing figure) | 53,000 |
| | 240,000 | | 240,000 |

## Cash payments for purchase of property, plant and equipment

Purchase of property, plant and equipment during a period can be calculated by means of a T account or a working table.

#### PROPERTY, PLANT AND EQUIPMENT

| | £ | | £ |
|---|---|---|---|
| Balance b/d | X | Disposals | X |
| **Additions** (balancing figure) | X | Balance c/d | X |
| | X | | X |

## Interactive question 2: Cash payments for PPE

A company's accounts show that at 31 December 20X7, it had property, plant and equipment at cost of £6,800,000. During the year, it disposed of assets that had a cost of £850,000. At 31 December 20X6, the company's property, plant and equipment at cost had been £5,100,000.

What were purchases of property, plant and equipment during the year?

### PROPERTY, PLANT AND EQUIPMENT

| | £ | | £ |
|---|---|---|---|
| | | | |

See **Answer** at the end of this chapter.

## Interest and dividends received

Returns received in cash from investments will include interest and dividends received. The cash flows can be calculated by using an interest received or dividends received T account. Both T accounts are very similar and are prepared as follows:

### INTEREST/DIVIDENDS RECEIVED

| | £ | | £ |
|---|---|---|---|
| Balance b/d (receivable) | X | **Cash receipt** (balancing figure) | X |
| Statement of profit or loss | X | Balance c/d (receivable) | X |
| | X | | X |

## Interactive question 3: Interest received

A company had interest receivable of £35,000 at the start of the year and interest receivable of £42,000 at the end of the year. The statement of profit or loss for the year shows interest income of £90,000. What were the cash receipts for interest received in the year?

### INTEREST RECEIVED

| | £ | | £ |
|---|---|---|---|
| | | | |

See **Answer** at the end of this chapter.

The pro-forma for investing activities

**Cash flows from investing activities**

Purchase of property, plant and equipment

Purchase of intangible assets

Proceeds from sale of property, plant and equipment

Proceeds from sale of intangibles

Interest received

**Net cash from/used in investing activities**

### Worked example: Cash flows from investing activities

Pearl Plc acquired a new factory in the year to 30 June 20X6 for a cost of £805,000. They sold their old factory for £425,000. They also received interest on surplus funds of £350,000. Calculate cash flows from investing activities.

### Solution

| | £ |
|---|---|
| **Cash flows from investing activities** | |
| Purchase of property, plant and equipment | (805,000) |
| Proceeds from sale of property, plant and equipment | 425,000 |
| Interest received | 350,000 |
| **Net cash flows from investing activities** | **30,000** |

## 2.7 Cash flows from financing activities

This section of the statement of cash flows shows the share of cash which the entity's capital providers have claimed during the period. This is an indicator of **likely future interest and dividend payments**. The standard gives the following examples of cash flows which might arise under this heading

Cash flows from financing activities

Proceeds from issue of shares

Movement in borrowings

Dividends paid

Net cash from/used in financing activities

### Cash received from issuing shares

The amount of cash received from new issues of shares can usually be calculated from the opening and closing statement of financial position figures for share capital and share premium.

As a general rule:

SHARE CAPITAL AND PREMIUM

| | £ | | £ |
|---|---|---|---|
| | | Balance b/d | X |
| Balance c/d | X | **Cash receipt** (balancing figure) | X |
| | X | | X |

This rule does not apply fully when the company makes a bonus issue of shares during the year, and some of the new share capital is obtained by means of reducing a reserve account other than the share premium. To calculate cash receipts from share issues in the year, the amount transferred to share capital from the other reserve account should be subtracted.

### Worked example: Cash received from share issue

Rustler plc's annual accounts for the year to 31 December 20X7 show the following figures.

|  | At 31.12.X7 £ | At 31.12.X6 £ |
|---|---|---|
| Share capital: Ordinary shares of 50p | 6,750,000 | 5,400,000 |
| Share premium | 12,800,000 | 7,300,000 |

There were no bonus issues of shares during the year. What amount of cash was raised from shares issued during the year?

### Solution

SHARE CAPITAL AND PREMIUM

|  | £ |  | £ |
|---|---|---|---|
|  |  | Balance b/d (5,400,000 + 7,300,000) | 12,700,000 |
| Balance c/d (6,750,000 + 12,800,000) | 19,550,000 | **Cash receipt** (balancing figure) | 6,850,000 |
|  | 19,550,000 |  | 19,550,000 |

### Interactive question 4: Bonus issue

Groat plc's accounts for the year to 31 December 20X7 show the following figures.

|  | At 31.12.X7 £ | At 31.12.X6 £ |
|---|---|---|
| Share capital: Ordinary shares of 10p | 22,500,000 | 10,000,000 |
| Share premium | 900,000 | 4,800,000 |

The company made a one for two bonus issue of shares at the start of the year. It used the share premium account and £200,000 from retained earnings to do this.

What amount of cash was raised from share issues during the year?

SHARE CAPITAL AND PREMIUM

|  | £ |  | £ |
|---|---|---|---|
|  |  |  |  |

See **Answer** at the end of this chapter.

### Worked example: Cash flows from financing activities

Spear Plc issued 87,500 £1 shares at par during the year to 31 December 20X6. Loans taken out increased from £18,000 at the beginning of the year to £30,000 at the end of the year. The company declared a dividend of 10p per share. Calculate the cash flows from financing activities.

|  | £ |
|---|---|
| Proceeds from issue of shares | 87,500 |
| Movements in borrowings | 12,000 |
| Net cash from financing activities | 99,500 |

Note that only dividends paid (as opposed to declared) in the period represent cash flows. Interest paid on the loans will be shown under cash flows from operating activities.

# Cash from raising a loan

The **cash** derived from **obtaining a new loan** during the year should be apparent from a comparison of the opening and closing statement of financial position figures for non-current interest-bearing borrowings. **An increase during the year represents new financing**, and should be taken as the amount of cash received from financing.

It is important that **all loans in the statement of financial position should be taken into consideration** in the calculation. There may be a loan that is within 12 months of repayment. If so, it will be included within current liabilities in the year-end statement of financial position as 'short-term borrowings', when it would have been a non-current liability in the statement of financial position at the start of the year. The loan has not been repaid during the year, **merely re-classified from non-current liability to current liability**.

## Repayment of non-current interest-bearing borrowings

In the same way, **a reduction in interest-bearing borrowings** indicates that a loan has been **repaid**, or that loan stock or debentures have been **redeemed**. It should be assumed that the loans are repaid or loan stock is redeemed for cash.

## Dividends paid

Cash flows from dividends paid should be **disclosed separately**.

Dividends paid by the entity can be classified in **one of two ways**.

(a) As a **financing cash flow**, showing the cost of obtaining financial resources (as in the worked example: cash flows from financing activities above). This is the presentation adopted in these Learning Materials.

(b) As a component of **cash flows from operating activities** so that users can assess the entity's ability to pay dividends out of operating cash flows.

Cash flows for dividends paid can be calculated using a T account.

## Worked example: Dividends paid

A company has declared preference dividends for the year of £7,000 (based on its 7% £100,000 redeemable preference shares in issue). At the start of the year the statement of financial position included a liability of £3,500 for preference dividends payable. At the end of the year no amount was owing to preference shareholders in respect of dividends.

The preference dividend paid for the year is not simply the £7,000 declared and reflected in retained earnings as this amount needs to be adjusted for any opening and closing liabilities.

### DIVIDENDS PAID

| | £ | | £ |
|---|---|---|---|
| Cash payment (balancing figure) | 10,500 | Balance b/d | 3,500 |
| Balance c/d | 0 | Retained earnings | 7,000 |
| | 10,500 | | 10,500 |

The cash paid during the year of £10,500 is the second half year preference dividend due from last year and the whole of this year's preference dividend (all paid during the year).

**Point to note:** Dividends paid may have to be derived from the retained earnings account.

## 2.8 Example: Direct method

The following example statements of cash flows are provided by IAS 7 using the direct method and the indirect method.

**XYZ PLC**

**Statement of cash flows (direct method)**

| | £'000 | £'000 |
|---|---:|---:|
| **Cash flows from operating activities** | | |
| Cash receipts from customers | 30,150 | |
| Cash paid to suppliers and employees | (27,600) | |
| Cash generated from operations | 2,550 | |
| Interest paid | (270) | |
| Income taxes paid | (900) | |
| *Net cash from operating activities* | | 1,380 |
| | | |
| **Cash flows from investing activities** | | |
| Purchase of property, plant and equipment | (700) | |
| Proceeds from sale of equipment | 20 | |
| Interest received | 200 | |
| Net cash used in investing activities | | (480) |
| | | |
| **Cash flows from financing activities** | | |
| Proceeds from issue of share capital | 250 | |
| Proceeds from long-term borrowings | 250 | |
| Payment of finance lease liabilities | (90) | |
| Dividends paid | (1,200) | |
| Net cash used in financing activities | | (790) |
| | | |
| | | |
| **Net increase in cash and cash equivalents** | | 110 |
| **Cash and cash equivalents at beginning of period** | | 120 |
| **Cash and cash equivalents at end of period** | | 230 |

## Example: Indirect method

**Statement of cash flows (indirect method)**

| | £'000 | £'000 |
|---|---:|---:|
| **Cash flows from operating activities** | | |
| | | |
| Profit before taxation | 3,350 | |
| Depreciation | 450 | |
| Investment income | (500) | |
| Interest expense | 400 | |
| | 3,700 | |
| Increase in trade and other receivables | (500) | |
| Decrease in inventories | 1,090 | |
| Decrease in trade payables | (1,740) | |
| Cash generated from operations | 2,550 | |
| Interest paid | (270) | |
| Income taxes paid | (900) | |
| **Net cash from operating activities** | | 1,380 |
| | | |
| **Cash flows from investing activities** | | |
| | | |
| Purchase of property, plant and equipment | (700) | |
| Proceeds from sale of equipment | 20 | |
| Interest received | 200 | |
| Net cash used in investing activities | | (480) |

**Cash flows from financing activities**

| | |
|---|---:|
| Proceeds from issue of share capital | 250 |
| Proceeds from long-term borrowings | 250 |
| Payment of finance lease liabilities | (90) |
| Dividends paid | (1,200) |
| Net cash used in financing activities | (790) |

| | |
|---|---:|
| **Net increase in cash and cash equivalents** | 110 |
| **Cash and cash equivalents at beginning of period** | 120 |
| **Cash and cash equivalents at end of period** | 230 |

# 3 Preparing a statement of cash flows

**Section overview**

- In essence, preparing a statement of cash flows is very straightforward. You should therefore simply learn the format and apply the steps noted in the example below.

Remember the way that the following items are treated. It might seem confusing at first, but the treatment is logical if you think in terms of cash.

(a) Increase in inventory is treated as negative (in brackets). This is because it represents a cash outflow; cash is being spent on inventory.

(b) An increase in receivables would be treated as negative for the same reasons; more receivables means less cash.

(c) By contrast an increase in payables is positive because cash is being retained and not used to pay off payables. There is therefore more of it.

**Worked example: Preparation of a statement of cash flows**

Kane Plc's statement of profit or loss for the year ended 31 December 20X2 and statement of financial position at 31 December 20X1 and 31 December 20X2 were as follows.

KANE PLC
STATEMENT OF PROFIT OR LOSS FOR THE YEAR ENDED 31 DECEMBER 20X2

| | £'000 |
|---|---:|
| Revenue | 720 |
| Cost of sales | (188) |
| Gross profit | 532 |
| Distribution costs | (18) |
| Administrative expenses | (94) |
| Profit from operations | 420 |
| Finance costs | (28) |
| Profit before tax | 392 |
| Income tax expense | (124) |
| Profit for the period | 268 |

KANE PLC
STATEMENT OF FINANCIAL POSITION AS AT 31 DECEMBER

|  | 20X2 | | 20X1 | |
|---|---|---|---|---|
|  | £'000 | £'000 | £'000 | £'000 |
| Non-current assets |  |  |  |  |
| Cost |  | 1,596 |  | 1,560 |
| Depreciation |  | (318) |  | (224) |
|  |  | 1,278 |  | 1,336 |
| Current assets |  |  |  |  |
| Inventory | 24 |  | 20 |  |
| Trade receivables | 66 |  | 50 |  |
| Recoverable corporation tax | 10 |  | 8 |  |
| Bank | 48 |  | 56 |  |
|  |  | 148 |  | 134 |
| Total assets |  | 1,426 |  | 1,470 |
| EQUITY |  |  |  |  |
| Share capital |  | 360 |  | 340 |
| Share premium |  | 36 |  | 24 |
| Retained earnings |  | 716 |  | 514 |
| Non-current liabilities |  |  |  |  |
| Borrowings |  | 200 |  | 500 |
| Current liabilities |  |  |  |  |
| Trade payables | 12 |  | 6 |  |
| Taxation | 102 |  | 86 |  |
|  |  | 114 |  | 92 |
|  |  | 1,426 |  | 1,470 |

Dividends totalling £66,000 were paid during the year.

During the year, the company paid £90,000 for a new piece of machinery.

Included in the cost of sales is depreciation of £118,000. A loss on disposal of £18,000 has been included in distribution costs.

**Requirement**

Prepare a statement of cash flows for Kane Plc for the year ended 31 December 20X2 in accordance with the requirements of IAS 7.

Solution

### Step 1.
Set out the pro-forma statement of cash flows with all the headings required by IAS 7. In the assessment this will be provided for you.

### Step 2.
Complete the cash flows from operating activities as far as possible. When preparing the statement from the statement of financial position, you will usually have to calculate items such as depreciation, profit or loss on sale of non-current assets and profit for the year (see Step 4). Remember to use parentheses to denote a negative figure.

### Step 3.
Calculate the figures for tax paid, purchase or sale of non-current assets, issue of shares and repayment of loans if these are not already given to you (as they may be). Note that you may not be given the tax charge in the statement of profit or loss. You will then have to assume that the tax paid in the year is last year's year-end provision and calculate the charge as the balancing figure.

## Step 4.
If you are not given the profit figure, open up a working for the statement of profit or loss. Using the opening and closing balances, the taxation charge and dividends paid you will be able to calculate profit for the year as the balancing figure to put in the statement.

## Step 5.
You will now be able to complete the statement by slotting in the figures given or calculated.

## Step 6.
Check that the net increase in cash and cash equivalents that you have calculated plus the cash and cash equivalents at the beginning of the period totals to the cash and cash equivalents at the end of the period.

KANE PLC
STATEMENT OF CASH FLOWS FOR THE YEAR ENDED 31 DECEMBER 20X2

### Statement of cash flows (indirect method)

| Cash flows from operating activities | £'000 | £'000 |
| --- | --- | --- |
| Profit before taxation | 392 | |
| Loss on sale of property, plant and equipment | 18 | |
| Depreciation | 118 | |
| Interest expense | 28 | |
| Increase in trade and other receivables | (16) | |
| Increase in inventories | (4) | |
| Increase in trade payables | 6 | |
| **Cash generated from operations** | **542** | |
| Interest paid | (28) | |
| Income taxes paid (W1) | (110) | |
| **Net cash from operating activities** | | **404** |
| **Cash flows from investing activities** | | |
| Purchase of property, plant and equipment | (90) | |
| Proceeds from sale of equipment (W2) | 12 | |
| Interest received | | |
| **Net cash used in investing activities** | | (78) |
| **Cash flows from financing activities** | | |
| Proceeds from issue of share capital (360 + 36 – 340 – 24) | 32 | |
| Proceeds from long-term borrowings (500 – 200) | (300) | |
| Dividends paid | (66) | |
| **Net cash used in financing activities** | | (334) |
| **Net increase in cash and cash equivalents** | | (8) |
| **Cash and cash equivalents at beginning of period** | | 56 |
| **Cash and cash equivalents at end of period** | | 48 |

WORKINGS

(1) **Corporation tax paid**

| | £'000 |
| --- | --- |
| Opening CT payable (86 – 8) | 78 |
| Charge for year | 124 |
| Net CT payable at 31.12.X2 (102 – 10) | (92) |
| Paid | 110 |

**(2) Non-current asset disposals**

**COST**

| | £'000 | | £'000 |
|---|---|---|---|
| At 1.1.X2 | 1,560 | At 31.12.X2 | 1,596 |
| Purchases | 90 | Disposals | 54 |
| | 1,650 | | 1,650 |

**ACCUMULATED DEPRECIATION**

| | £'000 | | £'000 |
|---|---|---|---|
| At 31.1.X2 | 318 | At 1.1.X2 | 224 |
| Depreciation on disposals | 24 | Charge for year | 118 |
| | 342 | | 342 |

| | £'000 |
|---|---|
| Carrying value of disposals | 30 |
| Net loss reported | (18) |
| Proceeds of disposals | 12 |

## Summary

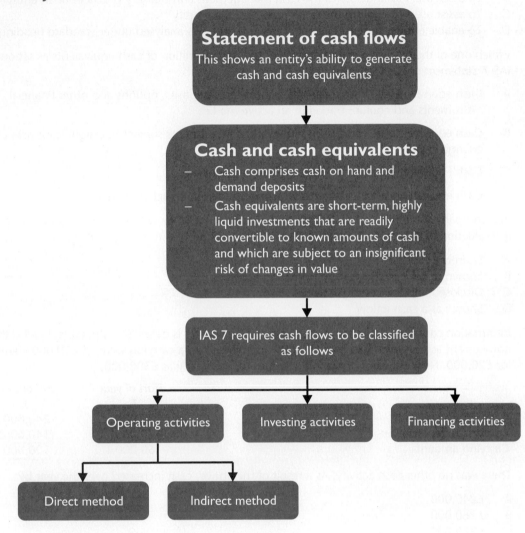

**Statement of cash flows**
This shows an entity's ability to generate cash and cash equivalents

**Cash and cash equivalents**
- Cash comprises cash on hand and demand deposits
- Cash equivalents are short-term, highly liquid investments that are readily convertible to known amounts of cash and which are subject to an insignificant risk of changes in value

IAS 7 requires cash flows to be classified as follows

Operating activities

Investing activities

Financing activities

Direct method

Indirect method

CHAPTER

13

## Self-test

Answer the following questions.

1   Which one of the following options best describes the objective of IAS 7 *Statement of Cash Flows*?

    A   To aid comparison of cash flows between entities
    B   To assist users to understand the cash management and treasury practices of an entity
    C   To assist users to confirm the going concern of an entity
    D   To enable entities to report cash inflows and outflows analysed under standard headings

2   Which one of the following statements gives the best definition of cash equivalents as set out in IAS 7 *Statement of Cash Flows*?

    A   Cash equivalents are cash, overdrafts, short-term deposits, options and other financial instruments and equities traded in an active market

    B   Cash equivalents are short-term highly liquid investments subject to insignificant risks of change in value

    C   Cash equivalents are readily disposable investments

    D   Cash equivalents are investments which are traded in an active market

3   In a company's statement of cash flows prepared in accordance with IAS 7 *Statement of Cash Flows*, a revaluation of non-current assets during the year will be:

    A   Entirely excluded
    B   Shown under cash flows from operating activities
    C   Disclosed under investing activities
    D   Shown as a cash inflow

4   Information concerning the non-current assets of Ealing plc is detailed in the table. During the year non-current assets which had cost £80,000 and which had a carrying value of £30,000 were sold for £20,000. Net cash from operating activities for the year was £300,000.

|  | Start of year £ | End of year £ |
|---|---|---|
| Cost | 180,000 | 240,000 |
| Aggregate depreciation | (120,000) | (140,000) |
| Carrying amount | 60,000 | 100,000 |

There was no other cash activity. As a result of the above, cash increased over the year by

    A   £240,000
    B   £260,000
    C   £320,000
    D   £180,000

5   Waterloo plc acquired a freehold building for cash, financed in full by issuing for cash 166,000 £1 ordinary shares at a premium of £2 per share.

In its statement of cash flows prepared in accordance with IAS 7 *Statement of Cash Flows* this transaction should be stated as:

    A   Inflow £498,000, outflow nil
    B   Inflow nil, outflow nil
    C   Inflow £498,000, outflow £498,000
    D   Inflow nil, outflow £498,000

6    Information from the statement of cash flows and related notes of Gresham plc for the year ended 31 December 20X1 can be found in the table below.

|                                                      | £      |
|------------------------------------------------------|--------|
| Depreciation                                         | 30,000 |
| Profit on sale of property, plant and equipment      | 5,000  |
| Proceeds from sale of property, plant and equipment  | 20,000 |
| Purchase of property, plant and equipment            | 25,000 |

If the carrying amount of property, plant and equipment was £110,000 on 31 December 20X0, what was it on 31 December 20X1?

A    £85,000
B    £90,000
C    £70,000
D    £80,000

Now go back to the Learning Objective in the Introduction. If you are satisfied you have achieved this objective, please tick it off.

## 1 Objective of the statement of cash flows

- The statement of cash flows should show the historical changes in cash and cash equivalents.

- Cash comprises cash on hand and demand deposits.                                IAS 7(6)

- Cash equivalents are short-term, highly liquid investments that are readily      IAS 7(6)
  convertible to known amounts of cash and which are subject to an insignificant
  risk of changes in value.

## 2 Presentation of a statement of cash flows                                    Appendix A

- Cash flows should be classified by operating, investing and financing activities.   IAS 7(10)

- Cash flows from operating activities are primarily derived from the principal    IAS 7(13–14)
  revenue-producing activities of the entity.

- There are two methods of presentation for cash flows from operating activities:

  - Direct method                                                                 IAS 7(19)

  - Indirect method                                                               IAS 7(20)

- Cash flows from investing activities are those related to the acquisition or
  disposal of any non-current assets, or trade investments together with returns
  received in cash from investments (ie dividends and interest received).

- Financing activities include:                                                   IAS 7(16)

  - Cash proceeds from issuing shares

  - Cash proceeds from issuing debentures, loans, notes, bonds, mortgages
    and other short or long-term borrowings

  - Cash repayments of amounts borrowed

  - Repayment of capital of amounts borrowed under finance leases

  - Dividends paid to shareholders

## Answer to Interactive question 1

### INCOME TAX PAID

| | £ | | £ |
|---|---|---|---|
| Cash payment (balancing figure) | 1,085,000 | Balance b/d | 940,000 |
| Balance c/d | 1,125,000 | Statement of profit or loss | 1,270,000 |
| | 2,210,000 | | 2,210,000 |

Alternatively this could be calculated as follows:

(£940,000 + £1,270,000 − £1,125,000) = £1,085,000

## Answer to Interactive question 2

### PROPERTY, PLANT AND EQUIPMENT

| | £ | | £ |
|---|---|---|---|
| Balance b/d | 5,100,000 | Disposals | 850,000 |
| Additions (balance) | 2,550,000 | Balance c/d | 6,800,000 |
| | 7,650,000 | | 7,650,000 |

The company started the year with PPE at cost of £5,100,000. It bought a further £2,550,000 of PPE, giving a total of £7,650,000 at cost. However, there were disposals of PPE with a cost of £850,000, bringing the year-end figure down to £6,800,000.

## Answer to Interactive question 3

### INTEREST RECEIVED

| | £ | | £ |
|---|---|---|---|
| Balance b/d | 35,000 | Cash received (balancing figure) | 83,000 |
| Statement of profit or loss | 90,000 | Balance c/d | 42,000 |
| | 125,000 | | 125,000 |

## Answer to Interactive question 4

### SHARE CAPITAL AND PREMIUM

| | £ | | £ |
|---|---|---|---|
| | | Balance b/d | 14,800,000 |
| Balance c/d | 23,400,000 | Retained earnings | 200,000 |
| | | Cash received (balance) | 8,400,000 |
| | 23,400,000 | | 23,400,000 |

# Answers to Self-test

1  D  To enable entities to report cash inflows and outflows analysed under standard headings. (IAS 7)

2  B  Cash equivalents are short-term highly liquid investments subject to insignificant risks of changes in value.

3  A  A revaluation of non-current assets during the year will be entirely excluded.

   Revaluations have no cash flow implications.

4  D  The correct answer is £180,000.

### NON-CURRENT ASSETS – COST

|  | £ |  | £ |
|---|---|---|---|
| Balance b/d | 180,000 | Disposals | 80,000 |
| Therefore purchases | 140,000 | Balance c/d | 240,000 |
|  | 320,000 |  | 320,000 |

### DEPRECIATION

|  | £ |  | £ |
|---|---|---|---|
|  |  | Balance b/d | 120,000 |
| Disposals | 50,000 | Therefore charge | 70,000 |
| Balance c/d | 140,000 |  |  |
|  | 190,000 |  | 190,000 |

### DISPOSALS

|  | £ |  | £ |
|---|---|---|---|
| Cost | 80,000 | Accumulated depreciation | 50,000 |
|  |  | Proceeds | 20,000 |
|  |  | Therefore loss | 10,000 |
|  | 80,000 |  | 80,000 |

|  | £ |
|---|---|
| Cash from operations | 300,000 |
| Cash inflow: |  |
| Disposal proceeds | 20,000 |
|  | 320,000 |
| Cash outflow: purchases of non-current assets | (140,000) |
| Therefore net cash increase | 180,000 |

Note that adjustments for depreciation and loss on disposal will already be included in net cash from operating activities.

5  C  Inflow £498,000, outflow £498,000.

   The outflow is classified under 'Purchase of property, plant and equipment'.

   The inflow is classified under 'Proceeds from issuance of share capital'.

6  B  £90,000

### PROPERTY (carrying amount)

|  | £ |  | £ |
|---|---|---|---|
| Balance b/d | 110,000 | Depreciation | 30,000 |
| Additions | 25,000 | Disposals | 15,000 |
|  |  | Balance c/d (bal. fig.) | 90,000 |
|  | 135,000 |  | 135,000 |

# CHAPTER 14

# Company financial statements under UK GAAP

Introduction

Examination context

**Topic List**

Summary and Self-test

Answers to Interactive questions

Answers to Self-test

## Learning objectives

- Record and account for transactions and events resulting in income, expenses, assets, liabilities and equity in accordance with the appropriate basis of accounting and the laws, regulations and accounting standards applicable to the financial statements

- Prepare an extended trial balance

- Identify the main components of a set of financial statements and specify their purpose and interrelationship

- Prepare and present  balance sheet, profit and loss account and cash flow statement (or extracts therefrom) from the accounting records and trial balance in a format that satisfies the information requirements of the entity

Specific syllabus learning outcomes are: 1d; 2c; 3a, c

## Syllabus links

The material in this chapter will be developed further in this paper, and referred to in the Professional Level module of Financial Accounting and Reporting.

## Examination context

Questions on the topics in this chapter will be set as multiple choice questions, some of which may involve calculations so that the correct answer can be selected. Very often double entry questions are phrased in terms of preparing a journal.

In the exam you may be required to:

- Identify what comprises UK GAAP

- Specify the key differences between UK GAAP and IAS formats of financial statements, especially in terms of the net assets UK GAAP balance sheet

- Use UK GAAP when identifying balances in preparing the profit and loss account and balance sheet of a company

- **You will not be asked to prepare company financial statements using UK GAAP.**

# 1 What is UK GAAP?

> **Section overview**
>
> - Financial statements are prepared under UK GAAP for most private, unlisted companies, partnerships and sole traders.

In this Study Manual so far we have looked at how financial transactions are recorded in books of original entry and in ledgers, and at the techniques that are then used (such as the profit and loss ledger account and/or the extended trial balance) to summarise those ledgers and produce statements

- Of the business's **financial performance** over a period of time (which we have called its **statement of profit or loss**), and

- Of the business's **financial position** at the end of that time period (which we have called its **statement of financial position**)

These techniques are universal, arising out of the key accounting principles of:

- Accruals
- Going concern
- Double entry bookkeeping

However, there are quite a number of issues in relation to which accounting practice around the world is diverse, in particular:

- Terminology
- The formats used to present financial statements

We have so far adopted an approach to these issues based on international accounting and financial reporting standards (specifically IAS 1) and on the *Conceptual Framework*. You need to be aware however that this 'international standards' approach currently only applies in the UK to a limited number of companies; the remainder still produce their financial statements under what has come to be called UK generally accepted accounting practice, or UK GAAP. Understanding the distinction, and being able to prepare accounts in accordance with UK GAAP will therefore be very important in the workplace, as well as for students who choose to study the UK GAAP FAR module.

> **Definition**
>
> **UK GAAP**: The rules, from whatever source, that govern accounting and financial reporting in the UK.

## 1.1 The constituents of UK GAAP

In the UK generally accepted accounting practice is a combination of:

- Company law (the Companies Act 2006)

- UK accounting standards

- The effects of stock exchange listing requirements (which apply directly to listed companies but which are influential more widely) and

- The effects of international accounting and financial reporting standards

GAAP is a dynamic concept: it changes constantly as circumstances alter through new legislation, standards and practice.

The problem of what is 'generally accepted' is not easy to settle, because new practices are obviously not generally adopted yet. The criteria for a practice being 'generally accepted' depend on factors such as whether the practice is addressed by UK accounting standards or legislation, or their international equivalents, and whether other companies have adopted the practice. Most importantly perhaps, the question should be whether the practice is consistent with the needs of users and the objectives of financial statements, and whether it is consistent with the 'true and fair' concept (see below).

To understand better the importance of UK GAAP we need to look briefly at why and how companies in the UK are required to publish annual financial statements, or 'published accounts'.

# 2 Published accounts

## Section overview

- UK companies are required by law to publish financial statements annually and file them with the Registrar of Companies ('published accounts').

- Such accounts must show a true and fair view.

- Listed companies are required by the Listing Rules to apply IASs in preparing and presenting their published accounts. Unlisted companies may choose to use UK standards.

## 2.1 Publishing annual accounts

Under the Companies Act 2006 UK limited companies must produce accounts (financial statements) annually, and large companies must appoint an independent person to audit and report on them. Once prepared, a copy of the accounts must be sent to the Registrar of Companies, who maintains a separate file for every company. The Registrar's files may be inspected for a nominal fee, by any member of the public. This is why the 'statutory accounts' are often referred to as **published accounts**.

## Definition

Statutory accounts: Financial statements which limited companies are obliged by law to publish in a particular form.

---

The company's directors must publish accounts which show a **true and fair view** (a phrase used in s393 Companies Act 2006) of the company's assets, liabilities, financial position and profit or loss (profit and loss account and balance sheet) for a financial year. The board evidences its approval of the accounts by the signature of one director on the balance sheet. Once this has been done, and the auditors have completed their report, the accounts are sent to shareholders and, in the case of a public company, are presented to the body of shareholders at a general meeting. When the shareholders have adopted the accounts they are sent to the Registrar for filing.

## 2.2 True and fair view

The Companies Act 2006 requirement that the accounts show a **true and fair view** is paramount. A company's accounts can show a true and fair view when prepared using **either** Companies Act (UK GAAP) formats **or** IAS formats.

Although the Companies Act 2006 lays down numerous rules on the information to be included in published accounts and the format of its presentation, any such rule may be **overridden** if compliance with it would prevent the accounts from showing a **true and fair view**.

When prepared under UK GAAP the accounts must include:

- A profit and loss account (equivalent to a statement of profit or loss)

- A balance sheet as at the date to which the profit and loss account is made up (equivalent to a statement of financial position)

- A directors' report, and a directors' remuneration report in the case of a quoted company

- An auditors' report addressed to the members (not to the directors) of the company

- A strategic report to inform members of the company and help them assess how the directors have performed their duty

All we are concerned with in the *Accounting* syllabus is the **profit and loss account** and **balance sheet**.

## 2.3 Published accounts of listed and unlisted companies

Listed companies must comply with the Listing Rules set out by the UK Listing Authority (part of the Financial Conduct Authority). These require that listed companies should prepare their published accounts under international accounting standards. This is permitted by the Companies Act 2006, as we have seen above.

The **terminology and formats** of international financial statements are different from the ones set out in the Companies Act 2006 and UK GAAP, however. In the UK therefore there is currently the situation whereby:

- **Listed companies** produce a statement of profit or loss and statement of financial position following international terminology and formats.

- **Non-listed companies** can choose between UK GAAP or international terminology and formats for their published accounts.

# 3 UK GAAP terminology and formats

### Section overview

- UK terminology and IAS terminology vary in a number of areas

- UK formats set down in the Companies Act 2006 apply a net assets approach to the balance sheet: total assets – total liabilities = total equity.

So far in this Study Manual we have exclusively used the international terminology and formats: we need now to introduce the UK GAAP versions.

## 3.1 UK GAAP terminology

FRS 102 actually uses international (ie IFRS) terminology, while the Companies Act 2006 uses terminology that is UK specific. In their published financial statements, UK non-listed companies tend to follow Companies Act 2006 and use the UK specific terminology which is as follows:

| International term | UK GAAP term |
|---|---|
| Statement of profit or loss | Profit and loss account |
| Statement of financial position | Balance sheet |
| Non-current asset | Fixed asset |
| Carrying amount | Net book value |
| Inventories | Stock |
| Receivables | Debtors |
| Irrecoverable debt | Bad debt |
| Irrecoverable debt expense | Bad and doubtful debts expense |
| Allowance for irrecoverable debts | Allowance for doubtful debts |
| Retained earnings | Retained profits (reserve) |
| Payables | Creditors |
| Non-current liabilities | Creditors: amounts falling due after more than one year |
| Current liabilities | Creditors: amounts falling due in less than one year |
| Revenue | Turnover |
| Finance costs | Interest payable |

## 3.2 UK formats

The format of the balance sheet and profit and loss account of a limited company under the Companies Act 2006 is shown below, with some simplifications (it is derived from the formats set down by the Companies Act 1985, which are adopted by the 2006 Act). Note in particular that the UK GAAP balance sheet presents **net assets,** with current liabilities deducted from current assets, and long-term liabilities deducted to arrive at net assets. The lower half of the balance sheet comprises the owners' interests only.

TYPICAL LIMITED COMPANY
BALANCE SHEET AS AT...

|  |  | £ | £ | £ |
|---|---|---|---|---|
| *Fixed assets* |  |  |  |  |
| Intangible assets | Development costs |  | X |  |
|  | Concessions, patents, licences, trademarks |  | X |  |
|  | Goodwill |  | X |  |
|  |  |  |  | X |
| Tangible assets | Land and buildings |  | X |  |
|  | Plant and machinery |  | X |  |
|  | Fixtures, fittings, tools and equipment |  | X |  |
|  | Motor vehicles |  | X |  |
|  |  |  |  | X |
|  |  |  |  | X |
| *Current assets* | Stocks |  | X |  |
|  | Debtors and prepayments |  | X |  |
|  | Cash at bank and in hand |  | X |  |
|  |  |  | X |  |
| *Creditors: amounts falling due within one year* |  |  |  |  |
|  | Debenture loans (nearing their redemption date) | X |  |  |
|  | Bank overdraft and loans | X |  |  |
|  | Trade creditors | X |  |  |
|  | Provisions | X |  |  |
|  | Taxation | X |  |  |
|  | Accruals | X |  |  |
|  |  |  | (X) |  |
| *Net current assets (liabilities)* |  |  |  | X |
| *Total assets less current liabilities* |  |  |  | X |
| *Creditors: amounts falling due after more than one year* |  |  |  |  |
|  | Debentures |  |  | (X) |
| *Net assets* |  |  |  | X |
| Capital and reserves |  |  |  |  |
|  | Equity shares |  |  | X |
|  | Preference shares |  |  | X |
|  | Share premium account |  |  | X |
|  | Other reserves |  |  | X |
|  | Retained profits |  |  | X |
|  |  |  |  | X |

The UK GAAP profit and loss account is as follows.

TYPICAL LIMITED COMPANY
PROFIT AND LOSS ACCOUNT FOR THE YEAR ENDED...

|  | £ |
|---|---|
| Turnover* | X |
| Cost of sales | (X) |
| Gross profit | X |
| Distribution costs | (X) |
| Administrative expenses | (X) |
|  | X |
| Other operating income | X |
| Operating profit | X |
| Interest payable and similar charges | (X) |
| Profit before taxation | X |
| Taxation | (X) |
| Profit after taxation | X |

\* Note that the turnover figure is net of trade discount, refunds and VAT, as the revenue figure is under IASs.

## 3.3 Fixed assets

### 3.3.1 Intangible fixed assets

Intangible fixed assets represent amounts of money paid by a business to acquire benefits of a long term nature. **Goodwill** and **deferred development expenditure** are two intangible assets; these were discussed in detail in Chapter 10 and the same principles apply under UK GAAP.

If a company purchases some **patent rights**, or a concession from another business, or the right to use a trademark, the cost of the purchase can be accounted for as an intangible fixed asset. These assets are subject to **amortisation** over their useful lives (called '**economic life**' under UK GAAP).

### 3.3.2 Tangible fixed assets

Tangible fixed assets are shown in the balance sheet at their net book value (ie at cost less accumulated depreciation).

Under UK GAAP a fixed asset note is normally needed to give the required detail. Alternatively on the face of the balance sheet we can present each item as follows:

|  | Cost | Accumulated depreciation | Net book value |
|---|---|---|---|
|  | £ | £ | £ |
| Land and buildings | X | (X) | X |
| Plant and machinery | X | (X) | X |
| Fixtures and fittings | X | (X) | X |
| Motor vehicles | X | (X) | X |
|  | X | (X) | X |

## 3.4 Current and long-term liabilities

The term '**creditors: amounts falling due within one year**' is used in the Companies Act 2006 to mean '**current liabilities**'.

Similarly, the term '**creditors: amounts falling due after more than one year**' is the Companies Act 2006 term for **non-current liabilities**.

## Worked example: Company financial statements

To see how UK GAAP is used when preparing financial statements, we shall work through a full practical example. **Note that you will not be asked to prepare financial statements under UK GAAP in your exam.** However, if you choose to continue your studies under UK GAAP, the following example will be very useful.

The accountant of Hartpeace Ltd has prepared the following trial balance as at 31 December 20X7.

|  | £'000 | £'000 |
|---|---|---|
| 50p equity shares (fully paid) |  | 350 |
| 7% £1 irredeemable preference shares (fully paid) |  | 100 |
| 10% debentures |  | 200 |
| Retained profit 1.1.X7 |  | 242 |
| General reserve 1.1.X7 |  | 171 |
| Freehold land and buildings 1.1.X7 (cost) | 430 |  |
| Plant and machinery 1.1.X7 (cost) | 830 |  |
| Accumulated depreciation: |  |  |
|    Freehold buildings 1.1.X7 |  | 20 |
|    Plant and machinery 1.1.X7 |  | 222 |
| Stock 1.1.X7 | 190 |  |
| Sales |  | 2,695 |
| Purchases | 2,152 |  |
| Debenture interest paid | 10 |  |
| Wages and salaries | 254 |  |
| Light and heat | 31 |  |
| Sundry expenses | 113 |  |
| Suspense account |  | 420 |
| Debtors | 464 |  |
| Creditors |  | 195 |
| Cash at bank | 141 |  |
|  | 4,615 | 4,615 |

### Notes

(a) Sundry expenses include £9,000 paid in respect of insurance for the year ending 1 September 20X8. Light and heat does not include an invoice of £3,000 for electricity for the three months ending 1 January 20X8, which was paid in February 20X8. Light and heat includes £20,000 relating to sales commission payable to employees.

(b) The suspense account is in respect of the following items:

|  | £'000 |
|---|---|
| Proceeds from the issue of 100,000 equity shares | 120 |
| Proceeds from the disposal of plant on 1.1.X7 | 300 |
|  | 420 |

(c) The freehold property was acquired 10 years ago, the buildings element being £100,000. Their estimated economic life was 50 years at the time of purchase.

(d) The plant disposed of on 1.1.X7 cost £350,000 and had a net book value of £274,000. £36,000 depreciation is to be charged on plant and machinery for 20X7.

(e) The debentures are not redeemable for some years.

(f) The directors wish to provide for:

   (i) Debenture interest due
   (ii) A transfer to general reserve of £16,000
   (iii) Audit fees of £4,000

(g) Stock as at 31 December 20X7 was valued at cost of £220,000.

(h) Taxation is to be ignored.

**Requirement**

Prepare journals and a draft profit and loss account and balance sheet for Hartpeace Ltd.

## Solution

WORKING for adjustment (f)

|  | £'000 |
|---|---:|
| Charge needed in profit and loss account for debenture interest (10% × £200,000) | 20 |
| Amount paid so far, as shown in trial balance | (10) |
| Accrual – presumably six months' interest now payable | 10 |

|  |  | £'000 | £'000 |
|---|---|---:|---:|
| (a) | DEBIT Prepayment (9,000 × 8/12) | 6 | |
| | CREDIT Sundry expenses | | 6 |
| | DEBIT Light and heat | 3 | |
| | CREDIT Accrual | | 3 |
| | *Accrual of electricity and prepayment of insurance* | | |
| | DEBIT Wages and salaries | 20 | |
| | CREDIT Light and heat | | 20 |
| | *Correction of misposting of sales commission* | | |
| (b) | DEBIT Suspense | 120 | |
| | CREDIT Share capital (100,000 × 0.5) | | 50 |
| | Share premium | | 70 |
| | *Being correct treatment of proceeds of share issue* | | |
| | DEBIT Suspense | 300 | |
| | CREDIT Disposals | | 300 |
| | *Being correct treatment of sales proceeds re plant* | | |
| (c) | DEBIT Disposals | 274 | |
| | Accumulated depreciation – Plant and machinery (350 – 274) | 76 | |
| | CREDIT Plant and machinery: cost | | 350 |
| | *Being disposal of plant on 1.1.X7* | | |
| | DEBIT Depreciation expense | 38 | |
| | CREDIT Freehold property: accumulated depreciation (£100,000/50) | | 2 |
| | CREDIT Plant and machinery: accumulated depreciation | | 36 |
| | *Being depreciation for 20X7* | | |
| (d) | DEBIT Debenture interest | 10 | |
| | Audit fee | 4 | |
| | CREDIT Accruals | | 14 |
| | *Being accruals of debenture interest and audit fee for 20X7* | | |
| | DEBIT Retained profit | 16 | |
| | CREDIT General reserve | | 16 |
| | *Being transfer to general reserve* | | |
| (e) | DEBIT Stock (balance sheet) | 220 | |
| | CREDIT Stock (profit and loss account) | | 220 |
| | *Being closing stock at 31.12.X7* | | |

Here is Hartpeace Ltd's draft profit and loss account and balance sheet, taken direct from the ETB before being 'tidied up' for publication.

HARTPEACE LTD
PROFIT AND LOSS ACCOUNT
FOR THE YEAR ENDED 31 DECEMBER 20X7

|  | £'000 | £'000 |
|---|---|---|
| *Sales* | | 2,695 |
| Less cost of sales | | |
| Opening stock | 190 | |
| Purchases | 2,152 | |
| Less closing stock | (220) | |
| | | (2,122) |
| *Gross profit* | | 573 |
| Profit on disposal of plant | | 26 |
| | | 599 |
| Less expenses | | |
| Wages and salaries | 274 | |
| Sundry expenses | 107 | |
| Light and heat | 14 | |
| Depreciation expense | 38 | |
| Audit fees | 4 | |
| Debenture interest | 20 | |
| | | (457) |
| *Net profit* | | 142 |

HARTPEACE LTD
BALANCE SHEET AS AT 31 DECEMBER 20X7

|  | Cost/val'n £'000 | Dep'n £'000 | £'000 |
|---|---|---|---|
| *Fixed assets* | | | |
| Tangible assets | | | |
| Freehold property | 430 | (22) | 408 |
| Plant and machinery | 480 | (182) | 298 |
| | 910 | (204) | 706 |
| *Current assets* | | | |
| Stock | | 220 | |
| Debtors | | 464 | |
| Prepayments | | 6 | |
| Cash | | 141 | |
| | | 831 | |
| *Creditors: amounts falling due within one year* | | | |
| Creditors | 195 | | |
| Accrued expenses | 17 | | |
| | | (212) | |
| *Net current assets* | | | 619 |
| *Total assets less current liabilities* | | | 1,325 |
| *Creditors: amounts falling due after more than one year* | | | |
| 10% debentures | | | (200) |
| | | | 1,125 |
| *Capital and reserves* | | | |
| Called up share capital | | | |
| 50p equity shares | | 400 | |
| 7% £1 preference shares | | 100 | |
| | | | 500 |
| *Reserves* | | | |
| Share premium | | 70 | |
| General reserve | | 187 | |
| Retained profits (226 + 142) | | 368 | |
| | | | 625 |
| | | | 1,125 |

## 3.5 Company financial statements for publication

Hartpeace Ltd's financial statements would appear as follows if presented for **external** purposes using the full standard Companies Act 2006 formats.

HARTPEACE LTD
PROFIT AND LOSS ACCOUNT FOR THE YEAR ENDED 31 DECEMBER 20X7

| | £'000 |
|---|---:|
| Turnover | 2,695 |
| Cost of sales | (2,122) |
| Gross profit | 573 |
| Administrative expenses (274 + 107 + 14 + 38 + 4) | (437) |
| Operating profit | 136 |
| Other operating income | 26 |
| Interest payable and similar charges | (20) |
| Profit before taxation | 142 |
| Taxation | 0 |
| Profit after taxation | 142 |

HARTPEACE LTD
BALANCE SHEET AS AT 31 DECEMBER 20X7

| | £'000 | £'000 |
|---|---:|---:|
| *Fixed assets* | | |
| Tangible assets | | 706 |
| | | |
| *Current assets* | | |
| Stocks | 220 | |
| Debtors | 464 | |
| Prepayments | 6 | |
| Cash at bank and in hand | 141 | |
| | 831 | |
| | | |
| *Creditors: amounts falling due within one year* | (212) | |
| *Net current assets* | | 619 |
| *Total assets less current liabilities* | | 1,325 |
| *Creditors: amounts falling due after more than one year* | | (200) |
| | | 1,125 |
| | | |
| *Capital and reserves* | | |
| Called up share capital | | 500 |
| Share premium account | | 70 |
| Other reserves | | 187 |
| Retained profits | | 368 |
| | | 1,125 |

Note that under UK GAAP in financial statements for publication there is less detail on the face of the balance sheet; the detail that we saw earlier in the Companies Act 2006 format is normally shown in notes to the financial statements.

## Interactive question 1: UK GAAP financial statements I

The following is an extract from the trial balance of Tafford Ltd, at 30 September 20X1:

|  | £'000 | £'000 |
|---|---|---|
| Machinery: |  |  |
| Cost: | 3,000 |  |
| Accumulated depreciation at 1 October 20X0 |  | 1,700 |
| Motor vehicles: |  |  |
| Cost | 1,180 |  |
| Accumulated depreciation at 1 October 20X0 |  | 500 |
| Stock at 1 October 20X0 | 13,000 |  |
| Sales |  | 41,600 |
| Purchases | 22,600 |  |
| Distribution costs | 6,000 |  |
| Administrative expenses | 5,000 |  |
| Allowance for doubtful debts, 1 October 20X0 |  | 1,300 |
| Bad debts written off | 600 |  |
| 10% Debentures (issued 20W9) |  | 10,000 |
| Interest paid on debentures | 500 |  |
| Suspense account |  | 100 |

### Notes

(1) Closing stock at 30 September 20X1 was £15,600,000.

(2) Bad debts written off and the movement on the allowance for doubtful debts are to be included in administrative expenses. The allowance for doubtful debts is to be reduced to £500,000.

(3) The balance on the suspense account is the disposal proceeds of motor vehicles, entered to the suspense account pending correct treatment in the records.

The vehicles were sold on 1 October 20X0. They had cost £180,000 and at 1 October 20X0 their net book value was £60,000. The vehicles sold were all used in distributing the company's goods. Any profit or loss is to be included in distribution costs.

(4) Depreciation is to be provided for on the straight line basis as follows:

Machinery          10%

Motor vehicles     25%

Depreciation of motor vehicles is to be divided equally between distribution costs and administrative expenses, and depreciation of machinery is to be charged wholly to distribution costs.

(5) Prepayments and accruals at 30 September 20X1 were as follows:

|  | Prepayments £'000 | Accruals £'000 |
|---|---|---|
| Distribution costs | 200 | 100 |
| Administrative expenses | 100 | 60 |

(6) The estimated tax charge for the year is £3,000,000.

### Requirement

For Tafford Ltd's profit and loss account for the year ended 30 September 20X1 calculate the figures to be included for (a) cost of sales, (b) distribution costs, (c) administrative expenses and (d) interest payable.

See **Answer** at the end of this chapter.

## Interactive question 2: UK GAAP financial statements II

The following information is available about the balances and transactions of Alpaca Ltd:

| BALANCES AT 30 APRIL 20X1 | £'000 |
|---|---:|
| Fixed assets – cost | 1,000 |
| – accumulated depreciation | 230 |
| Stocks | 410 |
| Debtors | 380 |
| Cash at bank | 87 |
| Creditors | 219 |
| Issued share capital – equity shares of £1 each | 400 |
| Retained profits | 818 |
| 10% Debentures | 200 |
| Debenture interest owing | 10 |

| TRANSACTIONS DURING YEAR ENDED 30 APRIL 20X2 | £'000 |
|---|---:|
| Sales | 4,006 |
| Purchases | 2,120 |
| Expenses | 1,640 |
| Interest on debentures paid during year | 20 |
| Issue of 100,000 £1 equity shares at a premium of 50p per share | |

There were no purchases or disposals of fixed assets during the year.

ADJUSTMENTS AT 30 APRIL 20X2

(1) Depreciation of £100,000 is to be charged.
(2) Bad debts of £20,000 are to be written off.

BALANCES AT 30 APRIL 20X2

| | £'000 |
|---|---:|
| Stocks | 450 |
| Debtors (**before** writing off bad debts shown above) | 690 |
| Cash at bank | 114 |
| Creditors | 180 |

### Requirement

Prepare Alpaca Ltd's balance sheet as at 30 April 20X2 under UK GAAP as far as the information available allows, including a working showing how the retained profits figure in the balance sheet is calculated.

See **Answer** at the end of this chapter.

## Summary

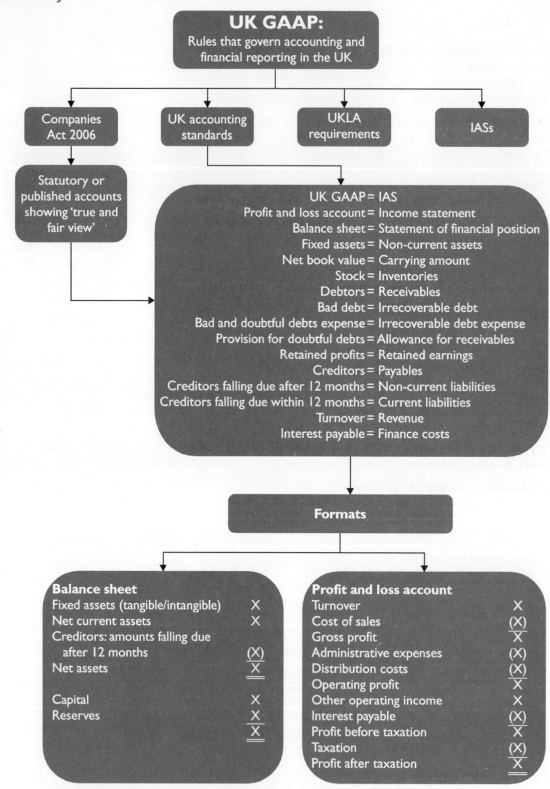

**UK GAAP:**
Rules that govern accounting and
financial reporting in the UK

| | | | |
|---|---|---|---|
| Companies Act 2006 | UK accounting standards | UKLA requirements | IASs |

Statutory or
published accounts
showing 'true and
fair view'

UK GAAP = IAS
Profit and loss account = Income statement
Balance sheet = Statement of financial position
Fixed assets = Non-current assets
Net book value = Carrying amount
Stock = Inventories
Debtors = Receivables
Bad debt = Irrecoverable debt
Bad and doubtful debts expense = Irrecoverable debt expense
Provision for doubtful debts = Allowance for receivables
Retained profits = Retained earnings
Creditors = Payables
Creditors falling due after 12 months = Non-current liabilities
Creditors falling due within 12 months = Current liabilities
Turnover = Revenue
Interest payable = Finance costs

**Formats**

**Balance sheet**

| | |
|---|---|
| Fixed assets (tangible/intangible) | X |
| Net current assets | X |
| Creditors: amounts falling due after 12 months | (X) |
| Net assets | X |
| | |
| Capital | X |
| Reserves | X |
| | X |

**Profit and loss account**

| | |
|---|---|
| Turnover | X |
| Cost of sales | (X) |
| Gross profit | X |
| Administrative expenses | (X) |
| Distribution costs | (X) |
| Operating profit | X |
| Other operating income | X |
| Interest payable | (X) |
| Profit before taxation | X |
| Taxation | (X) |
| Profit after taxation | X |

# Self-test

Answer the following questions.

1   Y Ltd purchased some plant on 1 January 20X0 for £38,000. The payment for the plant was correctly entered in the cash book but was entered on the debit side of plant repairs account.

   Y Ltd charges depreciation on the straight line basis at 20% per annum.

   How will Y's profit for the year ended 31 March 20X0 be affected by the error?

   | | | | |
   |---|---|---|---|
   | A | Understated by £30,400 | C | Understated by £38,000 |
   | B | Understated by £36,100 | D | Overstated by £1,900 |

2   The closing stock of X Ltd was £116,400 *excluding* the following two stock lines:

   - 400 items which cost £4 each, but which were expected to sell for £3 each, with selling expenses of £200 in total.

   - 200 different items which had cost £30 each, but which are defective. Rectification work will cost £1,200, after which they can be sold for £35 each, with selling expenses totalling £300.

   What will appear on X Ltd's balance sheet for stock?

   | | | | |
   |---|---|---|---|
   | A | £122,300 | C | £122,900 |
   | B | £121,900 | D | £123,300 |

3   At 1 January 20X0 the capital structure of Q Limited was as follows:

   | | £ |
   |---|---|
   | Issued share capital 1,000,000 equity shares of 50p each | 500,000 |
   | Share premium account | 300,000 |

   On 1 April 20X0 the company made an issue of 200,000 50p shares at £1.30 each, and on 1 July the company made a 1 for 4 bonus issue.

   Which of the following correctly states the company's share capital and share premium account at 31 December 20X0?

   | | Share capital | Share premium account |
   |---|---|---|
   | A | £750,000 | £230,000 |
   | B | £875,000 | £285,000 |
   | C | £750,000 | £310,000 |
   | D | £750,000 | £610,000 |

4   W Ltd bought a new printing machine at a cost of £80,000. The installation costs were £5,000 and the employees received training on how to use printing machines at a cost of £2,000. A regulatory test to ensure the machine functioned safely cost £1,000.

   What is the cost of the machine in the company's balance sheet?

   | | | | |
   |---|---|---|---|
   | A | £80,000 | C | £86,000 |
   | B | £85,000 | D | £88,000 |

5   The electricity account for the year ended 30 June 20X1 was as follows.

   | | £ |
   |---|---|
   | Opening balance for electricity accrued at 1 July 20X0 | 300 |
   | Payments made during the year | |
   | 1 August 20X0 for three months to 31 July 20X0 | 600 |
   | 1 November 20X0 for three months to 31 October 20X0 | 720 |
   | 1 February 20X1 for three months to 31 January 20X1 | 900 |
   | 30 June 20X1 for three months to 30 April 20X1 | 840 |

Which of the following is the appropriate entry for electricity?

|   | Accrued at 30 June 20X1 | Charge to profit and loss account year ended 30 June 20X1 |
|---|---|---|
| A | £Nil | £3,060 |
| B | £460 | £3,320 |
| C | £560 | £3,320 |
| D | £560 | £3,420 |

6   The year end of M Ltd is 30 November 20X1. The company pays for its gas by a standing order of £600 per month. On 1 December 20X0 the statement from the gas supplier showed that M Ltd had overpaid by £200. M Ltd received gas bills for the four quarters commencing on 1 December 20X0 and ending on 30 November 20X1 for £1,300, £1,400, £2,100 and £2,000 respectively.

Which of the following is the correct charge for gas in M Ltd's profit and loss account for the year ended 30 November 20X1?

A   £6,800          C   £7,200
B   £7,000          D   £7,400

7   Teasdale Ltd, whose year end is 31 December, bought a car on 1 January 20X0 for:

|  | £ |
|---|---|
| Cost | 10,000 |
| Road tax | 150 |
| Total | 10,150 |

The car was depreciated at 25% per annum reducing balance then traded in for a replacement vehicle on 1 January 20X3 at an agreed value of £5,000.

What was the profit on disposal of the car?

A   £718           C   £1,788
B   £781           D   £1,836

8   Which of the following items does NOT appear under the heading 'reserves' on a company balance sheet?

A   Share premium account          C   Debentures
B   Retained profits               D   General reserve

9   Which of the following statements regarding a company profit and loss account is correct?

A   The Companies Act 2006 defines the expenses which are reported under 'cost of sales'

B   'Depreciation' appears as a separate heading in the profit and loss account

C   Interest payable is deducted from profit after taxation

D   Bad debts are included under one of the statutory expense headings (usually administrative expenses)

10   At the end of its first year of trading on 30 June 20X7 Lindman Ltd's net assets are £324,854. It has equity 25p share capital of £100,000 issued at 50p each, and a retained profits reserve of £59,854.

In relation to Lindman Ltd's balance sheet which of the following statements could be true?

A   It has share premium of £115,000
B   It has a general reserve of £65,000
C   It has share capital of £200,000
D   It has a general reserve of £115,000

Now, go back to the Learning Objectives in the Introduction. If you are satisfied that you have achieved these objectives, please tick them off.

## Answer to Interactive question 1

TAFFORD LIMITED
PROFIT AND LOSS ACCOUNT FOR THE YEAR ENDED 30 SEPTEMBER 20X1

|  |  | £'000 |
|---|---|---|
| Turnover |  | 41,600 |
| (a) | Cost of sales (W1) | **(20,000)** |
|  | Gross profit | 21,600 |
| (b) | Distribution costs (W2) | **(6,285)** |
| (c) | Administrative expenses (W3) | **(4,885)** |
|  | Operating profit | 10,430 |
| (d) | Interest payable (10% × £10,000,000) | **(1,000)** |
|  | Profit before taxation | 9,430 |
|  | Taxation | (3,000) |
|  | Profit after taxation | 6,430 |

WORKINGS

**(1) Cost of sales**

|  | £'000 |
|---|---|
| Opening stock | 13,000 |
| Purchases | 22,600 |
|  | 35,600 |
| Less closing stock | (15,600) |
|  | 20,000 |

**(2) Distribution costs**

|  | £'000 |
|---|---|
| Distribution costs (6,000 – 200 + 100) | 5,900 |
| Depreciation: machinery (10% × £3,000) | 300 |
| motor vehicles (25% × ½ × £(1,180 – 180)) | 125 |
| Profit on sale of vehicles (100 – 60) | (40) |
|  | 6,285 |

**(3) Administrative expenses**

|  | £'000 |
|---|---|
| Administrative expenses (5,000 – 100 + 60) | 4,960 |
| Bad debts | 600 |
| Reduction in allowance for doubtful debts | (800) |
| Depreciation: motor vehicles (25% × ½ × £(1,180 – 180)) | 125 |
|  | 4,885 |

CHAPTER

14

## Answer to Interactive question 2

ALPACA LIMITED
BALANCE SHEET AS AT 30 APRIL 20X2

|  | £'000 | £'000 | £'000 |
|---|---|---|---|
| *Fixed assets* |  |  |  |
| Cost/ Accumulated depreciation (230 + 100) | 1,000 | (330) | 670 |
| *Current assets* |  |  |  |
| Stock |  | 450 |  |
| Debtors (690 – 20) |  | 670 |  |
| Bank |  | 114 |  |
|  |  | 1,234 |  |
| *Less Creditors: amounts falling due in less than one year* |  |  |  |
| Creditors | 180 |  |  |
| Accruals (W1) | 10 |  |  |
|  |  | (190) |  |
| *Net current assets* |  |  | 1,044 |
|  |  |  | 1,714 |
| *Less Creditors: amounts falling due after more than one year* |  |  |  |
| 10% Debentures |  |  | (200) |
|  |  |  | 1,514 |
| *Capital and reserves* |  |  |  |
| Share capital (400 + 100) |  |  | 500 |
| Share premium (100 × 50p) |  |  | 50 |
| Retained profits (W2) |  |  | 964 |
|  |  |  | 1,514 |

WORKINGS

(1) **Accruals**

DEBENTURE INTEREST

|  | £'000 |  |  | £'000 |
|---|---|---|---|---|
| Bank | 20 | Bal b/d |  | 10 |
| Bal c/d (bal fig) | 10 | P+L |  | 20 |
|  | 30 |  |  | 30 |

(2) **Retained profits**

|  | £'000 | £'000 | £'000 |
|---|---|---|---|
| Bal b/f |  |  | 818 |
| Sales |  | 4,006 |  |
| Opening stock | 410 |  |  |
| Purchases | 2,120 |  |  |
| Closing stock | (450) |  |  |
|  |  | (2,080) |  |
| Gross profit |  | 1,926 |  |
| Expenses | 1,640 |  |  |
| Depreciation | 100 |  |  |
| Bad debts written off | 20 |  |  |
| Debenture interest payable (W1) | 20 |  |  |
|  |  | (1,780) |  |
| Net profit for year |  |  | 146 |
| Balance c/f |  |  | 964 |

1   B   DEBIT          Fixed assets                                     £38,000
        CREDIT         Plant repairs                                                £38,000
        DEBIT          Dep'n expense (3/12 × 20% × £38,000)   £1,900
        CREDIT         Accumulated dep'n                                         £1,900

    Profit is understated by £38,000 – £1,900 = £36,100

2   C
                                                                                            £
        Draft figure                                                              116,400
        Line 1: (400 × £3) – £200                                            1,000
        Line 2: (200 × £35) – £300 – £1,200                              5,500
        Final valuation                                                         122,900

3   C
                                                                                            £
        Share capital @ 1.1.20X0                                           500,000
        Issue on 1.4.20X0 (200,000 @ 50p)                            100,000
        Bonus issue (1.2m / 4) @ 50p                                     150,000
        Share capital as at 31.12.20X0                                   750,000

                                                                                            £
        Share premium @ 1.1.20X0                                       300,000
        1.4.20X0 200,000 shares @ (130p – 50p)                   160,000
        Bonus issue (as above)                                             (150,000)
                                                                                        310,000

4   C
                                                                                            £
        Cost of machine                                                        80,000
        Installation                                                                 5,000
        Testing                                                                        1,000
                                                                                          86,000

    The employee training was general and not specifically related to bringing the asset into use, so its cost cannot be included.

5   C

### ELECTRICITY ACCOUNT

|              |                          | £     |                       | £     |
|--------------|--------------------------|-------|-----------------------|-------|
|              |                          |       | Balance b/fwd         | 300   |
| 20X0:        |                          |       |                       |       |
| 1 August     | Paid bank                | 600   |                       |       |
| 1 November   | Paid bank                | 720   |                       |       |
| 20X1:        |                          |       |                       |       |
| 1 February   | Paid bank                | 900   |                       |       |
| 30 June      | Paid bank                | 840   |                       |       |
| 30 June      | Accrual £840 × $^2/_3$    | 560   | Profit and loss a/c   | 3,320 |
|              |                          | 3,620 |                       | 3,620 |

6    A

### GAS SUPPLIER ACCOUNT

| | £ | | | £ |
|---|---|---|---|---|
| Balance b/fwd | 200 | | | |
| Bank £600 x 12 | 7,200 | 28 February | invoice | 1,300 |
| | | 31 May | invoice | 1,400 |
| | | 31 August | invoice | 2,100 |
| | | 30 November | invoice | 2,000 |
| | | 30 November | bal. c/d | 600 |
| | 7,400 | | | 7,400 |

### GAS ACCOUNT

| | | £ | | | £ |
|---|---|---|---|---|---|
| 28 February | invoice | 1,300 | | | |
| 31 May | invoice | 1,400 | | | |
| 31 August | invoice | 2,100 | | | |
| 30 November | invoice | 2,000 | 30 November | Profit and loss a/c | 6,800 |
| | | 6,800 | | | 6,800 |

7    B

| | £ |
|---|---|
| Cost | 10,000 |
| 20X0 Depreciation 25% | (2,500) |
| | 7,500 |
| 20X1 Depreciation 25% | (1,875) |
| | 5,625 |
| 20X2 Depreciation 25% | (1,406) |
| | 4,219 |
| 20X3 Part exchange value | (5,000) |
| Profit on disposal | 781 |

8    C    This is correct because debentures are accounted for as liabilities in the financial statements.

A and B are statutory reserves, while the general reserve can be created by the company if its constitution allows.

9    D    Correct, company will usually include this under distribution costs or administrative expenses.

A    Incorrect, the expenses in cost of sales are not defined by statute.

B    Incorrect, depreciation is included under the relevant statutory expense heading (eg office equipment depreciation goes into administrative expenses).

C    Incorrect, profit after taxation is calculated after interest has been deducted.

10    B

| | £ |
|---|---|
| Share capital | 100,000 |
| Share premium $\left( \dfrac{100,000}{25p} \times 25p \right)$ | 100,000 |
| Retained profits reserve | 59,854 |
| Balancing figure | 65,000 |
| Net assets | 324,854 |

This figure could be a general reserve of £65,000.

# CHAPTER 15

# Sole trader and partnership financial statements under UK GAAP

Introduction

Examination context

**Topic List**

### Learning objectives

- Record and account for transactions and events resulting in income, expenses, assets, liabilities and equity in accordance with the appropriate basis of accounting and the laws, regulations and accounting standards applicable to the financial statements

- Record and account for changes in the ownership structure and ownership interests in an entity

- Prepare an extended trial balance

- Identify the main components of a set of financial statements and specify their purpose and interrelationship

- Prepare and present a balance sheet, profit and loss account and cash flow statement from the accounting records and trial balance in a format which satisfies the information requirements of the entity

Specific syllabus learning outcomes are: 1d, e; 2c; 3a, c

### Syllabus links

You will encounter the accounting principles related to changes in ownership structure later in in the Professional Level module of Financial Accounting and Reporting.

### Examination context

Questions on the topics in this chapter will be set as multiple choice questions, some of which may involve calculations so that the correct answer can be selected. Very often double entry questions are phrased in terms of preparing a journal.

In the exam you may be required to:

- Manipulate opening and closing balance sheets for sole traders to identify profit for the year using the accounting equation

- Use UK GAAP terminology when identifying figures in the profit and loss account and balance sheet of a sole trader or partnership

- Identify the unique features of accounting for general partnerships, especially capital and current accounts, drawings, profit sharing ratios, interest on capital and drawings, salaries, the profit appropriation statement, guaranteed shares, and loans from partners

- Identify figures when accounting for changes in partnership structure, including goodwill

# 1 Sole trader financial statements

## Section overview

- Sole trader financial statements are similar in terminology and format to those of companies prepared under UK GAAP, but there are important differences.

- Tax is not included in sole trader accounts.

- There are no formal requirements as to headings in the profit and loss account.

- The ownership interest half of the balance sheet shows opening capital, plus capital introduced, less drawings, plus profits, less losses to arrive at the closing net assets figure at the balance sheet date.

In terminology sole trader financial statements are very similar to a profit and loss account and balance sheet prepared under UK GAAP for a limited company. Where they differ is in relation to:

- **Tax**: a business operated by a sole trader has no legal identity separate from its owner, so the liability to pay tax on profits is the owner's and not the business's. This means that there is no tax expense in the profit and loss account, and no tax creditor in the balance sheet.

- The **format** of the profit and loss account: there is no need to aggregate expenses under set headings.

- The **ownership interest half of the balance sheet**: sole traders do not have share capital or reserves. Instead they show the following (this should look similar to the capital part of the accounting equation):

|  | £ |
|---|---|
| Opening capital = net assets at start of period | X |
| Capital introduced in the period | X |
| Net profit/net loss of the period | X/(X) |
| Drawings (of cash, or of stock at cost) | (X) |
| Closing capital = net assets at end of period | X |

## Worked example: Sole trader financial statements

Wasto had the following trial balance as at 31 December 20X4:

|  | £'000 | £'000 |
|---|---|---|
| Owner's capital at 1.1.X4 |  | 450 |
| Bank loan |  | 613 |
| Freehold land and buildings | 430 |  |
| Freehold land and buildings – accumulated depreciation |  | 20 |
| Plant and machinery – cost | 830 |  |
| Plant and machinery – accumulated depreciation |  | 222 |
| Stock | 190 |  |
| Sales |  | 2,695 |
| Purchases | 2,152 |  |
| Loan interest | 10 |  |
| Wages and salaries | 254 |  |
| Drawings | 31 |  |
| Sundry expenses | 113 |  |
| Suspense account |  | 420 |
| Debtors | 464 |  |
| Creditors |  | 195 |
| Cash | 141 |  |
|  | 4,615 | 4,615 |

The following matters have now been discovered:

(a) On 1 January 20X4 Wasto injected a further £190,000 into the business. The only entry made was to debit cash.

(b) On 1 January 20X4 an item of plant that had cost £350,000 and on which depreciation of £74,000 had been charged was disposed of for £230,000. The only entry made was to debit cash.

(c) Depreciation of £36,000 needs to be charged on the remaining plant and machinery, and £5,000 on the land and buildings.

(d) Loan interest of £10,000 should be accrued at 31 December 20X4.

(e) Stock on hand at 31 December 20X4 cost £220,000.

**Requirement**

Prepare Wasto's ETB, his profit and loss account for the year ended 31 December 20X4 and his balance sheet at that date.

## Solution

Wasto's ETB is as follows:

| | Trial balance Debit £'000 | Trial balance Credit £'000 | Adjustments Debit £'000 | Adjustments Credit £'000 | P&L account Debit £'000 | P&L account Credit £'000 | Balance sheet Debit £'000 | Balance sheet Credit £'000 |
|---|---|---|---|---|---|---|---|---|
| Owner's capital at 1.1.X4 | | 450 | | | | | | 450 |
| Bank loan | | 613 | | | | | | 613 |
| Freehold land and buildings | 430 | | | | | | 430 | |
| Freehold land and buildings – accumulated depreciation | | 20 | | 5 | | | | 25 |
| Plant and machinery – cost | 830 | | | 350 | | | 480 | |
| Plant and machinery – accumulated depreciation | | 222 | 74 | 36 | | | | 184 |
| Stock | 190 | | 220 | 220 | 190 | 220 | 220 | |
| Sales | | 2,695 | | | | 2,695 | | |
| Purchases | 2,152 | | | | 2,152 | | | |
| Loan interest | 10 | | 10 | | 20 | | | |
| Wages and salaries | 254 | | | | 254 | | | |
| Drawings | 31 | | | | | | 31 | |
| Sundry expenses | 113 | | | | 113 | | | |
| Suspense account | | 420 | 420 | | | | | |
| Debtors | 464 | | | | | | 464 | |
| Creditors | | 195 | | | | | | 195 |
| Cash | 141 | | | | | | 141 | |
| Capital introduced | | | | 190 | | | | 190 |
| Disposals | | | 276 | 230 | 46 | | | |
| Depreciation expense | | | 41 | | 41 | | | |
| Accruals | | | | 10 | | | | 10 |
| | | | | | 2,816 | 2,915 | | |
| Net profit | | | | | 99 | | | 99 |
| | 4,615 | 4,615 | 1,041 | 1,041 | 2,915 | 2,915 | 1,766 | 1,766 |

WASTO: PROFIT AND LOSS ACCOUNT FOR YEAR ENDED 31 DECEMBER 20X4

|  | £'000 | £'000 |
|---|---|---|
| Sales |  | 2,695 |
| *Cost of sales* |  |  |
| Opening stock | 190 |  |
| Purchases | 2,152 |  |
| Closing stock | (220) |  |
|  |  | (2,122) |
| Gross profit |  | 573 |
| *Expenses* |  |  |
| Loan interest | 20 |  |
| Wages and salaries | 254 |  |
| Sundry expenses | 113 |  |
| Loss on disposal | 46 |  |
| Depreciation expense | 41 |  |
|  |  | (474) |
| Net profit |  | 99 |

WASTO: BALANCE SHEET AS AT 31 DECEMBER 20X4

|  | Cost £'000 | Acc. depn. £'000 | £'000 |
|---|---|---|---|
| *Fixed assets* |  |  |  |
| Freehold land and buildings | 430 | 25 | 405 |
| Plant and machinery | 480 | 184 | 296 |
|  | 910 | 209 | 701 |
| *Current assets* |  |  |  |
| Stock |  | 220 |  |
| Debtors |  | 464 |  |
| Cash |  | 141 |  |
|  |  | 825 |  |
| *Current liabilities* |  |  |  |
| Accruals |  | 10 |  |
| Creditors |  | 195 |  |
|  |  | 205 |  |
| Net current assets |  |  | 620 |
| *Non-current liabilities* |  |  |  |
| Bank loan |  |  | (613) |
|  |  |  | 708 |
| *Ownership interest* |  |  |  |
| Opening capital |  |  | 450 |
| Capital introduced |  |  | 190 |
| Profit for year |  |  | 99 |
| Drawings |  |  | (31) |
| Closing capital |  |  | 708 |

### Interactive question 1: Sole trader financial statements

In 20X5 Wasto takes drawings of £40,000 and ends 20X5 with net assets of £850,000. He did not introduce any capital in the year.

What was Wasto's net profit in 20X5?

See **Answer** at the end of this chapter.

# 2 Partnerships

**Section overview**

- A partnership is a business run by two or more people together; unless it is a limited liability partnership (LLP) it is not a separate legal entity so tax does not appear in the accounts.

- Parties agree how to appropriate the profits made by the business each year. Sometimes there are salaries, and there is always a profit sharing ratio (PSR).

A general **partnership** is an arrangement between two or more individuals in which they share the risks and rewards of a joint business operation, as if they were joint sole traders.

**Definition**

**Partnership**: The relationship which exists between persons carrying on a business in common with a view of profit.

Usually a general partnership is established formally with a written **partnership agreement**. However, if individuals act as though they are in partnership even if no written agreement exists, then it is presumed that a partnership does exist and that its terms are as laid down in the Partnership Act 1890.

## 2.1 The partnership agreement

A partnership agreement contains the terms of the partnership, in particular the financial arrangements between partners and how profit/loss should be appropriated. It should cover the following issues.

- **Capital**. Each partner puts in a share of the capital. Any minimum fixed amount should be stated.

- **Interest on capital**. Partners can pay themselves interest at an agreed rate on the capital they put into the business. **Interest on capital is treated as a profit appropriation**.

- **Partners' salaries**. Partners can pay themselves salaries. These are **not** salaries in the same way that an employee of the business is paid a wage or salary; **partners' salaries are an appropriation of profit, and not a profit and loss account expense**. Paying salaries gives each partner an income before the **residual profits** are shared out in PSR.

- **Profit-sharing ratio (PSR)**. Partners can agree to share **residual profits and losses after interest and salaries** in any profit-sharing ratio they choose. For example, three partners might agree to share profits equally, but if one partner does a greater share of the work, or has more experience and ability, or puts in more capital, the ratio of profit sharing might be different.

- **Guaranteed minimum profit shares**. Partners can agree that one or more partners should get a guaranteed minimum profit share, even if the partnership makes a smaller than expected profit, or a loss. If the amount allocated by using **interest on capital, salaries** and the **profit-sharing ratio** (PSR) is lower than this, the partner receives the guaranteed minimum profit share and the remaining profits are shared between the other partners in the profit-sharing ratio. Occasionally, **one partner will guarantee another partner's minimum profit share**. That partner will alone make up the difference.

- **Drawings**. Partners can withdraw profits from the business just like sole traders. They can agree to put a limit on how much they should draw out in any period, and they can be charged interest on their drawings during the year. **Interest on drawings is treated as a negative appropriation of profit**.

## 2.2 Appropriating partnership profit

The partnership's net profit is calculated in the same way as for a sole trader using a profit and loss ledger account, or the ETB. We then prepare an **appropriation statement**, which:

- **Allocates** interest on capital, interest on drawings, and salaries to each partner
- **Shares** out the **residual profit** in the PSR

### Worked example: Appropriating partnership profits

Bill and Ben are partners sharing profits in the PSR 2:1, after they each take a salary of £10,000 per year. Net profit **before** deducting salaries is £26,000.

How much profit is appropriated to each partner?

### Solution

First, the two salaries are deducted from profit, leaving £6,000 (£26,000 – £20,000).

This £6,000 has to be distributed between Bill and Ben in the ratio 2:1, so Bill will receive twice as much as Ben. (£4,000:£2,000)

**Profit appropriation statement**

| Ratio | 2 : | 1 | |
| --- | --- | --- | --- |
| | Bill | Ben | Total |
| | £ | £ | £ |
| Salary | 10,000 | 10,000 | 20,000 |
| Share of residual profits (£6,000 in ratio 2:1) | 4,000 | 2,000 | 6,000 |
| Total profit share | 14,000 | 12,000 | 26,000 |

### Interactive question 2: Profit share

Tom, Dick and Harry want to share out net profit of £170,000, in the ratio 7:3:5. Dick gets a salary of £20,000 pa. How much would each partner get?

See **Answer** at the end of this chapter.

## 2.3 Guaranteed minimum profit share

Partners can agree that one or more partners will receive a **minimum appropriation of profit,** even if the business makes a loss, or one partner is appropriated a loss while the others take all the profit.

### Worked example: Guaranteed minimum profit share

Sita, Nisha and Zelda share profits in the ratio of 2:2:1 but Zelda has a guaranteed minimum profit of £18,000. The net profit for the year is £75,000.

The sum of the ratio 'parts' is 2 + 2 + 1 = 5. Each part is worth £15,000 so if we just used the PSR the profits would be allocated as follows:

| Ratio | 2 : | 2 : | 1 | |
| --- | --- | --- | --- | --- |
| | Sita | Nisha | Zelda | Total |
| | £ | £ | £ | £ |
| Initial profit share | 30,000 | 30,000 | 15,000 | 75,000 |

However, this leaves Zelda with less than her guaranteed minimum, so a further reallocation of profits is made from the other two partners equally, because they share 2:2, to give her the minimum amount.

| Ratio | 2 | : | 2 | : | 1 | |
|---|---|---|---|---|---|---|
| | Sita | | Nisha | | Zelda | Total |
| | £ | | £ | | £ | £ |
| PSR | 30,000 | | 30,000 | | 15,000 | 75,000 |
| Reallocation (2:2) | (1,500) | | (1,500) | | 3,000 | 0 |
| Total profit share | 28,500 | | 28,500 | | 18,000 | 75,000 |

### Interactive question 3: Profit appropriation

Anna, Brian and Clare have a profit-sharing ratio of 3:2:1, with Clare due a salary of £8,000. Brian has a minimum profit share of £16,000 guaranteed by Anna. The partnership made a profit of £26,000 in the year.

How much profit will be appropriated to each partner?

See **Answer** at the end of this chapter.

## 3 Preparing partnership accounts

### Section overview

- Each partner's interest in the partnership is shown in a capital account and a current account.

- If a partner has made a loan to the partnership, this is treated the same as a third party loan, with interest deducted before arriving at net profit. Interest may be credited to the partner's current account rather than being paid in cash.

- A profit appropriation statement is used as a working to appropriate salaries, interest on capital, interest on drawings and residual profit share to each partner.

### 3.1 How does accounting for partnerships differ from accounting for sole traders?

Partnership accounts are **identical** in many respects to the accounts of sole traders.

(a) Assets and liabilities are like the **net assets** of any other business, and are accounted for in the same way. Even where a **loan to a partnership** comes from a partner, this is accounted for as if it were a third party loan, in the top half of the balance sheet.

(b) **Net profit** is calculated in the same way as the net profit of a sole trader. If a partner makes a loan to the business (as distinct from a capital contribution) then interest on the loan is an expense in the profit and loss account, in the same way as interest on any other loan from a third party.

(c) Just like a sole trader **tax** does not appear in partnership accounts.

There are two respects in which partnership accounts are **different**, however.

(a) The **ownership interest** of each partner must be shown.
(b) The net profit must be **appropriated** between the partners and shown in the accounts.

### Definition

Appropriation of profit: Sharing out profits in accordance with the partnership agreement.

## 3.2 Accounting for each partner's ownership interest

- Initial capital contributions are recorded in **capital accounts** for each partner. (Since each partner is ultimately entitled to repayment of capital it is clearly vital to keep a record of how much is owed to whom.)

- Profits and losses appropriated over time, less drawings, are shown in a **current account** for each partner.

### Definition

Current account: A record of the **profits retained in the business** by the partner.

A current account increases when the partnership makes profits, and decreases when the partner makes drawings, or when the partnership makes a loss.

**Differences between capital and current accounts** are as follows.

- The balance on the **capital account** remains **static** from year to year (with one or two exceptions).

- The balance on the **current account** is continually **fluctuating** up and down, as the partnership makes profits and losses which are shared out between the partners, and as each partner takes out drawings.

If the partnership agreement provides for interest on capital, partners receive **interest on the balance in their capital account, but not on the balance on their current account.**

If the amount of a partner's **drawings** exceeds the balance on his/her current account, the current account will show **a debit balance** brought forward at the beginning of the next period.

The **ownership interest** side of the partnership balance sheet will therefore consist of:

- Capital accounts for each partner.
- Current accounts for each partner.

## 3.3 Accounting for loans by partners

A partner making a loan to the partnership becomes its creditor. On the balance sheet the loan is shown separately as a long term liability (unless repayable within twelve months, in which case it is a current liability). **Interest on the loan is a deduction from profit to arrive at net profit, not an appropriation of profit.** Interest is payable at 5%.

**Interest on partners' loans is usually credited to the partner's current account** as this is administratively more convenient, especially when the partner does not particularly want to be paid the loan interest in cash immediately it becomes due.

## 3.4 Accounting for appropriation of net profit/loss

The net profit of a partnership is shared out in the PSR in an **appropriation account**, which follows on from the profit and loss ledger account itself.

The accounting entries for an individual share of profits for each partner are:

(a)  DEBIT      P & L ledger account with net profit c/d
      CREDIT    P & L appropriation account with net profit b/d

(b)  DEBIT      P & L appropriation account
      CREDIT    The current accounts of each partner

The steps to take are as follows.

## Step 1

Establish the net profit, after deducting interest on loans from partners.

## Step 2

Appropriate interest on capital and salaries first. These items are appropriations of profit and do not appear in the P & L account.

## Step 3

Charge partners interest on their drawings where relevant.

## Step 4

Residual profits are shared out between partners in the PSR.

## Step 5

Each partner's share of profits is credited to his/her current account.

The calculations involved in steps 2 to 4 are made in a **profit appropriation statement**.

In practice each partner's capital account will be a separate ledger account, as will their current account, but the examples which follow use a columnar form to show how it works.

### Worked example: Partnership accounts

Locke, Niece and Munster are in partnership and share profits in the ratio 3:2:1. They also agree that:

(a) All three should receive interest at 12% on capital.

(b) Munster should receive a salary of £6,000 per annum.

(c) Interest will be charged on drawings at the rate of 3% (a full year charged on any drawings in the year).

(d) The interest rate on the £6,000 loan from Locke is 5%.

Their capital and current accounts as at 1 January 20X5 are as follows:

|  | £ | £ |
|---|---|---|
| *Capital accounts as at 1.1.X5* | | |
| Locke | 20,000 | |
| Niece | 8,000 | |
| Munster | 6,000 | |
| | | 34,000 |
| *Current accounts as at 1.1.X5* | | |
| Locke | 9,500 | |
| Niece | 3,300 | |
| Munster | 8,800 | |
| | | 21,600 |

Drawings made during the year to 31 December 20X5 were:

|  | £ | £ |
|---|---|---|
| *Drawings in 20X5* | | |
| Locke | (6,000) | |
| Niece | (4,000) | |
| Munster | (7,000) | |
| | | (17,000) |
| | | 38,600 |

The net profit for the year to 31 December 20X5 was £24,870 **before** deducting loan interest.

**Requirement**

Prepare a profit and loss appropriation statement for the year to 31 December 20X5, and the partners' capital accounts and current accounts at that date.

## Solution

The interest payable to Locke on his loan is:

5% of £6,000 = £300

This is **debited** to net profit in the profit and loss account and **credited** to Locke's current account. As a result, the profit to be appropriated is:

| | £ |
|---|---|
| Draft net profit | 24,870 |
| Interest | (300) |
| | 24,570 |

The interest payable by each partner on their drawings during the year is:

| | | £ |
|---|---|---|
| Locke | 3% of £6,000 | 180 |
| Niece | 3% of £4,000 | 120 |
| Munster | 3% of £7,000 | 210 |
| | | 510 |

### LOCKE, NIECE AND MUNSTER: PROFIT APPROPRIATION STATEMENT

| Ratio | 3:<br>Locke<br>£ | 2:<br>Niece<br>£ | 1<br>Munster<br>£ | Total<br>£ |
|---|---|---|---|---|
| Interest charged on drawings | (180) | (120) | (210) | (510) |
| Salary | | | 6,000 | 6,000 |
| Interest on capital | | | | |
| 12% × £20,000 | 2,400 | | | |
| 12% × £8,000 | | 960 | | |
| 12% × £6,000 | | | 720 | 4,080 |
| Share of residual profit: (24,570 + 510 – 6,000 – 4,080) = £15,000 in 3:2:1 ratio | 7,500 | 5,000 | 2,500 | 15,000 |
| Total profit share | 9,720 | 5,840 | 9,010 | 24,570 |

### PARTNERS' CURRENT ACCOUNTS

| | Locke<br>£ | Niece<br>£ | Munster<br>£ | | Locke<br>£ | Niece<br>£ | Munster<br>£ |
|---|---|---|---|---|---|---|---|
| Drawings | 6,000 | 4,000 | 7,000 | Bal b/d | 9,500 | 3,300 | 8,800 |
| | | | | Interest | 300 | | |
| Bal c/d | 13,520 | 5,140 | 10,810 | Profit share | 9,720 | 5,840 | 9,010 |
| | 19,520 | 9,140 | 17,810 | | 19,520 | 9,140 | 17,810 |

### PARTNERS' CAPITAL ACCOUNTS

| | | | | | Locke<br>£ | Niece<br>£ | Munster<br>£ |
|---|---|---|---|---|---|---|---|
| | | | | Balance b/d | 20,000 | 8,000 | 6,000 |

## 3.5 Partnership accounts on the ETB

The ETB can be used to help prepare partnership accounts. The differences to sole trader ETBs are as follows:

- **Accrued interest on a partner's loan** is accounted for in the adjustments column and included in the cross-casts, so the net profit figure in the debit column of the profit and loss account is then the amount to be appropriated

| | | |
|---|---|---|
| DEBIT | Interest expense | £X |
| CREDIT | Current account | £X |

- Each partner's drawings are transferred in the adjustments columns from the drawings accounts to the current account

  DEBIT     Current accounts            £X

  CREDIT    Drawings accounts                 £X

- The profit appropriation statement is prepared as a separate working, then each partner's total profit share is accounted for as follows

  DEBIT     Profit and loss account      £X

  CREDIT    Current accounts (balance sheet)      £X

## Worked example: Partnership accounts on the ETB

Frank and Myra are in partnership sharing profits 2:1. Each partner has an annual salary of £6,750. Frank's loan to the partnership attracts interest at 5% per annum. Their trial balance at 30 June 20X4 is as follows

|  | Debit £ | Credit £ |
|---|---|---|
| Loan from Frank |  | 20,000 |
| Fixed assets – NBV | 100,000 |  |
| Stock at 1 July 20X3 | 15,000 |  |
| Debtors | 18,000 |  |
| Creditors |  | 14,000 |
| Sales |  | 85,000 |
| Purchases | 52,000 |  |
| Loan interest |  |  |
| Expenses | 12,500 |  |
| Drawings |  |  |
|   Frank | 14,000 |  |
|   Myra | 15,000 |  |
| Cash | 6,300 |  |
| Capital accounts |  |  |
|   Frank |  | 20,000 |
|   Myra |  | 20,000 |
| Current accounts at 1 July 20X3 |  |  |
|   Frank |  | 38,400 |
|   Myra |  | 35,400 |
|  | 232,800 | 232,800 |

You are told that closing stock cost £16,500.

**Requirement**

Prepare Frank and Myra's extended trial balance at 30 June 20X4.

## Solution

We process the adjustment for interest and the transfer of drawings as above, then make the adjustment for closing stock. Next we extend the ETB to calculate the net profit for appropriation:

| | Trial balance Debit £ | Trial balance Credit £ | Adjustments Debit £ | Adjustments Credit £ | P&L account Debit £ | P&L account Credit £ | Balance sheet Debit £ | Balance sheet Credit £ |
|---|---|---|---|---|---|---|---|---|
| Loan from Frank | | 20,000 | | | | | | 20,000 |
| Fixed assets – NBV | 100,000 | | | | | | 100,000 | |
| Stock | 15,000 | | 16,500 | 16,500 | 15,000 | 16,500 | 16,500 | |
| Debtors | 18,000 | | | | | | 18,000 | |
| Creditors | | 14,000 | | | | | | 14,000 |
| Sales | | 85,000 | | | | 85,000 | | |
| Purchases | 52,000 | | | | 52,000 | | | |
| Loan interest | | | 1,000 | | 1,000 | | | |
| Expenses | 12,500 | | | | 12,500 | | | |
| Drawings | | | | | | | | |
| Frank | 14,000 | | | 14,000 | | | | |
| Myra | 15,000 | | | 15,000 | | | | |
| Cash | 6,300 | | | | | | 6,300 | |
| Capital accounts | | | | | | | | |
| Frank | | 20,000 | | | | | | 20,000 |
| Myra | | 20,000 | | | | | | 20,000 |
| Current accounts | | | | | | | | |
| Frank | | 38,400 | 14,000 | 1,000 | | | | |
| Myra | | 35,400 | 15,000 | | | | | |
| Net profit for appropriation | | | | | **21,000** | | | |
| | 232,800 | 232,800 | 46,500 | 46,500 | 101,500 | 101,500 | | |

### PROFIT APPROPRIATION STATEMENT

| | | 2 Frank £ | 1 Myra £ | Total £ |
|---|---|---|---|---|
| Ratio | | | | |
| Salaries | | 6,750 | 6,750 | 13,500 |
| PSR (2:1) | | 5,000 | 2,500 | 7,500 |
| Total profit share | | 11,750 | 9,250 | **21,000** |

The final ETB is as follows:

| | Trial balance Debit £ | Trial balance Credit £ | Adjustments Debit £ | Adjustments Credit £ | P&L account Debit £ | P&L account Credit £ | Balance sheet Debit £ | Balance sheet Credit £ |
|---|---|---|---|---|---|---|---|---|
| Loan from Frank | | 20,000 | | | | | | 20,000 |
| Fixed assets – NBV | 100,000 | | | | | | 100,000 | |
| Stock | 15,000 | | 16,500 | 16,500 | 15,000 | 16,500 | 16,500 | |
| Debtors | 18,000 | | | | | | 18,000 | |
| Creditors | | 14,000 | | | | | | 14,000 |
| Sales | | 85,000 | | | | 85,000 | | |
| Purchases | 52,000 | | | | 52,000 | | | |
| Loan interest | | | 1,000 | | 1,000 | | | |
| Expenses | 12,500 | | | | 12,500 | | | |
| Drawings | | | | | | | | |
| Frank | 14,000 | | | 14,000 | | | | |
| Myra | 15,000 | | | 15,000 | | | | |
| Cash | 6,300 | | | | | | 6,300 | |
| Capital accounts | | | | | | | | |
| Frank | | 20,000 | | | | | | 20,000 |
| Myra | | 20,000 | | | | | | 20,000 |
| Current accounts | | | | | | | | |
| Frank* | | 38,400 | 14,000 | 1,000 | | | | 37,150 |
| Myra** | | 35,400 | 15,000 | | | | | 29,650 |
| Appropriated net profit | | | | | | | | |
| Frank | | | | | 11,750 | | | |
| Myra | | | | | 9,250 | | | |
| | 232,800 | 232,800 | 46,500 | 46,500 | 101,500 | 101,500 | 140,800 | 140,800 |

\*     Frank's current account balance is 38,400 – 14,000 + 1,000 + 11,750 = 37,150

\*\*   Myra's current account balance is 35,400 – 15,000 + 9,250 = 29,650

The profit and loss account for the partnership will be presented as for sole traders. The balance sheet is as follows:

FRANK AND MYRA
BALANCE SHEET AS AT 30 JUNE 20X4

| | £ | £ |
|---|---:|---:|
| *Fixed assets* | | 100,000 |
| *Current assets* | | |
| Stock | 16,500 | |
| Debtors | 18,000 | |
| Cash | 6,300 | |
| | 40,800 | |
| *Current liabilities* | | |
| Creditors | (14,000) | |
| *Net current assets* | | 26,800 |
| *Non-current liabilities* | | |
| Loan from Frank | | (20,000) |
| | | 106,800 |
| *Capital accounts* | | |
|   Frank | | 20,000 |
|   Myra | | 20,000 |
| *Current accounts* | | |
|   Frank | | 37,150 |
|   Myra | | 29,650 |
| | | 106,800 |

# 4   Accounting for changes in partnership structure

**Section overview**

- When a partner dies or retires, the remaining parties normally carry on the business, buying out the departing partner's share of the net assets, including goodwill.

## 4.1   Retirement or death of a partner

Any changes in a partnership require a new agreement. Unless the agreement specifically states otherwise, legally the old partnership is dissolved and a new partnership is created. However, from an accounting viewpoint, it is more realistic to treat the partnership as **continuing** but with a change in the partners and the PSR.

On the retirement or death of a partner, we need to:

- Calculate the profits up to the **date of change** and appropriate them according to the **old PSR**.
- Appropriate the profits **after** the date of change according to the **new PSR**.

**Worked example: Retirement**

Returning to the example of Locke, Niece and Munster, assume that Locke retired on 30 September 20X5 and Niece and Munster decided to continue the partnership on the same terms as before, but with a PSR of 1:1. Locke's drawings of £6,000 were taken in the period to 30 September 20X5 and Locke's loan remained with the partnership after his retirement.

**Requirement**

Prepare the relevant profit appropriation statements for the year to 31 December 20X5.

**Solution**

We need to treat the accounting year as being in two sections:

(a)   Period to 30 September 20X5 (9 months), with partners Locke, Niece and Munster.
(b)   Period from 1 October to 31 December 20X5 (3 months), with partners Niece and Munster.

Up to the date of retirement the profit to be appropriated net of interest is £24,570 × 9/12 = £18,427, since the loan was not repaid at retirement and we can assume that interest accrues evenly over the year.

**Locke, Niece and Munster: Profit appropriation statement**

| *Ratio to 30 September 20X5* | *3:* | *2:* | *1* | |
|---|---|---|---|---|
| | *Locke* | *Niece* | *Munster* | *Total* |
| | *£* | *£* | *£* | *£* |
| Interest charged on drawings (9/12 for N&M) | (180) | (90) | (158) | (428) |
| Salary 9/12 | | | 4,500 | 4,500 |
| Interest on capital | | | | |
| 12% × £20,000 × 9/12 | 1,800 | | | |
| 12% × £8,000 × 9/12 | | 720 | | |
| 12% × £6,000 × 9/12 | | | 540 | 3,060 |
| Share of residual profit: (18,427+ 428 – | | | | |
|    4,500 – 3,060)  = £11,295 in 3:2:1 ratio | 5,648 | 3,765 | 1,882 | 11,295 |
| Total profit share | 7,268 | 4,395 | 6,764 | 18,427 |

From Locke's retirement the profit to be appropriated net of interest is £24,570 × 3/12 = £6,143.

| *Ratio from 30 September 20X5* | *1:* | *1* | |
|---|---|---|---|
| | *Niece* | *Munster* | *Total* |
| | *£* | *£* | *£* |
| Interest charged on drawings (3/12) | (30) | (52) | (82) |
| Salary 3/12 | | 1,500 | 1,500 |
| Interest on capital | | | |
| 12% × £8,000 × 3/12 | 240 | | |
| 12% × £6,000 × 3/12 | | 180 | 420 |
| Share of residual profit: (6,143 + 82 – 1,500 – 420) | | | |
|    = £4,305 in 1:1 ratio | 2,152 | 2,153 | 4,305 |
| Total profit share | 2,362 | 3,781 | 6,143 |

## 4.2   Goodwill in the partnership accounts

Usually on a partner's retirement or death a **valuation of the partnership's net assets** is carried out, or the partners simply agree that as well as a share of the profits to the date of retirement the retiring partner should also take a **share in the partnership's goodwill**, in the form of **a settlement in cash or other assets** from the other partners. Once the partner has gone the goodwill is then removed from the accounts.

The principles behind how we account for retirement or death of a partner when there is a settlement which includes recognition of the value of the partnership's goodwill are the same as we used when converting and selling a sole trader's business.

In the example that follows we combine each partner's capital and current accounts for ease of explanation.

## Worked example: Death of a partner

George, Amanda and Henry have been in partnership for many years, sharing profits equally and preparing accounts to 31 December each year. As at 1 January 20X2 each partner's combined capital and current accounts were as follows:

|  | £ |
|---|---|
| George | 138,540 |
| Amanda | 95,400 |
| Henry | 125,950 |
|  | 359,890 |

During 20X2 the partnership made profits of £584,580 and each partner took drawings of £50,000.

On 31 December 20X2 Henry died. The remaining partners value goodwill at £300,000 at that date, but do not wish this valuation to remain in the accounts. George and Amanda will continue in partnership, sharing profits equally.

## Solution

Henry's estate is entitled to receive payment for his ownership of a share in the partnership. When Henry dies there are two options:

- Break up the partnership by selling all the assets and sharing out the net proceeds among George, Amanda and Henry's estate.

- A 'buy out' of Henry's share of the partnership by George and Amanda

The parties have agreed on the second option, but need to determine how much Henry's share is worth, and therefore how much his estate should be paid as consideration.

It is possible to determine how much the remaining partners will need to pay simply by using the capital/current accounts.

(a) Appropriate profits (£584,580/3 = £194,860 each)
(b) Share out the goodwill in old PSR: £300,000/3 = £100,000 each
(c) Calculate the amount Henry's estate will be paid in cash, being the balancing figure on the account
(d) Remove the goodwill in the new PSR: £300,000/2 = £150,000 each
(e) Carry down the balances on the remaining two partners' accounts

### PARTNERS' CAPITAL AND CURRENT ACCOUNTS

|  | George £ | Amanda £ | Henry £ |  | George £ | Amanda £ | Henry £ |
|---|---|---|---|---|---|---|---|
| Drawings | 50,000 | 50,000 | 50,000 | Bal b/d | 138,540 | 95,400 | 125,950 |
| Cash (bal fig) (c) |  |  | 370,810 | Profit share (a) | 194,860 | 194,860 | 194,860 |
| Goodwill (d) | 150,000 | 150,000 |  | Goodwill (b) | 100,000 | 100,000 | 100,000 |
| Bal c/d (e) | 233,400 | 190,260 |  |  |  |  |  |
|  | 433,400 | 390,260 | 420,810 |  | 433,400 | 390,260 | 420,810 |

To prove these calculations are correct we can reconstruct the balance sheet after the payment has been made:

|  | £ |
|---|---|
| Opening net assets = total of the three capital/current accounts at 1.1.X2 | 359,890 |
| Add net profit for the year | 584,580 |
| Less drawings (3 × £50,000) | (150,000) |
| Closing net assets at 31.12.X2 | 794,470 |
| Less cash paid to Henry's estate | (370,810) |
|  | 423,660 |
|  |  |
| George's capital/current account | 233,400 |
| Amanda's capital/current account | 190,260 |
|  | 423,660 |

## 4.3 Admission of a partner

When a new partner is admitted, a new agreement is needed to cover the appropriation of profits.

If the new partner introduces **additional capital** into the partnership, the total amount they bring in must be **credited** to their capital account.

The existing partners' share of the partnership's goodwill at the date of admission is credited to them in the old PSR and then (assuming they do not wish to retain goodwill in the accounts) debited in the new PSR. The result is that the new partner will be shown to have purchased a share of the goodwill by introducing cash.

### Worked example: Admission of a partner

Oil and Grease, equal partners in a vehicle repair business, agree to Detergent becoming a partner on 1 January 20X1. At that date Oil and Grease value the business's goodwill at £5,000 and their capitals are Oil – £12,000; Grease – £9,000. Detergent agrees to introduce £2,000 capital. The partners agree to share profits in the ratio – Oil 2: Grease 2: Detergent 1, and not to retain goodwill in the accounts.

The partners' capital accounts are as follows, showing that £1,000 of Detergent's cash introduced has actually been paid in equal shares to Oil and Grease in respect of their shares of the business's goodwill:

CAPITAL ACCOUNTS

| Ratio | 2:<br>Oil<br>£ | 2:<br>Grease<br>£ | 1<br>Detergent<br>£ | | 1:<br>Oil<br>£ | 1<br>Grease<br>£ | Detergent<br>£ |
|---|---|---|---|---|---|---|---|
| | | | | Balances b/d | 12,000 | 9,000 | |
| Goodwill in new PSR | 2,000 | 2,000 | 1,000 | Goodwill in old PSR | 2,500 | 2,500 | |
| Balances c/d | 12,500 | 9,500 | 1,000 | Cash introduced | | | 2,000 |
| | 14,500 | 11,500 | 2,000 | | 14,500 | 11,500 | 2,000 |

### Summary (1/2)

## Sole trader financial statements

- Less regulated, so can show expenses separately in profit and loss account
- Tax does not appear
- Ownership interest:

| | |
|---|---|
| Opening capital/net assets | X |
| Capital introduced | X |
| Net profit/(loss) | X/(X) |
| Drawings | (X) |
| Closing capital/net assets | X |

## Partnerships

- Business run by two or more people together
- Tax does not appear
- Partners agree:
  - Capital contributions
  - Whether interest on capital and/or drawings is paid
  - Whether salaries are to be paid
  - Profit-sharing ratio (PSR), including any guaranteed minimum
  - Loans from partners accounted for as if from third parties
- Financial statements:
  - Profit and loss account + net assets balance sheet like sole trader's
  - Ownership interest:

| | A | B | Total |
|---|---|---|---|
| Capital account | X | X | X |
| Current account | X | X | X |
| | X | X | X |

ICAEW

# Summary (2/2)

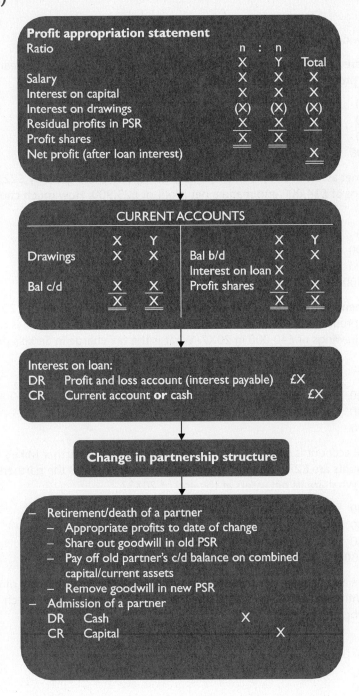

**Profit appropriation statement**

| | X | Y | Total |
|---|---|---|---|
| Ratio | n : | n | |
| | X | Y | Total |
| Salary | X | X | X |
| Interest on capital | X | X | X |
| Interest on drawings | (X) | (X) | (X) |
| Residual profits in PSR | X | X | X |
| Profit shares | X | X | |
| Net profit (after loan interest) | | | X |

**CURRENT ACCOUNTS**

| | X | Y | | X | Y |
|---|---|---|---|---|---|
| Drawings | X | X | Bal b/d | X | X |
| | | | Interest on loan | X | |
| Bal c/d | X | X | Profit shares | X | X |
| | X | X | | X | X |

Interest on loan:
DR    Profit and loss account (interest payable)    £X
CR    Current account **or** cash    £X

**Change in partnership structure**

– Retirement/death of a partner
  – Appropriate profits to date of change
  – Share out goodwill in old PSR
  – Pay off old partner's c/d balance on combined
    capital/current assets
  – Remove goodwill in new PSR
– Admission of a partner
  DR    Cash    X
  CR    Capital    X

CHAPTER

15

## Self-test

Answer the following questions.

1   A, B and C are in partnership with a profit sharing ratio of 3:2:1. For the year ended 31.12.X9, the partnership profits are £18,000. What is B's share of the profits?

    A   £3,000
    B   £6,000
    C   £9,000
    D   £18,000

2   Madro had net assets of £35,000 at 1 January 20X8, and these grew by £22,500 in the year. He took drawings of £14,000 and made a net profit of £23,900. How much capital did Madro inject in the year?

    A   £9,900
    B   £12,600
    C   £67,400
    D   £102,400

3   Serko commenced trading as a sole trader in 20X6 and made a profit of £20,000 in that year. He made a net profit of £50,000 in 20X7. He has calculated that tax at 25% is due on the 20X7 profit. Serko took drawings of £40,000 in 20X7. What is the tax charge in Serko's profit and loss account for 20X7?

    A   £0
    B   £10,000
    C   £12,500
    D   £17,500

4   Pam's capital account is £10,000 at the end of 20X3, and her partner Mike's is £20,000. Their current accounts are £27,820 and £16,910 respectively. In 20X3 the partnership made a net profit of £42,300. What are its net assets at the end of 20X3?

    A   £30,000
    B   £44,730
    C   £74,730
    D   £117,030

5   Rene, Hughie and Paul are partners sharing profit 4:3:1. Paul gets a salary of £12,000. Hughie retires 3 months into 20X4. In 20X4 a profit of £67,040 is made. How much profit is appropriated to Hughie when he retires?

    A   £5,160
    B   £6,285
    C   £6,880
    D   £20,640

6   Sarah has a minimum profit share of £10,000 guaranteed by Richard. On initial appropriation Sarah is allocated £8,000 and Richard is allocated £16,000. What is Richard's final appropriation of profit?

    A   £10,000
    B   £14,000
    C   £16,000
    D   £18,000

Now, go back to the Learning Objectives in the Introduction. If you are satisfied that you have achieved these objectives, please tick them off.

# Answers to Interactive questions

## Answer to Interactive question 1

| | £'000 |
|---|---|
| Opening capital | 708 |
| Capital introduced in the period | 0 |
| Net profit of the period (balancing figure) | 182 |
| Drawings | (40) |
| Closing capital = net assets | 850 |

## Answer to Interactive question 2

### Tom, Dick and Harry: Profit appropriation statement

| Ratio | 7: Tom £ | 3: Dick £ | 5 Harry £ | Total £ |
|---|---|---|---|---|
| Salary | 0 | 20,000 | 0 | 20,000 |
| Share of residual profit ((£170,000 – £20,000) in 7:3:5 PSR) | 70,000 | 30,000 | 50,000 | 150,000 |
| Total profit share | 70,000 | 50,000 | 50,000 | 170,000 |

## Answer to Interactive question 3

### Anna, Brian and Clare: Profit appropriation statement

| Ratio | 3: Anna £ | 2: Brian £ | 1 Clare £ | Total £ |
|---|---|---|---|---|
| Salary | 0 | 0 | 8,000 | 8,000 |
| Share of residual profit (£26,000 – £8,000) in 3:2:1 | 9,000 | 6,000 | 3,000 | 18,000 |
| Initial profit share | 9,000 | 6,000 | 11,000 | 26,000 |
| Reallocation from Anna to Brian | (10,000) | 10,000 | 0 | 0 |
| Total profit share | (1,000) | 16,000 | 11,000 | 26,000 |

1   B   Each 'share' is worth $\dfrac{£18,000}{6} = £3,000$. B's share is, therefore, £6,000.

2   B   35,000 + 23,900 − 14,000 − (35,000 + 22,500)

3   A   As the business is a sole tradership, no tax charge or tax liability will appear in the financial statements

4   C   (10,000 + 20,000 + 27,820 + 16,910) = £74,730. We ignore the net profit figure as we have been given the year-end capital and current account figures, after appropriation.

5   A   $\dfrac{(67,040 - 12,000)/4}{(4 + 3 + 1)} \times 3 = £5,160$

6   B   16,000 − (10,000 − 8,000) = £14,000

# Glossary of terms

| | |
|---|---|
| **AVCO (average cost)** | As purchase prices can change with each new consignment received, the average value of an item is constantly changing. Each item at any moment is assumed to have been purchased at the average price of all the items together, so inventory remaining is therefore valued at the most recent average price. |
| **Accounting equation** | ASSETS = CAPITAL + LIABILITIES. |
| **Accounts payable** | See trade payables |
| **Accounts receivable** | See trade receivables |
| **Accounting standards** | A set of accepted guidelines used by companies to prepare their financial statements. |
| **Accruals (accrued expenses)** | Expenses which are charged against the profit for a particular period, even though they have not yet been paid for. |
| **Accruals basis of accounting** | Items are recognised as assets, liabilities, equity, income and expenses (the elements of financial statements) when they satisfy the definitions and recognition criteria for those elements in the *Conceptual Framework*. |
| **Accumulated depreciation** | The total amount of the asset's depreciation that has been allocated to reporting periods to date. |
| **Allowance for receivables** | An amount in relation to specific debts that reduces the receivables asset to its prudent valuation in the statement of financial position. It is offset against trade receivables, which are shown at the net amount. |
| **Appropriation of profit** | Sharing out profits in accordance with the partnership agreement. |
| **Asset** | The *Conceptual Framework* states that an asset is a resource controlled by the entity as a result of past events from which future economic benefits are expected to flow to the entity. |
| **Asset register** | A listing of all non-current assets owned by the organisation, broken down by department, location or asset type, and containing non-financial information (such as chassis numbers and security codes) as well as financial information. |
| **Balance sheet** | See statement of financial postion. Under UK GAAP this is called a balance sheet. |
| **Bank reconciliation** | A comparison of a bank statement (sent monthly, weekly or even daily by the bank) with the cash book. Differences between the balance on the bank statement and the balance in the cash book should be identified and satisfactorily reconciled. |
| **Bank statement** | A record of transactions on the business's bank account maintained by the bank in its own books. |
| **Books of original entry** | The records in which the business first records transactions. |
| **Bonus issue (or capitalisation issue or scrip issue)** | An issue of fully paid shares to existing shareholders, free of charge, in proportion to their existing shareholdings. |
| **Business entity concept** | The concept that financial accounting information relates to the activities of the business entity and not to the activities of its owner(s). |
| **Capital** | The *Conceptual Framework* states that capital is the residual interest in the assets of the entity after deducting all its liabilities. |
| **Capital accounts (partnerships)** | The partnership capital account is an equity account in the accounting records of a partnership. It contains the initial investment by the partner. |
| **Capital expenditure** | Expenditure which results in the acquisition of long-term assets, or an improvement or enhancement of their earning capacity. |
| **Capital income** | Proceeds from the sale of non-current assets. |

| | |
|---|---|
| Carrying amount | Cost less accumulated depreciation. |
| Cash | Comprises cash on hand and demand deposits. |
| Cash book | The book of original entry for receipts and payments in the business's bank account. |
| Cash discount | A reduction in the amount payable in return for immediate payment in cash, or for payment within an agreed period. There are separate ledger accounts for cash discounts: one for discount allowed to customers, and one for discount received from suppliers. |
| Cash equivalents | Short-term, highly liquid investments that are readily convertible to known amounts of cash and which are subject to an insignificant risk of changes in value (maturity of three months or less from the date of acquisition). |
| Cash flows | These are inflows and outflows of cash and cash equivalents. |
| Comparability | Accounting policies used should be disclosed, to make it possible for users to compare the company's results with its own prior years and with the results of other companies. |
| Contra | When a person or business is both a customer and a supplier, amounts owed by and owed to the person may be 'netted off' by means of a contra entry. |
| Control account | Nominal ledger account in which a record is kept of the total value of a number of similar individual items. Control accounts are used chiefly for trade receivables and payables. |
| Conversion costs | Any costs involved in converting raw materials into final product, including labour, expenses directly related to the product and an appropriate share of production overheads (but not sales, administrative or general overheads). |
| Cost of sales | Opening inventory + purchases + carriage inwards – closing inventory = cost of sales. This amount is then deducted from revenue to arise at the business's gross profit. |
| Credit note | A document issued to a customer relating to returned goods, or refunds when a customer has been overcharged for whatever reason. It can be regarded as a negative invoice. It is a source document for credit transactions. |
| Creditor | Person to whom a business owes money. |
| Current account | A record of the profits retained in the business by the partner. |
| Current asset | An asset is current when it is expected to be realised in, or intended for sale or consumption in, the entity's normal operating cycle, or it is held for being traded, or it is expected to be realised within 12 months of the date of the statement of financial position, or it is cash or a cash equivalent. |
| Current liabilities | Debts of the business that must be paid within one year, or within the entity's normal operating cycle, or that are held to be traded. |
| Debtor | Person who owes money to the business. |
| Depreciation | The systematic allocation of the cost of an asset, less its residual value, over its useful life. |
| Discount | A reduction in the price of goods below the amount at which those goods would normally be sold to other customers. |
| Discounts allowed | Prompt payment discounts allowed to customers who pay within a certain period of time from the invoice date. |
| Discounts received | Prompt payment discounts received from suppliers for payment made within a certain time period from the invoice date. |
| Dividend | A sum of money paid regularly by a company to its shareholders out of its profits (or reserves) |
| Double entry | Each transaction has an equal but opposite effect. Every accounting event |

| | |
|---|---|
| bookkeeping | must be entered in ledger accounts both as a debit and a credit. |
| Drawings | Money and goods taken out of a business by its owner. |
| Economic value | (EV), or value in use: what the existing asset will be worth to the company over the rest of its useful life. |
| Equity | The amount invested in a business by the owners (IAS 1 refers to 'owners' rather than 'equity holders' or 'shareholders'). |
| Elements of financial statements | The Conceptual Framework lays out these elements as: Financial position in the statement of financial position, consisting of assets, liabilities and equity. Performance in the statement of profit or loss consisting of income and expenditure. |
| Equity share | See ordinary share |
| Equity share capital | The total capital raised from the issue of ordinary shares of a company. |
| Error of commission | A transaction that is calculated incorrectly |
| Error of omission | Failing to record a transaction at all, or making a debit or credit entry, but not the corresponding double entry. |
| Error of principle | Making a double entry in the belief that the transaction is being entered in the correct accounts, but subsequently finding out that the accounting entry breaks the 'rules' of an accounting principle or concept. A typical example of such an error is to treat revenue expenditure incorrectly as capital expenditure. |
| Expenses | Decreases in economic benefits over a period in the form of outflows or depletion of assets, or increases in liabilities, resulting in decreases in equity/capital (*Conceptual Framework*). Expense is a key element of financial statements. |
| FIFO (first in, first out) | Items are used in the order in which they are received from suppliers, so oldest items are issued first. Inventory remaining is therefore the newer items. |
| Fair presentation | The faithful representation of the effects of transactions, other events and conditions in accordance with the *Conceptual Framework*. |
| Faithful representation | Information that is complete, neutral and free from errors, so that users can understand the nature and significance of what is presented. |
| Financial accounting | A method of reporting the results and financial position of a business. |
| Financial reporting standards | See accounting standards. |
| General ledger | Ledger in which all asset, liability, capital, income and expense ledger accounts are kept. Also known as the nominal ledger. |
| Going concern concept | The assumption that the business will continue in operation for the foreseeable future. It is assumed that the entity has neither the intention nor the necessity of liquidation or of curtailing materially the scale of its operations. |
| Goodwill, purchased | The excess of the purchase consideration paid for a business over the fair value of the individual assets and liabilities acquired. |
| Gross profit | The profit from the trading activities of the business. Calculated as Sales less Cost of Sales. |
| Historical cost | Transactions are recorded at their cost when they occurred. |
| IASB | International Accounting Standards Board. International accounting standard setting body, responsible for the issue of IFRS |
| Impairment | If the carrying amount of an asset or cash generating unit exceeds its recoverable amount, that asset is said to be impaired |
| Impairment loss | The amount by which the carrying amount of an asset or cash generating unit exceeds its recoverable amount |

| | |
|---|---|
| Income | Increases in economic benefits over a period in the form of inflows or increases of assets, or decreases of liabilities, resulting in increases in equity/capital (*Conceptual Framework*). It can include both revenue and gains. Income is a key element of financial statements. |
| Income statement | The statement of profit or loss was previously referred to as an income statement |
| Inventories | Assets:<br><br>• Held for sale in the ordinary course of business<br><br>• In the process of production for such sale; or<br><br>• In the form of materials or supplies to be consumed in the production process or in the rendering of services. |
| Inventories, cost of | All costs of purchase, of conversion (eg labour) and of other costs incurred in bringing the items to their present location and condition. |
| Inventories, cost of purchase | The purchase price, import duties and other non-recoverable taxes, transport, handling and other costs directly attributable to the acquisition of finished goods and materials. |
| Irrecoverable debt | A debt which is not expected to be paid. |
| LIFO (last in, first out) | Items issued originally formed part of the most recent delivery, while oldest consignments remain in stores. This is disallowed under IAS 2 *Inventories*. |
| Liability | The *Conceptual Framework* states that a liability is a present obligation arising from past events, the settlement of which is expected to result in an outflow from the entity of resources embodying economic benefits. Liabilities are key elements of financial statements. |
| Loss | The excess of expenses over income. |
| Management accounting | Sometimes known as cost accounting, is a management information system which analyses data to provide information as a basis for managerial action. |
| Market value (of shares) | The price that the shares would sell for if traded on a stock market |
| Material | Omissions or misstatements of items are material if they could, individually or collectively, influence the economic decisions of users taken on the basis of the financial statements. Materiality depends on the size and nature of the omission or misstatement judged in the surrounding circumstances. The size or the nature of an item, or a combination of both, could be the determining factor. |
| Net assets | Assets less liabilities. |
| Net realisable value | The expected price less any costs still to be incurred in getting the item ready for sale and then selling it. |
| Nominal ledger | See general ledger. |
| Nominal value (of shares | By law, shares must have a nominal (or par) value. It can be any amount for example 1p, 5p, 10p, 25p, 50p, £1 an so on. The nominal value will rarely bear any relationship to either the issue price or the current market value of the shares. |
| Non-current assets | Assets acquired for continuing use within the business, with a view to earning income or making profits from their use, either directly or indirectly, over more than one reporting period. |
| Non-current liability | A debt which is not payable within one year. Any liability which is not current must be non-current |

ICAEW

| | |
|---|---|
| Ordinary share | A share entitling its holder to dividends which vary in amount depending on the performance and policy of the company |
| Par value (of shares) | See nominal value |
| Partnership | The relationship which exists between persons carrying on a business in common with a view of profit. |
| Payables ledger | The memorandum ledger for suppliers' personal accounts. It is not part of the nominal ledger nor part of the double entry system, but double entry rules apply to the payables ledger accounts. |
| Payroll | The book of original entry for recording staff costs |
| Petty cash book | The book of original entry for small payments and receipts of cash. |
| Preference share | A share which entitles the holder to a fixed dividend, whose payment takes priority over that of ordinary share dividends |
| Preference share (redeemable) | Preference shares which the company is entitled to buy back from its shareholders or 'redeem' at some future time. They are treated as non-current liabilities (debt capital) in the financial statements. |
| Preference share (irredeemable) | Preference shares which the company is not entitled to buy back or redeem at some stage in the future. They are treated as share capital in the financial statements. |
| Preference share capital | The total capital raised from the issue of preference shares in a company. |
| Prepayments (prepaid expenses) | Expenses which have been paid in one reporting period, but are not charged against profit until a later period, because they relate to that later period. |
| Profit | The excess of income over expenses. |
| Profit and loss account | See statement of profit or loss. Under UK GAAP this is called a profit and loss account. |
| Profit sharing ratio | This is the ratio in which the profits of a business are shared amongst the partners in a partnership |
| Provision | A liability of uncertain timing or amount. |
| Purchase day book | The book of original entry in respect of credit purchasesall. |
| Purchase returns day book | A listing of all credit notes received from credit suppliers. Sometimes known as the purchases returns journal. |
| Receivables ledger | The memorandum ledger for customers' personal accounts. It is not part of the nominal ledger nor the double entry system, but double entry rules apply to the receivables ledger accounts. |
| Reducing balance depreciation | The annual depreciation charge is a fixed percentage of the brought forward carrying amount of the asset. |
| Relevant financial information | Information which is capable of making a difference in the decisions made by users. |
| Replacement cost | The cost of an inventory unit is assumed to be the amount it would cost now to replace it. This is often (but not necessarily) the unit cost of inventories purchased in the next consignment *following* the date of the statement of financial position. |
| Residual value | The estimated amount that the entity would currently obtain from disposing of an asset, after deducting estimated disposal costs. |
| Retained earnings | A reserve used to accumulate the company's retained earnings. |
| Revenue | The gross inflow of economic benefits during the period arising in the course of the ordinary activities of an entity when those flows result in increases in equity, other than increases relating to contributions from equity participants. |

| | |
|---|---|
| **Revenue expenditure** | Expenditure which is incurred either:<br><br>• For trade purposes. This includes purchases of raw materials or items for resale, expenditure on wages and salaries, selling and distribution expenses, administrative expenses and finance costs, or<br><br>• To maintain the existing earning capacity of long-term assets. |
| **Revenue income:** | Income derived from<br><br>• The sale of trading assets, such as goods held in inventory<br>• The provision of services<br>• Interest and dividends received from business investments |
| **Rights issue** | New shares are offered to existing owners in proportion to their existing shareholding, usually at a discount to the current market price. |
| **Sales day book** | The book of original entry in respect of credit sales.all. |
| **Sales returns day book** | A listing of all credit notes sent out to credit customers. Sometimes known as the sales returns journal. |
| **Share premium** | The excess of the issue price of shares above their nominal value |
| **Standard cost** | All inventory items are valued at a pre-determined cost. If this standard cost differs from prices actually paid during the period the difference is written off as a 'variance' in the statement of profit or loss. |
| **Statement of changes in equity** | Financial statement that shows the changes in owners' equity (capital) invested in a business during the period. |
| **Statement of financial position** | A *list* of all the *assets controlled* and all the *liabilities owed* by a business as at a particular date: it is a snapshot of the financial position of the business at a particular moment. Monetary amounts are attributed to assets and liabilities. It also quantifies the amount of the owners' interest in the company: **equity**. |
| **Statement of profit or loss** | A statement displaying items of income and expense in a reporting period as components of profit or loss for the period. The statement shows whether the business has had more income than expense (a profit for the period) or *vice versa* (a loss for the period). |
| **Statutory accounts** | Financial statements which limited companies are obliged by law to publish in a particular form. |
| **Stocks** | See inventories |
| **Straight line depreciation** | The depreciable amount (cost less residual value) is charged in **equal instalments** to each reporting period over the expected useful life of the asset. (In this way, the carrying amount of the non-current asset declines at a steady rate, or in a 'straight line' over time.) |
| **Suspense account** | An account showing a balance equal to the difference in a trial balance. |
| **Timeliness** | Financial information should be available in time to be capable of influencing users' decisions. |
| **Trade discount** | A reduction in the cost of goods, owing to the nature of the trading transaction. It usually results from buying goods in bulk. It is deducted from the list price of goods sold, to arrive at a final sales figure. There is no separate ledger account for trade discount. |
| **Trade payables** | The amounts due to credit suppliers. Also known as trade accounts payable or simply payables. |
| **Trade receivables** | The amounts owed by credit customers. Also known as trade accounts receivables or simply receivables. |
| **Transposition errors** | When two digits in an amount are accidentally recorded the wrong way round. |

ICAEW

| | |
|---|---|
| **Trial balance** | A list of nominal ledger balances shown in debit and credit columns, as a method of testing the accuracy of double entry bookkeeping. The trial balance is not part of the double entry system. |
| **UK GAAP** | The rules, from whatever source, that govern accounting and financial reporting in the UK. |
| **Understandability** | Financial information needs to be capable of being understood by users 'having a reasonable knowledge of business and economic activities and accounting'. |
| **Useful life** | The estimated economic life (rather than the potential physical life) of the non-current asset. |
| **Verifiability** | Information is verifiable if different observers can broadly agree that a particular way of presenting an item is a faithful representation. |
| **Writing off (debt)** | Charging the cost of the debt against the profit for the period. |

# Index

**REVIEW FORM – ACCOUNTING STUDY MANUAL**

Your ratings, comments and suggestions would be appreciated on the following areas of this Study Manual.

| | Very useful | Useful | Not useful |
|---|:---:|:---:|:---:|
| *Chapter Introductions* | ☐ | ☐ | ☐ |
| *Examination context* | ☐ | ☐ | ☐ |
| *Worked examples* | ☐ | ☐ | ☐ |
| *Interactive questions* | ☐ | ☐ | ☐ |
| *Quality of explanations* | ☐ | ☐ | ☐ |
| *Technical references (where relevant)* | ☐ | ☐ | ☐ |
| *Self-test questions* | ☐ | ☐ | ☐ |
| *Self-test answers* | ☐ | ☐ | ☐ |
| *Index* | ☐ | ☐ | ☐ |

| | Excellent | Good | Adequate | Poor |
|---|:---:|:---:|:---:|:---:|
| *Overall opinion of this Study Manual* | ☐ | ☐ | ☐ | ☐ |

**Please add further comments below:**

**Please return completed form to:**

The Learning Team
Learning and Professional Department
ICAEW
Metropolitan House
321 Avebury Boulevard
Milton Keynes
MK9 2FZ
E learning@icaew.com